English with an Accent

Since its initial publication, *English with an Accent* has provoked debate and controversy within classrooms through its in-depth scrutiny of American attitudes toward language. Rosina Lippi-Green discusses the ways in which discrimination based on accent functions to support and perpetuate social structures and unequal power relations.

This second edition has been reorganized and revised to include:

- new dedicated chapters on Latino English and Asian American English
- discussion questions, further reading, and suggested classroom exercises
- updated examples from the classroom, the judicial system, the media, and corporate culture
- a discussion of the long-term implications of the Ebonics debate
- a brand-new companion website with an interactive bibliography, glossary of key terms, and links to audio, video, and images relevant to each chapter's content, available at: www.routledge.com/cw/lippi-green.

English with an Accent is essential reading for students with interests in attitudes and discrimination toward language.

Rosina Lippi-Green is an independent scholar and award-winning writer of fiction. She holds a PhD in linguistics from Princeton University, USA, and was a University of Michigan, Ann Arbor faculty member for ten years.

English with an Accent

Language, ideology, and discrimination in the United States

Second Edition

Rosina Lippi-Green

Routledge
Taylor & Francis Group

LONDON AND NEW YORK

This second edition published 2012
by Routledge
2 Park Square, Milton Park, Abingdon, Oxon OX14 4RN

Simultaneously published in the USA and Canada
by Routledge
711 Third Avenue, New York, NY 10017

Routledge is an imprint of the Taylor & Francis Group, an informa business

First edition published by Routledge 1997

British Library Cataloguing in Publication Data
A catalogue record for this book is available from the British Library

Library of Congress Cataloging-in-Publication Data
Lippi-Green, Rosina.
English with an accent: language, ideology and discrimination in the United States /
Rosina Lippi-Green. – 2nd ed.
p. cm.
Includes bibliographical references and index.
English language–Social aspects–United States. 2. English language Political aspects–United States. 3. English language–Variation–United States. 4. Speech and social status–United States. 5. Language and culture–United States. 6. Language policy–United States. 7. Discrimination–United States. I. Title.
PE2808.8.L57 2011
306.440973–dc23
2011024009

ISBN: 978–0–415–55910–2 (hbk)
ISBN: 978–0–415–55911–9 (pbk)
ISBN: 978–0–203–34880–2 (ebk)

Typeset in Janson and Akzidenz Grotesk
by Keystroke, Station Road, Codsall, Wolverhampton

In memory of my father, Arturo Lippi, 1911–1985
who had an accent I couldn't hear

Contents

The glossary and an extended bibliography with further reading can be found at
www.routledge.com/cw/lippi-green.

List of figures

List of tables

Preface[1]

Everyone is entitled to their own opinion, but not to their own facts.

Daniel Patrick Moynihan[2]

By almost anybody's modern U.S. standards, I have no accent. Because of the English I speak, the destructive and exclusionary practices you will read about in this book have never been directed at me.

But of course, I do have an accent. My English tells anybody who wants to listen to me who I am: a woman of European ancestry, middle-aged, who has lived most of her life in the heart of the country, in the Midwest. By fortunate circumstance, I had a longer and more exclusive education than most people have, which has also influenced my accent – because it took me away from the Midwest, primarily, but also because it put me in social circumstances which were foreign to me, against which I struggled and will always struggle, even as I adjust.

This is a written work, and so it is not by virtue of my accent but of my education that I am granted a voice. For that reason some would say that my authority derives exclusively from privilege. It is true that I cannot claim the authority of personal experience in the matters I am going to describe and discuss – except in the most trivial way – but I can and do claim the authority of careful observation and study, and of interest and participation.

I am taking a chance. My thoughts may be dismissed, my observations put aside. In a time when authorial voices are questioned very closely, I have no credentials which allow me to speak – nor do I wish to speak – for African Americans or Asian Americans. Because I am not a Latina or Lakota Sioux, because I am not from Mobile, the Bronx, Bombay, Singapore, or Nairobi, readers may question my data before ever considering my analysis and conclusions. In that case, I invite them to investigate for themselves before dismissing what I have to say. The purpose of this study is not to answer the questions raised in a definitive way, but to open up a discussion and examination which has been suppressed for too long.

There is another kind of chance I take here, one that is not new to me. Many people take strong exception to the ideas presented here. Beliefs about the way language should be used are passed down and protected in much the same way that religious beliefs are passed along and cherished. Some will call me a language anarchist and a liberal elitist; I know this, because I have been called such things before, and by colleagues I respect. This kind of reaction I take as further proof of the power of the standard language ideology that we are all exposed to.

In fact, some colleagues have suggested that you, the reader, could take offense at the material presented here. The concern is that you may consider yourself judged and found lacking. My own experience tells me that most university students have more intellectual rigor than they are given credit for, and will at least attempt to think critically before taking offense. This has been borne out by research classrooms where race and conflict are central themes:

The more comfortable instructors are to openly engage difficult dialogues (and not simply gloss over substantive issues), the more willing students are to share openly (Simpson *et al.* 2007). In addition, students are often willing to move into and through emotional tension when other class members move beyond blaming, condescending or patronizing (ibid.: 43). What we have learned generally from critical analyses of race (particularly whiteness) is that the analysis of student (and teacher) responses lends insight into the ways that whiteness is both challenged and reproduced in the everyday spaces of education (Cooks 2003; Johnson *et al.* 2008: 116; Warren 2001).

In the hope that it will provide some perspective, this quote from Murray Rothbard, an economist:

> It is no crime to be ignorant of economics, which is, after all, a specialized discipline and one that most people consider to be a "dismal science." But it is totally irresponsible to have a loud and vociferous opinion on economic subjects while remaining in this state of ignorance.
>
> (Rothbard 2000: 202)

With very few adjustments, this quote applies also to the study of language and linguistics. The primary difference is here: *economics is a specialized discipline that most people consider "dismal science."* In fact, people are generally very interested in language. Unfortunately, our institutions are very good at producing citizens who truly believe that they understand the inner workings of language, and that their understanding is enough to justify not only vociferous opinions but also to act on those opinions in ways that sometimes will be detrimental and even destructive to others. To put this another way: for the most part, the public does not see the difference between opinion and fact when it comes to language. Part of what I hope to accomplish here is to make the difference visible.

Of course, this text is not simply a list of facts. I cannot claim that this work is no more than a neutral presentation of observations about language. Where the facts end, interpretation and analysis begin and questions are raised which have consequence in the real world. My opinions are informed by careful thought and by research, but they are opinions. You are, of course, entitled – and encouraged – to disagree. I am not offended by disagreement; I do not equate it with personal animosity.

To be clear, I would summarize my stance with two general statements:

● There is something deeply inequitable and unacceptable about the practice of excluding the few from the privileges of the many not on the basis of what they have to say, but how they say it.
● The demand that the disempowered assimilate linguistically and culturally to please the empowered is – purely in linguistic terms – an impossibility. For that reason, such demands are misleading, unreasonable and demeaning.

There is a challenge here for the reader. Can you be objective about language? Can you examine what you think you know about your own language? And more difficult, are you willing to explore why you may be so very protective of common sense arguments about language which have no demonstrable basis in fact?

This book is about reluctance to acknowledge language for the social construct that it is, and the repercussions of such resistance. When I use this book as a classroom text, sooner or later someone asks me what I hope to accomplish. I can say with complete honesty that I have no illusions about saving the world or initiating an era of universal linguistic goodwill.

Walt Wolfram's version of this same question requires more thought. He asks:

> What approaches to the dissemination of sociolinguistic information must be adopted with communities and with the general public when language diversity is interpreted in terms of a prescriptive, correctionist model?
>
> (Wolfram *et al.* 2008)

This issue has been debated and will continue to be debated as long as there is life and movement in the discipline. That is good and right, because it is an important question. In the published work on this matter there are three principles that make sense to me:

1 *Principle of error correction*: "A scientist who becomes aware of a widespread idea or social practice with important consequences that is invalidated by his own data is obligated to bring this error to the attention of the widest possible audience" (Labov 1982: 172).
2 *Principle of debt incurred*: "An investigator who has obtained linguistic data from members of a speech community has an obligation to use the knowledge based on that data for the benefit of the community, when [the community] has need of it" (ibid.: 173).
3 *Principle of linguistic gratuity*: the obligation to "pursue positive ways in which [linguists] can return linguistic favors to the [fieldwork] community" (Wolfram 1993: 227; see also Wolfram *et al.* 2008).

In so far as teaching is concerned, Wolfram concludes that:

> [W]hile it is relatively easy to capitalize on people's inherent interest in language, it is sometimes difficult to convince the general public to accept the need for language study, a prerequisite to changing uninformed opinions and assumptions about language variation.
>
> (Wolfram *et al.* 2008: 1113)

One fall while I was teaching what was my signature course, Language & Discrimination, I had an unusual conversation with a student. He asked a question that took some courage.

"Okay," he said in class discussion. "I resisted, but I can see now that my reactions to certain kinds of errors [*sic*] are not based on fact but on ideology and emotion. Knowing that, I can still discriminate on the basis of language. I'm within my rights doing that. Right?"

To which there was only one response: of course. In so far as his behavior stays within the parameters of the law (he couldn't refuse employment to someone because of an Irish or Indonesian accent, for example), he was free to do as he wished. My hope was that he finished the book (and the course) with a wider understanding and perspective, so that he didn't rationalize his choices to himself or anyone else.

I hope that and more for everyone who comes across this book. I hope too that when others try to use language ideology to silence you, your family, your community, you will hear Eleanor Roosevelt reminding you: *no one can make you feel inferior without your consent.* And then you will speak up out of conviction, but armed with facts.

Please take advantage of additional materials (a full bibliography, a glossary, additional links and supplementary materials as well as discussion questions) available at the companion website www.routledge.com/cw/lippi-green. You'll see the logo in the margin when there is content on the website that is specific to that particular point of discussion.

Notes

1   Since the first edition of *English with an Accent* appeared in 1997, linguists (along with colleagues in anthropology, psychology, education, media studies and other disciplines) have produced a great deal of work on the linguistic, sociocultural and ideological aspects of English as it evolves and changes. Between 1999 and 2010 I added more than eight hundred books, chapters, articles, essays, newspaper reports, court cases, and government documents to my bibliography. I have never lacked for reading material.

   As a result, pretty much every sentence in *EWA* had to be rewritten, every source checked, reevaluated, replaced or brought up to date, and every conclusion challenged. The process was not an easy or pretty one, but I hope the results make *EWA* more relevant and useful, and that it will continue to work well for those who use it as a classroom text. I also hope that the people who are responsible for this great smörgåsbord of information will understand I just couldn't fit everything in. That has nothing to do with a lack of interest, but only restrictions on time and space.

2   A search of the Congressional Record provides no clear source for this statement, but it is attributed at various points to Senator Moynhan and to Senator Simpson.

Suggested further reading

Cooks, L. (2003) Pedagogy, Performance, Positionality: Teaching About Whiteness in Interracial Communication. *Communication Education* 52: 245–257.

Johnson, J., Rich, M. and Cargile, A.C. (2008) "Why Are You Shoving This Stuff Down Our Throats?": Preparing Intercultural Educators to Challenge Performances of White Racism. *Journal of International and Intercultural Communication* 1(2): 113–135.

Labov, W. (1982) Objectivity and Commitment in Linguistic Science: The Case of the Black English Trial in Ann Arbor. *Language in Society* 11(2): 165–201.

Simpson, J.S., Causey, A. and Williams, L. (2007) "I Would Want You to Understand It": Students' Perspectives on Addressing Race in the Classroom. *Journal of Intercultural Communication Research* 36: 33–50.

Warren, J.T. (2001). Doing Whiteness: On the Performative Dimensions of Race in the Classroom. *Communication Education* 50: 91–108.

Wolfram, W. (1993) Ethical Considerations in Language Awareness Programs. *Issues in Applied Linguistics* 4: 292–313.

Wolfram, W., Reaser, J. and Vaughn, C. (2008) Operationalizing Linguistic Gratuity: From Principle to Practice. *Language and Linguistics Compass* 2(6): 1109–1134.

Acknowledgements

There were dozens of people who contributed to writing the first edition of this book, many of whom were good enough to lend a hand this time around, too.

My sincere thanks to all friends and colleagues who were so generous with their time and expertise. Most especially I would like to thank John Rickford, Joe Salmons, Pam Beddor, Tricia Cukor-Avila, Jane Hill, Matthew Gordon, John Baugh, Carmen Fought, Walt Wolfram and Vershawn Ashanti Young.

Thanks to John S. Adams, Peter Gould, Ronald Abler, and Dolly Withrow for kindly allowing the use of their work.

Thanks also to the many people who helped me locate articles and other resources that eluded me, including Patricia Rosenmeyer, Lesley Milroy, Marcyliena Morgan, Rusty Barrett, Chad D. Nilep, Lauren Hall-Lew, Aneta Pavlenko, Tara S. Sanchez, Jessi Elana Aaron, Beth Markocic, Sharon M. Klein, Jennifer Leeman, Dennis Preston, Erik Thomas, Panayota Gounari, Mark Patkowski, Alicia Beckford Wassink, Jeff Siegel, Andrea L. Menz, Catherine Evans Davies, William Chin, Tracey L. Weldon, Monica MacCauley, George Aaron Broadwell, Valerie M Fridland, Thomas Purnell, Erik Thomas. Felisa Salvago-Keyes, my editor at Routledge, showed remarkable patience as she shepherded me along. I am thankful for her help. I am also indebted to my anonymous reviewers for helpful insights and suggestions.

I count myself very fortunate in friends and family, who keep me moving forward when things get rough: Penny Chambers, who asks me to read work in progress out loud and then really listens; my daughter Elisabeth for modeling courage in the face of adversity; my husband Bill. Everybody should be so lucky.

Introduction

Language ideology or science fiction?

> The American ideal, after all, is that everyone should be as much alike as possible.
>
> James Baldwin, *Notes of a Native Son* (1984: 64)

> If we choose, we can live in a world of comforting illusion.
>
> Noam Chomsky (http://tinyurl.com/4q7eej4)

This book is about language, but let's begin with a bit of science fiction. Imagine the following:

On January 1 of the next new year, each person residing in the United States wakes up to find themselves physically transformed: regardless of race or ethnicity, all adult males 18 and older will be exactly 6' tall and weigh 175 pounds; adult females, 5'9", at 140 pounds. All persons will show exactly the same physical measurements (length of tibia, diameter of wrist) and body fat ratios, with a differential arising from gender-specific roles in the propagation of the species. All persons newborn through age 17 will approach the adult model on a scale graduated exactly to age. Metabolism has adjusted so that the ratios of height to weight are maintained regardless of diet or development of musculature.

Let's take this strange idea a step further and imagine what this revolution would mean to us in our day-to-day lives. Some of the repercussions might be seen as positive:

- Tremendous behavior shifts in matters of mate selection and sexuality. Every woman will wear what is now a size ten, but as sizes are no longer relevant or meaningful, the social connotations of clothing sizes (petite or queen, extra tall, extra long, extra broad, extra narrow) will quickly be lost.
- The end of the diet industry.
- Sudden resolution of health problems related to weight. Heart disease, hypertension, anorexia – a whole range of difficult health problems greatly simplified or resolved overnight.
- Dramatic changes in the way we think about food. As metabolism is now fine-tuned to deal with excessive or insufficient calories, carbohydrate and fat intake, much of the culture and psychology about eating would evolve in new directions.
- Revolution in the design and manufacture of easy chairs, roller-skates, toothbrushes, gloves, skis, kitchen counters, bathtubs, lawnmower handles, car seats, bed sheets, violins, submarines, auditoriums, coffins and everything else which now makes allowance for variation in physical size. This would mean a tremendous economic advantage for businesses which can streamline production in ways never imagined.

● Sports, professional and otherwise, would change greatly. But because muscle tone, agility, speed, and strength would remain matters of life style, nutrition, and training, sports as we know them would not disappear, but shift in focus and nature.

These are just a few areas which would be changed. The list can easily be expanded as we anticipate the major social and cultural impact on our lives.

When I discuss this fictional United States with my classes, the students are eager to list things that would be easier, cheaper, more streamlined and efficient if this physical world were suddenly to become a reality. Slowly, different considerations begin to emerge, which students are sometimes reluctant to express. They have to do with issues which are more subtle, which touch on identity and self-awareness, aesthetic and value systems. It sounds like this would be a good thing overall, for us as a country, says one student. But my father and my grandfather and my great-grandfather were all 6'5" or bigger. With less of an apologetic tone, a Japanese-American woman tells the class "I can't imagine being that tall." Another student asks, "Who decided on these particular figures? Why 140 pounds for women – wouldn't 125 be more aesthetically pleasing?" And yet another comment: "Why shouldn't men and women be the same height?"

Before I let the class discuss these questions in any depth, there is one more step in the science fiction fantasy which we must consider.

Imagine now that this unanticipated and unwilled transformation does not take place. Instead, a junior Congresswoman rises before the House of Representatives and she presents a precise, well-written proposal for a law which dictates the physical world imagined above, in which a woman who is 6'2" or a man who weighs 225 pounds are either violating federal law willfully, or must be labeled handicapped.

In support of her proposal, the Congresswoman outlines the many social ills which will be instantaneously fixed, and the economic advantages for the manufacturing and business communities. She provides projections which promise that billions of dollars will be saved if this law is put into effect, money which can be put into education and job training. Her presentation includes complex essays and calculations by a panel of experts who have, on the basis of considerable study, determined what ideal heights and weights must be – what makes a superior, efficient, aesthetically pleasing human being.

"Let us all be one height and weight," she says. "For we are all one nation."

This is a funny idea; students laugh. What is wrong with it is so obvious as to be trivial, they tell me.

First, we cannot all be the same height and weight and physical type: variation and diversity are inescapable biological facts. Thus, this law would be unenforceable.

Second, even if this were not an impossibility, it would be wrong – an invasion of personal liberties – to require people to change their physical beings to approximate some model set up by others, in the name of perceived economic or social advance, even their own.

Third: People will find ways to differentiate themselves, to stand out, to be individuals, because that's part of human nature.

Fourth, and finally: The premise that we will be a better nation, a more unified nation, if we all look the same, is suspect.

Now what does this hypothetical world, this hypothetical Congresswoman and her proposal have to do with language, and more to the point, with language and discrimination? People will immediately claim that language cannot stand in for height and weight in this story. The argument will go that language is an ethereal, mutable thing, something we learn, something within our control. Height and weight are biological facts of the physical world, determined by genetics and nutrition in the first line, and by will and habit only secondarily. Language – which languages we speak, and how we speak them – is a matter of choice, people will argue, whereas height is not.

In the course of this book I will argue that language has more in common with height and weight than is readily apparent, and that the same reservations which are so self-evident when we talk about manipulation of our physical bodies can and must be applied to discourse about language, and the manipulation and evaluation of language. Language, a possession all human collectives have in common, is more than a tool for communication of facts between two or more persons. It is the most salient way we have of establishing and advertising our social identities. It may not be as tangible as height and weight, but the way we use language is more complex and meaningful than any single fact about our bodies.

The degree of control we have over language is limited. We can choose to be polite or obtuse, to use forms of address which will flatter or insult, to use gender-neutral language or language that is inflammatory; we can consciously use vocabulary which is easily understood, or we can purposefully mislead with language. But there are many dimensions of language which are not subject to conscious or direct control. And still, as speakers we are obsessed with the idea of authority over language: we talk a great deal about language as if it were an indispensable but often wayward and unpredictable servant, in need of our constant attention and vigilance if the job is to get done.

Crucial questions have been raised here which will occupy the rest of this study:

- What is the relationship between language and social identity? How do we use language to construct "self" and "other"?
- What is or is not mutable about language, specifically about phonetics and phonology (accent)?
- Do individuals have language rights which render the question of mutability irrelevant? That is, is it desirable or even possible to balance the individual's language rights with the needs of the community? Is this an appropriate matter for majority rule, or is it an area where the tyranny of the majority is a real threat, and individual liberties must be invoked?
- Who claims authority to make these decisions, how do they manage to do this, and why do people let them?

All of these questions are important to this study, but the last question is perhaps the most complex and difficult one. There is a common conception that there is a good English, and following from that, bad English. Further, there is a good deal of consensus on who speaks good English, and who has authority to decide what is good. While anyone would anticipate heated debate on the height/weight legislation (who has the authority to decide what an ideal person looks like, and on what aesthetic, biological or other grounds?), it is interesting to note that there is little debate at all about who sets the standards for spoken and written language, standards which have been the focus of legislation, standards which affect our everyday lives.

Before we can set out on an exploration of these issues, however, there must be some common ground, built of established facts about language structure and function. Be prepared to give up some dearly held beliefs – things your teachers and parents and mentors told you – as you forge ahead.

The linguistic facts of life

1

To disarm the strong and arm the weak would be to change the social order which it is my job to preserve. Justice is the means by which established injustices are sanctioned.

Anatole France, *Crainquebille* ([1901] 1949: iv)

All over the world, right at this moment, very young children are acquiring a first language, and every one of them is going through the same stages at just about the same ages. A child in Papua New Guinea and a child in Carson City, Nevada, born on the same day, will mirror one another as they go through those stages, even if one of them is acquiring Sign Language and the other a spoken language.[1] In Nairobi or El Paso, Okinawa or Bruges, the pattern is the same. It was the same for you, and for me and for those who come after us.

One of the most important linguistic insights of the last century was quite simple: this species-wide, universal phenomenon could not be coincidental. Noam Chomsky proposed what now seems obvious:

> The fact that all normal children acquire essentially comparable grammars of great complexity with remarkable rapidity suggests that human beings are somehow specially designed to do this, with data-handling or "hypothesis-formulating" ability of unknown character and complexity.

(Chomsky 1959: 62)

In other words, our brains are hard-wired for language; it's in our DNA. A child has the innate capacity to acquire language, something like a blueprint in the mind that makes it possible to recognize and absorb the structural patterns of language. He or she uses the data available in the environment to build a mother tongue by filling in and adapting those blueprints. Better understanding of this process came with the identification of one (and as yet, the only identified) of the genes that contribute to the language faculty. The FOXP2 gene was isolated by means of neuropsychological, neuroimaging and genetic investigations of three generations of one family with severe speech and language disorders (Gopnik 1990; Vargha-Khadem and Liégeois 2007).[2]

So while the primary focus in this study is American English, the language phenomena discussed here are relevant to every language community and every human being.[3] To understand these bigger issues, you will need to be familiar with some of those basic universal facts about the structure and function of human language. These are things you do not know, unless you've studied linguistics, in the same way you do not know how your brain causes your hand to turn the page of this book unless you've studied anatomy, physiology and neurology.

Some of the things you read here may seem at first counter-intuitive or just plain wrong, and in fact there are some obstacles to laying out these ideas.

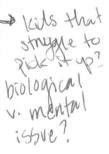

Linguists[4] do not form a homogenous club. Like any other group of scholars divided by a common subject matter, there are great rivalries, ancient quarrels, picky arguments, and plain differences of opinion. It could hardly be otherwise in a discipline diverse enough to include topics such as neurological structures and linguistic capacity, grammaticalized strategies for encoding social information in systems of address, and creolization. Thus it should be no surprise that those who study the rules which generate the ordering of words into sentences (syntacticians and cognitive grammarians, for example) are often openly disdainful of each other's approach, on theoretical grounds, and of the study of the social life of language, more generally. Linguists concerned with the relationship between structured variation in language and social identity (socio-linguists, variationists, some anthropological linguists) chide both syntacticians and cognitive grammarians for what they see as unreasonable abstractions and lack of reproducible results; phoneticians go about their business of understanding and theo-rizing the way humans produce and perceive sound – the architects and engineers of linguistics – and wonder what all the noise is about; historical linguists concern themselves with the written data of lost language communities and write complex formulas for the reconstruction of sounds that might have been heard around the early Roman explora-tions of central Europe, or in more extreme cases, when people first wandered from Asia to the North American land mass.

However, there is a great deal that linguists do agree about. For example, the statement *All living languages change* is one that no academic linguist would deny, unless they were to ask for a definition of "living" and to debate the parameters and implications of that term, just for the fun of it. And, of course, not all linguists find the fact that all living languages change to be equally interesting or worthy of study. The very subject of this book – how people think about language, how and why they try to control it, to what ends, and with what social repercussions – has received comparatively little attention.

Traditionally, linguists draw a strict line in the sand. They stand on one side with what they hope is their own objective, analytic approach to the study of language; on the other side they see prescriptivists who have a shallow understanding of human language, and whose primary purpose is to exert an authority that they have not earned (but see Chapter 5 for Lakoff's discussion of rationality as a philosophy).

More recently, however, linguists have been putting aside this strict division in recognition of the fact that how people think about language – no matter how ill-founded such beliefs might be – is in fact relevant to the study of language as a social construct.

Dennis Preston has produced a large body of work on the way attitudes toward language are relevant to the study of variation and change. He sees the juxtaposition as a matter of focus: is the study oriented toward the participants (speakers), or is the approach analyst-centric?

What linguists believe about standards matters very little; what non-linguists believe constitutes precisely that cognitive reality which needs to be described in a responsible sociolinguistics – one which takes speech-community attitudes and perception (as well as performance) into account (Preston 1993b: 26).

We begin with those linguistic facts of life that will be crucial to the issues raised in the course of this book:

- All spoken language changes over time.
- All spoken languages are equal in terms of linguistic potential.
- Grammaticality and communicative effectiveness are distinct and independent issues.

- Written language and spoken language are historically, structurally and functionally fundamentally different creatures.
- Variation is intrinsic to all spoken language at every level, and much of that variation serves an emblematic purpose.

This small collection of facts is where most linguists would come together. The irony is that where linguists settle down to an uneasy truce, non-linguists take up the battle cry. The least disputed issues around language structure and function, the ones linguists argue about least, are those which are most often challenged by non-linguists, and with the greatest vehemence and emotion.

Here I am concerned primarily with common beliefs and attitudes toward variation in American English (AE), and from there, I hope to demonstrate how such attitudes influence personal and institutionalized policy and practice, with very real severe consequences. This distinction between individual and institutionalized effects is quite purposeful, and the reason for that is laid out in *The Everyday Language of White Racism* (Hill 2008), Jane Hill's excellent and very detailed look at these topics from her viewpoint as an anthropological linguist:

> Critical theorists do not deny that individual beliefs figure in racism. But we prefer to emphasize its collective, cultural dimensions, and to avoid singling out individuals and trying to decide whether they are racists or not. Furthermore, critical theorists insist that ordinary people who do not share White supremacist beliefs can still talk and behave in ways that advance the projects of White racism.
>
> (Hill 2008: 7)

All spoken language changes

All language changes over time, in all linguistic subsystems: sounds (phonetics, phonology); the structure of words (morphology, lexicon), the way sentences are put together (syntax), and meaning (semantics). Only moribund, dead languages (languages that have no native speakers) are static.[5] This is as true in Asia as it is in on the North American continent, as it is for every language in the world.

Linguists base this assertion on observation, experimentation, and deduction, so that the statement *all living languages change* is not a matter of faith or opinion or aesthetics, but observable fact. And yet, some people – some of you reading this right now – are doubtful. There are many people who are uncomfortable with the idea that they cannot control all aspects of language.

For me as a sociolinguist, the interesting thing about this question is how it came to be asked in the first place. Why do so many people feel threatened by the idea of language change? Why do they contest the idea with so much emotion? How did the idea of a perfect, unchanging language become so deeply instilled? Even the most idealistic and nostalgic of language observers cannot argue that Chaucer, Shakespeare, Milton, Austen, Woolf, Wharton, Morrison and Erdrich (to take us from the fourteenth to the twenty-first century), some of the men and women who wrote what is commonly regarded as the great literature of the English-speaking world, all wrote the same English.

To take it one step further: Toni Morrison[6] does not write or talk like Shakespeare wrote and talked. Few people would claim that because that is true, Morrison's command of the language is faulty, that the English she speaks and writes is bad, less efficient, less capable of carrying out the functions for which it is needed. And still people will take up the battle cry and declare war on language change. All those attempts – and there have been a lot of them – are doomed to failure, unless they are instituted by means of genocide.[7]

Sometimes languages die a less sudden death, for example, when the community of speakers who use them disperse, succumb to plague, or otherwise are forcibly assimilated into dominant cultures (as in the case of most of the languages indigenous to the American continent); languages are born through the processes of pidginization and subsequent creolization.

?

Language standardization could be characterized as an attempt to stop language change, or at least, to fossilize language by means of controlling variation. We'll continue to explore that idea as a part of an in-depth consideration of the ideological structures which make standardization seem like such a good idea.

Finally, it is important to keep in mind that what we know about the history of English is subject to ideological retellings. It has been widely observed that when histories are written, they focus on the dominant class.[8] In the context of this study, that idea can be extended to language: the history of a language is written as the history of its language ideology. You may have heard this idea phrased differently, for example: histories are written by the winners, or even more concisely: consider the source.

Generally studies of the development of the language over time are very narrowly focused on the smallest portion of speakers: those with power and resources to control the distribution of information. Crystal's *The Stories of English* avoids this pitfall by looking at language in all its variation and stratification (Crystal 2005). So every living language changes, and every variety of every living language changes. It is important to keep this in mind when considering arguments put forward by prescriptivists based on a faulty and partial knowledge of the history of English.

All spoken languages are equal in linguistic terms

All spoken languages are equally capable of conveying a full range of ideas and experiences, and of developing to meet new needs as they arise. This claim by linguists is usually countered by non-linguists with examples of languages which have been deemed less sophisticated.

> I was writing the other day about a dull evening at the theater, but "dull" wasn't the word I wanted. Rodale's Synonym Finder gave me, among many others, vacuous, dense, obtuse, thick, slow, indifferent, sluggish, lethargic, torpid, lifeless, listless, apathetic, drowsy, tedious, tiresome, boring, wearisome, uninteresting, bland, insipid, jejune, vapid, prosaic, lackluster, anodyne, innocuous, soporific, oscitant and blah. Does anyone want to try that in Choctaw? Or in Spanish, Swahili or Norse?
>
> (Kilpatrick 1999)

Not so very long ago, in the larger scheme of things, English speakers did not have the vocabulary to talk about chemical weapons, aeronautical engineering, or genetic mapping. When our technology evolved to the point that we needed to discuss such things, so did our language.

Language is incredibly flexible and responsive; we make or borrow what we do not have. In this flexibility and ability to change and adapt when necessity or will arises, all languages

– all varieties of any given language – are equal. If through an unexpected shift in the world's economy the Arawakan speakers of Peru suddenly were sole possessors of some resource everyone else needed, then Arawakan would develop a variety of new vocabularies and grammatical strategies to deal with their new power on the world stage.

It is simply not a useful exercise to compare Swahili to Tagalog to Finnish in order to determine which one is the better or more efficient language: these are not cars. We cannot compare manufacturing costs, gas mileage, performance on rough terrain. Each language is suited to its community of speakers; each language changes in pace as that community and the demands of the speakers evolve. This applies not just to languages which are unrelated to one another, but also to varieties of a single language. Orange County and the Northwest side of Chicago, Boston Southie and the dialect of Smith's Island in Chesapeake Bay, while very different varieties of English in many ways, are all equally efficient as languages, although they do not enjoy the same degree of respect.

If efficiency and clarity in communication are the ultimate goal in language use, then it might be argued that English is neither efficient nor clear in terms of its pronouns, as a speaker cannot make clear, in purely grammatical terms, if she is addressing her comments to one speaker or more when she says: "I'd like to buy you dinner."

Of even more interest is the fact that the exchange in English happens without any indication of the social relationship between the speaker and the person or persons she is inviting. She might be a boss talking to two secretaries after a long day, or a mother talking to her son on the phone. She might be talking to a man she sees every day on the bus on her way home from work.

Other languages are not so lax: the Romance languages (and many others) distinguish between singular and plural personal pronouns, as well as between formal and informal uses.

Many languages also have a complex system of honorifics which requires that speakers situate themselves in social space in relationship to the person addressed. That is, the speaker will choose among as many as a dozen or more words or suffixes or tones to add to the utterance, and with that choice he or she will indicate the degree of respect (based on age, profession, kinship or other factors), friendship, or lack of respect felt toward the other person. In Thailand, young teenage girls – socially very low in the scheme of things – routinely end their sentences with the tag *I, little rat* (Simpson 1997).

Another example of a lack or hole in the structure of English is the fact that there is no impersonal third person singular pronoun. To the dismay of prescriptivists, we have only he or she, and thus must somehow cope in situations where we do not want to indicate gender. From the *Chicago Manual of Style* (2003): "Though some writers are comfortable with the occasional use of they as a singular pronoun, some are not, and it is better to do the necessary work to recast a sentence or, other options having been exhausted, use he or she."

In fact, the use of *they* (their, them) as singular pronouns is very old. Consider the following examples, dating back to early translations of the Bible:

A person can't help their birth.

(Jane Austen, *Emma*)

Whoever it is, I won't see them tonight.

(M.E. Braddon, *Aurora Floyd*)

God send every one their heart's desire!

(William Shakespeare, *Much Ado About Nothing*)

Who is in love with her? Who makes you their confidant?
(*King James Bible*, Matthew 18:35)

There are ways to avoid using *they* or *their*, but the usage of singular *they* is very firmly established. Using both female and male pronouns is considered awkward (*Whoever it is, I won't see him or her tonight*). Nor does it work to use the neutral single pronoun: (**Whoever it is, I won't see it tonight*).[9] Nevertheless, *The Chicago Manual of Style* and other authorities continue to take the stance that singular *they* is a recent and unhappy development.

It is a credit to the power of standard language ideology (SLI) that many people – and you may be one of them – will look at these examples and say, well, yes, now that you mention it, English is rather inefficient in these cases. But let's consider some facts.

First, a language which does not have an overt strategy for dealing with a grammatical or semantic distinction will have other ways of doing just that. We cannot claim that English speakers are incapable of making themselves clear on just who it is they are inviting to dinner. Social and regional varieties of English have developed a multitude of strategies for dealing with the singular/plural distinction. For example, in my own variety of American English, acquired in Chicago, we say *you/you guys*, in Belfast and some parts of the U.S. *you/youse*; in much of the Southern US *you/you'uns* or *ya'll*; in parts of Pennsylvania *you/yousns*.

An additional strategy employed by all speakers of English involves a range of lexical choices that might not engender negative social reactions, but which show strategic maneuvering: "Would you folks/people/chaps/fellows/kids like to . . .?"

These all come from regionally or socially restricted varieties of English. Idealized *Standard American English (a term we'll look at shortly; see p. 62) is bound, at least theoretically, by adherence to an inflexible grammar and thus is unable to change to address gaps in the language system. So then, isn't it reasonable to say that a standardized English is not as efficient as the social and regional dialects?

This is a tempting argument, but it cannot survive close examination. <u>All spoken language will cope with ambiguity of all kinds.</u> If socially motivated rules forbid reliance on certain grammatical strategies or lexical terms, then discourse, intonation and body language strategies can be called into play:

"Would you [single eye contact] like to have a meal with me?"
"Would you [multiple eye contact] like to have a meal with me?"

It is an odd thing that we should think about language as if it were a machine invented to serve the purpose of communication, and thus open to criticism on the same grounds in which we talk about our lawnmowers and food processors. In the next sections we will see that these misconceptions have less to do with inherent qualities of language than they do with a preoccupation with form (as opposed to function), which in turn originates in part with struggles over authority in the determination of language and social identity.

Grammaticality does not equal communicative effectiveness

Linguists and non-linguists both see grammar as a set of rules which must be obeyed, but they differ on the nature and origination of those rules. When linguists talk about grammar, they are thinking about the rule-driven structure of language. On the basis of those rules, individuals generate sentences. Children have acquired a working knowledge of this grammar of their native language by the age of 4.

A linguist would not call any of the following example sentences ungrammatical:

- If you're going out, I'm coming with.
- I might could stop at the store on the way home.
- You know Vicky be working after school.
- For reals, he won the lottery!
- If I had had three of them, you could've tooken one.
- Here are five things Joe should have went to jail for.
- I would of helped if I had known.
- We misunderestimated them.
- That's just what Maria said to Marcos and I.
- Ain't nobody can beat me no how.
- Which of the three boys was less troublesome?
- The house needs painted.
- He's the kind of guy that's always borrowing money.
- The data does not support your conclusion.
- Put it in your pocket.

The 'mistakes' in these sentences would be more or less obvious to people who concern themselves with such things, with the possible exception of the last two examples. In those cases, many academics probably would argue that the noun *data* must be used as a plural, with a plural verb (*The data do not support your conclusion*); particularly hardline prescriptivists would be sure to point out that things are put *into* a pocket.

For non-linguists, grammaticality is used in a much broader and fluid sense. It encompasses the spoken and written languages, and extends to matters of style and even punctuation. However, most important differences between the two approaches to grammar have to do with the concept of socially motivated grammaticality.

Pinker uses the example of a taxicab to illustrate the distinction. As it is a useful illustration I have adapted it here: "The Taxicab Maxim: A taxicab must obey the laws of physics, but it can flout the laws of the state of Michigan (or Massachusetts, or London, etc.)" (Pinker 1994b). To take a closer look at this idea, please consider the sentences in Table 1.1, and the way they are evaluated.

The last four examples are where the linguist and the non-linguist usually part ways. As any of these sentences could be – and are – heard in casual conversation every day on

Table 1.1 Grammaticality judgment comparison

	Grammaticality according to		Is the speaker's intent clear?	
	Linguist	Layperson	Linguist	Layperson
Colorless green ideas sleep furiously	Yes	Yes	No	No
Furiously sleep ideas green colorless	No	No	No	No
That house needs painted	Yes	No	Yes	Yes
I seen it yesterday when I got home	Yes	No	Yes	Yes
My daughter is taller than me	Yes	No	Yes	Yes
Dr. Hallahan might could give you a call	Yes	No	Yes	Yes

American streets, they are grammatical. A prescriptivist will take issue with the way the verbs have been used but even a prescriptivist could not claim that the meaning was unclear – we know exactly what it means if we hear somebody say *my sister is taller than me*. The hardline prescriptivist would say that the correct usage is *my sister is taller than I*. Formulated this way, the speaker would not be seen as well-spoken, but as odd or pretentious or perhaps, a non-native speaker.

Chomsky's famous demonstration of the difference between grammatical and well-formed was first published in 1957, and hasn't yet been replaced by a better one. Sentences (1) and (2) are equally nonsensical, but any speaker of English will recognize that only the former is grammatical.

1   Colorless green ideas sleep furiously.
2   Furiously sleep ideas green colorless.

(Chomsky 1957)

"*Furiously sleep ideas green colorless" is not grammatical for any speaker of English, descriptivist or prescriptivist. No child growing up in an English-speaking community would produce this sentence, just as you never have to remind a child about other points of language-internal, rule-governed grammaticality. When is the last time you heard somebody say to a child something like: "Susie! Stop putting your articles after your nouns!"

The concept of grammaticality might seem to be vague, because the methodology is so very simple: a person is asked if a given sentence suits their personal sense of well-formedness. A set of four sentences will help demonstrate how this works:

1   Sam put a red scarf on the dog.
2   George took the dog.
3   Linda asked what Sam put the red scarf on.
4   *George took the dog that Linda asked what Sam put a red scarf on.

The first three sentences are grammatical (they sound well-formed, as something you might say or hear said) for native speakers of English. The third one will make most people stop and think, but it can be unraveled. The last one cannot.

This process is used extensively by theoretical syntacticians, a field in which linguists are not interested in variation or change in language. When theoretical syntacticians come across native speakers who disagree on the grammaticality of a given utterance (which will happen quite often), they may note that as "noise," but otherwise abstract away from it.

Socially constructed grammar is what your parents or teachers were targeting when they corrected your language use. If Susie loudly announces "I gotta pee" during religious services, or if she says "I ain't got none," when she is asked about pets, some adult nearby may correct her, as you were possibly corrected (so long as the first language you acquired was English). Everyone seems to have memories of this kind, perhaps because such corrections can be quite harsh.

Linguists often keep notes on overheard conversations that illustrate such points. For example, in 1989, in Borders Books in Ann Arbor, an expensively dressed woman went rushing by, her son – maybe 10 years old – running to keep up with her. Over her shoulder she said to him: "I hate it when you use such ignorant, slovenly language. We don't talk like that."

I didn't hear what the boy had said to get this kind of rebuke, but the vitriol in the mother's voice, the dismissive tone in the way she corrected her son stuck with me. Suppose the boy had said, "Dad says the house needs painted."[10] This is a construction common in Michigan and some other areas in the Midwest, but it usually strikes non-Michiganders as odd. It still strikes me as odd, though I lived there for more than ten years. This usage is strongly marked for both region and socioeconomic status (Murray and Simon 1999).

If a boy growing up in Michigan used this construction, why would a parent correct him so abruptly? It's not that she didn't understand the message he was trying to get across; just the opposite. She was reacting to the social markers her son was using. The rules violated were not linguistic in nature; the objections rose out of socially constructed concepts of proper English and good language. *I do not identify with Michiganders,* the mother was saying, *and neither do you. Stop talking like them.*

Social conventions are a tremendously powerful source in our lives. Consider for a moment: A man wakes up one morning, ready to go to work. He'll be giving a speech he's been preparing for weeks, to an audience of a thousand employees. Everything hangs on this speech. His life goals, his career. Everything. If he handles it right, he'll be promoted to CEO. If he doesn't, his career at this company – and perhaps everywhere – is over. This is a once-in-a-lifetime opportunity, and he's prepared for it.

Except when he goes to his closet to get the polished shoes, freshly ironed shirt and crisp new suit, they aren't there. In fact, none of his clothes are there. He searches through the whole house, and finds not so much as one of his socks, anywhere. The only piece of clothing is a dress hanging in the guest room closet along with a pair of matching pumps, which look like they will actually fit him. The dress and pumps – and the boxers he wore to bed – are all he has.

His cell phone is dead, something he realizes just as the electricity goes out. No way to call for help. No neighbors within shouting distance. His car is missing – one more disaster – so he'll have to take the bus, too.

Does he wear the dress?

Our social conventions develop over time, along with a complex set of rationalizations. If a woman stands up in the middle of a restaurant eating linguini with clam sauce with her hands, the owner would probably feel justified in asking the customer to change her behavior or leave. Most people would consider this a reasonable request.

But what if when the owner went up to the woman to ask her to leave, she turned into a mouse and disappeared between the floorboards?

This possibility had not occurred to you, for the simple reason that it violates all the things we understand about the physical universe. The woman eating with her hands is ignoring the laws of socially acceptable behavior in public; when she turns into a mouse, she is flouting the rules of physics. Thus it is necessary to make a distinction between linguistic grammaticality and socially constructed grammaticality.[11]

I have put forward as facts that any language embedded in a viable speech community is capable of adapting to any linguistic need, and that every native speaker produces utterances which are by definition grammatical. What I have not claimed and cannot claim, is that message content can be judged in the same way. Take, for example, the sentence:

If we don't succeed, we run the risk of failure.

This sentence is grammatical in every sense of the word, but it makes no sense. It sounds well-formed but there isn't any content.

The fact is that each utterance, while grammatical, may or may not fulfill the purpose for which it was conceived and formulated, for a wide variety of reasons. Consider the following hypothetical responses (B1–B5) to a simple question, (A):

> A: Can I have your phone number?
> B1: I'll have a beer.
> B2: Uh, well, I'm not sure – what is my phone number, it's – ah –, I don't –.
> B3: What's a phone, and why does it have a number?
> B4: When hell freezes over.
> B5: It's 555-3333.

To determine linguistic grammaticality, a very simple question suffices: Can this utterance be generated by the grammar of the language? Each of the responses above is a grammatical construction for my own variety of English, and for many others. But an evaluation of content and socially construed well-formedness or efficiency moves to issues of intent, composition, and delivery. In each case, we could ask a number of questions to evaluate the responses given.

- Is the message clear?
- Is it easily broken down into its constituents?
- Does one point follow logically from the previous point?
- Is it couched in concise language and free of excess and overly complex construction?
- Is it persuasive?
- Is the delivery pleasing?

The five possible responses provided for the question "Can I have your phone number?" could be judged on the basis of clarity, logic, conciseness, persuasiveness, and delivery, but not until we have more information, because the communicative intent of both the question posed and the answer received are multidimensional. It is possible to imagine many underlying purposes to the question "Can I have your phone number?" depending on the context in which it is asked, and the relationship of speaker to listener. In one possible situation (in which one person is trying to establish a romantic or sexual relationship), the answer "Uh, well, I'm not sure – what is my phone number, it's – ah –, I don't –" may not be concise (in the sense of "succinct"), but the underlying message is, after all, a complex one: *I have evaluated you as a potential romantic and/or sexual partner and I find that you are not acceptable, but I have no wish to insult you directly or embarrass you, and in fact I am afraid of the social consequences of doing so.*

Within its social context, the reply is very clear, and it is also concise in that it gets its message across with fewer lexical items than the alternate proposed. Alternatively, *When hell freezes over* is a longer answer than *no*, but it is also much more descriptive and informative. A simple negation leaves room for interpretation of motive; *When hell freezes over* leaves very little doubt about the speaker's feelings.

In Europe in the medieval and early modern periods, liberal arts consisted in part of the study of grammar, logic, and rhetoric (the trivium), where rhetoric is taken to mean language used effectively and persuasively. This concern with effective language persists, although the term remains, as always, a subjective one.[12] If effectiveness in language is the sum of more specific qualifiers (clarity, logic, conciseness, persuasiveness, and delivery), then calculation of effectiveness is complicated by the fact that these are subjective rather than objective measures. Whether or not these are reasonable demands of language as a vehicle of communication is also debatable. Is language more effective when sentences are short, or long? When it is spoken fast, or slow? When the vocabulary used is primarily Germanic (help!), or Romance (assistance!)?

I will argue at various points in this book that the evaluation of language effectiveness can sometimes serve as a way of judging not the message, but the social identity of the messenger.

Political debate provides daily examples of highly educated and powerful people who speak what is generally considered *Standard American English (*SAE). Some of them do use language clearly and concisely, while others seem incapable of expressing simple ideas clearly. When the media draw attention to a politician's language use, not the content, but the variety of English itself – they are not accusing that politician of lying under oath or running Ponzi schemes or of dereliction of duty. Such commentary is not about policy or law; it is delivered in the manner of the finger-wagging way of children on the playground, the ones who police the social structure and keep people in their place. The fact is, the variety of English a person speaks, highly regarded or stigmatized, standard-like or vernacular, cannot predict the quality and effectiveness of any given utterance or that person's worth as a communicator.

What can be predicted is the fact that listeners will make assumptions about the speaker on the basis of language markers that signal alliance to certain social groups, primarily those having to do with race, ethnicity and economic factors.

Written language and spoken language are historically, structurally, and functionally fundamentally different creatures

In the history of mankind, widespread literacy is a relatively new development, one that trailed along behind technological advances in printing and the manufacture of paper.

Early printers had some things to work out, including the question of norms and standardization. If Caxton had to print the Bible in ten different dialects of English, there would be little or no profit in the venture, which was, of course, not acceptable. The solution was to print the Bible in one variety of English, and then to convince everybody that that was the best kind of English. Thus began the movement toward language norms and standardization of the printed (and then, written) language.

class → capitalism

It seems a matter of logic and convenience from a business perspective, but this narrowing-down and standardizing process was a long and arduous one. Who was going to make decisions about spellings and grammatical structures? Who was going to teach them, who would impose them, and how?

As it became possible to make key religious, literary and legal documents available on a wider basis, the standardized written language became a commodity of increasing value. In the first line, the control of this commodity was in the hands of those who were on the front line of teaching reading and writing. Trained clerks and lowly teachers claimed authority, and began to make a living out of telling people what their language should look and sound like. The job was not only to teach writing, but more important, to instill a respect for institutionalized authority in matters of language. This is still the case today.

The most salient feature which distinguishes an abstracted, idealized standard written or printed English from the reality of spoken language is conformity or the suppression of variation. That suppression is not easily achieved. It is a battle continually fought, and never completely won.

For linguists, the spoken language is of primary (and often, exclusive) interest. In this we linguists are pretty much alone; for most people involved in education – and many others, as well – the written language continues as a commodity of huge dimensions and complexity:

> Although the bias that speech is primary over writing has been extremely important in guiding research efforts within linguistics, it has not been widely accepted outside of linguistics. In fact, the historical view that written, literary language is true language continues as the dominant lay perception to the present time. Our children need to study English at school, which includes written composition and the prescriptive rules of writing, not speech . . . We expect our grammars and dictionaries to present the correct forms of written language; [when they instead] present both literate and colloquial vocabulary they are severely criticized for destroying the standards of English.
>
> (Biber 1988: 5–6)

The primacy of the spoken language is easy enough to bolster with factual evidence, but it is perhaps the single most difficult concept for non-linguists to fully grasp and accept. In our minds the spoken and written languages are so intertwined that we seem sometimes incapable of distinguishing between them. A LanguageLog post ("Pronouncing it by the book")[13] provides examples of the kind of extreme emotional investment some people put in the idea of the superiority of the written language:

> She was from Northern California, but had been born in the Midwest, and she acknowledged, "Everyone always assumes I'm British or something just because I'm more careful to pronounce words properly. It only sounds unusual because everyone simply ignores how words are spelled anymore." Everyone else at the table simply nodded as though that made all the sense in the world.

The internet abounds with examples of people who are proud to promote the superiority of the written language, and at the same time, to conflate written and spoken languages, adding punctuation to the mix: "Nothing destroys precision grammar and correct usage like raw, unmitigated anger [. . .] excessive use of capital letters, abundance of exclamation points, and lack of proper punctuation."[14]

In this weblog writer's view, too many exclamation points renders a piece of writing ungrammatical. I dislike exclamation points myself, but never once have I failed to understand a document because of them. Punctuation is irrelevant to the kind of work sociolinguists do, and has nothing to do with grammaticality. And yet, arguments about punctuation and the written word rage on: the misuse of semicolons, the insidious serial comma, the virus-like greengrocers' apostrophe sneaking into possessive nouns to herald the imminent fall of Western civilization.[15]

Arguments about usage are routinely settled by pulling out reference books (*The Chicago Manual of Style*, for example) or dictionaries. The dictionary is regarded as the highest authority in matters of language. Few people ever stop to ask how it is that the dictionary has taken – or has been given – such absolute authority. For the most part, individuals feel entitled to make pronouncements about language and to base those assertions on dictionaries or vague, never defined authorities, as in the case of a character on Showtime's *Californication*. Here the irreverent, quick-witted, curmudgeonly Hank Moody (played by David Duchovny) is rebelling against the intrusion of computers into life and language:

> People... they don't write anymore – they blog. Instead of talking, they text, no punctuation, no grammar: LOL this and LMFAO that. You know, it just seems to me it's just a bunch of stupid people pseudo-communicating with a bunch of other stupid people in a proto-language that resembles more what cavemen used to speak than the King's English.

Hank is a writer and as such, considers himself an authority on all matters having to do with language, written or spoken. He conflates the two without a pause or hesitation, and he is resentful because he believes others are ruining the language he (and the King) command. The offenders use language, as he sees it, without grammar. Note also that he refers to the *King's* English in spite of the fact that there is currently no king, but a queen in England. This is not insignificant, given Moody's character.

This kind of assertion about language, no matter how lacking in consistency or logic or factual underpinning, is received enthusiastically and repeated widely. In this case, Hank's testy ode to the decline of English was cited more than 3,000 times on the internet within a few months of the episode's first broadcast.

Prince Charles often demonstrates the same tendency in public speeches, as we see in the following example given in 1989 when he was judging a reading competition:

> If English is spoken in Heaven (as the spread of English as a world language makes more likely each year) God undoubtedly employs Cranmer as his speech-writer. The angels of the lesser ministries probably use the language of the New English Bible and the Alternative Service Book for internal memos.

I suppose we must be fair and point out that the Prince of Wales does not automatically assume that English is spoken in heaven. Nevertheless, his further assumptions are quite interesting. Those language authorities he cites as exemplary all draw their power from religious institutions. Thomas Cranmer was the Archbishop of Canterbury (the head of the Anglican Church) under Henry VIII; the Prince of Wales offers Cranmer as an authority because he simplified and translated the Latin prayer books into one English volume, the Book of Common Prayer. Then Henry VIII got a real lock on things by coming up with England's Act of Uniformity, which made the Book of Common Prayer the only acceptable book of its kind.

It is also interesting that the written documents which are cited here as appropriate models for the spoken language are British ones (in other places, Prince Charles has been very critical of the damage that has been done to English by its speakers on the North American continent). Most important to the discussion immediately at hand is the way this picture of language perfection takes as a departure point the idea that the various mediums of language are one and the same. Here we see mention of spoken language, speeches (which can be given as planned but extemporaneous speech, or the reading out loud of written language), and written language.

This proclamation by the future king of England builds on a tradition which goes back to Socrates, who suggested that the gods took a direct interest in language:

Hermogenes: And where does Homer say anything about names, and what does he say?

Socrates: He often speaks of them – notably and nobly in the places where he distinguishes the different names which gods and men give the same things. Does he not in these passages make a remarkable statement about the correctness of names? For the gods must clearly be supposed to call things by their right and natural names, do you not think so?

(Hamilton and Cairns 1961: 429–430)

More recently, in an event which is almost certainly apocryphal,[16] Miriam "Ma" Ferguson, the first female governor of the State of Texas, expressed the decisive argument against bilingual education (and unwittingly, for more and better history and geography instruction) by drawing on the (for her) ultimate authority: "If English was good enough for Jesus Christ," she declared, "then it's good enough for the schoolchildren of Texas" (*Handbook of Texas* 2009).

It has been pointed out that "writing and speaking are not just alternative ways of doing the same things; rather, they are ways of doing different things" (Halliday 1989: xv). That is, we write things that tax our ability to remember (genealogies, instruction manuals, legal documents), or to project our thoughts through space and time. We speak everything else. But aren't they the same thing, just as water is water whether it flows, or freezes so that we can walk on it? Isn't it just a matter of presentation? Can't speech and writing be treated as different manifestations of the same mental phenomenon? Wouldn't spoken language be more efficient if we treated it like written language?

Writing systems are a strategy developed in response to demands arising from social, technological and economic change. The purpose of writing systems is to convey decontextualized information. We write love letters, laundry lists, historical monographs, novels, mythologies, wound care manuals, menus, out to lunch signs, biochemistry textbooks. We write these things down because our memories are not capable of storing such masses of information for ourselves or those who come after us, or because we consider the message one worthy of preserving past a particular point in time.

The demands made on written language are considerable: we want it to span time and space, and we want it to do that in a social vacuum, without the aid of paralinguistic features and often without shared context of any kind. Thus, the argument goes, written language needs to be free of variation: it must be consistent in every way, from spelling to sentence structure.[17]

We might think of the difference between spoken and written language (see Table 1.2) as the difference between walking and machines built for the purpose of transporting human beings. Unless a child suffers a terrible turn of fate, she will learn to walk without focused instruction. No one must show her how to put one foot ahead of the other. She will experiment with balance and gait, and learn to move herself physically to pursue food and shelter, to come in contact with another human being, to explore her world. Over time, the human race developed a series of technologies to improve the ability to move themselves: they tamed horses, camels, oxen; they built carts, carriages, boats, trains, bicycles, cars, airplanes, skateboards. All of these things are faster than walking, and, if speed is the primary criterion by which we judge efficiency of movement, they are superior to the skill all humans have in common.

But it would not occur to us to set up standards for walking on the basis of the speed of any of these vehicles: it is a physical impossibility to walk 60 miles an hour. We cannot

Table 1.2 Written vs. spoken language traits

Spoken language . . .	Written language . . .
Is an innate human capacity which is acquired by all human children who are not isolated from other language users during the critical acquisition period	Is not universal, and must be consciously and rigorously taught. It is a skill which will be acquired with differing degrees of success
Draws heavily on paralinguistic features to convey information in more than one way: tone of voice, body language, facial expression, etc.	Must use punctuation, additional lexical items or constructions when written letters alone do not suffice
Primarily carried out face-to-face between two or more persons	Is carried out as a solitary pursuit, with an audience removed in time and space
Confusion and ambiguity resolved directly by repair and confirmation procedures	Confusion and ambiguity are not immediately resolvable
Happens in a social and temporal context, and thus brings with it a great deal of background information; draws on context to complement meaning and fill in that which is not said out loud	Without context, and thus more prone to ambiguity; intolerant of ellipses
Is planned or spontaneous	Is by nature planned
Is ephemeral	Can be permanent
Inherently and unavoidably variable on every level, language internally (structure) and externally (social); exploits variation to pass on information in addition to that of the surface message	Variation is actively suppressed and discouraged

walk like we ride. Why then do we not think anything of Prince Charles telling us that in heaven, people will speak like they write, as if this were the ultimate good, the ideal?

In their seminal work on authority in language, James and Lesley Milroy point to the underlying issue which may explain – in part – why we are so willing to see the spoken language subordinated to the written.

> As writing skills are difficult, our educational systems have concentrated on inculcating a relatively high degree of literacy, with little attention paid to the nature of spoken language as an everyday social activity. Training in the use of "English" . . . is usually assumed to be training in the use of written English . . . Spoken language is taken for granted. As a result of this constant emphasis on written language, there is an understandable tendency for people to believe that writing is somehow more complicated and difficult (and more important) than speech.
>
> (Milroy and Milroy 1999: 55)

This preoccupation with the written language to the exclusion of the spoken is quite easy to document. The National Association of Teachers of English, for example, publishes guidelines for the curriculum in English on a regular basis; of the twelve points addressed, only four include mention of spoken language skills, and then in a very vague and indirect way (a topic which will be taken up in more detail in Chapter 7).

From the spoken to the written language is a large step; it is another significant step from the written language to the possession of literacy.[18] However, the possession of a skill and the facility to use that skill to construct a product are cultural resources not equally available to all persons, and are heavily laden with social currencies. In the U.S., most people do not consider oral cultures as equal to literate ones. Some scholars have argued, with differing degrees of subtlety, that certain kinds or modes of thought cannot develop in oral cultures, and that for this reason literate cultures are superior.

This type of argument has come under attack on both methodological and theoretical grounds. One of the oldest but still most comprehensive examples of such tortured reasoning is Bernstein's (1966) theory of restricted and elaborated codes.[19] Bernstein attempted (and failed) to establish that children who spoke "elaborated" languages at home (he called those languages syntactically complex) were more capable of logical thought and other cognitive advantages, and that children who heard only restricted codes in the home were at a disadvantage.[20]

It is demonstrably true that in a literate culture, illiteracy is a *social* brand like few others. Cameron calls what goes on around the written language a *circle of intimidation*:

> [M]astering a complex and difficult craft gives you an inbuilt incentive to defend its practices. If I have invested time and effort learning how to write according to a particular set of prescriptions, it will take some convincing that those prescriptions are not necessary and desirable; to admit that the rules are both arbitrary and pointless is to devalue my own accomplishment in mastering them.
>
> (Cameron 1995: 14)

Gee goes a step farther when he outlines the complex associations and expectations of literacy:

> [L]iteracy leads to logical, analytic, critical and rational thinking, general and abstract uses of language, a skeptical and questioning attitude, a distinction between myth and history, the recognition of the importance of time and space, complex and modern governments . . . political democracy and greater social equity, economic development, wealth and productivity, political stability, urbanization, and contraception (a lower birth rate) . . . The literacy myth is, in fact, one of the master Myths of our society; it is foundational to how we make sense of reality, though it is not necessarily an accurate reflection of that reality, nor does it necessarily lead to a just, equitable, and humane world.
>
> (Gee 2007a [1996]: 36)

The literacy myth plays a role in the subordination of the spoken language to norms developed for the written language – norms that are in themselves arbitrary. This process is part of what Foucault has called the disciplining of discourse, or the way we decide who has the right to talk, and to be listened to (Foucault 1984), the major topic of interest in the later chapters of this book.

Variation is intrinsic to all spoken language at every level

Spoken language varies for every speaker in terms of speech sounds, sound patterns, word and sentence structure, intonation, and meaning, from utterance to utterance. This is true even for those who believe themselves to speak an educated, elevated, supra-regional English.

Variation is not a frivolous or sloppy or useless feature of language.[21] Quite the contrary, the variants available to the speaker to choose from are not neutral, and while the choice between them may not be conscious, it is often purposeful.

There are three main sources of variation in spoken language:

1. *Language internal pressures*, arising in part from the mechanics of production and perception.
2. *External influences on language*, such as geographic mobility and social behavior subject to normative and other formative social pressures.
3. *Variation arising from language as a creative vehicle of free expression*.

These forces can and do function in tandem, and any good study of language change in progress will consider at least the first two together.

Variation over space is the dimension that most people seem to be aware of, but in a limited way. There are language communities of well-established, self-contained or isolated religious groups that mark their English for insider/outsider status (the Amish and Mennonites in Pennsylvania; Mormons in Utah and Arizona; Jews in Williamsburg and the greater New York City area, Hassidic Jews in Brookline, outside of Boston). There are historical language communities which remain bilingual despite outside pressures (German in parts of Michigan and Texas, French (independent of the Creole communities in Louisiana) (Figure 1.1), bilingual pockets in New England and Louisiana.

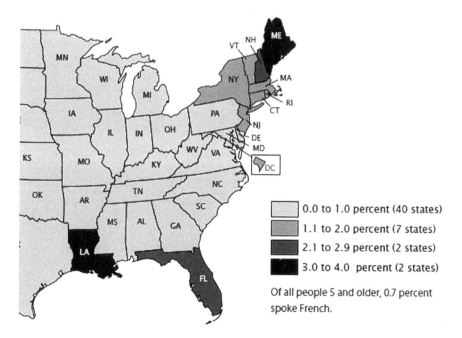

0.0 to 1.0 percent (40 states)
1.1 to 2.0 percent (7 states)
2.1 to 2.9 percent (2 states)
3.0 to 4.0 percent (2 states)

Of all people 5 and older, 0.7 percent spoke French.

Figure 1.1 French (and French Creole) spoken at home, 2007

Source: U.S. Census Bureau American Community Survey

Variation that is less likely to reach the level of consciousness has to do with the human neurological and vocal apparatus, which is architecturally and structurally universal and which accounts for the similarities in the way language is produced and perceived. As a young child acquiring language, every human being has potentially available to them the full range of possible sounds. The sounds which will eventually survive and become part of the child's language are arranged into language-specific systems, each sound standing in relation to the other sounds. In linguistic terms, the study of production and perception of speech sounds is the science of phonetics; concern with how sounds are organized into systems is called phonology.

It is in the production and perception of speech sounds as systematic entities functioning in relationship to each other that there is perhaps the greatest potential for variation in language, and following from that, variation leading to change. There are so many changes in progress at any given time that it would not be possible to catalog them all, but in Chapter 2 we consider a few changes that may well be active in your own variety of English.

To close this chapter I must point out what may seem obvious by now: linguists are outnumbered by prescriptivists, and outgunned, too. Prescriptivists are in a position to broadcast their opinions from positions of authority granted to them automatically, whereas linguists are confined to university settings and conferences. This makes it possible for prescriptivists to simply ignore – or mock – what linguists have to say about language. They make full use of this advantage and that is unlikely to change, ever.

By the end of this book you will be able to answer the crucial question for yourself: Are you comfortable with the institutional practices that are forced on individuals in the pursuit of proper English? If you are not – and not everyone will be – you must decide what you, as an individual, can do about it.

> Find out just what people will submit to, and you have found out the exact amount of injustice and wrong which will be imposed upon them; and these will continue until they are resisted with either words or blows, or both.
> (Frederick Douglass, *What to the Slave is the Fourth of July?*, July 5, 1852)

DISCUSSION QUESTIONS AND EXERCISES

- Browse through the Speech Accent Archive.
- Listen to speech samples from places you know well, where you have lived. How does your own variety of English compare? Do the samples on the website strike you as representative? Consider submitting a sample of your own speech to add to the archive (under "how to use this site").
- Pick one of the website resources provided above (but not the Speech Accent Archive) and report to the class on what it is, and how it might be of interest or use.
- Ask five people you don't know well why it's wrong to say "I seen it yesterday when I got home." Do not react to their response, and don't engage in conversation. Concentrate on taking notes. In class, compare the answers you received to those other students recorded. Similarities? Differences? Does gender or age make a difference? How does this exercise illustrate the taxicab maxim, if it does at all? In his essay "Standard English a Myth? No!"

Kilpatrick disputes the claim that all languages and language varieties are potentially equal, and uses this comparison to make his point: "And to assert that all languages and all dialects 'have the same expressive potential' is to assert that the ukulele ranks with the cello" (Kilpatrick 1999). Does this strike you as a valid comparison? Why or why not?

- Milroy and Milroy (1999) state: "As writing skills are difficult, our educational systems have concentrated on inculcating a relatively high degree of literacy, with little attention paid to the nature of spoken language as an everyday social activity." Can you conceive of ways that our schools might pay more attention to developing spoken language skills? What would the goals be?
- Is FOXP2 evidence to support Chomsky's innateness hypothesis?

Notes

1 Those stages are (1) babbling (repetitive consonant–verb patterns such as bababa or tatata); (2) one or two syllable words in isolation (duck, car, teddy); (3) two-word strings (more juice, get down, want that); (4) the telegraphic stage, where grammatical bits are mostly left out (Elmo kiss baby doll, Where mama going? I tie it myself). And onward to the acquisition of grammatical elements, complex structures and communicative competence.

2 There has been a lot of exaggeration and misinformation about FOXP2 from the popular press. It is factually incorrect to call it "the grammar gene." It does have something to do with articulation and fine motor control needed for speech. It also seems to control the behavior of some hundred other genes. FOXP2 is best understood as a starting point "for future studies of the molecular basis of language and human evolution" (source: http://goo.gl/3Zwgd).

3 While the more general language issues discussed here will be applicable to all English spoken on the continent, the exploration of specific authority and prescription issues focuses on the U.S. and with very few exceptions does not draw on material from other English-speaking countries.

4 I refer here specifically to academic linguists. Outside of the discipline, the definition of linguist is much broader, including, among other things, a linguist as a polyglot.

5 Any language which is no longer acquired as a first language, and is no longer used in day-to-day communication by a community of persons is considered to be dead, whether or not it survives in a literary form. Many languages have died and left no record behind; however, there are cases where moribund languages have been revived. Hebrew is an example of a dead (or "sleeping") language coming back to life. For two thousand years, Hebrew was preserved as a written and ritualistic language of the Jewish people only, and thus was dead by the technical definition. It is now spoken as a first language by a good proportion of the population of Israel.

6 Toni Morrison received the Nobel Prize for Literature in 1993. "[Morrison] made her debut as a novelist in 1970, soon gaining the attention of both critics and a wider audience for her epic power, unerring ear for dialogue, and her poetically-charged and richly-expressive depictions of Black America" (source: http://goo.g./ucXV5).

7 The modern-day systematic and violent repression of the Kurdish language and culture in Turkey is one extreme example. (Skutnabb-Kangas *et al.* 1994.)

8 This statement is generally attributed to Kwame Nkrumah, former president of Ghana and father of the pan-national African movement. It is also widely paraphrased as "Histories are written by the victors."

9 The standard linguistic convention is to put an asterisk in front of a sentence or word that is ungrammatical; that is, cannot be generated by the native speaker's grammar.

10 Murray (1986) takes a closer look at the need + past participle construction.

11 Milroy and Milroy draw a contrast between what they call Type 1 and Type 2 complaints about language. If the opposition expressed is to language change itself, they term this Type 1; Type 2 complaints are concerned with efficiency in written language. I do not adopt this distinction because I find it more important to take into consideration the conflation of written and spoken language and differing definitions of grammaticality.

12 The 1992 edition of *The American Heritage Dictionary of the English Language* points out that the word *rhetoric* has undergone a shift in usage:

> The word *rhetoric* was once primarily the name of an important branch of philosophy and an art deserving of serious study. In recent years the word has come to be used chiefly in a pejorative sense to refer to inflated language and pomposity. Deprecation of the term may result from a modern linguistic puritanism, which holds that language used in legitimate persuasion should be plain and free of artifice – itself a tendentious rhetorical doctrine, though not often recognized as such. But many writers still prefer to bear in mind the traditional meanings of the word. Thus, according to the newer use of the term, the phrase empty rhetoric, as in "The politicians talk about solutions, but they usually offer only empty rhetoric," might be construed as redundant. But in fact only 35 percent of the Usage Panel judged this example to be redundant. Presumably, it can be maintained that rhetoric can be other than empty.

> The mention of *linguistic puritanism* is surprising in this context; in fact, the tone might indicate that the editors are torn: they are surprised (and perhaps not quite satisfied) with the decision of their Usage Panel (in itself an interesting phenomenon), but they also point out the fact that rhetorical rules are not objective: they are doctrines.

13 Available at: http://languagelog.ldc.upenn.edu/nll/?p=2762.

14 Available at: http://writenowisgood.typepad.com/write_now_is_good/wordimage_combo/.

15 This issue is so much in the minds of the public that in October 2009, the *New York Times* reissued an article entitled "Minder of Misplaced Apostrophes Scolds a Town" that originally appeared in 2001.

16 Benjamin Zimmer's weblog post dated April 29, 2006, at Language Log looks at this legend very closely.

17 This is, of course, a fairly modern development. Early writing systems of Western European languages had no regulated orthography, no dictionaries or language pundits. Take, for example, the name Shakespeare, which shows up as Shakespeare, Shakespere, Shakespear, Shackspeare, Shake-speare, Shakspeare, and Shaxberd, to name just a few variants. It's very hard to imagine anyone in the present day being so lax with spelling. John Steinbeck does not show up as John Stenpeck or Stienpack. Our orthography is so set in stone that it lags centuries behind change in the spoken language.

18 In this discussion I have taken a short cut which some will find questionable, in that I have not considered in any depth what is meant by literacy, a term which has been

widely used and which stands at the center of much scholarly and educational debate. Here I use literate both in its narrowest way, as a reference to the skill needed to read and write, and in some of its broader connotations, as a measurement of cultural knowledge. The history of thought about literacy is one which I do not have time to explore here, but it is obviously both interesting and important. In particular, it would be useful to understand the point in our history in which our perceptions of the relationship of the written and spoken language began to change, as it seems that the subordination of spoken to written language may be a fairly new cultural phenomenon. I am very thankful to Deborah Keller-Cohen for valuable discussions on this topic.

19 While Bernstein never made explicit the connection between languages of oral cultures and "restricted" codes, or languages of literate ones and "elaborated" codes, my reading of his work is not an unusual one.

20 In a persuasive essay on the advantages of multiculturalism, Charles Taylor (1994) discusses examples of the kind of reasoning which ranks literate cultures as inherently more valuable than oral ones.

21 Earlier it was established that all living languages change; it can also be stated unequivocally that all change is preceded by variation. However, it cannot be claimed that all variation is followed by change.

Suggested further reading

Asking a linguist how many languages they speak is like asking a doctor how many diseases they have.

(Lynnequist, http://separatedbyacommonlanguage.blogspot.com/)

For those with little or no background in linguistics who would like to learn more, the following books and articles provide an introduction to a sampling of relevant topics. Note that some are more general and others more specific; some are more conversational in tone, and others more technical. Please also consult the Shortened bibliography on p. 337.

Morphology

Aronoff, M. and Fudeman, K.A. (2010) *What Is Morphology?* Malden, MA: Wiley-Blackwell.

Phonetics and phonology

Ashby, P. (2005) *Speech Sounds*. New York: Routledge.
Odden, D.A. (2005) *Introducing Phonology*. Cambridge: Cambridge University Press.

Syntax, grammar

Crystal, D. (2003a) Grammatical Mythology. In *The Cambridge Encyclopedia of the English Language*. New York: Cambridge University Press.

Crystal, D. (2003b) The Structure of Sentences. In *The Cambridge Encyclopedia of the English Language*. New York: Cambridge University Press.

Veit, R. (1999) *Discovering English Grammar*. Boston: Allyn and Bacon.

General introductions

Fromkin, V., Rodman, R. and Hyams, N.M. (2009) *An Introduction to Language*. Boston: Cengage Wadsworth.

Vanderweide, T., Rees-Miller, J. and Aronoff, M. (2001) *Study Guide for Contemporary Linguistics*. New York: Bedford/St. Martin's.

Language change and language history

Aitchison, J. (2001) *Language Change: Progress or Decay?* Cambridge: Cambridge University Press.

Crystal, D. (2005) *The Stories of English*. Woodstock, NY: Overlook Press.

History of American English

Bailey, R.W. (2004) American English: Its Origins and History. In E. Finegan and J.R. Rickford (eds.) *Language in the USA: Themes for the Twenty-First Century*. Cambridge: Cambridge University Press.

Sociolinguistics

Alim, H.S. (2009) Hip Hop Nation Language. In A. Duranti (ed.) *Linguistic Anthropology: A Reader*. New York: John Wiley and Sons.

Eckert, P. (2004) Adolescent Language. In E. Finegan and J.R. Rickford (eds.) *Language in the USA: Themes for the Twenty-First Century*. Cambridge: Cambridge University Press.

Ervin-Tripp, S., *et al.* (2004) "It Was Hecka Funny": Some Features of Children's Conversational Development. In *Proceedings of the Twelfth Annual Symposium* about *Language and Society*, Austin, TX, April 16–18. Available at: http://xrl.in/726q.

Winford, D. (2003) *An Introduction to Contact Linguistics*. Malden, MA: Blackwell.

Wolfram, W. and Schilling-Estes, N. (2006) Social and Ethnic Dialects. In *American English: Dialects and Variation*. London: Blackwell.

Uses and misuses of dictionaries

Nunberg, G. (2005) The Book of Samuels. November 29. Available at: http://people.ischool.berkeley.edu/~nunberg/johnson.html.

Language in motion

2

Eppur' si muove.[1]

Galileo Galilei

Changes in progress

There is a common belief that regional differences in U.S. English are eroding, and that as time passes, we all will sound more alike. The broadcast and print media outlets are believed to be the power that fuels this march toward homogeneity, and remarks on this topic show up in letters to the editor, on discussion forums, in human interest news stories and in weblogs. For example, "Dialects are becoming rare. TV and increased geographic mobility have us speaking more and more alike no matter where we're from. We're losing a portion of our culture" (Braiterman 2008).[2]

Where this idea originated is unclear. What we can be said with certainty is that regional varieties of English not becoming more alike over time, despite mass communication. Hard evidence makes it clear that just the opposite is true. Regional varieties of American English are changing, and many of the changes in progress are causing differences to intensify rather than lessen.

Salvucci (1999) synthesized all the major studies of language variation over space from 1968 to the late 1990s, and came up with the map shown in Figure 2.1. The linguists who contributed to this identification of dialect areas did so on the basis of bundles of linguistic features (or isoglosses) that constitute a kind of fluid linguistic border. Some of the changes in progress discussed in this chapter may seem unlikely to you, but closer examination might change your mind.

Each case is interesting for different reasons, and each case is vastly simplified here for our purposes. They are:

- the presence or absence of (r) after vowels;
- the Northern Cities Chain Shift;
- lexical variation and discourse markers;
- weak and strong verbs.

r-less in Manhattan[3]

The presence or absence of the /r/ sound after a vowel has been a sociolinguistic marker in the Eastern and Southern U.S. for a very long time, and it is also one of the most exhaustively studied. In the simplest terms, we are talking about /r/ when it occurs in the following positions or environments following a vowel:

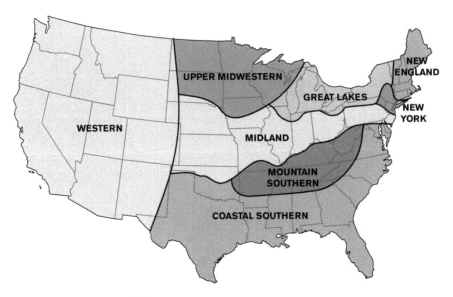

Figure 2.1 Language variation over space
Source: Adapted from Salvucci (1999)

| word final | whateve(r), butte(r), humdinge(r), floo(r), ca(r) |
| morpheme final or internal | sca(r)ed, ca(r)s, pa(r)ty, fou(r)th, ca(r)d |

The loss of (r) can result in homonyms as in the pair *pa(r)ty and potty* or *ca(r)ton and cotton*.
    One of the most famous and earliest studies of the connection between social identity and linguistic variation was William Labov's (1966) examination of postvocalic (r) in Manhattan (1972b). Since that time many more studies have been published (Table 2.1).

Table 2.1 Quantitative studies of (r) in the U.S.

Location of study	Year of publication	Ethnicity of speakers
New York, NY	1966 (1972)	White
Boston, MA	1967, 1971	White
Philadelphia, PA	1988	African American and White
Anniston, AL	1990	White
Memphis, TN	1997	African American
Philadelphia, PA	1998	White
Davenport, IA	2000	African American
Boston, MA, and Southern, NH	2007	African American and White
Stanstead, Quebec	2008	White
NH and VT, Upper Valley	2009	White
New York, NY	2009	White

Source: Adapted from Nagy and Irwin (2009)

From these studies it is quite clear that (r) is highly variable, and that its social significance is strongly dependent on place (as demonstrated in the New England studies), age, and race. In Boston and New Hampshire, (r) is variable across a wide variety of factors to the degree that "No speaker was either categorically r-ful or categorically r-less, and thus no social group was categorically r-ful or r-less" (Irwin and Nagy 2010).

At one point the absence of postvocalic (r) was common to most of New York City (and the East Coast more generally), but by the time Labov took up this study in the early 1960s, that had begun to change. Labov observed that in Manhattan, some people were r-less and others r-ful. He hypothesized that the shift toward r-fulness was linked to social prestige and thus that the variation would pattern to socioeconomic factors. In order to test that hypothesis, he conducted a field study which took place at three department stores in Manhattan: Saks, Macy's, and Klein's. The department stores represented three distinct socioeconomic classes: Saks's shoppers were well-to-do; Macy's were middle class; and Klein's were working class.

The fieldworkers in each store asked counter clerks for directions to a department they already knew to be on the fourth floor ("Excuse me, where are women's shoes?"). The clerk answered "Fourth floor," and the fieldworker walked around a corner to make notations. This methodology resulted in hundreds of tokens of the words "fourth floor" in both casual and emphatic speech (Figure 2.2).

Labov was able to pinpoint the effects of social class, prestige, style, gender, age, and other factors on the distribution of this data. The more socially elevated an individual was (or strove to be), the more postvocalic (r) sounds were retained in their speech. The simple conclusion would be that the lower the income level, the greater the r-lessness. But (r) is not simple. One way to get a sense of the range and distribution of postvocalic (r) is to watch reality television shows set on the East Coast between Philadelphia and Boston. The infamous *Jersey Shore* alone provides a lot of interesting examples.

Prestige is a complex concept, because it is so very relative. What is prestigious to one person may mean nothing to the next. More important: what is prestigious is one community may be a mark of disloyalty and highly stigmatized in the next, and thus the simplest truth about language variation: a speaker will gravitate to the variants tied to the community which is most important to him or her, despite possible negative repercussions.

Prestige is a notoriously relative concept, and is not always an issue of economics. Labov's study established that for (r), those who aspire to belong to the social upper crust

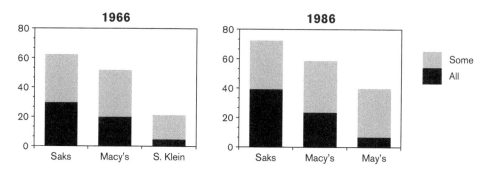

Figure 2.2 Percent r-fulness in three NYC department stores, rapid and anonymous data collection

Source: Adapted from Labov (1966), Fowler (1986)

are less likely to be r-less (Figure 2.3). Common sense alone should be enough to cast doubt on the idea that anybody in Manhattan who deletes postvocalic (r) is without ambitions, and disdainful of the trappings of social prestige. All around us we see people of all social and economic backgrounds trying to improve their lot in life; some work three jobs, wrack up huge school loans, buy lottery tickets, or invest in the latest widget. The fact is, some people strive for economic success and socially upward movement, but resist assimilation to the language habits of others who have successfully achieved that goal.

More recently new studies of r-lessness in Manhattan indicate that the distributions by socioeconomic class are stable (Fowler 1986). This is a good demonstration of the fact that variation is symbolic, that it is not necessarily unidirectional and further, that socioeconomic and sociolinguistic distributions do not necessary change at all. Speech that leans toward r-fulness is also very sensitive to formality and style issues, so that the more formal the situation, the more likely New Yorkers are to keep (r) after vowels (Fowler 1986; Labov 1994: 83–87).

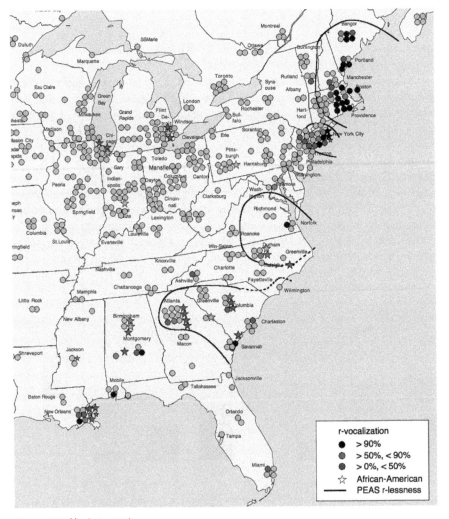

Figure 2.3 (r) after vowels

Source: Labov *et al.* 2006: 48. Reprinted by permission of the publisher, De Gruyter

The stability of the distribution of r-lessness in Manhattan is especially surprising when looking at other data on change over time. Elliott (2000) looked at films spanning most of the twentieth century, collecting data on an actor's use of (r), along with information on the individual's original variety of American English (Katherine Hepburn's native variety is r-less; Ginger Rogers' is r-ful) and other demographic information. One clear finding was that r-lessness was far more common earlier in the century, and that as the century progressed actors moved rapidly toward r-fulness. Figure 2.4 indicates that both groups – actors whose native variety of English is r-less (nonrhotic) and actors whose variety of English is r-ful (rhotic) – moved toward full r-fulness at about the same rate.

In the 1970s, Feagin undertook a similar investigation in Anniston, Alabama, and found a similar change in progress. Northerners tend to think of all Southerners as r-less, but Feagin established that postvocalic (r) was creeping in quite steadily. Another ten years provided enough data and perspective for her to conclude that the South was moving from r-less to r-ful in only three generations (Feagin 1990).

Elliott also found a great deal of stereotyping in the retention or deletion of (r), often within the same film for the same actress. For example, Patty Duke's character in *Valley of the Dolls* starts out as a prototypical good girl, at which point she is r-less no more than 9 percent of the time; by the end of the movie she is a drug addict with no hope, and her r-less rate has risen to 29 percent (ibid.: 121–122). It is no surprise that an actor manipulates language in the process of trying to establish character, a topic that will come up again in the discussion of accent in children's animated film.

So there is a wide range of factors that play a role in this change in progress. In addition to place, age is a strong predictor – the younger the speaker, the more postvocalic r-ful; so does education, so that people who have more formal education trend toward restoring (r). Race is more relevant still, as Labov (1972b) reports, "all other things being equal, African-American ethnicity lowers the frequency of (r) constriction by 32 percent."

African Americans tend to be r-less wherever they live, whether in Iowa (where postvocalic (r) is solid and categorical) or Alabama. Figure 2.5 indicates that New Hampshire is becoming more r-ful, while both Anglos and African Americans in Boston are resisting such a change. African Americans are more persistently r-less than Anglos. The two

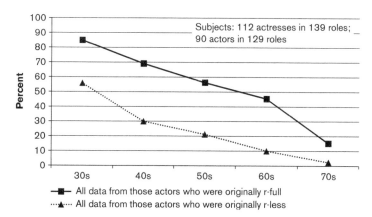

Figure 2.4 Five decades of film and the rate of change from r-less to r-ful, by actor's original rhoticity status whether r-ful or r-less

Source: Adapted from Elliot (2000: 105)

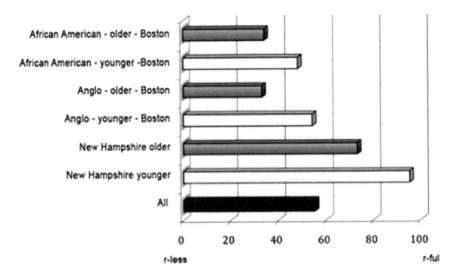

Figure 2.5 Percent postvocalic r maintenance by age, location, and race

Source: Adapted from Naggy and Irwin (2010)

groups' resistance to r-fulness may look similar on the surface, but the underlying motivations are certainly different.

This may be seen as following from many different factors, but the most important is likely the Great Migration. Between 1910 and 1940, roughly 1.5 million African Americans fled to the urban areas of the North to escape poverty and racism. After the interruption of World War II, another 1.5 million African Americans migrated North between 1940 and 1950, a trend that continued until about 1970.[4] For communities of African Americans recently who migrated from, for example, rural South Carolina to take up work in Detroit, postvocalic r-lessness was most likely a way to emphasize their solidarity and common history.

Recently linguists have argued for a more anthropological approach to the study of this kind of variation. Michael Silverstein (2003) proposed the concept of *indexical order* as an alternate way of studying language variation and change. Rather than assigning precise meanings to any given variable, for example, (r) deletion, it is more revealing and potentially more useful to think of variables as existing within a pool or field of potential meanings. Eckert (2008) has called this a "constellation of ideologically related meaning . . . The field is fluid, and each new activation has the potential to change the field by building on ideological connections." In a traditional sociolinguistic study, data would be analyzed quantitatively and the linguist would make observations. For example, the researcher might point to statistics to establish that the substitution of variant x for variant y is being propelled by adolescent males (or resisted by women of child-bearing age, etc.). The weakness of this approach is the way the focus on statistics has come to preclude study of less quantifiable aspects of language use. Thus a statement like *this change in progress is being led by middle-aged women* says nothing about the kinds of behavior and ideologies that underlie these patterns, what kinds of meaning people attach to the conservative and innovative variant, who does and does not fit the pattern and why (ibid.: 455).

Such a methodology would require a long period of observation to pinpoint those social categories which are truly relevant to the community in question, rather than simply trying to force the data into preconceived rubrics for class, ethnicity, race, etc. Eckert and Wenger point out that it is not social groups *per se* that are relevant to understanding distributions, but the "stances, activities and qualities" associated with those groups (2005: 584).

Variable postvocalic (r) is very complex and not quite what it seems on the surface: it's not that all well-educated or socially ambitious people in New York (or Boston, etc.) simply give in to rhoticity; there is an ebb and flow in way (r) is evaluated, adopted or rejected.

The Northern Cities Chain Shift (NCCS)

The Northern Cities Chain Shift (NCCS) involves the phonological system – specifically six vowels – which are shifting in a kind of domino effect in a large part of the Midwest (Gordon 2001).

Figure 2.6 is an abstraction of the shape of the human mouth which indicates the point of articulation for individual vowels. Any vowel can be described by its place of articulation (although a close transcription requires additional features be identified). To the right of the International Phonetic Alphabet's vowels are examples of each sound as it is realized in my own variety of English.

The linguistics lab at the University of Pennsylvania has been the site of many large-scale studies of change in progress, but the biggest and most exhaustive study, still ongoing, probably is the NCCS study. Simply put, six vowels are on the move, as seen in Figures 2.7 and 2.8.

The first stage of the series of shifts began sometime in the mid-twentieth century, most likely with the raising, tensing, and diphthongization of /æ/ (as in *bad*) moving toward the diphthong /ɪə/. If you say *be* + *at* together quickly, you'll end up with the shifted version of *bat* (bæt > bɪət). Another example: the woman's name *Ann* is pronounced like the man's name *Ian* where the NCCS has taken place.

As the first stage of the change goes forward and /æ/ moves out and into the diphthong system, the empty spot begins to be filled with the second stage shift, /ɑ/ > /æ/, and so on. In a series of phonological changes like this we talk about a chain, as if vowels fell in a neat

VOWELS

Figure 2.6 International Phonetic Alphabet and the author's vowel system

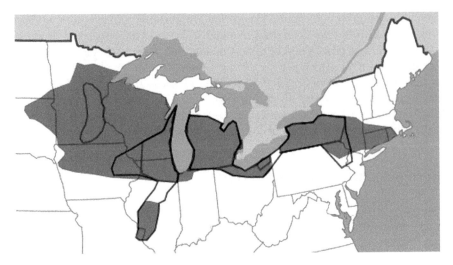

Figure 2.7 Geographic areas participating in the Northern Cities Chain Shift

Source: Adapted from Labov *et al.* (2006: 204)

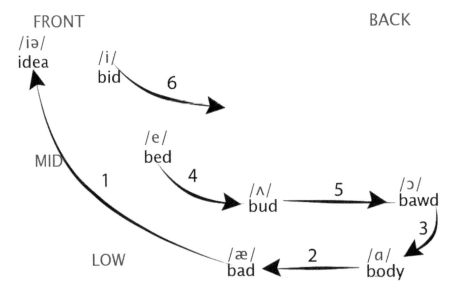

Figure 2.8 Northern Cities Chain Shift (abstracted)

Source: Adapted from Labov *et al.* (2006)

line, one after the other. In fact, it's a messy, drawn-out business that can only really be examined once it's well underway.

Sociolinguists are especially interested in how the stages of the NCCS relate to each other, and how they are motivated. Is there a social group who is driving the shift? Does it have to do with age or gender or economics or some complex interaction of all these and other social markers? For the NCCS, the questions are especially intriguing because the chain shift is such a large one (about 34 million people are taking part, in some or all parts), over a very large geographic area, and it's been gaining speed for a long time.

In my mid-twenties I moved from Chicago (where I was born and raised) to New Jersey. It was at that point that my own participation in the NCCS was terminated. By that I mean that because I was no longer living in a NCCS community, I was no longer exposed and thus I was immune to the social forces and pressures behind the shifts. Now, some twenty-five years later, I talk to friends still living on the Northwest side of Chicago once in a while, and it's always a bit of a surprise – even a shock – to hear how far the NCCS has progressed in the time I've been gone. I pronounce *block* with /ɑ/, but the people I grew up with now say it with /æ/, which to me sounds like the word *black*.

It's important to remember that a series of shifts like the NCCS rolls along well below the level of consciousness. No one makes a decision to participate or not participate. Of course, changes (in whole or part) can be and will be resisted, but by groups rather than individuals. For example, race and ethnicity have something to do with whether an individual participates in the NCCS, as Gordon established in a study of speakers in North-West Indiana (2000: 122). He found evidence that participation in the chain shift "generally serves to distinguish the speech of whites from that of Mexicans and African Americans."

Changes in progress proceed in tiny steps that go unnoticed by the participants until large-scale restructuring of the vowel system has become so distinctive that it begins to be identified with a particular geographic area. For example, many people today would say that Chicago has a distinctive accent; twenty-five years ago, it did not. That is, the NCCS has advanced to the point that people have come to notice it;[5] before this point, Chicago was just "Midwestern" English.

The NCCS is a hugely complex set of changes distributed over time, space and a dozen different social categories. You may be deeply invested in it, yourself.

Lexical variation

People are often quite aware of variation in word choice. Good-natured arguments about who says *tennis shoe* and who says *sneaker* are not uncommon. In Southeast Michigan, there are often classroom discussions on the use of *pop* (the variant most likely found farther West) versus *soda* (the variant found to the East) versus *coke* (the South). Michigan would seem to be on the boundary (or isogloss) between *soda* and *pop*; thus the spirited discussions. Such distinct variants over space are generally referred to as isoglosses; a bundle of isoglosses is a strong indicator that people on one side of the bundle consider themselves different (at least linguistically) from people on the other side of the bundle. The individual isoglosses seen in Figure 2.9 are primarily lexical. These include Dutch cheese (North of the bundle) and its equivalent, cottage cheese (South of the bundle) and (similarly) whinny (North) versus whicker or nicker (South).

Sociolinguists find this kind of variation less compelling, unless there is correlation to other points of variation which are more linguistically, socially or geographically complex.

There are also lexical items which function as discourse markers, however, and which are so complex in structural, social and stylistic terms that linguists spend a lot of time studying them (Barbieri 2009; Cukor-Avila 2002; Dailey-O'Cain 2000; Rickford *et al.* 2007; Tagliamonte and D'Arcy 2004).[6] Some terms (*like, you know, well,* and *but*) show us "how speakers and hearers jointly integrate forms, meanings, and actions to make overall sense out of what is said" (Schiffrin 1987: 49).

A particularly interesting discourse marker is *like*, which can be used in more than one way. As a focuser, *like* draws attention to a particular aspect of a sentence, as in "Well, it's

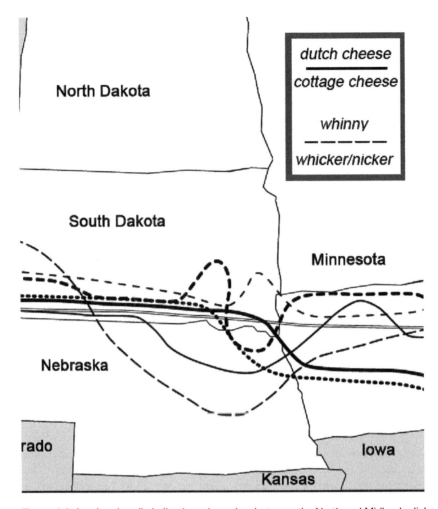

North Dakota

dutch cheese
———
cottage cheese

whinny
— — — —
whicker/nicker

South Dakota

Minnesota

Nebraska

rado

Iowa

Kansas

Figure 2.9 Isogloss bundle indicating a boundary between the North and Midlands dialect regions

Source: Adapted from Allen (1982)

not like wonderful, but it's okay" (Dailey-O'Cain 2000: 61). More commonly *like* (as a discourse marker) is a quotative and thus serves to signal a change in the source of the narrative: "My dad was constantly down on me. It's like, 'Get a job'" (ibid.: 62). At first glance it would seem that this must be nothing more than a random phenomenon and devoid of any significance, but that is not the case. For example, Dailey-O'Cain found that people talked one way about this use of *like* ("bad grammar") but did not necessarily evaluate speakers who used it negatively. Age always played an important role in both the use and perception of quotative *like*.

Rickford's (2007) study found distinct changes over time for the quotatives in both speech and popular media (chat, blogs, discussion boards) in California (Figure 2.10):

Sometimes an English language usage may seem to be unimportant or even trivial; certainly in this case, quotatives often invite mocking and humor. However, close

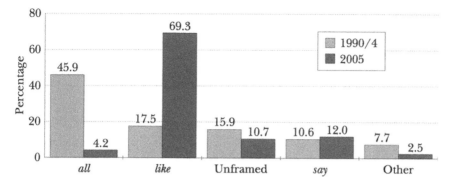

Figure 2.10 The use of quotative discourse markers over time in California

Source: Rickford (2007)

study of this kind of subtle marker can reveal a great deal about the community of speakers who use it.

Sociolinguists like to study quotatives for another reason. Whereas a vowel shift or a consonant cluster simplification[7] might stretch out over decades and require many years of study, quotatives change quickly. You may have observed this in your own speech or in the speech of those around you.

Variation in verb morphology: strong and weak verbs

Most English verbs fall into one of two groups: strong or weak. Weak (also called regular verbs) form the past tense and the past participle by the simple addition of a suffix (for example, -ed, *talked, smacked, climbed, cleaned*). Strong or irregular verbs are much harder to predict because the past forms are generated by a change to the vowel in the root syllable, and sometimes to consonants as well, for example, *shrink, shrank, shrunk*. Bybee and Slobin (1982) summarize the history and relationship between weak and strong verbs, and establish that while there are thousands of verbs that fall into the weak (-ed) class, only two hundred or so can be identified as strong. On the other hand, "of the 30 most frequent past-tense forms, 22 are irregular [strong]" (1982: 265). Since the Old English period, hundreds of strong verbs have weakened, for example.

Old English (strong)	*scūfan*	*scēaf*	*scofen*
	↓	↓	↓
Modern English (weak)	*shove*	*shoved*	*shove*

You might hypothesize that this movement from strong to weak verbs would be over and done with so many hundreds of years after it began, but in fact, it is still moving forward – and backward. Pinker's summary of the status of strong or irregular verbs is quite poetic:

> Do irregular verbs have a future? At first glance, the prospects do not seem good. Old English had more than twice as many irregular verbs as we do today. Not only is the

irregular class losing members by emigration, it is not gaining new ones by immigration. When new verbs enter English via onomatopoeia (to ding, to ping), borrowings from other languages (*deride* and *succumb* from Latin), and conversions from nouns (*fly out*), the regular rule has first dibs on them. The language ends up with dinged, pinged, derided, succumbed, and flied out, not *dang, pang, derode, succame*, or *flew out*.

(Pinker 1998)

Weak verbs have been metamorphizing into strong verb forms for a very long time. Pinker attributes this to the fact that strong verbs are generated by pattern, and human beings are prone to playing with patterns. Studies of children's speech regularly shows how they experiment, trying strong verb patterns on weak verbs (and weak on strong) to see how they'll fit. Bybee and Slobin provide examples from children's speech: bring–brang, bite–bote, and wipe–wope, but anyone who has had a part in raising a child will have their own examples. From the notes taken while my daughter was in this stage of language acquisition, for example: *He tooked Eliza's book, Her dress is all broked*, and *Look I clumed the stairs barefeeted*.

Adults find misapplications like these endearing or funny, but sometimes a strong rule pattern will stick to a weak verb. For example, there are areas in Great Britain and the U.S. where *sneaked* has become *snuck*, *dived* is now *dove*, and *dragged* is *drug*, to the horror of prescriptivists. In my own speech, *snuck* and *dove* are firmly entrenched.

This variation is active and vigorous, and has been widely documented. A Google search "dragged or drug?" brings up a million hits, which indicates real confusion in the language community. Speakers often show this kind of confusion and breakdown of contrasts when changes in progress are solidifying. An infamous example of such a case is the difference between *lie* and *lay*, a distinction that is now largely lost.

There are many other kinds and points of variation in the verb systems of American English, some of which have been tracked for a long time. For instance, the data for *A Survey of Verb Forms in the Eastern United States* (Atwood 1953) was collected at least five years earlier, or some 60 years ago. Atwood noted variation in distribution of the preterite and past participles in many verbs. Figure 2.11 is one of the maps from his atlas, this one showing the distribution of past tense variants for the verb *to drink*. In my own variety of American English, *drink* is a solidly strong verb (We drink Kool-Aid; we drank Kool-Aid) but there are areas where the verb is weak (We drinked Kool-Aid).

Verbs are a particular point of contention for most prescriptivists. My great-aunt Lillian used to wag her finger at me and intone "You may not abuse past participles in my home." Most likely you've had an experience something like this with a relative or teacher.

Structured variation: the hidden life of language

The examples of variation in language presented here might seem, at first glance, to be obvious and uncomplicated. In fact, sociolinguistic variation can be exceedingly complex and require advanced statistical techniques to tease out patterns.

Human beings choose among thousands of points of variation available to them not because the human mind is sloppy, or language is imprecise: just the opposite. We exploit linguistic variation available to us in order to send a complex series of messages about ourselves and the way we position ourselves in the world. We perceive variation in the

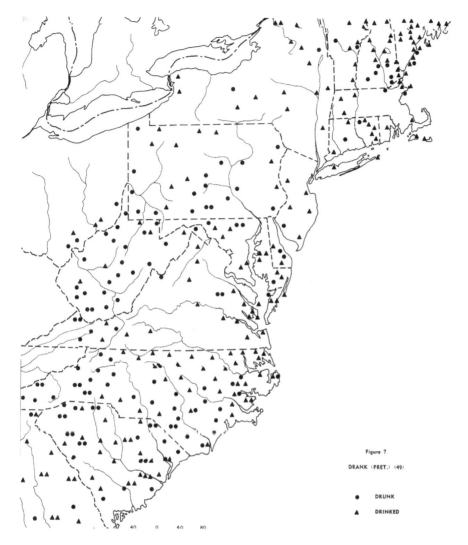

Figure 7

DRANK (PRET.) (49)

● DRUNK

▲ DRINKED

Figure 2.11 Past participles for *to drink* over space

Source: Atwood (1953: 20)

speech of others and we use it to structure our knowledge about that person. Listening to strangers calling into talk radio programs, it is more than verb morphology and vowel sounds that we evaluate, more than the content of their comments than we walk away with.

"What's a Dago know about the price of oil?" my father asked once while listening to an anonymous caller to a talk-radio program rant about the gasoline crunch in the late 1970s. My father, a native speaker of Italian, recognized the caller as socially and ethnically similar to himself and made a series of evaluations. We all have experiences like this: if you're far from home and in a crowd you hear someone who talks like you do, your attention turns in that direction.

The parameters of linguistic variation are multidimensional. In large-scale terms, these are social, stylistic, geographic, or temporal, and in any one case of active variation, more than one of these factors is probably at play. Different factors interact with each other, and with language-internal influences; the result is the variation you hear (or don't hear, but perceive).

When we choose among variants available to us – a process which happens well below the level of consciousness – we use those language signals that will mark us as belonging to specific social groupings, and distance us from others. We do this sometimes even when we are trying not to (in the next chapters we will return to this very relevant subject of mutability of language).

Individuals situate themselves in relationship to others; the way they group themselves, the powers they claim for themselves and the powers they stipulate to others are all embedded in language. Sociolinguistics becomes complicated (and gains in potential usefulness) as soon as we recognize that socially marked linguistic features only begin with geography, gender and age. Language markers can be emblematic for dozens of different kinds of social allegiances. National origin, socioeconomic class, ethnicity, occupation, religion, occupation, kinship: all these things and many more might be signaled linguistically. To add to this complexity, topic and setting put their own demands on variation.

This is what sociolinguists do: they look at active, socially structured variation to try to understand the process of language change. How it is initiated, how it moves, what it means. We try to identify universals in the power and solidarity structures which are relevant to language communities of all types, from inner city neighborhoods to remote Indonesian villages. And that is where sociolinguistics usually stops. Once we have understood, for example, the social correlates of *caught/cot* variation in Buffalo – the way changes in transportation and communication have effected diffusion of this change over generations – the job is done. We rarely ask why these facts are the way they are; traditionally, anthropological linguists pick up at this point.

We know who stigmatizes and avoids r-lessness in Manhattan and the South; we know who clings to it despite stigmatization, but we do not understand what the process itself is. Fairclough points this out as an unfortunate omission, and outlines questions he thinks should follow:

> How – in terms of the development of social relationships to power – was the existing sociolinguistic order brought into being? How is it sustained? And how might it be changed to the advantage of those who are dominated by it?
>
> (Fairclough 1989 [2001]: 7–8)

Sociolinguists have demonstrated beyond a doubt that variation is an intrinsic and functional feature of the spoken language. So then, what do people really mean when they talk about nonstandard or substandard or *SAE? How do these labels get attached to specific points of variation, and to what end? Before we pursue those issues, we need to consider terminology, starting with the idea of accent.

DISCUSSION QUESTIONS AND EXERCISES

● Consider the Salvucci map online: http://www.evolpub.com/Americandialects/Am DialMap.html, and read the descriptions he provided for each dialect area. How do they compare with your own understanding of the regional varieties of American English?

● Think you have a pretty good handle on American dialects? Try the synonym quizzes on the website of the *Dictionary of American Regional English*, http://dare.wisc.edu/?q= node/20.

● At the Harvard American Dialect Survey you will find the list of points of variation in American English that was included in that study. This is by no means a complete list of changes in progress, but there's quite a lot there. Before looking at the website and maps, identify three points of variation that you were aware of (in your own speech, or the speech of others you know) and three that you were not aware of.

● Look at the Dialect Map of /tɔk/ "talk" from the University of Texas linguistics department: http://www.utexas.edu/courses/linguistics/resources/socioling/talkmap/index.html and listen to the sound clips. Can you identify the vowels used in each geographic area? Can you hear the differences?

● A university or college campus often draws people from all over the country. Drawing on the diversity available to you for sampling, design a simple field study in which you look for the vowels in *cot* and *caught*, and map what you find. Where are the vowels distinct? Where are they merged? You might want to use Labov's (r) study as a model.

● Attached to the Wikipedia page for the Northern Cities vowel/chain shift is a "talk" page where people can comment or make suggestions about the article. A series of comments from late 2010 includes the following reaction to the idea of the shift itself. How does this illustrate the concepts introduced thus far on standard language ideology?

> I'm Ohio born and raised and I've never come across this, I think this whole thing is BS. The people on TV still sound exactly like us, I can't think of any person I've ever met who has started or had changed into the first shift, more prevalent is rural people saying warsh. Are there any examples or a video of people with this "shift"? . . . I know for a fact that I don't have a discernible accent and neither do most people I know.

● Consider the usage of *usta* (as in the sentence *I usta go out on Saturday nights, but now I'm broke*). Is it a verb, and if so, is it past or present tense? The answer is more complex and interesting than you might imagine, and you can read about it on Language Log, with this entry by Mark Liberman: http://languagelog.ldc.upenn.edu/nll/?p=2756.

● Galileo was the mathematician and astronomer who first observed that the earth revolves around the moon. This did not sit well with the Catholic Church, which taught that the earth was the center of the universe and everything revolved about it. They forced Galileo to recant his position, but afterward he is said to have mumbled (rebelliously) *Eppur' si muove*: And yet, it moves. How does this episode parallel the way people think about language in the present day?

Notes

1 "Nevertheless, it moves." See discussion topics in this chapter.
2 To look at this another way, some people see the broadcast media as immensely powerful and influential. So powerful, in fact, that the whole country is simply compelled to follow their example. This subject is pursued in greater depth in Chapter 8.
3 Please note the following notation conventions: slash brackets as in /r/ refer to phonemes; square brackets [r] to allophones; and parentheses (r) to sociolinguistic variables. The distinction between phoneme and allophone is a basic and a crucial one in phonetics and phonology, but will not be stressed here. For our purposes, it is enough to remember that (r) means the discussion focuses on sociolinguistic variation, while /r/ and [r] are references to the actual sounds (or classes of sound).
4 *In Motion: The African American Experience* has a wealth of historical documents, films, maps and essays about the Great Migration, here: http://www.inmotionaame.org/home.cfm.
5 Those who study accent as a phonetic and sociolinguistic phenomenon have come to the conclusion that accent can only really be defined from the perspective of the listener.
6 Some quotatives are also used as intensifiers, as for example in "My mom is all mad at me."
7 Consonant cluster reduction or simplification is common to many – even most – varieties of U.S. English. In the Midwest, a nasal (/n/ or /m/) followed by a stop (/b/ /p/ /t/ /d/) will usually reduce to a nasal alone, as in the word hunter which is pronounced *hunner*. This feature is so widespread that it is considered a *vernacular universal*: a feature that occurs regularly across stigmatized or peripheralized language varieties are proposed to be features of the human language faculty.

Suggested further reading

Aschman, R. (n.d.) http://www.aschmann.net/AmEng/.

Rick Aschman maintains an excellent and thorough website about the regional varieties of American English, with links to hundreds of audio and video clips to illustrate regionalisms. Aschman is not a linguist (thus his terminology is somewhat idiosyncratic), but he is a close and careful observer.

Elliott, N. (2000) A Study in the Rhoticity of American Film Actors. In R. Dal Vera (ed.) *Standard Speech and Other Contemporary Issues in Professional Voice and Speech Training*. New York: Applause, pp. 103–130.
Trudgill, P. (1997) Acts of Conflicting Identity: The Sociolinguistics of British Pop-Song Pronunciation. In N. Coupland (ed.) *Sociolinguistics: A Reader*. New York: St. Martin's Press.

Whether or not you have an /r/ sound after your vowels or at the end of words, you will probably find these articles of interest. Elliott's study looks at (r) in the speech of actors, while Trudgill examines the (r) variable in the recorded work of The Beatles and similar bands. Note the difference in dates on the articles. Read and compare them in terms of methodology and data. Does one seem better argued than the other? Do they complement each other? How might you approach a study like this in the present day?

Sultan, T. (2006) It's Not the Sights, It's the Sounds. *The New York Times*, March 17.

A non-linguist's view of linguistic fieldwork, based on observing William Labov.

The Language Lab website at the University of Pennsylvania is a bit confusing and could be better organized, but there's lots of interesting information about studies past and present, if you dig a bit.

The Harvard American Dialect Survey will allow you to look more closely at distributions over space. http://www4.uwm.edu/FLL/linguistics/dialect/index.html.

The Dictionary of American Regional English concentrates on lexical items, and provides very detailed background information and etymologies: http://dare.wisc.edu/?q=node/132.

The Great Pop/Soda Controversy is the subject of a detailed website, because, of course, you can never get too much sugar and caffeine. http://popvssoda.com:2998/.

The Phonological Atlas of North America website provides detailed information about language differentiation over space. "A National Map of the Regional Dialects of American English" is somewhat technical, but very interesting. http://www.ling.upenn.edu/phono_atlas/NationalMap/NationalMap.html.

The myth of non-accent

3

> The poets were not alone in sanctioning myths, for long before the poets the states and the lawmakers had sanctioned them as a useful expedient . . . They needed to control the people by superstitious fears, and these cannot be aroused without myths and marvels.
>
> Strabo (64 BC–AD 26), *Geographia*

You've got one too

Myth is understood broadly as a story with general cultural significance. In the study of myth, veracity is secondary to the way in which a story symbolizes human experience more generally. What is particularly interesting is the way that myths are used to justify social order, and to encourage or coerce consensual participation in that order.[1]

In general, linguists think of standard language and its corollary, non-accent, as abstractions. And in fact, this is a logical connection, as is borne out by the *Oxford English Dictionary*'s definition: "[an abstraction is] the idea of something which has no independent existence; a thing which exists only in idea; something visionary." From this follows quite neatly Milroy and Milroy's suggestion that standard language should not be understood as any specific language, but as "an idea in the mind rather than a reality – a set of abstract norms to which actual usage may conform to a greater or lesser extent" (1985: 22–23).

For our purposes, it is useful to consider both *standard language* and *non-accent* as myths. It is only by doing so that we can come to understanding how the collective consciousness came to be. Myths are magical and powerful constructs; they can motivate social behavior and actions which would be otherwise contrary to logic or reason.

We have come a good way into this discussion without defining the term *accent*. Perhaps the reason for that is clear by now: in so far as linguists are concerned, the term has no technical or specific meaning. It is widely used by the public, however, in interesting ways.

In a more technical sense, *accent* is used to distinguish stress in words (The accent is on the second syllable in *baNAna*) or intonation in sentences ("That's ANOTHER fine mess you've gotten us into!"); it can be used as a diacritic, but this is most often done in conjunction with the writing of other languages. More generally, accent is a loose reference to a specific "way of speaking." There is no official or technical specification for what this might mean in linguistic terms, but there are two widely recognized elements to what serves to distinguish one variety of a language from another in the minds of speakers:

1   *Prosodic features.* The study of the phonology of a language includes consideration of intonation, or patterns of pitch contours. This includes stress patterns, both at the lexical and at the sentence level, but it also touches upon other factors such as tempo of speaking. For example, speakers of English tend to call languages or varieties of

language which tend toward an upswing in stress at the end of words lilting, or sing-song, or some Romance languages rapid-fire. Currently in American English there is one very active point of variation having to do with stress, in a small set of words including *Thanksgiving, insurance, adult, cement.*

2 It seems that first syllable stress has been documented for these words in the South, while everywhere else in the country the stress is on the second syllable: *INsurance* (South) or *inSURance* (elsewhere). The first syllable variant has been showing up outside the South quite a lot over at least the past 20 years, which is when I started taking notes on it. The other words that follow this pattern in the South do not seem to be wandering North; my casual research has not uncovered use of *THANKSgiving, A-dult, CEment* or *UMbrella* on the West Coast, in the Midwest or on the East Coast.[2]

3 *Segmental features.* We acquire, as part of our first language, the sounds of the language which fall into two major categories: vowels and consonants. Each of these sounds exists in relation to one another in a phonological structure. In the discussion above, some speakers of U.S. English distinguish between the words *caught* and *cot*, while for others these are homonyms. This follows quite reasonably from the fact that there are many possible phonological systems for U.S. English.

Perspective

Linguists have struggled to find an accurate definition of the word *accent*, and for the most part, given it up as a bad job. Generally *accent* can only be understood and defined if there is something to compare it with. You travel to a small town in Kansas, and (unless you are actually from that area), your accent will be seen as the differences between your speech and the local speech. Those differences can be examined and identified, so that a linguist might make a study of how your prosodic features and phonology mark you as someone from someplace else. The "someplace else" can be another state, country, or social group.

Those who work on accent as a phonetic and sociolinguistic phenomenon seem to have come to the conclusion that while this is true, it is also not important. That is, in the serious study of accent, the object is not what comes out of one person's mouth, but what the listeners hear and understand. Derwing and Monro put it very simply: "From our perspective, listeners' judgments are the only meaningful window into accentedness and comprehensibility" (2009: 478).

And yet, it is important to distinguish between the two major kinds of accents: First Language (L1) and Second Language (L2).

L1 and L2 accents

What we call L1 accent is really no more than what we have been discussing all along: structured variation in language. Most usually we use geography as the first line of demarcation: a Maine accent, a New Orleans accent, an Appalachian accent, a Utah accent. But there are also socially bound clusters of features which are superimposed on the geographic: Native American accents, Black accents, Jewish accents. Gender, race, ethnicity, income, religion – these and other social identities are often clearly marked by means of choice between linguistic variants.

L1 accent is, then, the native variety of U.S. English spoken: every native speaker of U.S. English has an L1 accent, no matter how unmarked or marked the person's language may seem to be. This includes people like Rachel Maddow, Steven Colbert, Bill Maher, Bill O'Reilly and Ann Coulter, broadcast news and commentary personalities who are generally thought to be speakers of *SAE.

So where does accent end and dialect begin?[3] To be more specific: Why is Dutch considered a separate language from German, and Swiss German not? Why do people call the variety of English that many African Americans speak Black slang (or a Black accent or African American English) but call Cockney and Gullah dialects? Max Weinreich is widely quoted as pointing out that a language is a dialect with an army and a navy; I would like to add to that observation that a dialect is perhaps nothing more than a language that gets no respect. That is to say that *these questions are really about politics and history.* The features of the languages being discussed are secondary. However, if it is necessary to distinguish between accent and language variety on purely linguistic terms, then a rough division can be made as follows:

- Two varieties of a single language are distinguished by accent when differences are restricted primarily to phonology (prosodic and segmental features).
- If two varieties of a single language also differ in morphological structures, syntax, lexicon, and semantics, then they are different varieties, or dialects, of the same language.
- If two varieties of a common mother language differ in all these ways, and in addition have distinct literary histories, distinct orthographies, and/or geo-political boundaries, then they are generally called different languages.

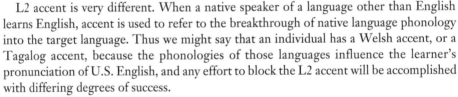

Style or code shifting is a term reflecting the speaker's ability to switch between languages or language varieties dependent on a large number of factors. It is a complicated process, and one that has been studied intensively. For our purposes, however, it is enough to say that when a speaker is shifting between two varieties of one language which are closely related, it will sometimes be appropriate to speak of "accent" and sometimes of "variety." Thus it is useful to retain the term *accent* to talk about phonology, but it is important to remember that this is a fluid category.

L2 accent is very different. When a native speaker of a language other than English learns English, accent is used to refer to the breakthrough of native language phonology into the target language. Thus we might say that an individual has a Welsh accent, or a Tagalog accent, because the phonologies of those languages influence the learner's pronunciation of U.S. English, and any effort to block the L2 accent will be accomplished with differing degrees of success.

Thus far it has been put forward that:

- all spoken human language is necessarily and functionally variable;
- one of the functions of variation is to convey social, stylistic and geographic meaning;
- the majority of the emblematic work of variation is carried out below the level of consciousness.

Given these facts, what is non-accent? And given the fact that *accent* is just shorthand for variable language (which is in some ways a redundant term), what can a 'standard' U.S. English be, but an abstraction?

In spite of all the hard evidence that all languages change, people steadfastly believe that a homogenous, standardized, one-size-fits-all language is not only desirable, it is truly a possibility. This takes us back to our opening science fiction scenario, in which the positive ramifications of a world in which we are all the same size and weight is so appealing, so enticing, that we overlook biological realities and the laws of physics.

Before we go on to ask how we are able to fool ourselves so thoroughly about language, we must first deal more carefully with the question of the mythical homogenous standardized spoken language. Until the impossibility of such a thing is established uncontrovertibly, people will continue to pine after it, and, worse, to pursue it.

So, can you lose one accent and replace it with another? A linguist's first impulse is to answer this question, very simply, no. It is not possible for an adult to substitute his native phonology (one accent) for another, consistently and in a permanent way.[4] But! The non-linguist will jump in. What about my Aunt Magda, who came here from the Ukraine and has no accent at all? What about Gwyneth Paltrow, who can switch from American English to British English without a moment's hesitation? And there's Joe's wife, who just gave up her Brooklyn accent when it caused her problems in medical school.

What does it mean to lose an accent? Are we talking about replacing one way of speaking for another, or adding a new phonology to a person's existing inventory? Are we demanding that a person sound one way for a brief period of time, or that he always sound that way? Consider a man who applies for a promotion and is told that his accent is too low-class for the job he wants to do.

James Kahakua, a native of Hawai'i, wanted to read prepared weather forecasts on the radio. He was refused promotion because his English marks him as a speaker of Hawai'ian Creole. When he sued, the radio station called an accent reduction specialist to testify on their behalf. The accent reduction specialist didn't mince words: Kahakua's English was deficient, wrong, unacceptable. Even given the demands of the job in question – rapid pronunciation of long and complex Native Hawai'ian language place names, the specialist (and the judge) found that Mr. Kahakua's bilingualism was a disadvantage the employer shouldn't have to tolerate. (A televised report on the Kahakua Title VII case can be seen at http://goo.gl/k12Bp.)

Accent reduction specialists like the one who testified in the Kahakua case are not objective parties. Such persons have a vested interest in the idea of *accent* and *standard*. If an accent reduction specialist could not convince the court that Mr. Kahakua's Hawai'ian accent was wrong and inappropriate, what would that mean for her career?

why, though?

Answers for all of these questions require a closer understanding of language acquisition. We begin with some generalizations which are more linguistic facts of life:

- There is a finite set of potentially meaning-bearing sounds (vowels, consonants, tones) which can be produced by human vocal apparatus. The set in its entirety is universal, available to all human beings without physical handicap.
- Each language uses some, but not all, sounds available.
- Sounds are organized into systems, in which each element stands in relationship to the other elements (phonology). The same inventory of sounds can be organized into a number of possible systems. Children are born with the ability to produce the entire set of possible sounds, but eventually restrict themselves to the ones they hear used around them.
- Children exposed to more than one language during the language acquisition process may acquire more than one language, if the social conditioning factors are favorable.

- At some time in adolescence, the ability to acquire language with the same ease as young children atrophies.[5]
- There are as yet poorly understood elements of cognition and perception which have to do with the degree of success with which an adult will manage to acquire a new phonology, or accent. In summary, the phenomenon that we call a foreign accent is a complex aspect of language that affects speakers and listeners in both perception and production and, consequently, in social interaction (Derwing and Munro 2005: 379).

These are very dry facts. Let's approach this in another way.

The Sound House

First, think of all the sounds which can be produced by the human vocal apparatus as a set of building materials. The basic materials, vowels and consonants, are bricks. Other building materials (wood, mortar, plaster, stone) stand in for things like tone, vowel harmony, and length, which are part of the articulation of vowels and consonants, but provide another layer of meaning-bearing sound in many languages. Thus far, we are talking about phonetics: the production and perception of the full set of possible sounds.

Children are born with two things: a set of language blueprints wired into the brain, which gives them some intuitive understanding of very basic rules of language. They also have a set of tools which goes along with these blueprints.

Now think of the language acquisition process as a newborn who begins to build a Sound House. The Sound House is the "home" of the language, or what we have been calling accent – the phonology – of the child's native tongue. At birth the child is in the Sound House warehouse, where a full inventory of all possible materials is available to her. She looks at the Sound Houses built by her parents, her brothers and sisters, by other people around her, and she starts to pick out those materials, those bricks she sees they have used to build their Sound Houses. She may experiment with other bricks, with a bit of wood, but in the end she settles down to duplicating the Sound Houses she sees around her. She sets up her inventory of sounds in relationship to each other; she puts up walls, plans the space: she is constructing her phonology.

The blueprints tell her that she must have certain supporting structures; she does this. She wanders around in her parents' Sound Houses and sees how they do things. She makes mistakes; fixes them. In the process, she makes small innovations.

Maybe this child has parents who speak English and Gaelic, or who are natives of Cincinnati and speak what they think of as standard American English, as well as African American English Vernacular. The parents each have two Sound Houses, or perhaps one Sound House with two wings. She has two houses to build at once. Sometimes she mixes materials up, but then sorts them out. Maybe she builds a bridge between the two structures. Maybe a connecting courtyard.

The child starts to socialize with other children. Her best friend has a slightly different layout, although he has built his Sound House with the exact same inventory of building materials. Another friend has a Sound House which is missing the back staircase. She wants to be like her friends, and so she makes renovations to her Sound House. It begins to looks somewhat different from her parents' Sound Houses; it is more her own. Maybe the Gaelic half of her Sound House is neglected, has a hole in the roof, a collapsing floor. Maybe she is at odds, because she loves her AAVE Sound House, but others criticize it as ugly and not worthy to be called a house at all. She might eventually abandon the AAVE Sound House and pretend it never existed. Now imagine this.

When the child turns 20, she notices another kind of Sound House, built by Spanish speakers, which she admires. She would like to build an extension to her own Sound House just like it. She looks for her blueprints and her tools, but they have disappeared. Puzzled, she stands on the street and looks at these Spanish Sound Houses. What is different about them? Look at that balcony. How do you build that? Why do the staircases look like that?

With her bare hands, she sets out to build an extension to her original Sound House. She sees bricks she doesn't have in her own inventory, but how to get back to the warehouse? She'll have to improvise. She's a smart woman, she can make a brick, cut down a tree. She examines the Sound Houses built by Spanish speakers, asks questions. The obvious things she sees right off: wow, they have fireplaces. The less obvious things: width of the doors, for example, slip right by her at first. She starts in on the long process. How did you build that chimney, she asks. I don't know, says her informant, a native speaker of Spanish. I was a kid at the time, and I've lost my blueprints.

If she's lucky, she has a guide – an informed language teacher – who can point out the difference between the extension she is trying to build and her own Sound House. Look, this guide will say. You're mixing up blue and ultramarine bricks! We use blue for this kind of wall, ultramarine for that. And you certainly can't put a pale pink brick next to a cerise one.

"Oh," says the woman building the new Sound House. "I hadn't noticed." And thus she will begin to differentiate more carefully, for example, between two very similar vowels which are distinctive in the language she is learning.

She works very, very hard on this extension. But no matter how hard she works, the balcony will not shape up; it is always rickety. There's a gap in the floor boards; people notice it and grin.

In absolute amazement, she watches her little sister build the exact same Sound House with no effort at all, and it is perfect. She points this out to her guide. "But your sister still has her blueprints and tools," says her guide. Then she sees a stranger, an older man, building the same extension and he is also taking less time, just galloping through. His Spanish Sound House looks like an original to her.

"Oh no," her guide tells her. "It's very good, no doubt, but look there – don't you see that the windows are slightly too close together? It would fool almost everybody, but those windows give it away."

She digs in her heels and moves into the extension, although the roof still leaks. She abandons her original English Sound House for months, for years, she is so dedicated to getting this right. She rarely goes back to the first Sound House anymore, and the Gaelic Sound House is condemned. When she does go back to the English Sound House, and first goes through the door it seems strange to her. But the structural heart of her Sound House is here, and it's still standing, if a little dusty. Very quickly she feels at home again.

When people come to visit her in her Spanish Sound House, they are amazed to find out that it's not her first construction. They examine everything closely. Some of them may notice very small details, but they don't say anything. There's the guy down the block, they tell her, he's been working on the same extension for longer than you and he'll never get it right.

This is not a perfect analogy; it has no way to account for the acquisition of syntax and morphology, or the use or production of language. A house cannot produce anything. But it is a useful analogy nonetheless, in as much as this limitation is recognized.

Adult language learners all have the same handicap in learning a second language: the blueprints have faded to near illegibility, and the tools are rusted. We must all build new Sound Houses with our bare hands. When the judge claimed that there was no physiological reason that James Kahakua could not speak the broadcast English the radio station demanded, he was simply wrong.[6]

It is crucial to point out that the structural integrity of the targeted second Sound House – which here stands in for accent – is distinct from the language learner's skill in actually using the target language. Accent has little to do with what is generally called communicative competence, or the ability to use and interpret language in a wide variety of contexts effectively.[7]

There is a long list of prominent persons who speak English as a second language and who never lost their accents. They never managed to build an English Sound House which would fool anybody into thinking that they are native speakers, but their ability to use English is clear. This group includes people like Isabel Allende, Derek Wolcott, Adriana Huffington, Arnold Schwarzenegger, the irritable John Simon, and Zbigniew Brzezinski, who represent the political and socio-cultural mainstream, but who do it in an accented English. Do people like these choose to speak English with an accent? Have they not worked hard enough, long enough to sound American? Are they not smart enough?

The same questions are relevant to native speakers of English with marked or stigmatized regional or social accents. When you think of Jimmy Carter, Jessie Jackson or Rosie O'Donnell, do we think of people who cannot express themselves? Whether you like or dislike them as individuals, they are all excellent communicators. Do they willfully refuse to give up Georgia, African American, or New York varieties of English for something less socially marked, or are they incapable of doing so?

Because two phonologies are similar, we think it must be easier to build a second Sound House. Why can't Mr. Kahakua – who after all has an English Sound House to begin with – just make a few adjustments that will transform it into what passes as a generic English Sound House? Stephen Moyer – a Brit born and raised – makes a very convincing Louisiana vampire on *True Blood*. Surely Mr. Kahakua could pull off sounding less Hawai'ian.

The answer is, actors can't automatically adopt a foreign accent, no matter how easy they make it look. In the filming process the camera rolls for short periods of time, and in a limited context. The actor has had coaching, most likely, from someone who is standing on the sidelines ready to pitch in if the actor's accent begins to disintegrate. If the actor gets it wrong, they stop and try again. Under these favorable circumstances, many people could imitate another variety of English quite admirably – but for others, not even this is possible.

There are many examples of actors criticized roundly for not pulling off an accent, in spite of expensive tutoring, and the possibility of many takes of each utterance. In either case, whether we have a very English Hugh Laurie who truly sounds – up on the screen – as if were a cranky doctor born and raised in the States (Fox's *House*), or Dominic West – born in Yorkshire – who tries but fails to convince us that he is a tough Baltimore homicide detective (HBO's *The Wire*), we are not talking about a permanent Sound House. These accents are fake store fronts that won't stand up to a strong and persistent breeze. And it takes an exceptional talent (a subject to be raised shortly) to achieve even this limited amount.

At a sociolinguistics conference some years ago, a colleague who studies the Northern Cities Chain Shift came to my presentation. Afterwards she said to me "You know, it was really fascinating to listen to you, – oh, and your talk was good too." The whole time I had been presenting my work, she had been listening closely to my vowels, and making notes to herself. When I was reading from prepared text, she told me, my vowels pretty much stayed put, but when I looked up from my papers and spoke extemporaneously, my vowels started to move: the chain shift in action. The more attention I pay to speech, the less I participate in the shift; this is an indication that some part of me feels compelled to move away from my background when I am speaking as an academic. But when I am involved in my subject, when I forget to monitor my speech carefully, my origins come forth: I am a native of Chicago, and I cannot pretend to be anything else. This has been pointed out to me by many non-linguists; people are proud to be able to listen to me (or to anybody else) for a minute and then put me on the map.

reading out loud v. talking

All this happens in spite of the fact that my professional training has made me aware of the way I use subtle choices available to me, and in spite of the fact that sometimes I don't particularly want to announce to the world where I am from. I have no choice but to live in the Sound House I first created as a child, which bears the structural hallmarks of the social being I am.

It is true, however, that some people are better at putting together second or even third and fourth Sound Houses in adulthood. Not perfect ones, but very good imitations. The differential ability to do this is something not very well understood, but strong circumstantial evidence indicates it has nothing to do with intelligence and not very much to do with how hard you work to learn the target language. On the other hand, it certainly does have something to do with cognition, and – for lack of a better or more precise term – with an ear for language.

There are many published studies which underscore the relevance and importance of age (and hence, the critical language period) to the successful learning of a natively-accented second language (Marx 2002; Munro *et al.* 2008; Munro and Mann 2005; Piske *et al.* 2001). The importance of other factors – length of residency (that is, exposure to L2), gender, formal instruction, and motivation – have not been sufficiently studied to draw any firm conclusions. Perhaps the most interesting factor is one that can hardly be studied in controlled circumstances, and that is what might be called talent. Early studies of possible links between musical ability have not established a connection, while other studies "have identified mimicry ability as a significant predictor of degree of L2 foreign accent" (Piske *et al.* 2001: 202).

Focused training – the process of drawing the adult language learner's attention to elements in the production of speech sounds she would not otherwise notice – can have some effect. It is possible to adjust an accent, to some degree. We can work on that second Sound House, with guidance. But it is not possible to substitute the second Sound House for the original. Accent reduction courses, if they are well done by persons thoroughly trained in phonology and phonetics, who understand the structural differences between the languages, may help people learning English as a second language toward a better pronunciation.

The true ability to build second and third Sound Houses past the language acquisition stage is undocumented. It may exist; there are certainly rumors enough of such persons, who as adults acquire another language with absolute and complete native fluency. A person who is capable of this would never let the phonology of their first language interfere with their second language, regardless of the topic being discussed, or the amount of emotion brought to the table. Such a person would have to be able to stand up to close phonetic analysis of her language – and not just by phoneticians, but also by native speakers, who are incredibly sensitive to the subtle variation in language. Perhaps most important, such a person would have to have complete control of the structured variation active in the target language.

To understand the importance of this, imagine yourself in another country, speaking a language you have studied in school for a number of years. Not only do you have to keep the subjunctive straight, for example, but you should be able to interpret tone of voice and lexical choice. If you can't interpret such language signals, you have no way of knowing if you are being taken seriously, or for a ride.

If there are adults who are capable of learning to absolutely and cleanly substitute one accent for another, they are as rare as individuals who can do long division instantaneously in their heads, or have photographic memories. If they do exist, it would be interesting and important to study them, because it would seem that these are adults whose language acquisition function – the hard wiring in the brain – failed to stop functioning at the usual time.

If a person is very dedicated, works hard, and has good guidance, it may be possible to fool some of the people some of the time. But there's a crucial question that hasn't been asked yet:

Who do we ask to jump through these hoops, and why? If *SAE is something logically and reasonably required of broadcast news reporters, why was it required of James Kahakua, and not of Peter Jennings (Canada) or Dan Rathers (Texas)?

And, a more difficult question: what is right or wrong about asking Mr. Kahakua to pretend? If he is capable of faking an accent, why shouldn't his employer ask him to do this, for those few minutes he is reading the weather on the radio?

A close and cynical reader of my arguments – of which there will be many – will point out that I have made two statements which seem to contradict each other. I have gone to some length to establish that all spoken language is variable, and that all languages change. Thus, the Sound Houses we build change over our lifetimes. At the same time, it seems that I am arguing that Sound Houses cannot be changed. I have been critical of speech therapists who claim this is possible.

A Sound House is a living, evolving product of our minds, a mirror of our changing social beings. We redecorate constantly, with a keen eye for what the neighbors are doing. Little by little, we may move a wall, rearrange the bricks, add windows. One person builds a patio, and maybe that catches on, in the same way that somewhere, one day (in a way sociolinguists have never been able to observe) hundreds of other changes caught on and began to gain linguistic and social currency.

We are all subject to the aging process; no one is exempt from those changes over time. Thus our Sound Houses do change over time but in ways which are outside direct control.

DISCUSSION QUESTIONS AND EXERCISES

- What does the idea of style shifting do to the Sound House analogy? Many people are bilingual or multilingual, and for each language they also have multiple styles. Is there a way to adapt the metaphor to account for this, or does it simply break down?
- How many prominent people (politicians, actors, policy-makers, educators, media personalities, etc.) can you think of who speak English with an L2 accent? What impact does a foreign accent seem to have on the individual's life?

- Interview some friends or family – a group of three or four people – and try to elicit how they feel about different varieties of English and different L2 accents. Take notes. On what do they agree? Where do they differ? (One might find accent x "friendly" while the other one finds it "unsophisticated," for example.) Can you account for the differences, or lack of differences? What surprised you?
- What accents do you personally dislike or find irritating? Describe a situation in which you reacted this way to a variety of English other than your own. After reading this far, do you have any insight into your own reactions?
- Think about this statement: Discrimination does not justify discrimination. How might this relate to the topic at hand?
- Do an internet search for "accent reduction" and "lose your accent." What kind of articles and advertisements come up? What credentials do the people offering these courses have? Do you see any patterns?

Notes

1   The *Oxford English Dictionary* divides the use of myth into three domains: (1) purely fictitious narratives which serve to illustrate and explain natural or social phenomena (The Legend of Hercules; Noah and the Ark); (2) fictional or imaginary persons, objects or places (Big Foot, Santa Claus, Shangri-La); and (3) untruths, or rumors.

2   For a longer, very interesting discussion about *THANKSgiving*, see Language Log at http://goo.gl/sYOju.

3   Dialect is a term which linguists use primarily to talk about language differences over geographic space. It is, however, a fairly prickly term. Laypersons often associate the word dialect as something less developed, capable, or worthy, and hence always subordinate to a "real" language. This is an unfortunate and miscast use of the term and for that reason I avoid dialect more generally and use, as many linguists do, the term *variety*.

4   For a very accessible overview of the research on second language acquisition, the critical phase hypothesis, and the issue of accent, see Hyltenstam and Abrahamson (2000).

5   There is controversy among linguists about what has been called the critical period or the critical period hypothesis (CPH). Some linguists dismiss the concept entirely, and others have proposed amendments. In his chapter "Baby Born Talking – Describes Heaven," Pinker summarizes the view of the majority of linguists:

> In sum, acquisition of a normal language is guaranteed for children up to the age of six, is steadily compromised from then until shortly after puberty, and is rare thereafter. Maturational changes in the brain, such as the decline in metabolic rate and number of neurons during the early school-age years, and the bottoming out of the number of synapses and metabolic rate around puberty, are plausible causes. We do know that the language-learning circuitry of the brain is more plastic in childhood; children learn or recover language when the left hemisphere of the brain is damaged or even surgically removed (though not quite at normal levels), but comparable damage in an adult usually leads to permanent aphasia.
>
> (2007: 293)

6 For a first person account of accent issues in the acquisition of a second language as an adult, see Marx (2002).
7 I avoid an in-depth discussion of communicative competence here, because it raises the issue of cultural and stylistic appropriateness, which will be addressed later.

Suggested further reading

Derwing and Munro's *Putting Accent in Its Place: Rethinking Obstacles to Communication* (2009) provides an excellent overview of research on the sociolinguistic aspects of foreign accent, along with an extensive bibliography.

Other articles that would supplement this chapter include:

Finegan, E. (2004) American English and its Distinctiveness. In E. Finegan and J. Rickford (eds.) *Language in the USA: Themes for the Twenty-First Century*, Cambridge: Cambridge University Press.
Siegel, R. (1999) Commentary: Foreign Accent May Be a Detriment to an Immigrant. In transcript of *All Things Considered*, National Public Radio, October 26.
Tagliamonte, S. (2001) Come/Came Variation in English Dialects. *American Speech* 76: 42–61.
Tan, A. (1990) Mother Tongue. *The Threepenny Review* 43: 7–8.
Wolfram, W. and Schilling-Estes, N. (2006) Social and Ethnic Dialects. In *American English: Dialects and Variation*. Oxford: Blackwell.

The standard language myth

4

I therefore claim to show, not how men think in myths, but how myths operate in men's minds without their being aware of the fact.

Lévi-Strauss (1964)

It should be clear by now why linguists consider the idea of a spoken standardized language to be a hypothetical construct. In his survey of the evolution of the concept of a standard, Crowley (2003) uses the term *idealized language*, which captures the sense of an honorable and rightful perfection.

Not much has changed since Jonathan Swift wrote his "A proposal for correcting, improving and ascertaining the English tongue" (1712). Those who take it upon themselves to protect English from its speakers are still quite sure of their right to do so. James Kilpatrick is a modern-day example of someone who brings tremendous emotion and more than a little melodrama to what he clearly sees as a battle for the one true English:

▷ person who compiles dictionaries.

The lexicographer's job is to distill the grapes of usage at the different levels. Thus, "he doesn't go there anymore" conveys the same information that is transmitted by "he don't go there no more," but the one is standard American English and the other is not.

Is the one "inferior" to the other? Of course. Who says so? This is the silent, common judgment of writers, editors, teachers and prescriptive lexicographers. The setting of standards in language is a contentious business, but somebody has to do it. Without standards, without definitions, without structural law, we lapse into linguistic anarchy.

(Kilpatrick 1999)

Google searches provide a sense of how large these issues loom in the minds of people more generally (Table 4.1). A survey of discussions on the topic of grammar brings up hundreds of examples. A large portion of them have not to do with grammar in the way it has been defined here, but with matters of punctuation. No matter the topic, the tone can be affronted, sarcastic, condescending, servile and, on occasion, silly to the point of absurdity as in an unattributed adaptation of a Nazi poster originally designed for posting in Holland (Figure 4.1).

Table 4.1 Number of Google hits for grammar terms

Google term search	No. hits early October 2009
"bad grammar"	8,410,000
"grammar advice"	6,630,000
"English grammar errors"	5,050,000

Figure 4.1 Bad grammar destroys nations

The idea of a standard language is constructed and re-constructed on an on-going basis by those who have a vested interest in the concept. At this juncture, it is necessary to consider in some detail exactly what this mythical beast called U.S. English is supposed to be.

Standard (American) English

Non-linguists[1] are quite comfortable with the idea of a standard language, so much so that the average person is very willing to describe and define it, much in the same way that most people could draw a unicorn, or describe a being from *Star Trek*'s planet Vulcan, or tell us who King Arthur was and why he needed a Round Table. For the most part people will undertake describing any of these even though they know that the thing they are describing is imaginary. That is, your description of a unicorn would be a great deal like everybody else's, because the concept of a unicorn is a part of our shared cultural heritage. You picked up your mental image (a horse with a single pointed horn growing from its forehead) someplace along the line; most probably you don't remember when or where.

The same is true for what has been called, to this point, Standard American English. A comparison of published definitions for this term reveals some common themes. From *Pocket Fowler's Modern English Usage*:

> Standard American English. The term has been variously defined and heavily politicized, but essentially it is the form of English that is most widely accepted and understood in an English-speaking country and tends to be based on the educated speech of a particular area . . . It is used in newspapers and broadcasting and is the form normally taught to learners of English.

A more recent definition from *Merriam-Webster's Dictionary* (2009), which proclaims itself *The Voice of Authority*:

> Standard American English: the English that with respect to spelling, grammar, pronunciation, and vocabulary is substantially uniform though not devoid of regional differences, that is well established by usage in the formal and informal speech and writing of the educated, and that is widely recognized as acceptable wherever English is spoken and understood.[2]

Both definitions assume that the written and spoken language are equal, both in terms of how they are used, and how they should be used. *Merriam-Webster* sets spelling and pronunciation on common footing, and compounds this error by bringing in both formal and informal language use.

While the definitions make some room for regional differences, they make none at all for social ones, and in fact, it is quite definite about the social construction of the hypothetical standard: it is the language of the educated.

What is meant by "educated" is left unstated and neither are the implications explored anywhere else in the dictionary. People who are not educated – whoever they may be – are drawn into the definition by its final component: "Standard American English is acceptable wherever English is spoken and understood." The lexicographer assumes that those with lesser education will bow to the authority of those with more education, because that is what we are trained to do.

SAE as a means of asserting authority

Cambridge Advanced Learner's Dictionary's (2009) definition is more succinct, but it also draws on the idea of educated people as the source of acceptable English: "[The] language described as standard is the form of that language which is considered acceptable and correct by most educated users of it: Most announcers on the BBC speak Standard British English."

More specific information on exactly how the lexicographer draws on the language of the educated is provided by interviews with the pronunciation editor at *Merriam-Webster*, which followed from the dictionary's tenth edition. It falls to the pronunciation editor to decide which possible pronunciations are included in the dictionary, and how they are ordered. "Usage dictates acceptability," he is reported as saying. "There is no other non-arbitrary way to decide" (Nemy 1993).

In order to pin down usage, the editor listens to "talk shows, medical shows, interviews, news, commentary, the weather" (ibid.) on the radio and on television. The editorial preface to the dictionary is more specific about this procedure; the list of those who are consulted about pronunciation includes politicians, professors, curators, artists, musicians, doctors, engineers, preachers, activists, and journalists:

> In truth, though, there can be no objective standard for correct pronunciation other than the usage of thoughtful and, in particular, educated speakers of English. Among such speakers one hears much variation in pronunciation . . . [our attempt is to] include all variants of a word that are used by educated speakers.
>
> (*Merriam-Webster* 2009: 83)

The editors claim an objective standard (the language of the educated) and at the same time they acknowledge variation among educated speakers. This apparent inconsistency is resolved by the policy which includes *all variants* that are used by educated speakers. A close look at the pronunciations listed in the dictionary, however, indicates that this cannot be the case. An entry with three or more possible pronunciations is rare. If *Merriam-Webster's Dictionary* truly intends to include all pronunciations of the educated, then this definition of educated must be very narrow.

The goal is to be representative, but how do the editors of the dictionary go about gathering a representative sample? If the primary source of data comes from broadcast media, then the sample is very shallow indeed. How many people appear regularly in a forum which is broadcast to a wider audience? The lesser educated, who by the dictionary definition must constitute the greatest number of native speakers of English, are rarely heard from.

Maybe there is no way to compile a dictionary which is truly descriptive in terms of pronunciation; maybe it is necessary to choose one social group to serve as a model. Perhaps there is even some rationale for using those with more education as this group. But there is nothing objective about this practice. It is the ordering of social groups in terms of who has authority to determine how language is best used.

The rationale for this ordering derives at least in part from the perceived superiority of the written language. Persons with more education are more exposed to the written language and literary traditions; they may, in simple terms, be better writers than those with less education. Why this should mean that their pronunciation and syntax are somehow more informed, more genuine, more authoritative – that is never made clear.

Definitions of standard language supplied by people who do not edit dictionaries for a living echo many of the themes already established, but they sometimes become very specific. According to CompuServe (1995): *SAE is . . .

- having your nouns and your verbs agree.
- the English legitimatized by wide usage and certified by expert consensus, as in a dictionary usage panel.
- the proper language my mother stressed from the time I was old enough to talk.

[handwritten margin note: The use of "educated" as a social marker here is bugging me]

● one that few people would call either stilted or "low," delivered with a voice neither guttural nor strident, clearly enunciated but not priggish about it, with no one sound having a noticeably distinctive character. It is a non-regional speech but clearly and easily understood in all regions . . . Standard American English uses, in general, only one syllable per enunciated vowel so most accents from the South and West are not to the pattern.[3]

These references to the authority of educational institutions and unnamed experts correspond to the dictionary definitions in a fairly predictable way. Like the dictionary definitions, the written and spoken languages are being considered as one and the same thing. What is different about these personal definitions is the willingness to identify specific grammatical and phonological points which distinguish the hypothetical standard, and a highly emotional and personal element in the definitions. People feel strongly about language and will defend it: "In extreme cases . . . the tone is quasi-religious, even apocalyptic . . . The ideological basis of the most extreme complaints . . . is authoritarian and, seemingly, transcendental" (Milroy 1999: 20).

The most extreme ideological definitions of standard language come from those who make a living promoting the concept. Writers like Edwin Newman, John Simon and James Kilpatrick have published extensively on how English should be spoken and written. They do not address the source of their authority directly; that is taken for granted. They assume you will grant them authority because they demand it, and because it has always been granted. These men, and other men and women like them, have made careers for themselves as prescriptivists because they meet a demand they created.

The social domain of the standard has been established: it is the language of the educated, in particular those who have achieved a high level of skill with the written language (the lack of logic here will be discussed later) or those who control the written or broadcast media. However, this attempt at a simple definition of *SAE begins to falter when language variation over space is added to the mix.

Dennis Preston has compiled a body of empirical studies in which he has quantified and summarized non-linguists' beliefs about the geographic distribution of a standard language. In "Where they speak correct English," he asked 76 young white natives of Southern Indiana to rank all 50 states as well as New York City and Washington, DC. The best English was 1, and the worst, 52. Figure 4.2 provides Preston's visual representation of the means for the respondents' rankings.

If a high level of education is a primary characteristic of the hypothetical *SAE, then the opinions of these college students from Indiana would seem to provide relevant information about just where that language is spoken. Preston's analysis indicates that these informants found the most correct English in five areas: North Central (including their own speech); Mid-Atlantic (excluding New York City); New England; Colorado; and the West Coast. Standard deviations indicated that the students are most consistent in their positive evaluation in the case of Michigan, Minnesota and Wisconsin, with their agreement decreasing as they move Eastward through Ohio, Pennsylvania, Maryland, Delaware and finally Washington, DC (which showed little consistency in ranking with a standard deviation of 15.67). The worst standard deviation is for New York City. Preston hypothesizes this has to do with conflicting stereotypes about the city: from the center of culture to the center of crime.

Most interesting perhaps is the incredibly high level of consistency in the way his subjects found a lack of correct English in the South. Mississippi ranked last in terms of

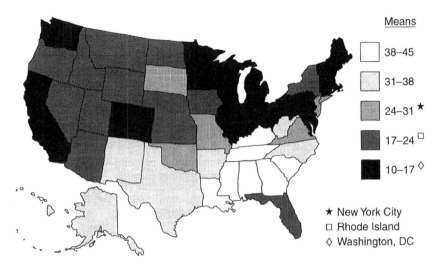

Figure 4.2 Ratings of the fifty states, New York City, and Washington, DC, for language "correctness" on a scale of 1 to 52 (lowest = '"best" by seventy-six young, first- and second-year, white undergraduates from Southern Indiana

Source: Preston (1989b: 54)

correct English and also was the most consistently ranked state. Preston takes the scores for the Southern states as "further proof of the salience of areas seen as nonstandard" (1989b: 56).

From these various definitions, a picture begins to emerge. The hypothetical Standard is the language spoken and written by persons:

● with no regional accent;
● who reside in the Midwest, Far West or perhaps some parts of the Northeast (but never in the South);
● with more than average or superior education;
● who are themselves educators or broadcasters;
● who pay attention to speech, and are not sloppy in terms of pronunciation or grammar;
● who are easily understood by all;
● who enter into a consensus of other individuals like themselves about what is proper in language.

It seems that we want language to be geographically neutral, because we believe that this neutrality will bring with it a greater range of communication. The assumption, of course, is that Midwest is neutral – at least, that is the way students in Indiana see it. Standard language ideology is responsible for the fact that a large percentage of students from other parts of the country agree with them.

We want language to be structured and rule-governed and clear. Something as important as language cannot be left to itself: normal people are not smart enough, not aware enough, to be in charge of their own language. There must be experts, persons in charge, structured authority. In the minds of the respondents, the areas of the country in which the hypothetical Standard is not spoken (the South, New York City), are the logical home of accent. From this assumption it follows that everybody else speaks the hypothetical Standard and thus, has no accent. A native of Mississippi or Brooklyn may have exactly the same educational background, intelligence, and point to make as their counterparts in Ohio and Colorado, but many believe that the accent must compromise the quality of the performance.

This mindset is set down quite clearly in the *Oxford English Dictionary* (1989):

> [Accent is] The mode of utterance peculiar to an individual, locality, or nation, as "he has a slight accent, a strong provincial accent, an indisputably Irish, Scotch, American, French or German accent" . . . This utterance consists mainly in a prevailing quality of tone, or in a peculiar alteration of pitch, but may include mispronunciation of vowels or consonants, misplacing of stress, and misinflection of a sentence. The locality of a speaker is generally clearly marked by this kind of accent.

The judgmental tone is quite evident even without the heavily significant choice of *mispronunciation*, *misplacing*, and *misinflection*. It follows from this definition that there is a correct regional pronunciation, but it is not explicitly identified.

From a legal perspective, Matsuda notes the similarities between the construction of the hypothetical Standard, or English without an accent, on one hand, and hidden norms codified in our legal institutions, on the other:

> As feminist theorists have pointed out, everyone has a gender, but the hidden norm in law is male. As critical race theorists have pointed out, everyone has a race, but the hidden norm in law is white. In any dyadic relationship, the two ends are equidistant from each other. If the parties are equal in power, we see them as equally different from each other. When the parties are in a relationship of domination and subordination we tend to say that the dominant is normal, and the subordinate is different from normal. And so it is with accent . . . People in power are perceived as speaking normal, unaccented English. Any speech that is different from that constructed norm is called an accent.
>
> (Matsuda 1991: 805)

The myth of standard language persists because it is carefully tended and propagated, with huge, almost universal success, so that language, the most fundamental of human socialization tools, becomes a commodity. This is the core of an ideology of standardization which empowers certain individuals and institutions to make these decisions and impose them on others.

Words about words

One very thorny problem that is not raised very often by sociolinguists is the fact that we are, as individuals and as a group, just as hampered by language ideology as the rest of the population (Bucholtz 2003; Eckert 2008; Gal 2005; Winford 2003; Wolfram 2007). This is best illustrated by the fact that most sociolinguists continue to use terms like *standard* and (worse still) *non-standard* even while they are arguing that these terms are ideological and inaccurate.[4] Labov's seminal paper "The Logic of Non-Standard English" (1972c), is a tour-de-force (and purposefully polemic) demonstration of the fact that the young men who speak AAVE are just as capable of constructing logical arguments (and sometimes better at it) as young men who speak other varieties of English. In the forty years since it was first published there have been hundreds of studies that reinforce Labov's findings.

The persistence of the terms *standard* and *non-standard* among linguists is a testament to the deep roots of language ideology. This is a problem with no easy solution. Coupland summarizes:

> "Standardness" and "non-standardness" are too deeply ingrained into sociolinguistic theory and methods for us to dispense with received perspectives and begin again, conceptually. Even so, there are good reasons to move on from ontological perspectives that reify, describe and account for Standard American English as a "natural" or "necessary" sociolinguistic reality.
>
> (2002: 632)

In the first edition of this book I attempted to sidestep the use of standard and non-standard by borrowing *mainstream* as a reference to the varieties of American English which were broadly considered to be correct by prescriptivists. In the years since then, I have come to the conclusion that *mainstream* is just as inaccurate as the term *standard*. Thus in this revised edition, I will use a term which, while not perfect, is an improvement on both standard/nonstandard and mainstream/peripheral.

If you recall, syntacticians use an asterisk to mark utterances which are judged grammatically inauthentic. I am adapting that practice here, and will use *SAE to refer to that mythical beast, the idea of a homogenous, standard American English.

There is also the issue of names and labels for language varieties, race and ethnicity. The Census Bureau's terminology for race (Table 4.2) can be challenged on many levels, but it does observe the distinction between race and ethnicity. You'll note that there are no terms in this list for someone whose family originated in a Spanish-speaking country. That is because Latinos (or Hispanics – more about this below) can be and are any race.

In this volume my policy is to use those labels that people choose for themselves.[5] In the case of Spanish-speaking Americans, the situation is far more complex in part because there are so many different cultures represented, a topic that will be discussed in Chapter 14 in more detail.

"White" as a category used by the Census Bureau is a descriptive term that does not parallel "African American" or "Asian." European American is awkward and inexact; in Canada *Anglophone* has come to refer to their English-speaking (rather than French-speaking) population. Historically *Anglo* has to do with the Anglo-Saxons in the British Isles, but the term has gained wider usage. Here I will use Anglo, Anglo-American, and sometimes, White.

Table 4.2 U.S. Census Bureau naming conventions and alternatives

Naming convention	Alternative
White	Anglo, White
Black or African American	African American, Black
Hispanic	Latino/a*
American Indian	American Indian*
Asian	Asian*
Native Hawai'ian	Hawaiian

For the African American language community I use *African American Vernacular English* (AAVE), *African American English* (AAE), or *Black English*. I will not use the term Ebonics except in quotations of work that is not my own, or in discussion of the term itself. Sclafani relates an anecdote which is an excellent illustration of the corruption of the term:

> I was once lectured by a retired airline pilot at a wedding reception on the difference between African American English and Ebonics; he held that the former was a "legitimate language" and the latter was "that horrible slang you hear on cable TV."
>
> (Sclafani 2008: 508)

→ AAVE gives it the respect it deserves

DISCUSSION QUESTIONS AND EXERCISES

● The Free Online Dictionary's (2009) definition of *SAE is interesting. How does the usage note relate to the definition? Is it complementary, or contradictory?

> Standard American English: The variety of English that is generally acknowledged as the model for the speech and writing of educated speakers.

> Usage note: People who invoke the term *SAE rarely make clear what they have in mind by it, and tend to slur over the inconvenient ambiguities that are inherent in the term. Sometimes it is used to denote the variety of English prescribed by traditional prescriptive norms, and in this sense it includes rules and usages that many educated speakers do not systematically conform to in their own speech or writing, such as the rules for use of who and whom. In recent years, however, the term has more often been used to distinguish the speech and writing of middle-class educated speakers from the speech of other groups and classes, which are termed nonstandard . . . Thus while the term can serve a useful descriptive purpose providing the context makes its meaning clear, it shouldn't be construed as conferring any absolute positive evaluation.

● English Plus+ (Bair 2009; http://englishplus.com), a website that offers resources to prepare for the SAT, provides a definition of *SAE which covers every possibility:

> Standard American English, also known as Standard Written English or SWE, is the form of English most widely accepted as being clear and proper.

> Publishers, writers, educators, and others have over the years developed a consensus of what *SAE consists of. It includes word choice, word order, punctuation, and spelling.

> Standard American English is especially helpful when writing because it maintains a fairly uniform standard of communication which can be understood by all speakers and users of English regardless of differences in dialect, pronunciation, and usage. This is why it is sometimes called Standard Written English.

> There are a few minor differences between standard usage in England and the United States, but these differences do not significantly affect communication in the English language.

> Please note that most dictionaries merely report on words that are used, not on their grammar or usage. Merely because a word appears in a dictionary does not mean that it is standard.
>
> ● How does this definition compare to the others quoted in this chapter? How is it different? Consider the last paragraph especially, which strikes a very different tone. The author seems to be challenging the authority of dictionaries. Why might that be?
> ● Consider these two statements:
>
> > The fact that a word appears in a dictionary means ____.
> >
> > The fact that a word does not appear in a dictionary means ____.
>
> Can you come up with clear, consistent and factually accurate ways to finish these thoughts? If not, why not?
> ● In this book I use *SAE to refer to the concept of a standardized, idealized American English. How does this term fit, or fail to fit? Can you come up with a better solution?

Notes

1 Sociolinguists are still debating the parameters of such crucial terms as prestige, education, and standard: "Other[s] might share my sense of institutional frustration at how far sociolinguistics is from being able to present a consistent and persuasive set of principles and perspectives on [*SAE]" (Coupland 2000: 623). See also Milroy (2004a) for a discussion of the importance of resolving these very basic matters.

2 The equivalent variety of British English will be referenced as *SBE.

3 These definitions were answers to queries posted to various CompuServe discussion forums in summer 1995 requesting personal definitions of *SAE. Answers came from adults in all parts of the country who provided answers with the knowledge that they would be used here in whole or part.

4 A parallel challenge has to do with how we think about and define race. In sociology, race is not seen as a matter of genetics or biology. Race is not a thing at all, but a very complex process, the application of a set of stereotypes through institutions (Omi and Winant 1994). That is, race is a social construct, an idea that is imposed by the same institutions that promote language ideology.

 In a series of studies Baugh has approached this issue from various directions (1991, 2005, 2006a) in which he carefully teases apart the question of racial identity to the point that terms like "African American" mean very little. "It Ain't About Race: Some Lingering (Linguistic) Consequences of the African Slave Trade and Their Relevance to Your Personal Historical Hardship Index" (2006a) is an examination of the greater sociopolitical, historical and linguistic context of race in the aftermath of Hurricane Katrina.

5 For example, when writing about American Indians or Native Americans, I make an attempt to identify the tribe. This raises the question: Do the Hopi have a different variety and accent of English than the Navaho or the Chippewa?

Suggested further reading

Crowley, T. (2003) *Standard American English and the Politics of Language.* Basingstoke: Palgrave Macmillan.

McWhorter, J. (1998) The Heart of the Matter. In *The Word on the Street: Fact and Fable about American English.* New York: Plenum Trade.

Nunberg, G. (2007) The Persistence of English. In *The Norton Anthology of American Literature.* New York: W.W. Norton.

Shaw, S. (1999) Who Wrote Your Dictionary? Demystifying the Contents and Construction of Dictionaries. In R. Wheeler (ed.) *Language Alive in the Classroom.* Westport, CT: Praeger Publishers.

Wolfram, W. and Schilling-Estes, N. (2006) Dialects, Standards and Vernaculars. In *American English: Dialects and Variation.* New York: Blackwell.

Language subordination

5

> The primary function of myth is to validate an existing social order. Myth enshrines conservative social values, raising tradition on a pedestal. It expresses and confirms, rather than explains or questions, the sources of cultural attitudes and values . . . Because myth anchors the present in the past it is a sociological charter for a future society which is an exact replica of the present one.
>
> Ann Oakley (1974)

> When I read some of the rules for speaking and writing the English language correctly, I think any fool can make a rule, and every fool will mind it.
>
> Henry David Thoreau, Journal entry, February 3, 1860

Close to fifty years of empirical work in sociolinguistics have established that language is flexible and constantly flexing, and that emblematic marking of social allegiances is not random. We use variation in language to construct ourselves as social beings, to signal who we are, and who we are not and do not want to be. Speakers choose among sociolinguistic variants available; their choices group together in ways which are obvious and interpretable to other speakers in the community. This process is a functional and necessary part of the way we interact. It is not an optional feature of the spoken language.

When an individual is asked to reject their own language, we are asking them to drop allegiances to the people and places that define them. We do not, cannot under our laws, ask a person to change the color of her skin, her religion, her gender, her sexual identity, but we regularly demand of people that they suppress or deny the most effective way they have of situating themselves socially in the world:

- I don't care about the color of our skin, but speak that dialect of yours someplace where it won't insult my ears.
- You were a successful engineer in the Ukraine, sure, but why can't you speak real English?
- If you just didn't sound so corn-pone, people would take you seriously.
- You're the best salesperson we've got, but must you sound gay on the phone?

It is hard for most younger people to imagine a time when Congress and the courts did nothing to prevent violence against people of color while the media looked the other way. It is even more difficult to acknowledge how slowly things began to improve after the Emancipation Proclamation. It's true that progress was made; Harry Truman achieved some significant advances by establishing a committee on civil rights, and then charging the committee to design policies that would eliminate discrimination and segregation in employment, the civil service, the armed forces, housing, access to health care, public accommodations, voting, and interstate transportation.[1]

But it's also true that anti-lynching legislation came before the Senate some two hundred times after the Emancipation Proclamation and before the passage of the Civil Rights Act, and two hundred times the Senate did not vote, even once, on that legislation; senators from the South went to extraordinary lengths to block such bills by keeping them in committee. The House did pass the Dyer Anti-Lynching Bill in 1922; this made it possible for such cases to be tried in federal courts rather than state and local courts, which were biased in favor of the person or persons charged with inflicting bodily harm. In 2005, the Senate apologized officially for the lack of action on their part, but yet, in 2005, ten senators voted against that resolution (Anon 2005).

All the evidence indicates that there is still blatant discrimination in employment, housing, education, the media, the courts and in everyday interaction. Despite the passing of Civil Rights legislation, despite what we would like to think of as a more enlightened attitude about social issues, discrimination persists. Civil Rights legislation has brought about some positive change, but it has also driven those who wish to discriminate underground, where alternate, more subtle approaches to exclusion have been crafted.

In the wake of ever tighter antidiscrimination laws, language and accent have become an acceptable excuse to publicly turn away, to refuse to recognize the other or acknowledge their rights. *Recognition* and *misrecognition* are concepts that have interested philosophers for a long time. Ricoeur (2005) notes that human beings have a common constitution, and that our commonalities demand mutual recognition, something that we resist. Everyone struggles "against the misrecognition of others at the same time that it is a struggle for recognition of oneself by others" (ibid.: 258).

Taylor describes the opposite of recognition as misrecognition:

> [O]ur identity is partly shaped by recognition or its absence, often by the misrecognition of others, and so a person or group of people can suffer real damage, real distortion, if the people or society around them mirror back to them a confining or demeaning or contemptible picture of themselves.
>
> (1994: 25)

If you look closely at language-focused discrimination, you will find that it is not language *per se* that is relevant; instead we need to understand the individual's beliefs about language and following from those beliefs, institutional practices. In short, these beliefs and practices are the way in which individuals and groups are denied recognition. In this study I use ideology as a framework to examine and understand the subordination process. That is, I am interesting in exploring how arguments for standardization reproduce "cultural conceptions which are partial, contestable and contested, and interest-laden" (Woolard and Schieffelin 1994: 58; see also Schieffelin *et al.* 1998; Silverstein 1998; Woolard 2008).

For our purposes, ideology is defined as: "the promotion of the needs and interests of a dominant group or class at the expense of marginalized groups, by means of disinformation and misrepresentation of those non-dominant groups."

More specifically, standard language ideology (SLI) is defined as:

> a bias toward an abstracted, idealized, homogenous spoken language which is imposed and maintained by dominant bloc institutions and which names as its model the written language, but which is drawn primarily from the spoken language of the upper middle class.[2]

Silverstein's work on language ideology (1979, 1998) initiated a long discussion of how ideology functions, while Foucault considered the way in which discourse is "controlled, selected, organized and redistributed," or disciplined. In concluding that "discourse is the power to be seized" (1984), Foucault was anticipating some of the arguments about rhetorical framing which will be raised in later chapters.

SLI proposes that an idealized nation-state has one perfect, homogenous language. That hypothetical, idealized language is the means by which (1) discourse is seized, and (2) rationalizations for that seizure are constructed. It is also a fragile construct and one that needs to be protected.

It might be argued that in a culture such as ours which obliges everyone to participate in the educational system, everyone has access to discourse. In theory, marginalized groups can, by coming through the educational system, make themselves heard. Foucault antici- pates part of this argument by pointing out the fallacy of the assumption of education as an evenly distributed and power-neutral cultural resource: "Any system of education is a political way of maintaining or modifying the appropriation of discourses, along with the knowledges and powers which they carry" (ibid.: 123).

The educational system may not be the beginning, but it is the heart of the standard- ization process. To suggest that children who do not speak *SAE will find acceptance and validation in the schools is, in a word, ludicrous. A child who tells her stories in stigmatized varieties of English is quickly corrected. She must assimilate, or fall silent. Sledd sees this as an institutionalized policy to formally initiate children into the linguistic prejudices (and hence, language ideology) of the middle classes (Sledd 1972, 1988). Dominant institutions promote the notion of an overarching, homogenous standard language which is primarily Anglo, upper middle-class, and ethnically middle-American. Whether the issues at hand are large-scale sociopolitical in nature or more subtle, whether the approach is coercion or consent, there are two sides to this process: first, devaluation of all that is not (or does not seek to be) politically, culturally or socially marked as belonging to the privileged class, and second, validation of the social (and linguistic) values of the dominant institutions. The process of linguistic assimilation to an abstracted standard is cast as a natural one, necessary and positive for the greater social good.

What we do not seem to understand clearly, what is mysterious and important, is not so much the way in which the powerful deny others acknowledgement and permission to be heard in their own voices, but more so how and why those groups cooperate. How do the dominant bloc institutions manage to convince whole groups of human beings that they do not fully or adequately possess an appropriate human language? And, more mysteriously, why do those groups hand over this authority?

Eagleton puts a more personal face on this question when he summarizes one way ideology works with the simple but striking observation that critical language theory tries to understand "*how people come to invest in their own unhappiness*" (Eagleton 2007: emphasis added).[3]

When speakers of devalued or stigmatized varieties of English consent to the standard language ideology, they become complicit in its propagation against themselves, their own interests and identities. Many are caught in a vacuum: If an individual cannot find any social acceptance for her language outside her own speech communities, she may come to denigrate her own language, even while she continues to use it.

A standard language ideology provides a web of (supposedly) common-sense arguments, in which the vernacular speaker can get tangled at every turn: at school, in radio news, at the movies, while reading novels, at work, she hears that the language which marks her as

Chilean, Muslim, or a native of Mississippi is ugly, unacceptable, incoherent, illogical. This is countered, daily, by her experience: she does communicate, effectively, with the people who are closest and most important to her, who mark their language similarly. She even manages to communicate with the people who are criticizing her, in spite of their complaints. The things they say about her language and her social allegiances make her uncomfortable and unhappy. The things they promise her if she were to change this behavior may be very seductive: more money, success, recognition. She may think about trying to change the way she talks, and pay some attention to pronunciation points which have been brought to her attention. It isn't clear to her that her phonology – her accent – will be very difficult to change.

This day-by-day, persistent devaluation of her social self has repercussions. It might eventually bring her to the point of resistance, on a personal level. If there is a group of people like her going through the same experience, it might bring organized resistance. There are occasional signs of this: An accent reduction class scheduled in a South Carolina school which must close because of lack of student interest (Riddle 1993); a movement to validate Hawai'ian Creole in public forums (Verploegen 1988); a group in Wisconsin which publicizes their commitment to AAVE and their wish to have it recognized for the functional language it is (Hamblin 1995); a Cambodian-American who takes his employer to court for telling him that to get a promotion he must "sound American" (Xieng 1991; Court case Xieng 1993: 93, see Appendix).

In the rest of this book we will see that the institutions that embody language ideology do not let these small acts of resistance go by unnoticed; they strike back, and strike hard. The institutions which see themselves as protectors of the values of the nation-state work hard to validate their favored status in that state, in part on the basis of language. This process of resistance and counter-resistance which pits the empowered against small groups or individuals who struggle for recognition is an on-going process. It is reminiscent of Antonio Gramsci's recasting of Marxist social theory in terms of what he called hegemony, or ideology as struggle.[4]

What concerns us in the remainder of this book is the process of linguistic domination itself. The arguments which are used to legitimize the values of the mainstream and to devalue non-conforming language varieties are well established, and so accepted that they are often quite openly used.

Before we look at specific instances of the process of misrecognition, it will be useful to focus attention on two analytical tools. The first is a working model of the way institutions subordinate linguistically. The second is a brief consideration of the way this language subordination model is realized in the uneven distribution of what will be called the communicative burden.

A model of the language subordination process

The steps in the language subordination process included in this model (Figure 5.1) have been compiled from an analysis of a wide range of reactions or actions of dominant bloc institutions when a threat to the authority of the homogenous language of the nation-state has been perceived. The elements in this model grew out of analysis of many kinds of public commentary on language use and language communities, but they are similar to other models of ideological processes.[5]

Language is mystified.

> *You can never hope to comprehend the difficulties and complexities of your mother tongue without expert guidance.*

Authority is claimed.

> *We are the experts. Talk like me/us. We know what we are doing because we have studied language, because we write well.*

Misinformation is generated.

> *That usage you are so attached to is inaccurate. The variant I prefer is superior on historical, aesthetic, or logical grounds.*

Targeted languages are trivialized.

> *Look how cute, how homey, how funny.*

Conformers are held up as positive examples.

> *See what you can accomplish if you only try, how far you can get if you see the light.*

Non-conformers are vilified or marginalized.

> *See how willfully stupid, arrogant, unknowing, uninformed and/or deviant these speakers are.*

Explicit promises are made.

> *Employers will take you seriously; doors will open.*

Threats are made.

> *No one important will take you seriously; doors will close.*

Figure 5.1 The language subordination model

Mystification is a basic tool in the application of any ideology but the fact is that people do communicate with each other in the vernacular, and they do so daily, without specialized knowledge of language. The claim that spoken language is so complex that mere native speakers can never sort things out for themselves is countered by evidence, but the mystification message is so strong that many people really believe they don't speak their own language well.

A particularly striking case of self-denigration comes out of England, where John Prescott, a prominent politician, was a constant object of mockery in the print media not so much for his policies, but for his English (Wooding 2008). It's certainly nothing unusual for newspapers to target an individual for grievances, real or imaginary. What was unusual in this case was the target's complicit agreement:

Mr. Prescott said:

> It's something I've not mastered – the language or the grammar – and that's caused a problem for me. It goes back to the education. Secondary modern school education wasn't the greatest, but there were lots of people who learned the grammar – I didn't. It's often used as part of my characterization – mangle the language.

Since the popularization of the internet, examples of trivialization abound. Later we'll be looking at two examples: the explosion of websites mocking Ebonics after the 1997 controversy (Ronkin and Karn 1999), and similar tactics undertaken to peripheralize and trivialize Spanish speakers (Hill 1995, 2008).

Any speaker of a stigmatized vernacular is promised large returns if he or she will adopt *SAE. Persons who persist in their allegiance to stigmatized varieties of English will be cut off from the everyday privileges and rights of citizenship at every turn, regardless of inherent talent or intelligence.

At its most brutal, this turns into personal attacks on whole groups of people. The most salient example of this will be seen in the way *SAE speakers and adherents react to any attempt to cast a stigmatized variety in a positive or legitimate light. Dominant bloc institutions lead the charge in cases like these, and the results are loud and shrill. The best recent example of this happening on a large-scale basis is what is generally called the Oakland Ebonics controversy, something we will look at in more detail in Chapter 16.

In this model linguistic form and social structures are connected by means of ideology (here used simply in the sense of "what people believe"), an approach that originated in its current form with Silverstein (1979), as well as in the work of other anthropological linguists and sociolinguists. In fact, all three of these nodes are bound, each to the other (Figure 5.2). Ideology cannot be abstracted away; no one can suspend the way they think about language from the process of interpreting language.

Before moving on, it will be useful to consider the nature of communication as a collaborative act between two or more persons.

Rejecting the gift: the individual's role in the communicative process

The most common rationalizations for discrimination against non-*SAE accents and languages have to do with communication. "I've got nothing against [Taiwanese, Appalachians, Kenyans]," the argument will go. It is not hard to find people who won't hesitate to put these opinions into words in a public forum:

> I cannot stand anyone with a thick Black Southern accent, it sounds racist but I seriously cannot understand when the people try to communicate to me. Example: I called my cell company and I needed help with why my email pop system did not work. The guy had a half Ebonics/Southern slang accent. Trying to explain to me technical shit I had to do. It was super annoying. I had to have him keep repeating to me what the hell he was saying, it was embarrassing me [*sic*] for me, and probably for him or not.
>
> (*Electrical Audio*, November 30, 2008)

Communication seems to be a simple thing: one person talks and another listens; they change roles. But the social space between two speakers is rarely completely neutral. Think

Figure 5.2 **Ideology as the bridge or filter between language change and social structures**

of the people you talked to today. Each time you begin an exchange, a complex series of calculations begins: Do I need to be formal with this person? Do I owe her respect? Does she owe me deference? Will she take me seriously, or reject me out of hand? What do I want from her, or she from me? Those calculations are more conscious in unusual encounters; for example, if you suddenly were introduced to the Queen of England, without preparation, would you be comfortable talking to her? For those you interact with every day, the calculations are fast and sure and well below the level of consciousness.

In any situation, a person can simply refuse to communicate. In an adversarial position, we may understand perfectly what our partners, parents, friends say to us, but still respond with "I cannot understand you." We can also reject how what we say has been understood: We say "You just don't understand" when in fact the issue is not comprehension, but difference of opinion.

When a person rejects the message in this way, he or she is refusing to accept responsibility in the communicative act, and the full burden is put directly on the other. "I can't understand you" may mean, in reality: "You can't make me understand you."

Clark's cognitive model of the communicative act is based on a principle of mutual responsibility, in which participants in a conversation collaborate in the establishment of new information. This involves complicated processes of repair, expansion, and replacement in iterative fashion until both parties are satisfied:

> Many purposes in conversation, however, change moment by moment as the two people tolerate more or less uncertainty about the listener's understanding of the speaker's references. The heavier burden usually falls on the listener, since she is in the best position to assess her own comprehension.
>
> (Clark and Wilkes-Gibbs 1986: 34)

When native speakers of U.S. English are confronted with an accent which is foreign to them – either unfamiliar varieties of English, or foreign (L2) accented English – the first decision they make is whether or not they are going to participate. What we will see again and again in the examples that follow, is that members of the dominant language group (in the cases we will examine, those who classify themselves as *SAE speakers) feel perfectly empowered to reject their responsibility, and to demand that a person with an accent carry the majority of the burden in the communicative act. Conversely, when an *SAE speaker comes in contact with another *SAE speaker who is nonetheless incoherent or unclear, the first response is not to reject the communicative burden, but to take other factors into consideration and work harder at establishing understanding.

The whole concept of units of conversation in which two partners work toward mutual comprehension assumes a certain state of mind on the part of the participants, and to an extent, the question of skill. Intercultural competence is as crucial to successful communication as underlying motivation, solidarity or hostility. Work in accommodation theory (Gallois *et al.* 2004; Giles 1984; Giles *et al.* 1991) suggests that a complex interplay of linguistic and psychological factors will establish the predisposition to understand or to refuse to understand.

Thakerar, Giles and Cheshire (1982) conducted a series of empirical tests to examine accommodation behavior; they were not working directly with L2 accented speech, but their findings are generally typical of such studies, which verify something known intuitively: listeners and speakers will work harder to find a communicative middle ground and foster mutual intelligibility when they are motivated, socially and psychologically, to do so. Conversely, when the speaker perceives that the act of accommodating or assimilating linguistically may bring more disadvantages than advantages, in in-group terms, he or she may diverge even farther from the language of the listener.

Degree of accentedness, whether from interference of a native language other than English, or a socially or geographically marked language variety, cannot predict the level of an individual's competency in the target language or skill as a communicator. In fact, high degrees of competence are often attained by persons with especially strong foreign language accents. Nevertheless, accent will sometimes be an issue in communication, especially in the case of non-native speakers of English who are in the early stages of learning the language

Accent, in the general way it has been used here, can sometimes be an impediment to communication even when all parties involved in the communicative act are willing, even eager, to understand. In many cases, however, breakdown of communication is due not so much to accent as it is to negative social evaluation of the accent in question, and a rejection of the communicative burden.

When we are confronted with a new person we want to or must talk to, we make a quick series of social evaluations based on many external cues, one of them being the person's language and accent. On the phone, of course, the only cues we get are linguistic in nature.

Based on our personal histories, our own backgrounds and social selves which together comprise a set of filters through which we hear the people we talk to, we will take a communicative stance. Most of the time, we will agree to carry our share of the burden (Figure 5.3). Sometimes, if we are especially positive about the configuration of social characteristics we see in the person, or if the purposes of communication are especially important to us, we will accept a disproportionate amount of the burden.

Each of us would group the accents we come across in different configurations. For the majority of Americans, French accents are positive ones, but not for all of us. Many have strong pejorative reactions to Asian accents, or to African American Vernacular English, but certainly not everyone does. The accents we hear must go through our language ideology filters. In extreme cases, we feel completely justified in rejecting the communicative burden, and the person in front of us:[6]

- The supervisor explained that workers would . . . ask the plaintiff what he wanted them to do, and then simply walk away, unable to understand. The supervisor refused to attribute such incidents to the plaintiff's accent, but offered no other explanation. He said they just couldn't understand him "like normal people with normal language."
- I signed up for this chemistry course but dropped it when I saw the Teaching Assistant. I shouldn't have to have TAs who can't speak English natively.
- She put on a really excellent presentation to the committee, but if she had applied for a job on the phones sounding like she does, we wouldn't have hired her.

What we have yet to fully understand is how the subjugation process works, why it works, and why we let it. We will see that standard language ideology is introduced by the schools, vigorously promoted by the media and entertainment industries and further institutionalized by the corporate sector. It is enforced in subtle and not so subtle ways by the judicial system. Thus, it is not surprising that many individuals do not recognize the fact that for spoken language, variation is systematic, structured, and inherent, and that *SAE is an abstraction. What is surprising, even deeply disturbing, is the way that many individuals who consider themselves democratic, even-handed, rational and free of prejudice, hold

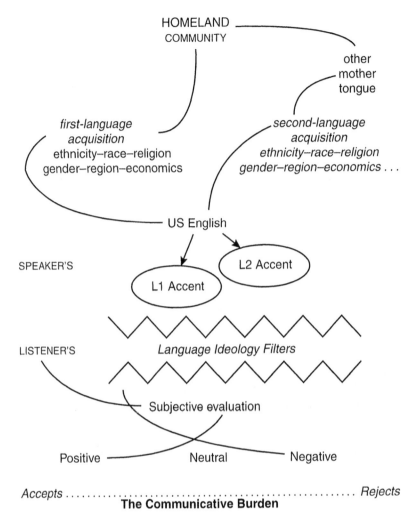

Figure 5.3 Accepting or rejecting the communicative burden

on tenaciously to a standard ideology which attempts to justify rejection of the other because of race, ethnicity, or other facet of identity that would otherwise be called racism.

Accent discrimination can be found everywhere in our daily lives. In fact, such behavior is so commonly accepted, so widely perceived as appropriate, that it must be seen as the last back door to discrimination. And the door stands wide open.

DISCUSSION QUESTIONS AND EXERCISES

● From Nunberg (2009 1983/1997) consider this paragraph from "The Decline of Grammar":

> If we are bent on finding a decline in standards, the place to look is not in the language itself but in the way it is talked about. In the profusion of new books and articles on the state of the language, and in most new usage books, the moral note, if it is sounded at all, is either wavering or shrill. What is largely missing is the idea that there is any pleasure or instruction to be derived from considering what makes good usage good. Rather, grammar comes increasingly to be regarded as a mandarin code that requires only ritual justification. And, for all the heated polemics over the importance of grammar, it appears that each party at least implicitly accepts this view.

What is it that Nunberg wants? Is he appealing to linguists, prescriptivists or both? On what basis? The entire piece is available online, for a deeper understanding of his position.

● How might Accommodation Theory serve as a tool to analyze disagreement more generally? Can you reconstruct an argument you've had (or can imagine having) using the idea of the communicative burden?

● Do you remember an occasion when you witnessed or overheard one person refusing to understand another, though the communicative content was clear? Why was the communicative burden rejected?

● Discuss how standard language ideology has been a positive or negative force in your own life or your family's. Has it afforded you advantages, or disadvantages? How have you used language ideology yourself?

● Consider the contribution from *Electrical Audio* to an online discussion of accents that are attractive or displeasing on p. 71. How is (or isn't) this an example of language ideology at work? If not language ideology, what is going on here?

● Read "Help for today's Eliza Doolittles," a newspaper article that appeared in the *Christian Science Monitor* (Gardner 1999). How does this article demonstrate the language subordination process? What steps are used? Why is the tone relevant?

● Consider two (unlikely, but useful) scenarios:

  ● Walking along the street in London, you come around a corner face to face with Mick Jagger. He's wearing a torn concert t-shirt and ripped jeans, and he grabs you by the arm. His breath is bad, and he's slurring his words. He is looking for his runaway terrier and he's talking very fast. You don't understand everything he says in his high agitation, but it's clear he wants your help.

  ● You're waiting for a bus in a small crowd of people when a shabbily dressed stranger who looks a lot like Mick Jagger approaches you, slowly and with deference. In a very heavily accented English (maybe it's Polish, you think, or some other Eastern European language) this person asks for directions.

● Are you equally willing to help in both situations? Do you in fact help both these people? If not, how do you handle it?

Notes

1 The committee issued their report, *To Secure These Rights*, in October 1947. During this same period, The United Nations began to put together the Universal Declaration of Human Rights , which establishes that all people are entitled to basic human rights without regard for race, color, sex, language, religion, political or other opinion, national or social origin, property, birth or other status. In his study *The Universal Declaration of Human Rights: Origins, Drafting, and Intent*, Morsink (2000) provides insight into the discussions that went on behind the scenes while the declaration was being drafted.

2 The term *standard language ideology* was coined by James and Lesley Milroy. Their work in this area was the first impetus for much of my own thinking on this issue, which has been further influenced in particular by the work of Fairclough, Silverstein, Eagleton, Bakhtin, Bourdieu and Foucault as well as by linguists Eckert, Bucholtz, Schieffelin, Woolard, *et al*. The definition I provide here has evolved from those provided in earlier publications.

3 A classical Marxist might look at the way language ideology works and find it an excellent example of "false consciousness," or the process by which the working class is manipulated into accepting a status quo which denies their own claims while preserving the interests of those with property and power, because it is right and good and common sense to do so. But the Marxist ideological model has limitations; its unidirectionality does not resemble the give-and-take process of standardization well enough to make it useful in this discussion.

4 The more common use of hegemony is in the sense of dominance or domination, but here I use the Gramscian definition. Gramsci provides an interesting example of an attempt to bend linguistic facts to a particular end. In his writings he argues strongly for teaching the lower and working classes a standardized Italian, and equates this process with passing on literacy, a necessary tool to fight oppression. Gramsci's confusion of symptom with cause (he sees friction following from the fact of language heterogeneity) and his rejection of rural values would seem to be at odds with his goals more generally. He was apparently able to deal with language as if it were a commodity to be willfully manipulated and cleansed of regional and social variation on command. This is particularly strange as he very early recognized the relationship between the rise of public discourse around language and accelerated shifting in the established power structures and hegemony (ibid.).

5 See Gitlin's (1980) model for analysis of the media's representation of the Vietnam War and elsewhere.

6 Examples are from (1) Anthony Dercach v. Indiana Department of Highways (in paraphrase); (2) student questionnaires on language attitudes from my own research; (3) my interviews with employers in the Chicago area; (4) discussion board entry.

Suggested further reading

Bell, L.A. (2010) *Storytelling for Social Justice: Connecting Narrative and the Arts in Antiracist Teaching*. New York: Routledge. See especially Chapters 1 and 2 on the importance of storytelling as a model for understanding racism.

Freeden, M. (2003) *Ideology: A Very Short Introduction*. Oxford: Oxford University Press.

Goldberg, S. (2003) *Fads and Fallacies in the Social Sciences*. Amherst, NY: Humanity Books.

Nunberg, G. (1983/1997) The Decline of Grammar. *The Atlantic Monthly*, November 3.

Silverstein, M. (1998) The Uses and Utility of Ideology. In B.B. Schieffelin, K.A. Woolard and P.V. Kroskrity (eds.) *Language Ideologies: Practice and Theory*. New York: Oxford University Press.

Woolard, K.A. (1998) Introduction: Language Ideology as a Field of Inquiry. In B.B. Schieffelin, K.A. Woolard and P.V. Kroskrity (eds.) *Language Ideologies: Practice and Theory*. New York: Oxford University Press.

The educational system   **6**

Fixing the message in stone

> The situation of our youth is not mysterious. Children have never been very good at listening to their elders, but they have never failed to imitate them.
>
> James Baldwin, "Nobody Knows My Name" (1985b: 208)

Education is commonly understood to be the key to success of all kinds, and formal education is built on the cornerstone of literacy. School is first and foremost the place where children learn to read and write.

The majority of children in the United States are educated in state-run and financed schools, where attendance is mandatory and the curriculum goes well beyond reading and writing. We hold schools responsible for turning the children in their care into a productive body of citizens capable of critical thought. The goal is an informed electorate, one which will accept and perpetuate the values of the nation-state.

The National Council of Teachers of English (NCTE) explicitly links goals in literacy to those of citizenship: "Standards [in language arts education] can help us ensure that all students become informed citizens and participate fully in society" (National Council of Teachers of English 1996).[1] Thus the primary educational goal in our schools equates the acquisition of literacy with the adoption of both a spoken and written *SAE.

Teaching is a difficult profession, a particularly challenging way to make a living, undertaken by people who are for the most part deeply dedicated and truly wish to do well for the children in their charge. A teacher is both an authority figure and a role model and as such has tremendous influence in a child's life. What follows in this chapter is an examination of the beliefs and practices of educators in so far as they address language issues, and how language ideology affects goals in both abstract and concrete ways. This is not a frontal attack on the crucial but undervalued profession of teaching, but a consideration of how inequality and disadvantage are perpetuated – for the most part unwittingly – in the classroom.

There is a large body of work on the way teachers' attitudes play out in the classroom, and it is remarkably consistent in its findings. For example, Briggs and Pailliotet (1997) undertook a study of education majors who had had extensive coursework emphasizing process-based (rather than error-based) evaluation of student work. In this study, the education majors were asked to correct a number of essays but despite their training, the subjects were highly consistent in attributing usage errors with student carelessness, laziness, and incompetence. These findings supplemented Briggs and Pailliotet's own observations on the power of language conventions, and provided some insight into "how grammatical instruction remains a locus of power and control in English instruction at any level" (ibid.: 1).[2] There is a crucial question without any clear answer: Most teachers are aware of the power and control they have, but how many of them realize how very influential their personal opinions are in student success?[3] Ideology is indeed most powerful when it is least visible; the invisibility of ideology also makes it much easier to propagate in a classroom.

Language ideology in education is a multi-faceted and complex subject that cannot be addressed by means of a handful of academic studies; instead, I focus here on two specific angles: first, children who speak stigmatized varieties of English (Appalachian English, British West Indian English, Sea Islands Creole, Gullah, Mexicano English, Hawai'i Creole English, among many others) and how they cope, or fail to cope. Second, I'll look briefly at the language spoken by the teachers themselves. When a teacher who grew up speaking a stigmatized vernacular is assigned to teach a first grade class in his old neighborhood, what does institutional policy tell him about the kind of English he should use with those children? Do teachers in this position follow prescripted usage rules, or do they simply use whichever language works best in reaching the children? How do they talk to children about their language? What advantages and disadvantages might there be to this? This second issue will be taken up again in Chapter 9, which deals with cases where teachers have sued their schools and school districts for language-focused discrimination under Title XII of the Civil Rights Act.

The setting of goals

Figure 6.1 provides some insight into one of the most difficult and intractable problems in public education: there are large populations of children who do not learn to read.[4] This is not a new problem, but it is one that has evaded solutions. While educators, social scientists, government agencies, psychiatrists and linguists spend a lot of time trying to figure out (1) what's going wrong, and (2) how to fix it, whole generations of children leave school unprepared and perhaps even worse, uninspired. Certainly language conflicts are relevant, but whether they are a part of the cause or simply a symptom, that is yet to be

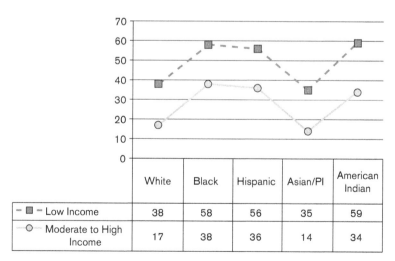

	White	Black	Hispanic	Asian/PI	American Indian
- ■ - Low Income	38	58	56	35	59
-○- Moderate to High Income	17	38	36	14	34

Figure 6.1 Percentage of 4th graders who scored less than "basic" reading skills, by race and income

Source: Adapted from Fiester (2010)

fully determined. When the subject comes into the public consciousness, it is almost always in connection with issues of race and ethnicity, bilingualism and stigmatized varieties of English. Despite strong evidence that poverty is at the root of many of the problems, the subject is rarely raised (but see especially Baugh 1999: 115 ff.).

Educators are aware of larger language-related issues as well. In 1972, the executive committee of the Conference on College Composition and Communication[5] passed a statement which was ratified by the membership in 1974:

> We affirm the students' right to their own patterns and varieties of language – the dialects of their nurture or whatever dialects in which they find their own identity and style. Language scholars long ago denied that the myth of a standard American dialect has any validity. The claim that any one dialect is unacceptable amounts to an attempt of one social group to exert its dominance over another. Such a claim leads to false advice for speakers and writers, and immoral advice for humans. A nation proud of its diverse heritage and its cultural and racial variety will preserve its heritage of dialects. We affirm strongly that teachers must have the experiences and training that will enable them to respect diversity and uphold the right of students to their own language.

Despite these clearly defined and articulated goals and a great many dedicated professionals who believe in the stated principles, more than 30 years have not seen much progress in terms of large-scale policies.[6] Nevertheless, the discussion continues and individuals have been working on ways to incorporate these goals into their research and teaching methodologies (Bruch and Marback 2005; Kinloch 2005; Katz *et al.* 2009; Scott and National Council of Teachers of English 2009). Kinloch (2005) has taken an integrative approach, encouraging her colleagues

> [to] reimagine our educational commitments, our shared values, in ways that mobilize public and professional attitudes circulating around the education of monolingual and multilingual students. This mobilization, I believe, needs to be grounded in linguistic and cultural negotiation and not in a wrong language/right language debate.
>
> (2005: 94)

Consider that every child comes to school with a home language (sometimes, more than one). They arrive fully fluent in that language. The child must now learn a series of concrete and abstract skills – reading and writing as well as an understanding of how and when different varieties are used to greatest effectiveness.[7] But it is at this point that trouble arises. The solid and reasonable arguments for literacy are now attached to the spoken language without discussion or pause. If Student A can learn to read and write, this mindset seems to go, then Student A can also learn to speak a different language variety. The two goals (mastering the standardized written language, and replacing one spoken language with another) have different underlying motivations, and in fact they stand in opposition to each other. What may seem minor in the first grade (reminding students to use a certain verb form) can mushroom into broad exclusionary practices that go beyond issues of spelling to the silencing of discourse, to the detriment of everybody (Gee 2007a [1996]: 221). This is an issue that is always close to the surface in the African American community, in part because of what Baugh has called educational malpractice stemming from educational apartheid (1999: 4). According to June Jordan (1989): "Black children in

America must acquire competence in white English, for the sake of self-preservation. But you will never teach a child a new language by scorning and ridiculing and forcibly erasing his first language."

Appropriacy arguments

The National Council of Teachers of English (NCTE), together with the International Reading Association (IRA) regularly reviews, revises and publishes Standards for the English Language Arts, a 12-point list which emphasizes reading and reading comprehension skills. The spoken language is mentioned only three times. A survey of language arts textbooks provides a similar picture, in which the focus is primarily the written language. In this view of education, children are potentially productive members of literacy communities rather than language communities (National Council of Teachers of English 1996: 3).

One variety of English can be targeted for culling with a ready-made but shallow set of appropriacy rationalizations.

Tightly bound to the concept of linguistic appropriacy is that of communicative competence, a term first coined by anthropological linguists, but appropriated by educational theorists. Taken in its loosest form, to become communicatively competent, a child learns how to adapt speech and writing on the basis of context, audience, and intention. Add to this the subjective nature of social appropriacy which is rarely challenged and the stage is set. If communicative competence is taken as a speaker's ability to use language appropriately in social context, and we do not challenge the construction of "appropriacy," then we have opened a back door to exclusion on the basis of another kind of "correctness" logic.[8]

Appropriacy judgments that cloak subjective, culturally bound judgments of "correct ness" might be made clearer by the contrast between two statements:

1   It is inappropriate for a law student to pose a question in Hawai'ian Creole English in the classroom.
2   It is inappropriate for a wife to contradict her husband.

While the second statement was once unremarkable, it would now evoke resounding criticism in most quarters. The first statement might still pass without comment, although the underlying issue; silencing of voices considered unworthy or unequal, is the same.[9] To challenge the first statement in the U.S. educational system is to question the primacy of one language variety over all others.[10]

At the same time, it is important to remember that ideologies and social strategies for the limitation of one language over another are not limited to one segment of the population. The following statements indicate that the concept of appropriacy has a wider, and quite relevant place in the discussion of the distribution of language varieties over social space:

1   A child who is a native speaker of Hawai'i Creole English may be criticized for using her home language rather than *SAE in the classroom.
2   A child who is a native speaker of Hawai'ian Creole English may be criticized for speaking "school English" rather than her family's home language at the dinner table.

The varieties of English spoken in peripheralized communities persist because they are a primary way to establish solidarity and loyalty. Minority language community ideologies can be just as powerful as the ideologies and strategies of the dominant bloc institutions, and both are worthy of study. Individuals caught between competing ideologies must learn to deal with this "push–pull."

The argument put forth by teachers in support of *SAE-only classrooms and schools generally sounds something like this:

*Student A must give up her home language in certain situations for her own good. This doesn't mean she has to give it up completely; there's no reason to deny that language; instead, redirect the student's use of that language to those environments and circumstances in which it is appropriate. At the same time, give the student another language (*SAE) – for those situations in which it will be the only socially acceptable language. This is necessary if she is to pursue a career or education in the wider world where potential employers would otherwise reject her because of the variety of English she speaks.*

The NCTE guidelines for teaching the English language arts includes this very idea, but in different terms:

> All of us who speak English speak different varieties of English depending on whom we are communicating with, the circumstances involved, the purpose of the exchange, and other factors. Indeed, creative and communicative powers are enhanced when students develop and maintain multiple language competencies.
>
> Nonetheless, some varieties of English are more useful than others for higher education, for employment, and for participation in what the Conference on College Composition and Communication (1993) in a language policy statement calls "the language of wider communication." Therefore, while we respect diversity in spoken and written English, we believe that all students should learn this language of wider communication.
>
> (National Council of Teachers of English 1996: 22–23)

Teachers are directed to appreciate and respect the otherwise stigmatized languages of peripheral communities, but at the same time, reminded that those languages must be kept separate. This faux-egalitarianism is well known to African Americans and others who fought for the reversal of the *separate but equal* doctrine. As has always been the case, the divide between socially stigmatized and socially sanctioned language runs along very predictable lines: certain vernacular varieties of U.S. English should be restricted to the home and neighborhood, to play and informal situations, to the telling of folktales and stories of little or no interest to the wider world.

With both feet firmly planted on the false assumptions of the standard language ideology and the literacy myth, a teacher may be adamant about the need to weed out the bad language and replace it with the good. To give children what they really need, these educators believe, they must supply them with a currency they don't have: *SAE, which is defined by default; it is not what these children speak.

What is more destructive than this reliance on the idealized *SAE, however, is the way in which these targeted varieties of English are devalued. Official policies draw strong distinctions: *SAE is preferred, obligatory, appropriate, widely used, while Other Languages are narrow, inappropriate, and something to be tolerated rather than accepted. Fairclough, looking at similar problems in the English school system, highlights the underlying ideology in formal policy statements and finds wording that "lifts the veil on a tradition of prescriptive bigotry towards non-standard varieties which is largely absent from the [Cox] Report" (1992: 37).

Teachers and school administrators are not hesitant to put forward appropriacy arguments in public, as was the case with the head of the Philadelphia School Board, an African American woman, in explaining why it was necessary to "drum Standard English into the heads" of AAVE speakers:

> In the process of young people applying for jobs, employers would ask them a question which would elicit a response, "I bees ready for coming here next week." This – um – utilization of the word and insertion of bees is rampant and I think really throws an employer off in terms of what the young person's talking about. "Uh, now that you're finished with me I bees going home." . . . If we relegate them only to that narrow, limited, provincial dimension of life and language, we do them a disservice because I see that they will not go beyond the borderlines of their immediate neighborhood. And we have no right to do that to any child.
>
> (McCrum *et al.* 1986)

The misinformation offered here is not uncommon: while AAVE invariant "be" is one of those points of contrast between AAVE and other varieties of English which elicits a lot of negative response, it is quite silly to claim that it would cause a breakdown in understanding among speakers of English. What this administrator is really saying is that employers have a negative emotive reaction to this feature of AAVE, which may well cause them to reject their fair share of the communicative burden.

And she is right in this point. Language-focused discrimination does exist in the wider world, and it does have a negative impact on individuals. From this, her logic follows, it is necessary to eradicate this offending grammatical feature and all of AAVE in favor of the language – and the prejudice – of the employer. Here AAVE is narrow, limited, provincial – by which she means that it is restricted to inner city Philadelphia. This kind of appropriacy rhetoric can be found again and again across the country in arguments for the subordination of languages and language varieties out of social favor. Sometimes the argument is that the subordinated language must be eradicated (as in the Philadelphia case); at other times the message is softened by arguments for supplementation in the form of an uneven bilingualism, a separate-but-equal language policy which relegates home languages to the peripheral and disposable.

In contrast, a Massachusetts teacher of Puerto Rican students makes no economic argument at all, but one which is purely ideological and unapologetically racist:

> These poor kids come to school speaking a hodge podge. They are all mixed up and don't know any language well. As a result, they can't even think clearly. That's why they don't learn. It's our job to teach them language – to make up for their deficiency. And, since their parents don't really know any language either, why should we waste time on Spanish? It is "good" English which has to be the focus.
>
> (cited in Zentella 1995: 8–9)

In this second approach, a teacher has effectively summarized all of the conclusions drawn from Basil Bernstein's theories of restricted and elaborated codes, also known as *verbal* *deficit theory* (1966). In Bernstein's view, children who do not speak *SAE do not possess sufficient human language to think or reason, and must be helped to overcome these language and cultural handicaps. The fact that Bernstein's theories and the resulting pedagogical innovations were thoroughly and resoundingly debunked some 40 years ago[11] is an indication of how receptive teachers can be to such rhetorical strategies.

It seems to be easier to approach language as a one-size-fits-all proposition. If there is only one proper language for the children in our care, and only one proper variety of that language – which happens to be the language of the socially and economically dominant – then it becomes easy, even prudent to dismiss the work that comes along with making teaching a dialogue rather than a lecture.

Yet another approach to rationalizing linguistic subordination is seen in the essay "Standard English vs. the American Dream" (Winsboro and Solomon 1990) which consolidates appropriateness and economic arguments with assimilationist rhetoric:

> While we must continue to manifest pluralistic approaches to integrating Black English into the curriculum, as necessary, we must simultaneously teach those who speak with a dialect that a realistic chance of success in American society is frequently based on mastery of Standard English.

Studies consistently demonstrate that educators manifest a generally negative reaction to the "less familiar dialect" in favor of *SAE. Black educators are candid about the socio-economic disadvantages of speaking AAVE in a predominantly Anglo society. Often, African Americans are the most vehement supporters of *SAE and intolerant of the very idea of AAVE. To further complicate this issue, those educators are understandably hesitant to consider what it means if the language ideology they have embraced turns out to be based on fallacies.

Vershawn Ashanti Young is an example of an African American teacher and scholar who has looked carefully at these complex and sensitive issues, which he has experienced from both sides: as a boy growing up in Chicago's Horner Projects, and as someone who left that life behind himself and became a professor of rhetoric. Young writes about a student, Cam, who comes into his classroom and deliberately uses AAVE to draw attention to things that Young has taken great pains to suppress in himself. Young asks: "What had I really achieved if Black males like Cam were coming to college and being successful? And would not my validating his use of the vernacular in order to affirm his Black masculine identity demean my own?" (Young 2007: 93).

Evidence clearly suggests that speakers of Black English and Hawai'i Creole English are presented with more obstacles to educational success than professed speakers of *SAE. The consequences are broad, not only in the way individuals are silenced, but also because the community as a whole is deprived of those voices, and the contributions that would have been.

Those who argue that it is right and good to help those children substitute *SAE for their home languages never seem to carry the argument to its ultimate conclusion. First, it has been established that teachers discriminate against speakers of stigmatized varieties of English; second, it is agreed that in such an atmosphere of rejection, no child can thrive. From these two facts come the conclusion that *SAE must be acquired and the vernacular put aside. This may seem to be common sense and logical, but it is in fact logical only in so far as one accepts the underlying premise of linguistic superiority and the primacy of economic motivations.

FACT: Language A and Language B are equal in linguistic and cultural terms. →
FACT: Language B is rejected by teachers and employers. →
FACT: Rejection has a negative effect on the speakers of Language B.

↓

*CONCLUSION: Language B must be discarded in favor of Language A.

When successful middle-class African Americans argue that AAVE must not be tolerated in public forums, the tone is often highly defensive, and one reason for that must be the awareness of the undeniable conclusion that to take such a stance is "surrendering to prejudice" (Young 2007: 108–109).

The teacher discriminates because the employer does; the child pays the price of that discrimination by accommodating and assimilating. The only way to achieve pluralistic goals, we are told, *is to make everyone alike*. In a confrontation between the powered and the disempowered, it is very rarely the empowered who must give way in the resolution of conflict. It is never suggested that speakers of language A stop and consider the nature of their prejudice, and how to end it.

The results of appropriacy argumentation

By the time they finish their elementary education, most children are firm believers in the appropriacy argument. If they are native speakers of a language other than *SAE, they will confess their uneasiness: "The more you get into [learning *SAE]," says a student in South Carolina, "the more I realize not how bad I sound but how much better I could sound" (*ABC Evening News*, December 15, 1991).

"I don't want my accent to hurt my self-esteem anymore," says a native speaker of Spanish. "I know I can get my point across in English, but I don't want to feel uncomfortable every time I say something" (Hernandez 1993: 1).

In a series of studies using matched-guise testing, Carranza and Ryan (1975) showed that African American, Anglo and Hispanic students all found Spanish-accented English to be lacking in prestige and inappropriate for a classroom setting. According to Ryan, Carranza and Moffie (1977) "Small increments in accentedness were found to be associated with gradually less favorable ratings of status, solidarity, and speech characteristics" (as summarized in Eisenstein 1983: 173).

In the teaching of language, there is a very striking division between educational psychologists and theorists, on the one side, and boards of education and classroom teachers, on the other. The NCTE circulates a publication list to its 90,000 members which includes titles such as *Kids Come in All Languages* (Spangenberg-Urbschat and Pritchard 1994) and (more than 20 years ago) *Affirming Students' Right to Their Own Language* (McCrum et al. 1986). For the most part, these are well-balanced reports on those factual issues which should be clear to every teacher involved in language instruction.

In spite of the availability of such resources, however, the language arts classroom is one of the best places to watch the way that language communities and individuals who do not use *SAE are subordinated by means of misinformation, trivialization, and a carefully constructed set of threats and promises.

Good enough English

In the second half of the nineteenth century, the U.S. government was hard pressed to find some kind of lasting resolution for the on-going conflicts with the continent's indigenous peoples. Disease, warfare and systematic routing had reduced the great variety of native cultures to a handful. Tribes that were not wiped out entirely were decimated often to less than 10 percent of their original numbers (Stannard 1992). By the mid-nineteenth century, the Native American diaspora and the accelerated western push by European immigrants had increased pressure to find a lasting solution. A remedy was needed which moved beyond the writing of treaties which the U.S. government drew up and signed, but ignored at whim.

In a series of policy statements written between 1868 and 1887, the Federal Commissioner of Indian Affairs put down a very clear strategy which involved moving away from traditional warfare to a policy which depended on forcibly breaking up family and tribal units to speed up the process of assimilation. Very astutely, the commissioner pinpointed the matter of language as crucial. Without tribal languages which functioned as the primary marker of social identity and provided a cohesive force in the face of so much turmoil, the indigenous peoples could be more easily drawn into the fold. His reasoning is worth quoting at length:

> The white and Indian must mingle together and jointly occupy the country, or one of them must abandon it . . . by educating the children of these tribes in the English language these differences would have disappeared, and civilization would have followed at once. Nothing then would have been left but the antipathy of race, and that, too, is always softened in the beams of a higher civilization . . . through sameness of language is produced sameness of sentiment, and thoughts; customs and habits are molded and assimilated in the same way, and thus in process of time the differences producing trouble would have been gradually obliterated . . . in the difference of language to-day lies two-thirds of our trouble . . . schools should be established, which children should be required to attend; their barbarous dialects should be blotted out and the English language substituted . . .The object of greatest solicitude should be to break down the prejudices of tribe among the Indians; to blot out the boundary lines which divided them into distinct nations, and fuse them into one homogeneous mass. Uniformity in language will do this – nothing else will . . .There is not an Indian pupil whose tuition and maintenance is paid for by the United States Government who is permitted to study any other language than our own vernacular – the language of the greatest, most powerful, and enterprising nationalities beneath the sun. The English language as taught in America is good enough for all her people of all races.
> (Atkins 1887, as quoted in Crawford 1992: 48–49)

Reading this passage, one is calmed, somewhat, by its date. This was written over a hundred years ago, the rationalization might go. We have a more democratic and fair-handed approach now. We are making slow progress on the rights of the continent's indigenous peoples.

In matters of indigenous language use and retention, there is some evidence that the native peoples are determining their own educational language policies and looking for ways to encourage use of the mother tongue. New Mexico, in particular, has instituted procedures by which state educational administrators work together with tribal authorities to set up bilingual education policies acceptable to the tribal administration. This would seem to be a necessity in a state where 73.1 percent of the population was born in Mexico (U.S. Census Bureau, 2006–2008 American Community Survey Three-Year Estimates).

As a part of these policies, the New Mexico Department of Education worked together with the Pueblo Indian community, for example, to establish an assessment protocol for those Pueblos who teach in the bilingual education program (Sims 1992). Because each tribe has a different set of views on bilingual education, each designs its own program.[12] More recently, New Mexico has instituted a path to alternative certification that has provided a way for American Indian language speakers to teach language and culture in public schools. Even more important, it gave tribes in New Mexico the means to conceive and develop internal tribal certification processes of their own (see especially American Indian Language Policy Research and Teacher Training Center 2008). In a similar way, there are healthy and growing immersion schools for the Kanien'kehaka (Mohawk) – primarily in Canada – where policy and curriculum are directed exclusively by and for that language community.

But these are questions of bilingualism, it must be pointed out, and since the first boarding school for Native Americans was opened at Carlisle in Pennsylvania (Coleman 1993), the language issue for Native Americans has become complicated by the development of varieties of English distinct both from tribal languages and the English of non-Native Americans. Thus, much like Mexican-Americans, Native Americans are confronted with educational challenges of two types: bilingualism, and bidialectalism. Leap (1992) makes the salient point that for each Native American tribal language there is a distinct and functioning variety of English with phonological, morphological, syntactic and discourse features specific to it. This variety of English must be taken into consideration in the classroom, and not just as an object to be replaced with another, less socially stigmatized *SAE.

In the current day, language education policies are rarely overtly racist or Eurocentric, and it is precisely for that reason that they work so well. There are no conspiracy plots to kidnap Mexican children in Texas or Chinese children in San Francisco or Arabic children in Detroit. Educators do not suggest that children of a specific ethnicity or race would be better off if they were removed from their homes. We ask those children to learn English, the argument goes, but it's for their own good. The more they willingly submit to mainstreaming, the better the mainstream will treat them.

The most commonly heard position on this issue of the appropriate language of education was summarized quite saliently by William J. Bennett, a former Secretary of Education:

> Our origins are diverse. Yet we live together as fellow citizens, in harmony . . . Each of us is justly proud of his own ethnic heritage. But we share this pride, in common, as Americans, as American citizens. To be a citizen is to share in something common – common principles, common memories, and a common language in which to discuss our common affairs. Our common language is, of course, English. And our common task is to ensure that our non-English-speaking children learn this common language . . . We expect much of [our schools] – to impart basic skills, to help form character, to teach citizenship. And we expect our schools to help teach all of our students, the common language that will enable them to participate fully in our political, economic, and social life.
>
> (Bennett 1988)

Maybe we would like to believe that current-day policies are more enlightened, that things have improved over the past 20 years, but evidence indicates that the opposite is true. Reading academic work on issues of language rights in the schools, one established theme comes repeatedly to the surface: separate but equal language policies are ugly, but necessary.

Valencia and Solórzano provide a sobering overview of educational policies founded on the idea of language deficit, and come to a simple conclusion: "Whether its rationale is genetics, poverty, culture and language, or home environment, the end result is that the deficit ideology defrauds marginalized students" (2004: 125).

The debates around bilingual education seem to pose very simple questions:

- Should children be required to learn English, and learn in English, regardless of their own home languages and the primary languages of their communities?
- Can one policy – based on allegedly common views of the responsibilities of citizenship – be just for all students in all schools, whether that child is a native speaker of Navajo, Arabic, or Spanish?

Despite many years of debate and experimentation no resolutions have been found, but a different question might help clarify some of the issues: If by magic it were possible to make every school-aged child in the nation instantaneously bilingual, equally proficient in English and in their native language, would the problem of discrimination in the schools go away?

Teacher talk

Formal expectations about teachers' language skills are easy enough to document. Each state has a complex administrative body which is responsible for reviewing and licensing teachers, and each publishes those guidelines openly. Guidelines for Michigan, New Mexico, California and New York, for example, all have similar language about the native language skills of any teacher, which include phrases such as "demonstrates excellent skills of pronunciation and grammar" and "carries out instruction in content areas of the curriculum using a standard variety of the native language" (New Mexico guidelines, effective July 1, 1989). Whether or not this latter expectation is realistic or enforceable is never addressed.

While the official pronunciation and accent test once administered by New York City to prospective teachers is no longer used, such policies have been employed elsewhere: in the 1970s, speakers of Chicano English were still failing the speech test required for teacher certification in California (Pelosa 1981: 8), while in 2010 Arizona Governor Jan Brewer signed a controversial Anti-immigration Act into law. As a result, the Board of Education initiated a purge that would remove teachers with "heavy accents" from classrooms. These measures were met with great enthusiasm by Tom Horne, Superintendent of Public Instruction, who had long been agitating for the exclusion of ethnic studies from those Tucson schools where Mexican American students were rude to him and critical of his administration. Note that it is on the basis of his dislike of a "small group of students" that he argues for abandonment of the entire Ethnic Studies curriculum. Note also the blatant partisanship:

An open letter to the citizens of Tucson . . .
The citizens of Tucson, of all mainstream political ideologies, would call for the elimination of the Tucson Unified School District's ethnic studies program if they knew what was happening there . . . I personally observed this at the Tucson Magnet School. My Deputy, Margaret Garcia Dugan, who is Latina and Republican, came to refute the allegation made earlier to the student body, that "Republicans hate Latinos." Her speech was non-partisan and professional, urging students to think for themselves, and avoid stereotypes. Yet, a small group of La Raza [Ethnic studies] students treated her rudely, and when the principal asked them to sit down and listen, they defiantly walked out. By contrast, teenage Republicans listened politely when Delores Huerta told the entire student body that "Republicans hate Latinos." In hundreds of visits to schools, I've never seen students act rudely and in defiance of authority, except in this one unhappy case. I believe the students did not learn this rudeness at home, but from their Raza teachers.

(Horne, June 11, 2007)

Just three years after this letter was made public, Arizona citizens passed laws that brought Horne's vision of a homogenous and obedient student body closer to realization:

While much condemnation has rightly been expressed toward Arizona's anti-immigrant law, SB 1070, a less-reported and potentially more sinister measure is set to take effect on January 1, 2011. This new law, which was passed by the conservative state legislature at the behest of then-School Superintendent (and now Attorney General-elect) Tom Horne, is designated HB 2281 and is colloquially referred to as a measure to ban ethnic studies programs in the state. As with SB 1070, the implications of this law are problematic, wide-ranging and decidedly hate-filled . . . With HB 2281, the intention is not so much to expel or harass as it is to inculcate a deep-seated, second-class status by denying people the right to explore their own histories and cultures. It is, in effect, about the eradication of ethnic identity among young people in the state's already-floundering school system, which now ranks near the bottom in the nation.

(Amster 2011)

Even in parts of the country where ethnic studies and bilingual education are less volatile subjects, it is not difficult to find school systems with formal guidelines designed to winnow teachers with social and regional accents out of the teaching force. In a telephone interview, a high-level administrator in a major eastern school district was quite candid, speaking on the matter of accent in the teaching force. He noted that in the evaluation of potential employees, there are different sets of expectations, so that

if you are interviewing for a laboratory specialist who has no contact with the students, then you have lower expectations. An African-American accent would be more acceptable in a phys ed teacher, for example, than it would be in a teacher of speech.

(Director of Evaluation Programs, interviewed June 1994)[13]

These issues rarely come to the attention of the public, unless the news media takes interest in some particular case, as in the 1992 controversy around teachers with foreign accents in Westfield, Massachusetts, a town of about 36,000 people and a broad ethnic mix.[14]

In July of that year, a petition signed by 403 residents was presented to the school board in protest of a decision to reassign two bilingual education teachers to positions as regular classroom teachers. The petition specifically addressed the issue of accent, urging that no teacher be assigned to first or second grade classrooms "who is not thoroughly proficient in the English language in terms of grammar, syntax, and – most important – the accepted and standardized use of pronunciation."

George Varelas, former mayor of Westfield and simultaneously the chair of the city's school committee, had spearheaded the effort behind this petition, promoting it vocally and with the press. Mr. Varelas is himself a native speaker of Greek and speaks English with that accent, but he found this proposal to the school board a compelling one.

"Persons like myself – and I cannot be confused with someone from Boston or Alabama – should not be in a self-contained classroom for a full year teaching 5- and 6-year olds the multitude of phonetic differences that exist in the English language," the Mayor said in an interview. "I would only impart my confusion and give them my defects in terms of language" (*New York Times*, July 5, 1992, Sec. 1, p. 12).

A debate ensued between Mr. Varelas and Piedad Robertson, a native of Cuba, former kindergarten teacher and at the time of the petition, Massachusetts Secretary of Education. Ms. Robertson openly called for the rejection of the petition: "instead of fostering the acceptance of cultural diversity, [it] would appear to encourage bigotry, racism, and discrimination" (ibid.).

In the end, the school board voted down the petition quite resoundingly, but whether or not this was out of conviction of the wrongness of the proposal or the fact that the State Attorney General had pointed out that it would violate Title VII of the Civil Rights Act, is unclear. After the issue settled, a number of questions had yet to be answered. Commentators observed that the parents feared not so much that the teachers would be incomprehensible, but that their children would pick up the teacher's accent.

In linguistic terms, this fear has no foundation. Children learn their phonologies first from their families and then from their peers, and that process is largely finished by the time they get to school. Phonetics and phonology do not pass from adult to children like viruses. A teacher provides a language role model, certainly, but of a different type: with schooling the lexicon and stylistic repertoire expands, but these are additions to the basic structure or the grammar of language, which is well established by age 6. In terms of the Sound House analogy used in Chapter 3 of this book, a child has already constructed a Sound House by the time they enter school. If any major remodeling is done (and it can be done at this age), the moving of walls or the addition of a staircase, it is done out of wanting to imitate the Sound Houses of other children. In contrast, the stylistic effects of certain grammatical strategies and lexical items might be seen as interior decorating with drapes and carpets, fabrics and colors, and will be greatly affected by the acquisition of literacy and hence by interaction with the teacher. Accent is not an issue; communicative effectiveness may be, but that is true whatever the native language of the teacher.

While these fears are easily addressed, the underlying issues remain. There is considerable resistance in this country to teachers with foreign accents, and nowhere is that resistance so loudly voiced as in the university setting. Most large research universities with graduate programs employ graduate students to teach, or assist in teaching, large introductory courses in their areas of expertise and scholarship. This is both a reasonable part of the training of future teachers, and an economic necessity in larger institutions. Many of these graduate students come from outside the U.S., and speak English as a second language and with an L2 accent. Emotions on the matter of graduate student instructors in the classroom sometimes run very high. The following examples all originate at the University of Michigan, during my tenure there:

A more recent experience concerns my daughter, a recent graduate of the engineering college. Most of her undergraduate experience was with TAs, many of whom were ill equipped to communicate the language let alone ideas. For $10,000 a year in out-of-state tuition we expected more.

> (Fall 1993; letter to the "Alumni Voices" section of the University of Michigan LSA magazine)

The ONE problem with Ann Arbor (aside from construction, too many coffee shops): Graduate Student Instructors who don't know how to speak English.

> (From a column in the student paper, *The Michigan Daily*, April 18, 1996)

Of course it's hard to understand them, and of course I resent it. Why can't I get what I pay for, which is a teacher like me who talks to me in my own language that I can understand?

> (From a questionnaire distributed annually to incoming students in a linguistics course)

The issues raised here, directly and indirectly, have to do with unmet student expectations. One set of expectations has to do with the contract between student and university, both formal and implied. Whether or not that contract is fairly interpreted to include student preferences on the nationality or ethnicity of instructors and faculty cannot be taken up here. What is relevant to this discussion are the issues of accent, comprehensibility, and communication.

In response to complaints from the University of Michigan student body on this issue, the university administration took a number of steps to ensure that graduate student instructors were indeed prepared to teach in English. The Center for Research on Learning and Teaching, in cooperation with the English Language Institute, also provided extensive training for teaching assistants whose first language was not English, including a three-week intensive workshop.[15] International TAs must successfully complete the workshop and also must pass an oral proficiency screening before being allowed to teach. Those who do not pass the oral screening continue to take English classes until their English is acceptable.

In an open letter to the student body, the Dean of the College of Liberal Arts and Sciences drew up a set of proposed remedies for the students' unhappiness about faculty with foreign accents. While the university recognizes its responsibility in screening and training non-native speakers of English who will be given teaching responsibilities, there is no parallel recognition of the need to educate undergraduates to discern between real communicative difficulties and those stemming not from language, but from stereotype and bias.

These issues are also relevant for faculty with advanced degrees; a Ph.D. cannot render anyone accentless. Undergraduate complaints, however, focus almost exclusively on graduate student teachers, which indicates that the underlying issues are complicated by the power and authority structures of any university setting. Undergraduates who come into the university system directly from high school are often very unclear on the organization of the faculty and the degree system; they might not even realize what roles a graduate student instructor plays. As a body, graduate student teachers seem to occupy a role in the minds of the undergraduates which is both subordinate and superordinate: because they teach, evaluate and grade, they have a significant amount of power. Conversely, because they are themselves still in training and perhaps close in age to their undergraduate students, they may be perceived as socially subordinate in ways which clash with origin, academic expectations and language, thus undergraduate willingness to challenge the graduate students' authority seems to rise exponentially (Table 6.1).

A small body of research has been established which moves beyond the anecdotal data usually called forth in this debate. A few studies have concentrated on the undergraduate's ability to distinguish between accents and make fair assessments of English proficiency. Orth (1982) found that undergraduates were not very good at making such assessments; their evaluations of non-native English-speaking instructors were biased by the grades they anticipated receiving from the instructor. More recently, a group of Canadian and American scholars have looked very closely at issues of comprehensibility, intelligibility and the importance of listener attitude for students of English as a second language (please see suggested additional readings at the end of this chapter).

Such studies indicate that success in communication between L1 and L2 speakers is far more complex than has been suggested here. For example, native speakers of Chinese, Japanese, Polish, Spanish and English listened to the same set of recordings of English spoken with a foreign accent. Despite the differences in their native languages, they showed an unexpected degree of agreement on the intelligibility and accentedness of the recordings (Munro *et al.* 2006). That is, a native Japanese speaker is no more or less able to understand Japanese-accented English than a native English speaker, which suggests that the properties of speech itself are important in how accent is perceived.

Rubin and Smith (1990) found that students were not always able to distinguish between different levels of accentedness and yet perceptions, right or wrong, served as a very good predictor of how the student rated the teacher. Thus, if students assessed an instructor with a very slight Cantonese accent as highly accented, they also found that person to be a poor teacher. In another study that drew a great deal of attention, Rubin (1992) used an interesting technique to see how students' expectations of foreign instructors played into their attitudes and learning experience.

In that study of how expectations built around accent and race affected student perceptions and performance, 62 undergraduate native speakers of English participated. Each undergraduate listened to a 4-minute lecture on an introductory topic, pre-recorded on tape. There were two possible lectures, one on a science topic and the other on a humanities topic. While listening, the student saw a projected slide photograph which was meant to represent the instructor speaking. Both of the recordings heard were made by the same speaker (a native speaker of English from central Ohio), but there were two possible projected photographs: half of the students saw a slide of a Caucasian woman

Table 6.1 Language conflict in the university classroom

Problem	Proposed solution
Graduate student speakers of English as a second language have special hurdles to deal with in order to become effective classroom teachers	Increased and more diligent screening and training of non-native English-speaking graduate student teachers
Undergraduates have stereotypes and biases which, if not put aside, interfere with a potentially positive and valuable learning opportunity	None

lecturer, and the other half saw a woman similarly dressed and of the same size and hair style, but who was Asian. Both were photographed in the same setting and in the same pose, and in fact no difference was registered between the Caucasian and the Asian photographs in terms of physical attractiveness.

Immediately after listening to the 4-minute lecture, each student completed a test of listening comprehension, and then a testing procedure which was designed to test homophily, which in effect asks the respondents to compare the person speaking to themselves and to judge the degree of similarity or difference. This measurement has been found to be very useful in studying communicative breakdown across cultural boundaries. Studies indicate that students "respond more positively to teachers of optimal homophily" (ibid.: 513). There were other items included in this questionnaire which asked the students to rate accent (speaks with an American accent, speaks with an Asian accent), ethnicity, and quality of teaching.

Figures 6.2 and 6.3 indicate that students clearly perceived the difference in ethnicity in the slides they looked at. As hypothesized, the Asian instructor was perceived to be more "Oriental/Asian" than was the Caucasian instructor, regardless of the subject of the lecture.

These figures indicate that perceived ethnicity on the basis of the photograph did have a great deal of significance on the way students evaluated language. Depending on the slide projected, the students evaluated the same native speaker of U.S. English as having more or less of a foreign accent. To put it more bluntly, some students who saw an Asian

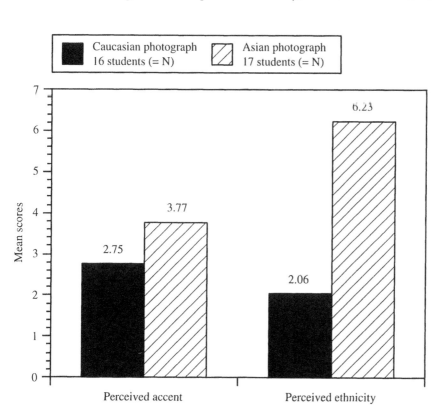

Figure 6.2 Student evaluation of lecturer's ethnicity and accent, recorded humanities lecture

Source: Rubin (1992)

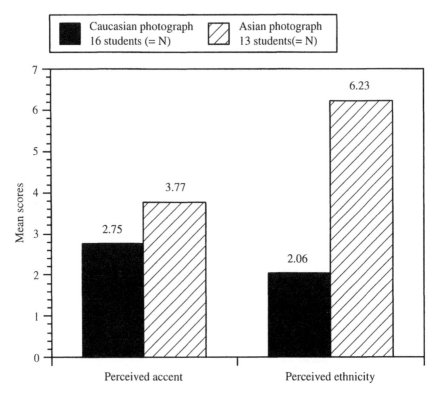

Figure 6.3 Student evaluation of lecturer's ethnicity and accent, recorded science lecture
Source: Rubin (1992)

were incapable of hearing objectively. It can be stated with absolute certainty that the pre-recorded language they listened to was native, non-foreign-accented English; students looking at an Asian face, however, sometimes convinced themselves that they heard an accent. Here it becomes clear that the students' negative preconceptions are at work.

Even more interesting is the fact that overall, students scored lower in the comprehension test when they believed that the lecturer was Asian (Figure 6.4). Not only were some of these students incapable of hearing objectively when confronted with an Asian face, their block extended to the way they absorbed and understood factual material. This was more extreme in the case of the science lecture, something not totally unpredictable. Rubin notes:

> For many undergraduates, introductory courses in mathematics and the natural sciences have reputations as extremely inhumane courses designed to winnow out marginal students. And it is well known that [non-native English speaking graduate student teachers] are disproportionately assigned responsibility for such high-anxiety classes.
>
> (1992: 512)

Thus it seems likely that preconceptions and fear are strong enough motivators to cause students to construct imaginary accents, and fictional communicative breakdowns.

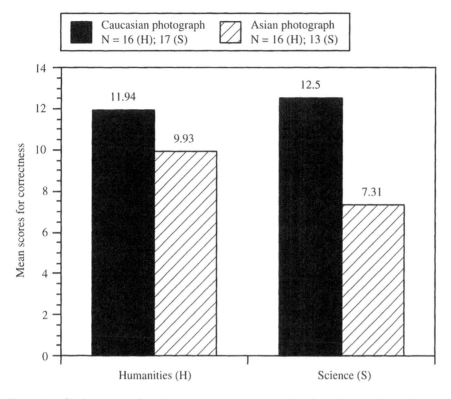

Figure 6.4 Student comprehension scores, by ethnicity of slide viewed and subject of lecture
Source. Rubin (1992)

The proposed rationale for the rejection of instructors with foreign accents in teaching must be carefully examined:

ACCENT → COMMUNICATIVE BREAKDOWN → POOR
CLASSROOM/LEARNING EXPERIENCE

Rubin's study indicates that whether or not an instructor actually does need further training in English may be irrelevant, if racial and ethnic cues are more important than degree of accentedness. If any cue is enough to shift the communicative burden entirely to the other party, the formula takes on another dimension:

INSTRUCTOR'S PERCEIVED ACCENT → STUDENTS' NEGATIVE
EXPECTATIONS
↓
COMMUNICATIVE BREAKDOWN → POOR CLASSROOM
EXPERIENCE

Of course, it is possible that a true communicative breakdown may cause difficulties between a non-native speaker of English and a student. One important difference remains, though. A student new to the lecture hall has no way of knowing whether or not the person teaching the course is going to be a good communicator and dedicated teacher or not, but the native language of the instructor is incidental to this question. Native speakers of English are usually given the benefit of the doubt; some turn out to be good teachers, and others do not. However, non-native speakers of English – specifically, speakers of Asian, African and South American languages – are often not given a chance at all.

While universities and colleges across the country are trying hard to deal with the complicated issue of graduate student instructors who are not native speakers of English, it seems that policies to address the question of quality of classroom instruction have to take a broader view. Foreign students need help in acclimating to a very different academic and social culture, in a variety of matters. Language is of primary importance, and deserves careful attention. In addition to the training of the foreign students, it must be noted that our own students have to be educated about matters of language and communication in the classroom, and be taught to take a reasonable amount of responsibility for a successful educational experience.

Summary

Educators have a difficult job. We want them to provide our children with a great variety of skills, from reading and writing to job training. Furthermore, we entrust them with teaching our children the basics of good citizenship and responsible behavior as social and sexual beings; we charge them with occupying and entertaining, even on occasion with passing on parenting skills. On top of all these expectations, we want the teacher to give our children that mythical perfect spoken language we call *SAE, a language which is grammatically homogenous and accentless. Whether or not the child can do anything constructive with that language is in many instances secondary to the social construction of accent.

Teachers have responded to these expectations by developing authority structures around language – written and spoken – which are projected as absolute and inviolate. We trust their intuitions and whims above all others. This authority is sometimes abused. Teachers are for the most part firm believers in a standard language ideology which rejects or marginalizes those varieties of U.S. English which are markedly non-middle-class, middle American, and colorless. Arguments for this overt limitation of discourse which affects huge numbers of children are usually based in economics. If asked about a wider possible view, and policies of acceptance, every teacher will point to the other institutions which support and propagate a standard language ideology. Employers have expectations, they will argue. There will be repercussions.

The teachers themselves are capable of seeing this circular logic: "Since English teachers have been in large part responsible for the narrow attitudes of today's employers, changing attitudes toward dialect variations does not seem an unreasonable goal, for today's students will be tomorrow's employers" (The National Council of Teachers of English 1974), but actual attempts to resolve this conflict are harder to find.

Are there no examples of educators with more informed and enlightened approaches to diversity in language? Teachers who strive to teach children to read and write, and at the same time respect the wholeness of the home language and the social identity attached to it? Are there teachers who question underlying assumptions?

Of course there are. At a college in the Midwest, there is at least one single English teacher who does not find it necessary to eradicate one variety of English to teach reading and writing in another. *The Chicago Tribune* found this method so remarkable that they ran an article on the approach, and highlighted a classroom practice of "[not] scold[ing] Black students . . . when they said 'ax,' rather than 'ask'" (Warren 1993: 2). In New Mexico, the Hopi Nation oversees the training and evaluation of bilingual teachers who come from the community and teach in the community, so that the experiences of Luther Standing Bear do not have to be repeated. A Sioux enrolled in an English-Only boarding school, he wrote, "How hard it was to forego the consolation of speech" (Standing Bear 1928, as cited in Reyhner and Eder 2006).

These stories of teachers and administrators who resist the process of language subordination are rare. What our schools do, for the most part, is to insist that some children forego the expressive power and consolation of speech which is the currency of their home communities. This gesture of denial and symbolic subordination is projected as a first and necessary step to becoming a good student and a good citizen.

DISCUSSION QUESTIONS AND EXERCISES

- Write your own linguistic history. Where did your influences come from? What ideologies were you exposed to? Which did you accept, and to what degree? Have you studied any foreign languages? Do you feel as though you could survive in a country where that language is spoken? What would it take?
- Do you have any memories of being corrected for the way you said something? Who did the correcting? What reason was given, and how did you react? Anger? Shame? Confusion?
- Describe your own experiences in school. Were there speakers of stigmatized varieties of English in your classroom? Were you one of those speakers? How did perceptions make things easier or harder for them (or you)?
- Search online in communities that discuss education and look for terms such as "standard English," "non-standard English," "dialect," "grammar," and "ugly." Was it easy or hard to find discussions of the issues covered in this chapter? What trends (if any) did you come across?
- Interview a friend who has never taken a linguistics class. Ask that person for definitions of "standard" and "non-standard" English, and be sure to ask for examples. Don't give away your thoughts or reactions, just record what your informant has to say, no matter how much you agree or disagree. Compare your findings with others in the class.
- Consider this box:

  INSTRUCTOR'S PERCEIVED ACCENT → STUDENTS' NEGATIVE EXPECTATIONS

  ↓

  COMMUNICATIVE BREAKDOWN → POOR CLASSROOM EXPERIENCE

  How accurate do you think this is? What might be missing?

- Have the materials in this chapter raised questions for you? Doubts? Do you feel the same way you did before this course on matters of language in the classroom?
- Write a short list of guidelines you might go over with a biology class where all of the teaching assistants are non-native speakers of English. How can the students contribute to making communication work? Are there concrete steps to take when communication breaks down?
- Interview a graduate teaching assistant or a professor or instructor who speaks English with a strong accent of any kind that contrasts with the average person on campus. For example, someone with a strong Texas accent teaching in Northern California, or someone whose first language is Japanese teaching in Cincinnati. Ask what experiences they have had because of accent. Positive, negative, neutral?

Notes

1 Between 1996 until the writing of the second edition of this book, there has been no official or published revision to the NCTE's Standards for the English Language Arts.

2 A 2003 study went one step further, asking non-academic professionals to evaluate 66 written sentences, each with one error (and a few with no errors, as a control). Their choices were "does not bother me," "bothers me a little," "bothers me a lot," or "no error." The researchers found that the professionals were very inconsistent and sometimes incorrect in their evaluations, and more interesting still, "while nonacademics are less bothered by usage errors, the errors that they find most bothersome are still common dialectical features" (Gray and Heuser 2003). In other words, the subjects had retained bias and ideology better than the grammatical rules they had been taught.

3 Here I touch only briefly on the question of children who come to school speaking a language other than English. Native speakers of Russian and Portuguese, for example, face a different set of institutionalized challenges. Bilingual education is an important – and very large – topic that cannot be addressed in any depth here.

4 The U.S. Department of Education is the home of the NAEP (National Assessment of Educational Progress) which is the "primary federal entity for collecting and analyzing data related to education" (NAEP website at: http://nces.ed.gov/). NAEP makes their raw data available to other public and private organizations, one of which is the Annie E. Casey Foundation. The NAEP uses a three-level assessment of achievement levels, in which reading skills are ranked as basic, proficient or advanced (http://tinyurl.com/4o35xco).

5 "Since 1949, the Conference on College Composition and Communication (CCCC) has been the world's largest professional organization for researching and teaching composition, from writing to new media." See http://www.ncte.org/cccc.

6 Smitherman (2003b) provides some insight into the evolution of this resolution in her essay "The Historic Struggle for Language Rights in the CCCC."

7 There comes a point where the argument for a strictly standardized written language will also collapse. In creative writing of all kinds, the rules of the written standard are sacrificed for the sake of story.

8 Cameron (1995: 234–235) explores this unfortunate turn in linguistic argument at length.

9 The issues that confront native speakers of AAVE in the classroom are very similar to those of Hawai'i Creole English speakers. Outside of Hawai'i, HC (Hawai'i Creole)

does not evoke the same kind of strong reactions that AAVE does, which makes it especially useful in trying to grasp the issues discussed here.

10 Appropriacy arguments are not always inappropriate, and often quite necessary when it comes to matters of public behavior. Children who get into a fight on the playground hear words like *inappropriate* and *unacceptable*.

11 See especially Labov's "The Logic of Non-Standard English" (1972c), which is purposefully polemic but also illustrates the inaccuracy of Bernstein's theories very clearly.

12 I am grateful to Mary Jean Habermann, Director of the Bilingual Multicultural Education Unit of the New Mexico Department of Education, for her helpful discussion on these policies and for the materials she provided.

13 Quotes in this section originate from a series of telephone interviews conducted with school administrators in four states: two in the Northeast, one in the Midwest, one in the Southwest. I also interviewed a key employee in a large company which develops and administers the testing and evaluation procedure for an entire state. Most parties agreed to be interviewed and quoted only if they remained anonymous. Notes from these interviews as well as partial transcripts are on file with the author. Questions were posed about the way teachers were evaluated in matters of language, and the hiring process more generally.

14 The sources and citations in this recounting of the Westfield school case are taken from a discussion on the LINGUIST list, an on-line forum for linguists at linguist@tamsun.tamu.edu. The discussion is summarized under 3.563: Accents in Classroom, dated July 14, 1992. Contributors to the discussion included Victor Raskin (who provided the summary), Barbara Partee, Michael Covington, Catherine Doughty, and Susan Ervin-Tripp.

15 Beyond issues of accent and intelligibility, faculty from other countries have the additional but necessary burden of adjusting to a new culture, both in education and teaching methods, and off.

Suggested further reading

On language issues in the classroom

Curkovic, K.D. (2000) Accent and the University: Accent as Pretext for National Origin Discrimination in Tenure Decisions. *Journal of College and University Law*, 26(4): 727–754.

Gee, J.P. (2007) The Literacy Myth and the History of Literacy. In *Social Linguistics and Literacies*. New York: Routledge.

Kinloch, V. (2005) Revisiting the Promise of Students' Right to Their Own Language: Pedagogical Strategies. *College Composition and Communication*, 57(1): 83–113.

Santa Ana, O. (2004) *Tongue-Tied: The Lives of Multilingual Children in Public Education*. Lanham, MD: Rowman & Littlefield Publishers.

Siegel, J. (2006) Language Ideologies and the Education of Speakers of Marginalized Language Varieties: Adopting a Critical Awareness Approach. *Linguistics and Education*, 17(2): 157–174.

Smitherman, G. (2003) *Talkin That Talk: Language, Culture, and Education in African America*. New York: Routledge.

Tamura, E.H. (2002) African American vernacular English and Hawai'i Creole English: A Comparison of Two School Controversies. *The Journal of Negro Education*, 71(1/2): 12–30.

Valdes, G. (1999) Nonnative English Speakers: Language Bigotry in English Mainstream Classrooms. *ADFL BULLETIN*, 31(1): 43–48.

On perception, attitude and comprehensibility in intercultural communication

Derwing, T.M. and Munro, M.J. (2009) Putting Accent in its Place: Rethinking Obstacles to Communication. *Language Teaching*, 42: 476–490.

Derwing, T.M., Rossiter, M. and Munro, M.J. (2002) Teaching Native Speakers to Listen to Foreign-Accented Speech. *Journal of Multilingual and Multicultural Development*, 23: 245–259.

Flege, J.E., Munro, M.J. and MacKay, I.R. (1995) Factors Affecting Strength of Perceived Foreign Accent in a Second Language. *The Journal of the Acoustical Society of America*, 97: 3125–3134.

Gallois, C., Ogay, T. and Giles, H. (2004) Communication Accommodation Theory: A Look Back and a Look Ahead. In W. Gudykunst (ed.) *Theorizing about Intercultural Communication*. Thousand Oaks, CA: Sage Publications, Inc., pp. 121–148.

Giles, H., Williams, A., Mackie, D.M. and Rosselli, F. (1995) Reactions to Anglo- and Hispanic-American-Accented Speakers: Affect, Identity, Persuasion, and the English-Only Controversy. *Language & Communication*, 15: 107–120.

Kavas, A. and Kavas, A. (2008) An Exploratory Study of Undergraduate College Students' Perceptions and Attitudes toward Foreign Accented Faculty. *College Student Journal* 42(3): 879–890.

Munro, M.J. and Derwing, T.M. (1999) Foreign Accent, Comprehensibility, and Intelligibility in the Speech of Second Language Learners. *Language Learning*, 49: 285–310.

Teaching children how to discriminate

7

(What we learn from the Big Bad Wolf)[1]

> We are faced first-off with indexical facts, facts of observed/experienced social practices, the systematicity of which is our central problem: are they systematic? If so, how?
>
> Silverstein (1992: 322)

> "Poor little guy! He just makes mistakes. He doesn't know any better. I'll just have to be patient and teach him the right way to do things," said Mickey.
>
> Disney Inc., "Mickey Mouse and The Boy Thursday" (1948)

Storytellers, Inc.

This chapter is about the ways children are systematically exposed to a standard language ideology by means of linguistic stereotypes in film or television entertainment.

Stories are more than entertainment, of course. Stories are in fact essential to the species and "second in necessity apparently after nourishment and before love and shelter" (Price 1978: xiii). As all human beings dream, we also all think and structure our understanding of the world in terms of narrative. A child takes in his or her family and community's stories and begins to experiment with storytelling at a young age. This process is crucial to socialization; thus, it is fair to say that storytellers have a crucial role to play in the lives of children.

Since the early twentieth century, the broadcast media have steadily increased in importance as agents of socialization. While we tend to think of Disney as a magical kingdom (mostly because Disney has convinced us this is so), in fact it is first and foremost a large and complex corporation. As such, its first and primary concern is its shareholders, and shareholders are primarily interested in profit, something a former head of Disney made clear in a memo to his staff: "We have no obligation to make history. We have no obligation to make art. We have no obligation to make a statement. To make money is our only objective" (Rowan 2005; Stepakoff 2007: 170).

To maintain and increase its customer base, Disney constantly reintroduces children to their world view. What sets Disney apart from other corporations is the fact that all this goes on in an indulgent atmosphere where critical discussion is actively discouraged (Giroux and Pollock 2010; Ward 2002). For example, while there may be scattered protests about gender roles, racism and historical inaccuracies in Disney films, those complaints never seem to have much of an impact on box-office numbers.

Giroux suggests reasoning for pursuing the questions raised here:

> Questioning what Disney teaches is part of a much broader inquiry regarding what it is parents, children, educators and others need to know in order to critique and challenge, when necessary, those institutional and cultural forces that have a direct impact on public life.
>
> (2001: 10–11)

To look at this from another angle, most people reading this book will consider themselves to be free of racism. If that is truly the case, then a question comes up that few people are comfortable discussing: in this enlightened twenty-first century, how is it that inequality persists?

Bonilla-Silva suggests that this conflict (we are not racists; racism persists) is one that the privileged resolve by looking elsewhere for explanations – the concept of market forces is a favorite stand-in or pretext for racism, as will be seen in Chapter 14 when employers are asked directly about the way field workers are hired. In this way the dominant group develops standardization ideologies which can be called upon when the conflict becomes too visible for comfort (Bonilla-Silva 2009: 3–11). The privileged have become expert at talking about race without talking directly about race. This is something to keep in mind while reading this chapter.

The purpose here is not to condemn Disney or any other producer of animated film;[2] but neither is it reasonable to simply overlook, rationalize or laugh off discriminatory and exclusionary behaviors, especially given the ubiquitous presence of Disney in the lives of children. That is, while nothing may be gained by latching onto what seem to be trivialities, neither is any progress made by refusing to look more closely at systematic patterns that have a profound impact on the way children come to see the world.

To discuss Disney's role in the socialization of young children, it is first necessary to demonstrate that their products have a regular, systematic effect on children on a day-to-day basis, and that children are influenced by the content of what they are seeing.

The ubiquitous mouse

In a 2009 report, the Nielson Company[3] calculated that children aged 2–5 watch more than 32 hours of television each week, while the 6–11-year-olds watch slightly less. These figures include what they call time-shifted programming (broadcasts recorded to be viewed at another time) and digital video. Roberts and Foehr (2004: 324) found that 4-year-olds spent about 60 percent of their total media time (which includes everything from video games to reading) in front of television or movie screens. With the rapid increased exposure to additional types of digital media, these numbers jumped significantly between Roberts and Foehr's (2004) and Robert's (2008) reports.

In the present day, safeguards have been put in place to protect the youngest and most vulnerable from unhealthy or dangerous everyday items such as toys, food, and clothing. The broadcast entertainment industry is subject to the same kind of inspection, but in a way that is far less consistent. Some producers of child-focused materials have an extraordinary amount of unquestioned access to children, and relatively little or perfunctory oversight. Disney is probably the most prominent of the companies who rely on reputation and nostalgia to deliver a message.[4] It is also true that a great deal of overtly discriminatory material has come out of all the animation studios from the earliest days of the industry. There is a large body of animated short films or cartoons that denigrate, trivialize or mock the mentally ill, the handicapped, Native Americans, African Americans, Africans, Asians, Middle Easterners, Eskimos, Italians, Latinos, Jews, the English, Irish, Scots, Russians and just about every other nationality and ethnicity.

Disney is the focus here because it holds such a large share of the market; for example, among its holdings are five film studios in addition to a majority share in twenty different television stations (Giroux and Pollock 2010: 285).

There is another kind of authority that Disney has claimed for itself that is rarely acknowledged or questioned. That is, Disney has systematically appropriated traditional stories and retold them in ways that isolate and exclude other storytellers and cultures. Zipes refers to this as the *Disney Spell*:

> It was not once upon a time, but at a certain time in history, before anyone knew what was happening, that Walt Disney cast a spell on the fairy tale, and he has held it captive ever since ... [He] used his own "American" grit and ingenuity to appropriate European fairy tales [so that] his signature has obfuscated the names of Charles Perrault, the Brothers Grimm, Hans Christian Andersen, and Carlo Collodi.
>
> (Zipes 1995)

In my own experiences teaching Disney film I have come across students who are under the impression that *Beauty and the Beast* was conceived and written in 1990 specifically to be animated in the Disney studios. They are surprised and sometimes unsettled to learn that the story was originally titled *La Belle et la Bête* (first published in France – in French – in 1740). At various points I have had students who assumed that *The Legend of Sleepy Hollow* (Irving 1819) and *Winnie the Pooh* (Milne 1926)[5] originated with and belong to Disney.

Stories are retold, by everyone, again and again; in this, Disney has not broken any sacred ground. The problem is that Disney appropriates and reinterprets stories and legends with significant meaning and importance to specific cultures without acknowledging what they are doing. This habit of appropriating cultural icons is not limited to English language stories; for example, the Chinese have expressed dismay over Disney's appropriation and remodeling of one of China's most beloved legends in *Mulan* (Dong 2010). Disney's versions are often the first and sometimes the only versions children see and hear. And because the sociocultural values are consistent from film to film, the cumulative effect is considerable.

The film that has garnered the most severe criticism in this regard is *Pocahontas* (Buescher and Ono 1996; Dundes 2001; Edgerton and Jackson 1996; Jhappan and Stasiulis 2005; Ono and Buescher 1996, 2001). Some have condemned Disney's version of this film: "Disney commodifies the past into digestible bits of information for the U.S. palate ... Indeed, Pocahontas transforms an historical abomination into kid's candy – genocide into a contemporary romance" (Ono and Buescher 2001: 35).

Others are simply dissatisfied with the historical inaccuracies, but even those who take note will often just shrug, as in the *Globe and Mail*'s (1994) review of a live-action Disney film *Squanto*. The reviewer acknowledges the liberties Disney took but notes that "history is written by the winners, and you can't get much more victorious than Daddy Disney" (5 November 1994, as cited in Schaffer 1996). There is often debate and difference of opinion about Disney's portrayal of American Indian history. In the case of *Pocahontas*, while most were critical of the film, there were a few who thought it showed positive and forward movement in the way native cultures are portrayed. These contrasting views play out both inside and outside Native American circles.[6]

The fact that children are exposed to broadcast media of all kinds on a regular, systematic basis has been established. Now the question must be: so what? Little kids – so this argument goes – don't really pay much attention to details, there's so much going on. They couldn't possibly be taking notes from Bugs Bunny or King Louie on how to be prejudiced. But children – even very young children – are tireless observers of human behavior, and research indicates that they do indeed take in what they see and put it to use.

Language acquisition is part and parcel of cognitive development more generally. While one part of the 4-year-old's mind is sorting through strategies for passive constructions, another is working on categorization and category awareness. Categorization is a universal cognitive strategy, a tool humans use to cope with the complexity of the world. It is also the very cornerstone of stereotype and following from that, prejudice (Brown 2010). Some aspects of learning to differentiate and categorize are not well understood, but it is clear that children use similarity in this process. Furry creatures with four legs – dogs, goats, horses – are all doggies or waggies or something similar to 2-year-olds. By age 4, the same child can identify a dog reliably. The important thing to note here is that children see patterns in the data the world presents on a day-to-day basis, and those patterns are put to use.

That is, children are not passive vessels who sit in front of the television and let stories float by them. What they take in is processed and added to the store of data on how things – and people – are categorized. Children absorb things both abstract and concrete. Rice and Woodsmall (1988) conducted an experiment in which 3- and 5-year-olds were shown two 6-minute animated television programs. Included were twenty words which were not known to the children prior to the viewing, in normal conversational context. After a single viewing of the two clips, 3-year-olds gained an average of 1.56 new words, while 5-year-olds retained 4.87 new words.

Now given this general and vastly simplified information about children, language, cognition, and identity, consider the fact that by age 4, some children begin to exhibit prejudicial attitudes (Persson and Musher-Eizenman 2003: 531). In fact, numerous studies indicate that preschool children not only categorize by race, they also demonstrate bias (Aboud 2003, 2005; Katz 2003). Working with children between the ages 3 and 5 in a racially and ethnically diverse day care center, Van Ausdale and Feagin (2001) found that the children used racial categories to identify themselves and others in conversation, to include or exclude others from activities, and to "negotiate power in their own social/play networks."

The use and manipulation of language variation to establish character are long-established practices in storytelling; Disney is by no means the first or only practitioner. Long before Disney came on the scene, stage actors used language accent to draw character quickly, building on well-established, preconceived notions associated with specific regional loyalties, ethnic, racial alliances or economic status. This shortcut to characterization means that certain traits need not be laboriously demonstrated by means of a character's history and actions and an examination of motive. The blatant use of stereotype in any kind of storytelling (print, small or large screen, stage) may sometimes be used for satirical effect, but more usually stereotypes indicate lack of imagination, laziness, bias, or some combination of the three.

However, the issue here is not the quality of the storytelling; more important is the way storytelling behaviors and reactions reflect deeper beliefs and opinions. As we will see, stereotypes do not have to be overtly negative to be problematic and limiting.

The wolf's backstory

In 1933, while the U.S. was in the depths of a severe depression, Walt Disney's animators created a short cartoon which would make an $88,000 profit in the first two years of its release (Grant 1993: 56). By 1930 there were some 20,000 motion-picture theaters in business, serving 90 million customers weekly (Emery and Emery 1988: 265) and the price of admission was approximately 25 cents.[7] Thus Disney's animated *The Three Little Pigs*, a familiar story with a message of hard work in the face of adversity, was widely seen from the early days of entertainment film. The theme of good triumphing over evil was clearly a timely and popular one, and one that has not gone out of favor: Disney's *The Three Little Pigs* is still shown with regularity, in part or whole, on Disney's cable television channels. It has also been released numerous times on video, laserdisc, and DVD, in at least four distinct editions.

One of the topics which is often discussed in relation to this particular Disney animated short is a scene included in the original release, in which the wolf – in yet another attempt to trick the pigs into opening the door to him – dresses as a Jewish peddler (Grant 1993; Kaufman 1988; Precker 1993a). Kaufman interprets this in a way that is deferential to Disney:

> Ethnic stereotypes were, of course, not uncommon in films of the early Thirties, and were usually essayed in a free-wheeling spirit of fun, with no malice intended. By the time the film was reissued in 1948 . . . social attitudes had changed considerably.
>
> (Kaufman 1988)

Kaufman's claim that such stereotypes came across as fun and free-wheeling with no malice intended cannot be taken at face value and must be examined more closely. It serves as an excellent example of the general inclination to isolate Disney from critical commentary.

Disney's caricature of a Jewish peddler stands out for the way it mirrors the anti-Semitic propaganda coming out of Germany in the same time period. Disney would not allow a screenshot of the original animation of the wolf as Jewish peddler to appear in this book (or anywhere else, for that matter). This refusal to allow reproduction of the image protects their corporate image, but it also stifles discussion about the role of animated film in the socialization of children and the history of anti-Semitism in the U.S.[8]

It is likely that many younger readers are not familiar with the visual stereotypes that were so common prior to World War II. These images include features which are visual shorthand for *Jew*, a context that is provided by the poster in Figure 7.1. The poster was designed to advertise an exhibition called *The Eternal Jew* (*Der ewige Jude*) in Germany in the late 1930s (Hippler *et al.* 1940, directors).

The similarities between the Disney version of the Big Bad Wolf as Jewish peddler and the Nazi propaganda are more than simply striking. Both images have large hook noses, straggly beards and wear side locks; both wear long black coats and a dark hat similar to those worn by some Orthodox Jews; both hold out a palm full of coins, a common way to invoke the stereotype of Jews as unscrupulous and greedy moneylenders. We know that,

Figure 7.1 The Eternal Jew

Source: Poster: Exhibition Der ewige Jude. Reprinted from Getty Images

because all of these virulent anti-Semitic statements were published openly in the "The Eternal Jew" exhibit itself, and also in the film based on the exhibition. This text which accompanied one set of still shots from the film provides a representative sample: "While millions of long-established native Germans were propelled into unemployment and misery, immigrant Jews achieved fantastic wealth within a few years. Not by means of honest work, but rather through usury, swindling, and fraud" (Hippler 1940: translated from the original German by this author).

There is no direct evidence that the Disney animators and film makers shared in any of these beliefs, but still it is not possible to overlook the similarities of the images produced.[9] Kaufman (1988) recounts that the anti-Semitic depiction of the wolf as a Jewish peddler remained intact until *The Three Little Pigs* was re-released in 1948, 14 years later. At that time the Jewish peddler was replaced with an all-around rough guy, and then only because of pressure from the Hays Office, which brought the issue of Jewish sensibilities and the Holocaust to Disney's attention.[10] Grant (1993: 54) reports that Disney later admitted that the original scene was in bad taste.[11]

In addition to the visual clues, the actor who supplied the voice for the wolf used a distinctive Yiddish accent to make the stereotype complete.[12] That is, while Disney did change the animation in 1948, the peddler's Yiddish accent was left intact for much longer. At an unspecified date the segment was finally revoiced: "[I]n case the Yiddish dialect of the original scene might itself be found offensive, the dialogue was changed as well. Now the Wolf spoke in a standard 'dumb' cartoon voice" (Kaufman 1988: 43–44). This means that even after that part of *The Three Little Pigs* was reanimated to remove the offensive stereotyped image, the wolf continued to *speak* with a Yiddish accent. Thus the underlying message rooted in anti-Semitism and fear of the other was maintained, establishing a link between the evil intentions of the wolf and Jewish identity. Grant also relates that the newer animation and dialogue still leaned on more general stereotypes and fears, in that the "disguised wolf no longer has Hebraic tones or mannerisms, instead saying: "I'm the Fuller brush-man. I workin' me way through college" (Grant 1993: 54).

Grant and Kaufman both claim that the original image of the Wolf-as-Jewish-Peddler had been edited out upon urging of the Hays Office. In 1997, I bought a VHS tape of three classic Disney cartoons from an official Disney store, however, and found, to my surprise and disquiet, that the original animation of the Wolf with a yarmulke and side locks, large nose and peddler's pack was intact. How – and why – this release of the cartoon came to include this particular redacted scene is unclear.

In 1992, a similar controversy would arise over the portrayal of characters in Disney's *Aladdin*, a movie set in an imaginary, long ago Arabic kingdom. An offending line of dialogue in an opening song "Where they cut off your ear if they don't like your face/It's barbaric, but hey, it's home" was partially changed in response to complaints from the American-Arab Anti-Discrimination Committee (AAADC), but as the representative of the AAADC pointed out, the accents of the characters remained as originally filmed:

> [They] particularly objected to the fact that the good guys – Aladdin, Princess Jasmine and her father – talk like Americans, while all the other Arab characters have heavy accents. This pounds home the message that people with a foreign accent are bad.
> (Precker 1993b)

Talking the talk

Any actor necessarily brings to a role his or her own native language. In many cases, the variety of English (we are still focused here on film and theater in the United States) is irrelevant to the characterization and can be left alone. Some actors are infamous for never trying to portray an accent other than their own, regardless of the nature of the story or the character. Jimmy Stewart, John Wayne, Ricky Gervais, Diane Keaton all made or make public statements about their unwillingness to attempt an accent other than their own.

More often, however, the director and actor, working together, will target a particular social, regional or L2 accent, perhaps because it is intrinsic to the role and cannot be sacrificed. U.S. audiences may or may not suspend disbelief when Robin Hood sounds like he grew up in Nevada, but it would be harder to cast someone with an upper-class British accent as Ronald Regan or Richard Nixon and not do serious harm to credibility, audience expectations and reception.

In a similar way, non-native speakers of English who come to the U.S. to be actors bring their L2 accents to their work. This accent may restrict the roles they can play, or they may have roles written or rewritten to suit the immutable nature of their accents (Arnold Schwarzenegger, Djimon Hounsou, Javier Bardem, Penelope Cruz, Chow Yun-Fat, Marion Cotillard, Benecio del Toro, and Juliette Binoche provide examples). American actors may undergo accent training of various kinds in an attempt to learn to imitate what they need for a particular role, although there are many examples where this effort fails despite expensive and careful tutoring, even in the limited way it is asked of them during filming.

What is particularly relevant and interesting in this context, however, is the way that actors attempt to manipulate language as a tool in the construction of character, sometimes successfully, sometimes not. Educational programs for the training of actors for stage and screen often include classes on speech, dialogue, and the contrivance of accent. Simply put, with a lot of hard work and good editing it may be possible to fool some of the people, some of the time.

The materials used in actor-oriented accent courses are interesting in and of themselves, because the approach often includes not just the mechanics and technicalities of one particular regional or foreign accent, but also issues of content and approach.

> Dialect actors must avoid going so far with certain speech traits that they end up creating ethnic or linguistic stereotypes . . . language or dialect background does not dictate character actions. Characters with accents must have the same range of choices available to them as characters whose speech is identical to yours.
>
> (Karshner and Stern 1990: Preface)

This is an enlightened and realistic position, certainly. Other materials prepared for actors are not always so even-handed, as seen in *Foreign Dialects: A Manual for Actors, Directors and Writers* (Herman and Herman 1943 [1997]). The pointers on how to imitate one particular national dialect (an abstraction in itself) are chock full of stereotypes. The 1997 edition has been stripped of the worst passages but some stereotypes remain, such as the advice on how to talk like an Irishman: "The pace is a bit faster than American but this is because of the Irishman's ability to voice his thoughts quickly and easily and also because of his habit of falling back on verbal clichés and other hackneyed expressions" (Herman 1997: 67).

Of course, a person using Herman's book to learn a particular accent for a particular role on stage or screen would not necessarily buy into Herman's characterizations of whole nations. But it's not adult viewers at the center of this discussion; we are looking at entertainment media and the way children are bombarded with stereotypes.

In a film set in a country where English is not spoken, the writers and director have to come to an initial decision: they could hire actors who are native speakers of the language that is spoken in that setting and use subtitles; they could have the dialogue spoken in English, each actor using his or her native variety and simply abstracting away from the question of logical language spoken; or the more common approach, at least in recent times: Native English-speaking actors speak English, but sometimes take on the accent of the language they would logically be speaking in the time and setting of the story.

If a French accent is meant to remind viewers that the story is taking place in France, then logic would require that all the characters in that story speak with a French accent. But this is not the case in animated or live action; for the most part, in movies set outside English-speaking countries only a few actors will contrive the accent of that country. The decision about which actors will try to sound French, for example, is not random, but follows logically from the dominant stereotypes (or in some cases, from the actor's native language). Consider Disney's *Beauty and the Beast* (Trousdale and Wise 1991, directors) set in France (Table 7.1). All of the major characters speak English with American accents with three exceptions: the sexy chamber maid, the amorous butler, and a temperamental cook are voiced by actors contriving French accents.

The exact opposite approach was taken with *The Hunchback of Notre Dame*, also set in France; in this case, there were no French accents used, but those voice actors who were portraying the dark-skinned Romani took on inconsistent and unidentifiable L2 features.

A final consideration that is very relevant to analysis of language manipulation in these films has to do with a new direction in casting that began in the 1960s with the production of *The Jungle Book*. This was the first animated feature in which voice actors were cast on the basis of public recognition and popularity. Actors and musicians who had already established a personality and reputation with the movie-going public were drawn, quite literally, into the animation and story-telling process so that the relationship between voice, popularity, language and characterization in Disney film entered a new era. This strategy was not greeted with enthusiasm by all film critics:

> [B]reathing heart and soul into a film is not so easily accomplished. *The Jungle Book* lacked this quality, and substituted for it a gallery of characters whose strongest identity was with the stars who provided their voices. The animators enjoyed working with people like George Sanders, Louis Prima, and Phil Harris, and incorporated elements of their personalities into the animated characters. Audiences naturally responded, so the animators felt justified in continuing this practice. "It is much simpler and more realistic than creating a character and then searching for the right voice," [producer] Reitherman contended.
>
> (Maltin 1987: 74–75)

The issue of recognizable voice actors will be relevant in the discussion of AAVE language features in specific films.

Table 7.1 Animated characters speaking French-accented English

Setting	Character	Role	Film
France	Lumière Stove Cherie	Maître d', steward Chef Chambermaid	*Beauty and the Beast*
Elsewhere	Louis Unnamed	Chef Waiter	*The Little Mermaid* *The Rescuers*

Time and place

Disney's animated films are set in a wide range of places and time periods (Table 7.2). It must be noted that in some cases Disney seems unconcerned with the setting and time and simply puts modern-day people and sensibilities in exotic places. *Tarzan* takes place in the Victorian era, somewhere on the African continent – which we must take on faith, as there are no local (African) humanoids in speaking roles. *The Lion King* is set in Africa, but again the story does not involve human beings; here we know it is Africa because the writers go out of their way to remind the audience. *The Jungle Book* is set in India, with a single human character – Mowgli – to establish that this story is set somewhere else. In extreme cases the film makers seem to want to draw on the atmosphere and cultural awareness associated with specific times and places, but the more pressing concern is how to engage the interest of the viewers by making the setting familiar and comfortable.

In all of these movies, the logical setting dictates a particular language or set of languages, but there is no attempt to try to build those social behaviors into the story. It makes a certain amount of sense to set aside issues of logical language use and simply tell the story in English, especially if the audience is very young. However, in most cases the directors or actors continue to draw on language-focused social differences to establish character. A case in point here is Tarzan's best friend, another smart-aleck sidekick with a strong Brooklyn accent (voiced by Rosie O'Donnell).

The Emperor's New Groove (Dindal 2000, director) is probably the most extreme case of a disconnect between the proposed time and place and the way the story is told. *Groove* is set in Incan Peru, a fact that is never explicitly named or identified in the film itself (Silverman 2002), but was spoken about freely when the creative staff were interviewed. Animators and producers talked at length about research into Incan culture and the fact that they went through many centuries of archeological artifacts to find those which appealed to them as supportive of a light-hearted, comedic plot. Silverman, an archeologist, estimates that as it is presented the film contains elements that span 3,000 years and 275,000 square kilometers of space (ibid.: 309). As a result, "In Disney's hands, *Groove* so significantly departs and appropriates from the archaeologically known Inca Empire and other pre-Columbian civilizations of ancient Peru, that it is a textbook example of hyperreality and simulacra." The terms *hyperreality* and *simulacra* are often used in media studies; simulacra are copies of an original that no longer exists, or as in this case, that never existed to begin with. That is, Disney's ancient Peru looks as though it is meant to be a copy of the original, but in fact is created out of whole cloth. Baudrillard (1994: 1) calls this *hyperreality*, or a map that precedes the territory it supposedly describes.

Table 7.2 Disney's animated films over space and time

Displaced in time; outside the U.S.	Mythical, fantastic or science fiction settings	Here and now
Nineteenth-century India and Africa	Atlantis	New Orleans
Sixth-century China	Outer space	African savannah
Seventeenth-century Persia	Unnamed kingdoms	Australia
Fifteeenth-century Peru		California
Ancient Greece		
Ice Age North America		New York

It could be argued that *Groove* is simply a well-intentioned but failed attempt to represent Incan culture. Images and icons might be seen as nothing more than an attempt to establish an unusual and exotic setting. In fact, the feel of the film is distinctly present-day U.S. in narrative strategy, social conventions, humor, and language.

This is a case where all voice actors use their own varieties of English. There are no attempts at an accent that would evoke Incan culture, because the story, in reality, has nothing to do with that time and place. The goal seems to be to evoke other cultures only in so far as they will mesh with the expectations of an American audience. This is done by assimilation and objectification, and the result is children's film which strips an entire culture of its history and trivializes what is left behind. And accomplishes all this in some 90 minutes.

The unfortunate result of all this is that the majority of children who see this movie – many more than once – will retain Disney's version of Incan culture because it is the only version they will ever be exposed to. Few American students will have an opportunity to learn in more detail about the more complex – and interesting – history of the Incan people.

Animated films offer a unique way to study how a dominant culture reaffirms its control over subordinate cultures and nations by re-establishing, on a day-to-day basis, their preferred view of the world as right and proper and primary. Precisely because of animation's (assumed) innocence and innocuousness, the film makers have a broader spectrum of tools available to them and a great deal more leeway:

> As non-photographic application of photographic medium, [animators] are freed from the basic cinematic expectation that they convey an "impression of reality" . . . The function and essence of cartoons is in fact the reverse: the impression of reality, of intangible and imaginary worlds in chaotic, disruptive, subversive collision.
>
> (Burton 1992: 23–24)

A study of accents in animated cartoons over time reveals the way linguistic stereotypes mirror the evolution of national fears: Japanese and German characters in cartoons during World War II, Russian spy characters in children's cartoons in the 1950s and 1960s (Natasha and Boris meet Rocky and Bullwinkle), Middle Eastern characters in the era of hostilities with Iran and Iraq. All of this in addition to long-standing prejudices against people of color and minority religious groups.

In the following discussion of systematic patterns found in a defined body of children's animated film, the hypothesis is a simple one: animated films entertain, but they are also a vehicle by which children learn to associate specific characteristics and life styles with specific social groups, and to accept a narrow and exclusionary world view. In fact, they are particularly adept at this precisely because they do entertain, an irony that might be called *A Spoonful of Sugar*.[13]

Disney feature films

A large-scale study was carried out for the first edition of this book, in which 371 characters in 24 full-length animated Disney films were analyzed. The 24 films represented everything available at that time on VHS (DVD technology was not yet commonly available). For this second, revised edition, an additional 14 films were watched and analyzed (Table 7.3).[14] To be included, a film had to be: (1) fully animated – no live action; (2) full length (i.e., not a short film or cartoon); and (3) produced by Disney. This last restriction excludes films that were produced by Pixar but distributed by Disney, a step taken for the sake of consistency.

Even a cursory look is enough to get a sense of the range of social and linguistic stereotypes Disney presents to young children repeatedly. Before the advent of the VCR, repeated viewings of *Cinderella*, for example, was simply not possible. Since the technology boom, however, Disney films can be rented or purchased and watched over and over again, so that the messages and morals become deeply ingrained (Buescher and Ono 1996; Edgerton and Jackson 1996; Giroux and Pollock 2010; Lacroix 2004). With this comes the merchandising storm. In the months prior to the release of any full-length animated film, Disney begins to release marketing tie-ins, which include "toys, apparel, accessories,

Table 7.3 Disney animated films included in the 1997 and 2010 studies

1997 study	2010 study	Animated full-length feature	Release year	$US gross
X		Snow White and the Seven Dwarfs	1937	184,925,485
X		Pinocchio	1940	84,300,000
X		Dumbo	1941	2,500,000
X		The Reluctant Dragon	1941	Not available
X		Bambi	1942	102,797,000
X		Cinderella	1950	85,000,000
X		Robin Hood	1953	9,500,000
X		Peter Pan	1953	87,400,000
X		Lady and the Tramp	1955	93,600,000
X		Sleeping Beauty	1959	9,404,008
X		101 Dalmatians	1961	153,000,000
X		The Sword in the Stone	1963	22,182,353
X		The Jungle Book	1967	141,843,000
X		The Aristocats	1970	55,675,257
X		The Rescuers	1977	48,775,599
X		The Fox and the Hound	1981	43,899,231
X		The Great Mouse Detective	1986	23,605,534
X		The Little Mermaid	1989	111,543,479
X		Duck Tales: Treasure of the Lost Lamp	1990	18,075,331
X		The Rescuers Down Under	1990	27,931,461
X		Beauty and the Beast	1991	171,340,294
X		Aladdin	1992	217,350,219
X		The Lion King	1994	328,539,505
	X	Pocahontas	1995	141,579,773
	X	The Hunchback of Notre Dame	1996	100,138,851
	X	Hercules	1997	99,112,101
	X	Mulan	1998	120,620,254
	X	Tarzan	1999	171,091,819
	X	The Emperor's New Groove	2000	89,296,573
	X	Atlantis: The Lost Empire	2001	84,052,762
	X	Lilo & Stitch	2002	145,771,527
	X	Treasure Planet	2002	38,120,554
	X	Brother Bear	2003	85,336,277
	X	Home on the Range	2004	50,026,353
	X	Chicken Little	2005	135,386,665
	X	Meet the Robinsons	2007	97,822,171
	X	Bolt	2008	114,053,579
	X	The Princess and the Frog	2009	104,374,107

footwear, home furnishings, home décor, health, beauty, food, stationery and consumer electronics" (The Walt Disney Company Fact Book 2008, http://goo.gl/P9UrJ).

Stereotypes (whether or not language and accent are manipulated) are not subtle, ranging from *Lady and the Tramp*'s cheerful, musical Italian chefs to *Treasure of the Lost Lamp*'s stingy, Scottish-accented McScrooge. In the post-1997 films this trend continued; for example, Disney continues to portray side-kicks as scrappy inner city tough guys with hearts of gold. Consider the following:

- *Bolt* (Howard and Williams 2008, directors), in which the side-kick street-smart character is a cat voiced by Susie Essmann, a native of Brooklyn.
- *Mulan* (Bancroft and Cook 1998, directors) where the main character has a small, very scrappy guardian dragon called Mushu voiced by Eddie Murphy. The illogic of a sidekick who speaks twentieth-century AAVE in ancient China seems to have been secondary to the need for this particular character type.
- *The Hunchback of Notre Dame*'s (Trousdale and Wise 1996, directors) Quasimodo has only three friends, stone gargoyles (inanimate objects who become animated for him alone) two of which speak American English with distinctly urban accents (Hugo, voiced by Jason Alexander, and Laverne, by Mary Wickes).

While Disney did not hesitate to include an AAVE-speaking sidekick in *Mulan* (set in ancient China), someone involved in the production of *Brother Bear* (Blaise and Walker 2003, directors) balked at that particular jump in logic. Instead, the odd side-kick characters – two moose – speak with the caricatured Canadian accent made popular by the fictional *Great White North* SCTV hosts Bob and Doug McKenzie (comedians Rick Moranis and Dave Thomas). Note also that in all of these cases, the characters who speak with stigmatized accents appear in animal or inanimate form, a pattern that will be seen elsewhere as well.

Original study methodology

This body of animated films was chosen because the Disney Corporation is the largest producer of such films, as seen in Figure 7.2. Together Disney and the rest of the Buena Vista empire[15] produced about half of the one hundred top grossing animated films between 1980 and the present, which means that they took in about 6 trillion US dollars in that time period, for one set of films only. Clearly Disney reaches many people, and a good proportion of them are children. This would be reason enough to study their films, but they are also the most highly marketed and advertised of the field.

The movies listed under the label 1997 in Table 7.3 were analyzed by a group of advanced graduate students and myself. In that process, each character was coded for a variety of language and characterization variables. The detailed linguistic description for each character consisted of a mix of phonetic transcription, quotes of typical syntactic structures, and marked lexical items.

In cases where an actor is clearly contriving an accent, a decision was made as to what language variety was most likely intended to be portrayed. For example, a poorly executed British accent was still counted as such for the creators and (most) viewers. In *Aladdin*, one of the minor characters, a thief, speaks primarily Midwestern or West Coast American English, but also has some trilled r sounds – definitely not a feature generally associated

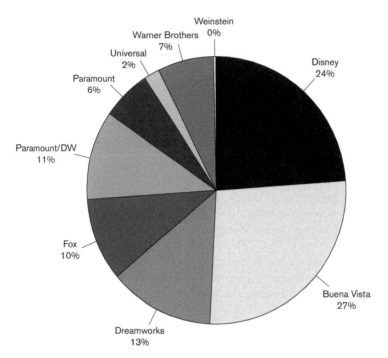

Figure 7.2 Percent of $12.8 billion (total box office gross) by studio, for the top 100 grossing animated films, 1980–2010

Source: http://boxofficemojo.com

with American English. This particular character's accent was still classified as *SAE, however, since only one atypical feature appeared in his phonology. Another character whose speech exhibits features from two or more dialects is Cogsworth, the butler/clock in *Beauty and the Beast*. He speaks with a contrived British accent in which some American features crop up unpredictably; thus, though it is not an accurate imitation of a middle- or upper-class British dialect, for the purposes of this study it is classified as such.

Disney's world

Of the 371 characters with speaking roles in the 24 movies examined in 1997, 259 or 69.8 percent are male (Figure 7.3). Female characters make up the other just over 30 percent. A look at the way female and male characters are deployed, overall, indicates that within the proportions established, they are equally distributed as major and minor characters. Female characters are rarely seen at work outside the home and family; where they do show up, they are mothers and princesses, devoted or (rarely) rebellious daughters. When they are at work, female characters are waitresses, nurses, nannies, or housekeepers. Men, conversely, are doctors, waiters, advisors to kings, thieves, hunters, servants, detectives, and pilots. The situation is roughly the same in the newer films added to the analysis (but see the discussion of *The Princess and the Frog*).

The universe displayed to young children in these films is one with a clear division between the sexes in terms of life style and life choices. Traditional views of the woman's

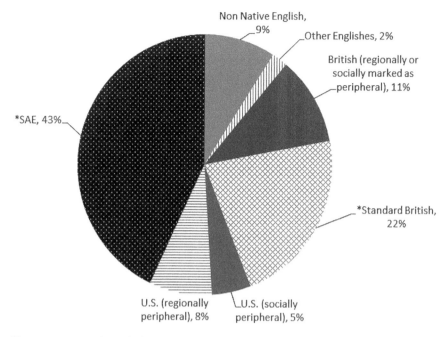

Figure 7.3 **371 animated characters by language spoken**

role in the family are strongly underwritten, and in Disney films, from *Snow White* to *Meet the Robinsons*, the female characters see, or come to accept, their first and most important role in life as that of wife and mother. What does an examination of language use have to add to this observation? What do characters, male and female speak?

For the most part (43.1 percent) they speak something approximating *SAE. Another 13.9 percent speak varieties of U.S. English which are associated with particular geographic area, racial, ethnic or economic groups. Less stigmatized varieties of British English are spoken by 21.8 percent.

While 91 of the total 371 characters occur in roles where they would not logically be speaking English, there are only 34 characters who speak English with a foreign accent.

The tendency to use foreign accents to convey the setting of the story is confirmed by these distributions; there are twice as many characters with foreign-accented English in stories set in places like France and Italy.

Of particular interest are the two movies set in Africa, *Tarzan* (Buck and Lima 1999, directors) and *The Lion King*. It is not unreasonable to assume that for stories set in Africa the logical language would not be English. There is no acknowledgement of this fact in *Tarzan*, but some of the characters in *The Lion King* are derived from Swahili. The good-natured but dumb warthog is called Pumbaa, or *simpleton*; Shenzi, the name of the leader of the hyena pack, means *uncouth*.

However, the only character who actually uses traces of Swahili and a contrived Swahili accent is Rafiki (Swahili for *friend*), the wise and eccentric baboon who fulfills the role of spiritual guide. Why there are not more characters in these settings who speak with an accent is a logical question, and one which will be addressed below.

Some 90 percent of all the characters speak English natively, with an American or British English or Australian accent. However, a closer look (Figure 7.3) makes it clear that

60 percent of all the characters appear in stories set in English-speaking countries; thus, a significant number of English-speaking characters appear in stories set outside the U.S.

Sometimes these are Americans abroad, as was the case in *Treasure of the Lost Lamp*; sometimes these are characters who are not logically English-speaking, given their role and the story, as is the case for all the characters in *Aladdin*. Here three language settings are considered: stories set in English-speaking lands, those set in non-English-speaking countries, and finally, those set in mythical kingdoms where it would be difficult to make an argument for one language or another as primary (*The Little Mermaid*, for example, seems to take place in a Caribbean setting) (Figure 7.4).

Since a contrived foreign accent is often used to signal that the typical or logical language of the setting would not be English, it is not surprising to see that the highest percentage of characters with foreign-accented English occur in the second type of language setting. But it is also significant that even more characters with foreign accents appear in stories set in the U.S. and England (Figure 7.5).

The breakdown of characters by their language variety (Figure 7.4) becomes interesting when we examine that variety in relationship to the motivations and actions of the character's role. Disney films rely heavily on traditional themes of good and evil, and with very few exceptions they depend also on happy endings. Characters with unambiguously positive roles (185 of them) constitute 49.9 percent; those who are clearly bad or even evil, only 19.4 percent. The remainder is divided between characters who change significantly in the course of the story (always from bad to good) and those characters whose roles are too small and fleeting to make such a judgment (86, or 23.2 percent of the total).

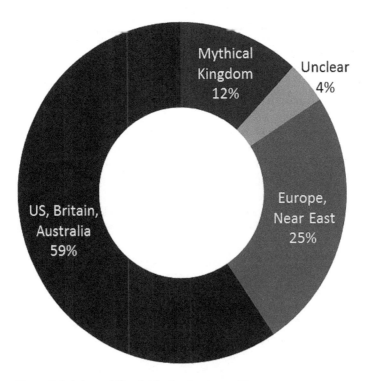

Figure 7.4 Animated film distribution by story setting

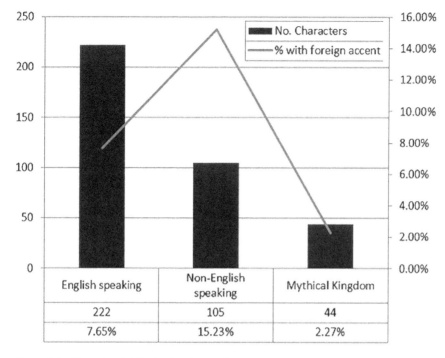

	English speaking	Non-English speaking	Mythical Kingdom
	222	105	44
	7.65%	15.23%	2.27%

Figure 7.5 Character distribution by story setting

Further, female characters are more likely to show positive motivations and actions (Figure 7.6). Unlike male characters who sometimes are bad and then become good, bad females show no character development. At this point it seems that there is no relationship between non-native English accents and the portrayal of good and evil.

There are 72 characters who are truly bad, in major and minor roles. They include the poacher and would-be child-murderer Percival McLeach in *Rescuers Down Under* with his contrived Southwestern accent and idiom ("purty feather, boy!" "I whupped ya'll!" "Home, home on the range, where the critters 'r ta-id up in chains"), and the whip-and-cleaver-wielding Stromboli of *Pinocchio*, with his threats of dismemberment, incredible rages, and florid, contrived Italian accent. Of these evil 72, however, a full 85 percent are native speakers of English; almost half are speakers of U.S. English. Bad guys with foreign accents account for only 15 percent of the whole (Figure 7.7 and Table 7.4).

Taken in context, however, this impression cannot stand firm. In Figure 7.8, which compares positive, negative and mixed motivations (the marginal characters have been removed for the sake of this discussion) by major language groups, it becomes clear the overall representation of persons with foreign accents is far more negative than that of speakers of U.S. or British English. About 20 percent of U.S. English speakers are bad characters, while about 40 percent of non-native speakers of English are evil.

Additional interesting patterns come forward when we examine the representation of specific languages linked to national origin, race, or characterization.

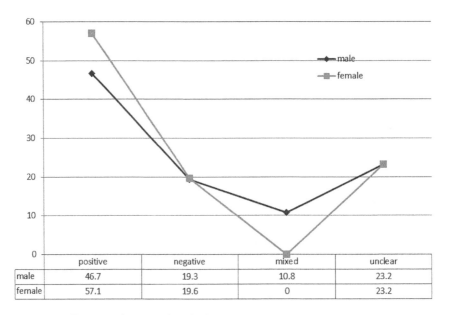

	positive	negative	mixed	unclear
male	46.7	19.3	10.8	23.2
female	57.1	19.6	0	23.2

Figure 7.6 Characters by sex and motivation

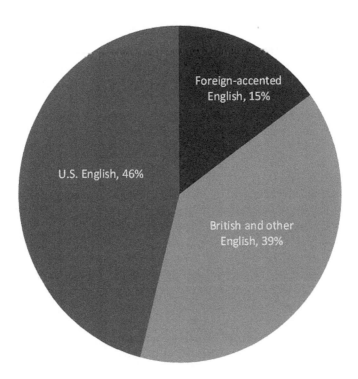

Figure 7.7 Negative characters by variety of English

Table 7.4 Characters by language traits and evaluation of motivations, N = 371

Motivations:	Positive	Negative	Mixed	Unclear	Total	(%)
U.S.	122	33	11	42	208	56.1
British	53	28	11	37	127	34.8
Foreign	10	11	6	7	34	9.2
Total	185	72	28	86	371	
(%)	49.9	19.4	7.5	23.2		100

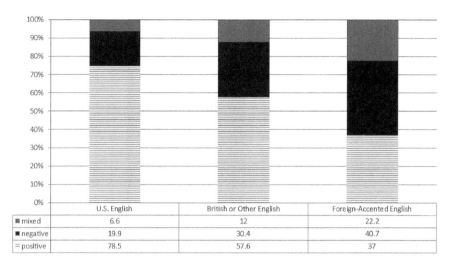

	U.S. English	British or Other English	Foreign-Accented English
mixed	6.6	12	22.2
negative	19.9	30.4	40.7
positive	78.5	57.6	37

Figure 7.8 Animated characters by positive, negative, and mixed motivations by major language groups

Getting the hang of Technicolor

Race and ethnicity are particularly sensitive issues in all Disney animated films. The company has repeatedly and soundly offended different segments of the population, but the most glaring missteps have to do with the representation of African Americans and people of color more generally. Examples include irresponsible Latinos and gregarious Italians (*Lady and the Tramp, Oliver and Company, The Lion King*), nefarious Asians (*Lady and Tramp, Mulan, The Aristocats*), smart-mouthed, lazy, disrespectful African Americans (*Dumbo, The Lion King, Song of the South, The Princess and the Frog, The Little Mermaid*), and savage Native Americans (*Peter Pan, Pocahontas*).

Table 7.5 is an attempt to draw together all characters from the animated films who fulfill one or more of the following categories:

- The voice actor is African American.
- The voice actor was most likely cast on the basis of voice recognition, regardless of race.
- The animated character is Black either in actuality or symbolically.
- The animated character speaks English with some degree of AAVE inflection or other salient markers (that is, the character's English would be heard as African American in origin).

Table 7.5 African American animated characters

Film	Name (Character)	Animal/human	Behavior evaluation	Race/ethnicity or appearance	Characteristics of English; sounds like? voice profiling?	Contrived?	Voice recognition?	Actor (Voice actor)	Actor's race/ethnicity	Native Language	Logical language (Setting)
Dumbo	Crows Jim Crow	a	m	Black	AAVE	n	u	Cliff Edwards	African American	English	English
	Straw Hat	a	m	Black	AAVE	n	u	Jim Carmichael	African American	English	English
	Dandy	a	m	Black	AAVE	n	u	James Baskett	African American	English	English
	Glasses	a	m	Black	AAVE	n	u	Nick Stewart	African American	English	English
Jungle Book	King Louie – Orangutan	a	m	Red	Scat/AAVE	n	y	Louis Pima	Italian American, Anglo	English	Hindi*
The Fox and the Hound	Big Mama – Owl	a	p	Grey	AAVE	n	y	Pearl Bailey	African American	English	English
The Aristocats	Scat	a	p	Black/Grey	Scat/AAVE	n	u	Scatman Crothers	African American	English	English
Atlantis	Dr. Joshua Strongbear Sweet	h	p	Black	*SAE	n	n	Phil Morris	African American	English	English
The Lion King	Simba – Lion	a	p	Brown/Tan	*SAE	n	u	Jonathan Taylor (cub) Matthew Broderick (adult)	U.S., Anglo	English	Swahili*
	Scar – Lion	a	n	Black/Tan	*SBE	n	y	Jeremy Irons	British	English	
	Timon – Meerkat	a	p	Tans	U.S. New York urban	n	y	Nathan Lane	English	English	
	Pumbaa – Warthog	a	p	Browns	U.S. urban	u	u	Ernie Sabella	U.S., Anglo	English	
	Mufasa – Lion	a	p	Brown/Tan	*SAE	n	y	James Earl Jones	African American	English	

Character	(a)nimal/(h)uman	p/n	Color	Language / Accent	y/n/u	Actor	Ethnicity	Typical Language	
Nala – Lion	a	p	Tans	*SAE	n	Niketa Calame	African American	English	English,
Shenzi – Hyena	a	n	Dark Grey	US Urban AAVE	n	Whoopi Goldberg	African American	English	Creole,
Banzai – Hyena	a	n	Grey	US Urban LatiN	y	Cheech Martin	U.S. Latino	English	Cajun
Rafiki – Mandrill ape	a	p	Multi	Pseudo Swahili accented	y	Robert Guillaume	African American	English	
Zazu – Hornbill	a	p	Multi	*SBE	n	Rowan Atkinson	British	English	
Sarabi	a	p	Pale Tan	*SAE	n	Madge Sinclair	African American	English	
The Princess and the Frog — Tiana	h	p	Black	South/AAVE	n	Anika Nni Rose	African American	English	
Prince Naveen	h	p	Dark	Foreign accent, U	y	BruNCampos	Brazilian	Portugese	
Dr. Facilier	h	n	Black	M Cajun, Creole, English	n	Keith David	African American	English	
Mama Odie	h	p	Black	French Creole	u	Jenifer Lewis	African American	English	
Eudora (Tiana's mother)	h	p	Black	South/AAVE	y	Oprah Winfrey	African American	English	
James (Tiana's father)	h	p	Black	AAVE	u	Terrence Howard	African American	English	
Buford (Tiana's boss)	h	n	u	m	u	Michael Colyar	African American	English	
Ray (firefly)	a	p	n/a	Cajun	u	Jim Cummings	U.S. Anglo	English	
Louis – Alligator	a	p	Green	AAVE	n	Michael-Leon Wooley	African American	English	
Lilo & Stitch — Cobra Bubbles	h	u p	Black	AAVE intonation	n	Ving Rhames	African American	English	

KEY: (y)es (n)o (u)ncertain (m)ixed (h)uman (a)nimal *hypothetically; NOTE: The category "typical language" is based on the country in which the story is set. Most of the movies are set in the U.S., thus the typical language is English. *Jungle Book* is set in India, and *The Lion King* in Africa. The typical languages of these stories could be any one of many native languages spoken in those places; I have chosen one of the many possible languages in such cases.

m = mixed, p = positive, n = negative

The ability to identify an individual's race or ethnicity on the basis of voice alone is a phenomenon that has been referred to as linguistic profiling, a topic that will be taken up in more detail in the discussion of discrimination in the housing market.

Baugh's work on linguistic profiling and the role of vowel shapes, intonation, timing and voice quality in social and racial identification becomes potentially relevant in this context (Thomas and Reaser 2004). Unfortunately, no studies have been done, to date, of the way linguistic profiling might work in an entertainment setting such as animated films.

It needs to be stated quite clearly that this discussion does not include the sum total of all African American actors who have ever had speaking roles in Disney animated film. For example, a thorough examination would require close study of *The Song of the South*, which Disney has yet to release on VHS tape or DVD for reasons that may or may not have to do with concerns about image and racism.

The most ideology-laden of the films examined here is probably the *Lion King*, which fulfills all four of criteria listed above. *The Lion King* is set in Africa, which may be the reason why many of the voice actors were African American. Of the three major roles, two of the voice actors are Anglo (Simba and Scar, his uncle), and one is African American (Mufasa). Mufasa is voiced by the immediately recognizable James Earl Jones; Mufasa's evil brother Scar is voiced in an exaggerated and distinctly effeminate British English (Jeremy Irons). This falls into a well-established practice of rendering evil geniuses as Brits (see, for example, *Aladdin* and *Bolt*), but it also portrays homosexuality as evil, untrustworthy, and inauthentic. Scar is also the only lion with a black mane.

But it is the casting of the primary character – Simba – which stands out. As cub and as an adult lion, Simba is voiced by Anglos. That is, the prince, the son of African Americans, is white, a fact that did not go unnoticed by the critics and scholars who consider race and ethnicity (Benshoff and Griffin 2009; Martin-Rodriguez 2000; Sun 2008; Walker 1994),[16] gender issues, sexuality and sexism (Benshoff and Griffin 2009: "Case study: The Lion King") or class, power and hegemony (Gooding 1995; Morton 1996; Sun 2008).

What the directors and producers were thinking when they cast the voice actors cannot be known; if notes on this process exist, they are not available to researchers, nor do the producers respond to requests for interviews. Nor is there any way to know which voice actors were considered for the role of Simba, whether young African American actors were considered and auditioned, or if the entire pool of candidates was Anglo. It is unfortunate that so much of the process remains out of the public eye, as that information would provide invaluable insights.

More subtle is stratification of characters voiced by actors who are recognizably African American. James Earl Jones (Mufasa) has a deep and commanding voice without AAVE intonation or grammatical structure; Whoopi Goldberg shifts in and out of AAVE as the leader of the pack of hyenas who do Scar's bidding. Thus the message is a familiar one: AAVE speakers occupy the dark and frightening places, where Simba does not belong and should not be; he belongs on the sunny savannah where *SAE speakers like his father live.

The three primary hyenas who threaten Simba are composed of the AAVE-speaking Shenzi, Ed, a hyena who slobbers and grunts without any language, and Banzai, voiced by Cheech Martin. Martin shifts in and out of Latino-accented English, throwing in Spanish at one point (¿*que pasa?*) to make sure there is no mistake about his ethnicity.

At the same time, none of the characters, whether they speak *SAE or AAVE, show any clear connection to things African with the exception of the wise baboon, Rafiki, who occupies a special but peripheral role in the film's story.

Other types of entertainment media use these same strategies, of course, as bell hooks
has observed:

> [It is the] current trend in producing colorful ethnicity for the white consumer
> appetite that makes it possible for blackness to be commodified in unprecedented
> ways, and for whites to appropriate black culture without interrogating whiteness or
> showing concern for the displeasure of blacks . . . white cultural imperialism . . . allows
> white audiences to applaud representations of black culture, *if they are satisfied with*
> *the images and habits of being represented.*
>
> (hooks 1996: 223)

The role of King Louie – an orangutan – in *The Jungle Book* provides an example of another
kind of stereotype: the African American entertainer, the jokester or trickster. Louis Prima,
who voiced the role of King Louie, was an Italian American who grew up in New Orleans
in the early twentieth century and spent a lot of time with the blues and jazz musicians,
primarily African Americans, in the French Quarter. Given his musical training, background and reputation for scat singing, it's not surprising that movie viewers generally
believe that King Louie is voiced by an African American. This might be seen as a fairly
neutral case of linguistic profiling.

Much has been made of King Louie and his manipulation of Mowgli, the only human
being in this story. He convinces Mowgli and the audience that he has one goal in life,
and that is to be the one thing he is not: a human being, a man. African American males
who are not linguistically assimilated to the sociolinguistic norms of a middle and colorless
United States are allowed very few possibilities in life, but they are allowed to want those
things they do not have and cannot be.

Other infamous stereotypes occur in *Dumbo* (the shiftless, aimless but friendly crows
who advise Dumbo speak and sing AAVE – one of them is called Jim Crow), and *The Fox*
and the Hound where the protective and wise Big Mama is voiced by Pearl Bailey.

While in the first study 161 *SAE speakers appear in proportions of 43.1 percent
humanoid, 54.4 percent animal and 2.5 percent inanimate creatures (such as the talking
teapot in *Beauty and the Beast*), all AAVE-speaking characters appear in animal rather than
humanoid form. Given the low overall number of AAVE speakers, however, it is hard to
draw any inferences from that fact. The issue is further complicated in that every character
with a Southern accent appears in animal rather than humanoid form as well. Further
examination of unambiguously positive and negative characters indicates that a full 43.4
percent of 90 characters in human form show negative actions and motivations while only
18.6 percent of the 156 animal characters are negative.

This correlation of African American to animal held true until *Atlantis:The Lost Empire*
(Trousdale and Wise 2001, directors) and the character of Dr. Joshua Strongbear Sweet.
Dr. Strongbear Sweet is presented in human form, clearly African American in appearance.
Like Mufasa, Dry Strongbear Sweet doesn't use AAVE features so that another correlation
is maintained: powerful, educated = *SAE.

Following *Atlantis*, Disney made some progress away from these stereotypes with *Lilo*
& Stitch and the 2009 film *The Princess and the Frog*. *Lilo & Stitch* stands apart for its sensitive
portrayal of Hawai'i, Hawai'ian culture and people of color. The difference here had to
do with the way the film was made: Chris Sanders and Dean DeBois were given "near-
complete creative control as co-writers, storyboard artists and directors – a first for a
Disney film" (Davis 2002). Lilo, her older sister and her sister's boyfriend have features

that are not Anglicized, and their lives are neither romanticized nor trivialized; they all speak with Hawai'i Creole (HC) intonation and rhythms, and HC is heard now and then in the background. The one African American character is Cobra Bubbles, a social worker who looks a great deal like a professional weight lifter. His looks are frightening and his voice – distinctly African American – is imposing, but this character is in fact one of the good guys, sincere in his concern for the orphaned sisters. Unfortunately Disney did not repeat this unusual arrangement, and the usual style of production oversight was restored for *The Princess and the Frog,*

The story is set in New Orleans in the 1920s, and features a young African-American woman as the main character, one who has both father and mother as the story opens.[17]

The issue of language variety and accent was made somewhat easier for Disney because all the characters – humanoid and animal – speak a variety of English marked, at the very least, as Southern. It's important to recognize that the film makers made an effort to acknowledge the wide variety of language and language varieties spoken in New Orleans and environs in that time period: beyond African American English, there are also speakers of Southern American English, Cajun and French Creole. How well they handled these various languages is a subject worthy of close examination, and cannot be undertaken here.

The language of the main African American characters is only slightly distinct from that of their Anglo counterparts, in part because the voice actors restrict themselves to intonation patterns. There are no AAVE grammatical constructions or idioms that would make that Anglo/African American differences more distinct. One of the strongest speakers of AAVE – Tatiana's father – dies before the story ever really starts.

The issue of language variety is sidestepped in the case of the Prince, as well. The character, while charming and handsome, as are all the Disney princes, is also not American. Neither is he African American, nor is he Anglo. The voice actor is a native of Brazil, which freed the writers and directors of dealing with the issue of AAVE. Many critics and commentators took note of this equivocation, pointing out that by turning both prince and princess into frogs, the issue of color could be set aside. Some see this as a maneuver by Disney to anticipate and nullify the potentially explosive topic of miscegenation (Gehlawat 2010: 424). Others took a more sarcastic tone: "They say it ain't easy bein' green, but it's certainly a hell of a lot easier than being black" (Foundas 2009). Commentary on the web was often emotional and angry, as was the case on Black Voices, an AOL discussion forum where commentators faulted the prince's light skin color. Commentator Angela Bronner Helm wrote: "Disney obviously doesn't think a black man is worthy of the title of prince. His hair and features are decidedly non-black. This has left many in the community shaking their head[s] in befuddlement and even rage" (as quoted in Barnes 2009).

Lovers and mothers

Romance is a major plot device in many of Disney's animated films. Of the 24 stories examined in the first study, 13 depend in part or whole on the development of a relationship between a male and a female character which has not to do with friendship, but love and mate selection. Those characters who are young and in search of a potential mate or love interest provide some of the most interesting material in these films overall. There has been much commentary in the popular press on the extreme and unrealistic portrayal of young people's physical beings, for both sexes. Doe-eyed heroines with tiny waists and heroes with bulging necks and overly muscular thighs have been roundly criticized, with little effect. There is little or no discussion of the language spoken by lovers, however.[18]

In spite of the setting of the story or the individual's ethnicity, lovers and mothers speak mainstream varieties of U.S. or British English, with some interesting exceptions (Tables 7.6 and 7.7). Of the male characters, only two can be said to be logically and certainly speakers of U.S. English: Bernard who appears twice (*Rescuers* and *Rescuers Down Under*) and Jock (*Lady and the Tramp*). All the other characters are speakers of British or Australian English, or of languages other than English. The languages of the three princes (from *Cinderella*, *Snow White* and *The Little Mermaid*) are debatable: the Disney version never specifies where these magical kingdoms are located (whether in the country of the story's origin or elsewhere).

Two of the male romantic leads speak socially marked varieties of U.S. English: in *The Aristocats* O'Malley (voiced by Phil Harris, a popular entertainer and singer of his day and cast on the power of voice recognition) does nothing to change or disguise his own English, which is rich in those characteristics which are often thought of as "working class" (simplified consonant clusters, double negative constructions, and other stigmatized

Table 7.6 The language of mothers and fathers in Disney animated films

Language	Mothers	Fathers
*SAE	15	8
Socially marked U.S.	–	–
Regionally marked U.S.	–	1
British	2	8
Socially or regionally marked British or other English	2	4
Foreign accented English	1	1

Table 7.7 Lovers and potential lovers in Disney animated films

Language variety	Male	Female
*SAE	Gaston (*Beauty and the Beast*)	(no mate)
	The Beast (*Beauty and the Beast*)	Belle (*Beauty and the Beast*)
	Bernard (twice) (*Rescuers, Rescuers Down Under*)	–
	Aladdin (*Aladdin*)	Jasmine (*Aladdin*)
	Prince Charming (*Cinderella*)	Cinderella (*Cinderella*)
	Prince Philip (*Sleeping Beauty*)	Aurora (*Sleeping Beauty*)
	Prince Erik (*The Little Mermaid*)	Ariel (*The Little Mermaid*)
	Snow White's Prince (*Snow White*)	Snow White (*Snow White*)
	Simba (*The Lion King*)	Nala (*The Lion King*)
		Lady (*Lady and the Tramp*)
Socially marked U.S.	Jock O'Malley (*Lady and the Tramp*)	(no mate)
Non U.S. English	Robin Hood (*Robin Hood*)	Maid Marion (*Robin Hood*)
	Jake (*Rescuers Down Under*)	(no mate)
	Pongo (*101 Dalmations*)	Perdita (*101 Dalmations*)
	Roger Radcliff (*101 Dalmations*)	Anita Radcliffe (*101 Dalmations*)
Foreign accented English		Miss Bianca (twice) (*Rescuers, Rescuers Down Under*)
		Duchess (*The Aristocats*)

phonological and grammatical features). This is also the case with Jock from *Lady and the Tramp*. Both of these characters are prototypical rough lovers, men with an edge who need the care and attention of good women to settle them, and both are rewarded with such mates – females who speak non-stigmatized varieties – because they prove themselves worthy. There are no male romantic leads with foreign accents.

There is even less variation among the female romantic leads. There are no rough, working-class equivalents of O'Malley and Jock. In fact, there is only one unambiguous case of a character who would logically speak U.S. English: Lady of *Lady and the Tramp*. The use of a typical or logical language for the part and background of the character is clearly less important in this case than a consistent portrayal of an ideal lover and potential mate which stresses the lack of "otherness."

However, there are two female characters (one of which occurs in two movies, *Rescuers* and *Rescuers Down Under*) with foreign accents, but they are both voiced by the same woman, Eva Gabor. The Gabor sisters were widely known and recognized in U.S. culture in the 1950s and 1960s for their glamor and demanding behavior in many highly publicized affairs with rich men. They were recognizable on the basis of their Hungarian accents, and they brought with them a set of associations about sexually aware and available females that resulted in typecasting. The roles that Eva Gabor voiced for Disney were thus of elegant, demanding and desirable females and as such have to be considered separately from other characters with foreign accents.

In short

Film producers like Disney are primarily concerned with engaging the audience and filling seats in the theater. As professional storytellers they understand a great deal about characterization, plot, setting, and all the other elements that make or break a production. Is it too much to expect film makers to consider other issues, as well? Does the storyteller have any obligation to the viewers? These are questions that cannot be answers in this context, but they require close consideration.

As one of the primary storytellers in the life of American children of all colors and ethnicities, Disney's films have a deep and long-lasting effect on socialization and the development of identity – for both self and other. There is a growing body of scholarship which looks at Disney in a wider context and without apologist rhetoric, and that work makes clear how systematically Disney animated film goes about setting up conceptions of good and evil with strong correlations to race and ethnicity. (Giroux's *The Mouse that Roared: Disney and the End of Innocence* (2010) provides an overview of this literature.) The manipulation of accent is part of that process, and it works very well.

DISCUSSION QUESTIONS AND EXERCISES

- Compile a list of Disney characters who speak English with a clear Anglo-New York City area accent. What do these characters have in common? Look at sociocultural characteristics, personality traits, motivations, style, and role in the plot? How do your findings support or contradiction the idea that stereotype does not have to be overtly negative to be limiting and prejudicial?

- Murnane (2007) proposes that Disney films can be used in the classroom to teach multiculturalism. See: http://www.historycooperative.org/journals/whc/5.1/murnane.html. Choose one of the Disney animated films and outline a middle school lesson plan that would accomplish such a goal. Be sure to include some aspect of language use and accent manipulation and to cite the sources of your information.
- Read "Demonizing in Children's Television Cartoons and Disney Animated Films," a short quantitative study of the concept of evil in Disney films (Fouts *et al.* 2006). How do the findings of this paper contradict or support the data and conclusions drawn in this chapter?
- Consider the way you and others talk about Disney. Do you hear phrases such as "allowances have to be made for the times," or "that's the way things were," or "everybody felt that way," or "come on, it's supposed to be funny"? Where do such reactions originate, and are they meant to move discussion forward, or to shut down discourse and critical analysis? For close readings of examples of this kind of reasoning, see especially Hill (2008).

Notes

1 Since the first edition of this book appeared in 1997, formal study of all aspects of the Disney empire has grown significantly (Doherty July 21, 2006). Of the work released over the last decade, perhaps most relevant to the issues raised here is Giroux's *The Mouse that Roared: Disney and the End of Innocence* (2010: 2nd edn).

  Over that same period of time, Disney has released a number of full-length animated films. Given technical limitations, it is not possible to include those films in the quantitative analysis used for the pre-1997 films, which remains intact. Instead, I have viewed and analyzed the newer films, and where they best fit into the discussion, I include my qualitative analysis.

2 Fisch (2005) presents arguments for the constructive aspects of television viewing for children, who are exposed to positive role models and educational exercises in programming such as *Sesame Street*.

3 Nielsen Media Research produces Nielsen ratings to measure U.S. television audience size and composition.

4 Of course, other broadcast entertainment venues for children are not given a free pass. Consider the widely broadcast accusations of homosexuality among *Teletubbies* and *Sesame Street* characters (*New York Times*, February 11, 1999; Mikkelson 2007), or of satanic worship in the *Harry Potter* books.

5 Disney bought the rights to *Winnie the Pooh* after Milne's death in 1956.

6 Paula Giese provides a compilation of Native American comments and discussions about Pocahontas on her website at http://www.kstrom.net/isk/poca/. Note also that Russell Means, a Native American rights activist, was very vocal with his unconditional praise of Disney's version of Pocahontas. His opinion is rendered suspect, however, because he took a prominent acting role in it.

7 In 1924, tickets averaged a quarter; by 1929 the average price was 35 cents. Prices dropped again during the Depression. In 1965, the average movie ticket price rose above $1.00 for the first time (Picture Show Man n.d.).

8 Giroux provides more background on the way Disney has limited access to its archives

and use of materials in academic publications for those scholars and academics whose work conflicts with the image they want to project. This may well be within their legal rights, but in the end it amounts to limiting and censoring discourse.

9 There has been a great deal of speculation about Walt Disney's ties to Nazi Germany and his anti-Semitic feelings more generally. While some evidence points to that conclusion, there is certainly not enough of it to make any claims along these lines.

10 In 1930, the Motion Picture Producers and Distributors of America (MPPDA) created a self-regulatory code of ethics. The office charged with this duty was put under the direction of Will H. Hays, and went into effect on July 1, 1934. The Hays Office outlined general standards of good taste and specifically forbade certain elements in film. The code specified that "no picture shall be produced which will lower the standards of those who see it. Hence the sympathy of the audience should never be thrown to the side of crime, wrongdoing, evil or sin." The specific regulations included (in paraphrase): (1) Revenge in modern times shall not be justified. (2) Methods of crime shall not be explicitly presented. (3) The sanctity of the institution of marriage and the home shall be upheld. (4) Miscegenation (interracial sexual relationships) is forbidden. The Code specifically addressed the inadvisability of caricaturing national origin groups or portraying them in offensive ways. In 1968 a Rating system was put into effect, and the Code was no longer used.

11 Brode (2005: 101–103) argues that the representation of the wolf as Jewish peddler is not racist. As a part of his argument he acknowledges that such stereotypes existed (and he knows this because this is part of his own family history). "Besides, cartoons – with their extremely (and, for anyone who understands the medium, necessarily) broad form of portraiture – rely more heavily on caricature than any other cinematic form." Brode goes on to add this odd bit of rationalization: "Disney may have created the wolf, but it is the wolf – the film's villain – who invokes ethnic stereotyping" (ibid.. 103).

12 Yiddish is a variety of German that originated in Jewish communities in Eastern Europe and spread to Jewish communities all over the continent. It was the first language of many Jews who immigrated to the United States in the last two centuries. While Yiddish spoken in Russia and the East is still vigorous, Western European Yiddish is dying out. In the U.S. about 150,000 people report speaking Yiddish at home, most of them resident in New York or Florida, with smaller populations in California, Pennsylvania and Illinois.

13 It might be argued that many aspects of animated films are actually aimed at the adults.

14 Included in the study were full-length feature films (generally between one and a half to two hours in length); specifically excluded short features and compilations of shorts grouped together for thematic reasons. Only fully animated films were included, excluding those that combine live-action sequences with animation (*The Song of the South, Three Caballeros*). Animated film created for adult audience (the war-time film *Victory through Air Power* is one example) were also omitted, as were Pixar films which are not produced by Disney. All characters with speaking roles of more than single word utterances were included in the analysis.

15 Note that Buena Vista is an umbrella term used for all aspects of Disney's business entities.

16 This reversal also occurs in *The Hunchback of Notre Dame*: Quasimodo, the son of two dark-skinned Romani (gypsies), has the milky complexion of a red-headed Irishman. A hero may be physically disabled, but he must also be Anglo, and his speech must sound Anglo.

17 *Princess* certainly represents an improvement over *The Lion King* in terms of stereotype

and language markers but other patterns are still there, if muted. Critics have questioned the fact that the young African American main character spends about three-quarters of the film as a frog:

> To make the first African American princess a frog, then, seems to literally conflate her with animality. Tiana, mixing her dreams of success with a lack of intelligence and reason, is a black girl who must hop around like a frog in the way early twentieth-century black actors had to don blackface and hop around like dogs.
>
> (Gehlawat 2010: 418)

18 Characters of an age to pursue a partner who do not do so in the story line are usually portrayed as awkward, fat or ugly (examples include the stepsisters in *Cinderella*, the witch-like Cruella de Ville in *101 Dalmatians*, and LaFou in *Beauty and the Beast*).

Suggested further reading

Bonilla-Silva, E. (2009) *Racism without Racists: Color-Blind Racism and the Persistence of Racial Inequality in the United States.* Lanham, MD: Rowman & Littlefield.

Do Rozario, R. (2004) The Princess and the Magic Kingdom: Beyond Nostalgia, the Function of the Disney Princess. *Women's Studies in Communication* 27(1): 34 ff.

Fouts, G., Callan, M., Piasentin, K. and Lawson, A. (2006) Demonizing in Children's Television Cartoons and Disney Animated Films. *Child Psychiatry and Human Development* 37(1): 15–23.

Nazzi, T. and Gopnik, A. (2001) Linguistic and Cognitive Abilities in Infancy: When Does Language Become a Tool for Categorization? *Cognition* 80(3): B11–B20.

Quintana, S. (2008) *Handbook of Race, Racism, and the Developing Child.* Hoboken, NJ: John Wiley & Sons.

Sayers, F. C. (1965) Walt Disney Accused. *Horn Book* 41: 602–611.

Van Ausdale, D. and Feagin, J.R. (2001) *The First R: How Children Learn Race and Racism.* Lanham, MD: Rowman & Littlefield.

Wright, B. (2007) American Cartoons of the Vietnam Era: A Study of Social Commentary in Films and Television Programs, 1961–1973. *Journalism History* 33(1): 62–63.

Zipes, J. (1979) The Instrumentalization of Fantasy: Fairy Tales, the Culture Industry, and the Mass Media. In *Breaking the Magic Spell: Radical Theories of Folk and Fairy Tales.* New York: Methuen, pp. 93–128.

The information industry

8

All media exist to invest our lives with artificial perceptions and arbitrary values.
Marshall McLuhan, *Understanding Media: The Extensions of Man*, 1965

Media manipulation in the U.S. today is more efficient than it was in Nazi Germany, because here we have the pretense that we are getting all the information we want. That misconception prevents people from even looking for the truth.
Mark Crispin Miller, *The Project on Media Ownership*

The voice of authority

There is a large and very active community of academics who study the history, structure and function of the media, in all its guises. In contrast, the focus of this book is quite narrow, and can be summarized in a single question: how does the mass media – specifically the broadcast and print media outlets concerned with the dissemination of news – use the language subordination model presented in Chapter 5?[1]

Media representatives claim authority in matters of language, and use that manufactured authority as a tool to coerce agreement on a wide range of public issues. This is a conscious, focused goal, as openly acknowledged in *The Art of Editing:* "The copy editor plays a major role in protecting the language against abuse" (from the chapter "Protecting the Language" in Baskette *et al.* 1986, cited in Cotter 1999: 175).

The same is true of all dominant institutions, but the media have one advantage over the others. Educational institutions begin the formal process of inculcating individuals into an SLI, but at a certain age everyone moves beyond school and educational influence loses some or all of its intensity. Some – but not all – employers require adherence to an SLI. A skilled forklift driver is not likely to be scolded about the variety of English she speaks; nor is a shipping clerk in an auto parts store likely to be called onto the carpet because of her phonology;[2] only the tiniest proportion of the population will ever submit a complaint or start legal proceedings on the basis of language-focused employment discrimination, and thus few will ever experience the way the judicial system and courts claim authority in these matters.

But a very large proportion of the population has regular and intense exposure to broadcast or print news media of one kind or another.

Language – the intrinsic and functional variability of language – is far more deeply integrated into our understanding of the world than any external symbol of wealth or influence. Linguistic variation linked to social identity is far more subtle. One way to think about this is by means of what Bourdieu calls *the linguistic marketplace*. In this theoretical model, an exchange between speaker and listener is about more than deciphering surface meaning. Sociolinguistic markers are "also signs of wealth, intended to be evaluated and appreciated, and signs of authority intended to be believed and obeyed" (Bourdieu and Thompson 1991: 66). A speech act's value is based on power relations that have already been established, such as the mastery of linguistic competences marked for class.

Linguistic utterances or expressions are always produced in particular contexts or markets, and the properties of these markets endow linguistic products with a certain "value" (ibid.: 18). It is important to note that there are multiple linguistic marketplaces, so that in some contexts a stigmatized variety of vernacular U.S. English may in fact have more persuasive power and capital than the smoothest talking National Public Radio reporter. This complexity was absent in the theory as Bourdieu first developed it, but other scholars – in particular, anthropological linguists – have refined it (Gal 2005; Schieffelin *et al.* 1998; Seargeant 2009; Woolard 2008).

Media representatives have claimed for themselves a spot as national role models. And in fact, we allow them to chide us when our language differs from those varieties of English they speak, or think they speak. They have convinced us that they have the right to do this, and we do not challenge them. That unwillingness or inability to question such claims of authority does the real damage. "The most successful ideological effects are those which have no need for words, *and ask no more than complicitous silence*" (Bourdieu 1987: 188, emphasis added).

In what follows, the focus is on the media as a powerful institution that plays a major role in the stability and perpetuation of the nation-state, and the way language serves as both a tool and a target in that process. Consider, for example, the phrase "voice of authority."

In the 1990s, ABC News produced a print advertisement featuring a head-shot of Peter Jennings, then senior editor and chief anchor of the news desk. Beneath the image of the photogenic Jennings was a single line of text: "The Voice of Authority." Regardless of Jennings' skill and the quality of his reporting, it requires a jump of faith to accept him – or any one person – as the ultimate voice of authority in the interpretation and reporting of current events.[3]

A study of the various media outlets provides many examples of how representatives see themselves and want to be seen. Sometimes the claims are very boldly stated, as in the following during a (2005) National Public Radio broadcast:

> NPR is considered by many to be the standard bearer for Standard American English. Listeners from around the country and around the world say that they find NPR English is the clearest and most comprehensible broadcast English available. They can hear that crisp American English on NPR member stations, on their Web sites, on line at npr.org or on the listeners' shortwave receivers.

(Dvorkin 2005)

As is often the case when authority is claimed in public forums, the identity and credentials of the cited expert are left conveniently in the shadows. The passive construction "considered by many" is a classic dodge in the tradition of "mistakes were made" (Broder 2007).

Such claims are not the largest part of the media's participation in the language subordination process, which requires that the non-compliant be dealt with summarily. The newscasters and reporters seem to have two primary methods for drawing attention to non-conformers: mocking or condescension. In looking at how this works, there are two types of data to be considered: commentary made about matters of language, often derisive or condescending and news reports which are language focused. The following examples come from both broadcast and print new media.

> The idea is to teach them how to speak English so that it sounds like English, and not, as Henry Higgins might put it, like warmed-over grits. Think of them as prisoners – prisoners of their own accents.

> We like Hahn, 34, who was born in South Korea and whose positions on controlling growth are much like our own. Unfortunately, we think his heavy accent and some-what limited contacts would make it difficult for him to be a councilman.

> For all the damage now being done to the English language there are people who continue to care about its health. Dr. Grammar is one of them.

> No matter how qualified a person is, a voice twisted by regional or ethnic influences can be a stumbling block socially and professionally. If others can't understand you or your words are too richly flavored with down-home spice, you could find all your skill and intelligence thwarted by a telltale tongue.[4]

Newspaper headlines alone are sometimes quite sufficient evidence of a particular slant on language issues: "Bad English Spoken Here" (McKenzie 1992); "Language is the Guardian of Culture" (Nenneman 1992); "Speak English, Troops" (Hamel 1989); "Black English Not Spoken Here" (Jarrett 1979a); "Oy Gevalt! New Yawkese an Endangered Dialect?" (Sontag 1993); "Today's Youth's Inability to Speak Proper English" (*Quad-City Herald* 2004).

A new business venture may begin with a hole in the market – a real need which has not been filled – or with a need that has been placed in the mind of the public. Whiter teeth, for example, have been extensively promoted through advertising media. Someplace along the way such a need for a better, more efficient, more elegant language was created in the minds of Americans.[5] This followed not because speakers of English were suddenly no longer able to communicate with each other and required a solution, but because they were made to feel inadequate or ashamed.

The parties sounding dire proclamations about the decline of spoken English are, not coincidentally, the ones with the cure to sell – those right-thinking and right-speaking individuals who are able to set the public on a straight and narrow path to the one true way of speaking.

Opinion, spin, propaganda

Editorial opinions are not out of place in any kind of information media, as long as they are clearly marked as such. The presentation of alternate interpretations is a public service, and an important one. In the past twenty years, however, the distinction between editorial commentary and news, between news and entertainment has given way to what has been called *infotainment* (Thussu 2011).

Objectivity is a theoretical concept and hardly attainable in real-world communication, even by the best trained, widely experienced and most professional and sincere journalists. Every exchange of information comes with a context that is relevant to understanding the speaker's intent. The purposeful lack or withholding of information is just as significant as the presentation of demonstrable fact. It might be more useful to speak of a continuum from absolute, unvarnished truth to purposeful, unapologetic falsehood; from a theoretical *purely objective* to *purely subjective*. On this continuum, *spin* sits somewhere between the center point and the purely subjective.

Everybody practices spin in communication. If you do very poorly on a performance review, you might tell your co-workers by starting with the fact that you had the flu that day, or that everybody came in below the 70 percent mark, or that you were thinking of changing jobs anyway. You might not mention it at all. You might deny you were reviewed. Or, if you state the fact outright "My performance review came back totally unsatisfactory," the people you're talking to might provide the spin for you and remind you that you had the flu that week, or that nobody did very well because the manager conducting the reviews is a jerk. One of the most fruitful areas for study of spin and objectivity is the political campaign.

The study of political language can take many points of departure. There are studies of style in public debate, audience focus, rhetorical tropes, metaphor, ritual insulting, and the use of humor, to name a few (Cienki and Mueller 2008; Clayman 1995; Dillard and Pfau 2002; Lim 2008; Santa Ana 2002). George Lakoff (Lakoff 2004, 2006, 2008; Lakoff and Rockridge 2006) is one of very few linguists whose theories have come to the attention of the public. This happened at least in part because his work in discourse analysis and cognitive linguistics aroused the interest of a senior members of the Democratic Party, who were scrambling for new, more effective ways of reaching the public (Bai 2005). Lakoff became a consultant to many politicians who were interested in the concept of rhetorical framing.

Lakoff's work suggests that success in swaying public opinion has to do with a more effective and consistent set of rhetorical strategies, or a frame of reference so that "through cultural narratives, metaphors, and frames . . . we understand and express our ideals (Lakoff 2008).

In the late twentieth and early twenty-first centuries, Republicans have tended to be much better at getting their message out to the public, and getting the public to listen. They do this, in part, by coining new, ideologically laden and emotive terminology and repeating those terms until they become embedded in the public consciousness. Two things are crucial to such a strategy: uniformity of style and rhetoric across the party, and repetition.

In *Whose Freedom?*, Lakoff claims that liberals run into trouble because they operate on the basis of a self-defeating political rationalism, which is "a myth about reason and its relationship to politics" (Lakoff 2006: 249–251). Some primary characteristics of political rationalism are: (1) its defining nature for humans (it distinguishes us from other life forms); (2) its universality (everyone is rational); and (3) the fact that rational thought is a conscious process.

A person who believes strongly in the value of rationalism will conclude that once the public has the facts, they will come to the same reasonable conclusion. Elections are (in Lakoff's view) the proof that this model is simply wrong: "The facts alone will not set you free. If the frames that define common sense contradict the facts, the facts will be ignored" (ibid.: 251).

The topic of frames will come up again shortly, but in the meantime, it is good to keep in mind that rational thought or rationalism is often called upon, but rarely proves useful as a tool to combat the language subordination process. It can be seen as a type of spin, and thus must be carefully examined.

Propaganda goes far beyond spin and is generally understood to be the planned, systematic distribution of disinformation to achieve a particular end, as in the manufacture of consent, a concept that is central to this chapter. In matters of language, we can also speak of propaganda, albeit of a more subconscious and subtle variety. In as much as language about language is factually incorrect or misleading, it becomes self-referential propaganda: it serves as both the vehicle of disinformation and its object. This process is a difficult one to look at closely, for while it is not so hard to reconstruct the motivations for the media's positive representation of, for example, the outcome of the 2000 presidential election, given the corporate structure and economic dependencies of broadcast and print journalism, the motivations that underlie the limiting of discourse are carefully masked.

Among the wealth of material about propaganda in political discourse, there are two schools of thought which might be familiar to the general public. The first is George Orwell's extensive writing on the subversion of power by means of language manipulation, most particularly by the media in reporting on politics. The second is the concept of doublespeak (often falsely attributed to Orwell), which William Lutz describes as deliberate, calculated misuse of language (Lutz 2004; Orwell 2005). In both cases, the emphasis is on the use and manipulation of language by individuals associated with the government, politics, and the media.

As an American, Lutz never denied the importance of freedom of the press as a basic liberty clearly stated in the Bill of Rights: "Congress shall make no law . . . abridging the freedom of speech, or of the press. As a nation we are proud of the rights established by the first ten amendments to the Constitution and generally very protective of those rights." But the Founders did not define what they meant by "press" or "speech," nor did they address the question of truthfulness or objectivity in reporting; that is, the idea of a fair and balanced press does not originate in our Constitution. The evolution of this idea is complex and worthy of close examination on its own. And yet, it seems that there is no official journalistic stance on issues such as spin, propaganda, framing and rationalism. Currently the Society of Professional Journalists has a Code of Ethics (http://www.spj.org/ethicscode.asp):

> Public enlightenment is the forerunner of justice and the foundation of democracy. The duty of the journalist is to further those ends by seeking truth and providing a fair and comprehensive account of events and issues. Conscientious journalists from all media and specialties strive to serve the public with thoroughness and honesty. Professional integrity is the cornerstone of a journalist's credibility.

In the first line, the setting of standards and ethics for journalists is not a matter of law, but of self-governance. That is, organizations like the Society of Professional Journalists can discuss what journalism can and should be; they can publish guidelines; they can even hold journalists who fail to meet those guidelines up for peer review and public criticism. In an extreme case, where a journalist has broken hard-line rules (quoting non-existent sources, knowingly presenting fiction as fact; direct plagiarism), he or she will simply no longer be unemployable as a journalist. If poor journalistic standards exceed a certain point, then the law may come into play.

There are external watchdog organizations which take up the task of monitoring journalists and news sources – Fairness and Accuracy in Reporting and FactCheck.org are two of many. For the most part these non-profit groups are scrupulously fair, pointing out misrepresentations and exaggerations in both the Democratic and the Republican campaign rhetoric, for example. But beyond bringing questionable practices to the public's attention, there is little they can do.[6]

Traditional and new media outlets claim to strive for objectivity, but study of practices over time provides evidence that bias is widespread. Media outlets are businesses like any other, one that must answer to corporate owners; this fact necessarily influences the context in which they do their work. The media's most effective tool in forming public opinion is quite obvious: they control the flow of information, what we hear about, for how long, how that subject is framed, and in what detail. This is so widely acknowledged that dozens of organizations publish lists of the most underreported news stories at the end of every year.[7] For example, there has been very little news from the mainstream outlets on the excesses of Immigration and Customs Enforcement (ICE), which maintains more than a hundred secret facilities where persons suspected of immigration violations are warehoused (Stevens, January 4, 2010).[8]

Not so long ago, the traditional media's ability to withhold, misrepresent or trivialize potentially important or relevant news was a tool that could stop major legislation. More recently the rise of the internet and alternate media has made it much harder – and sometimes impossible – to bury a story.[9] However, the media can still lift a story into the spotlight and keep it at the forefront for as long as it likes. In extreme cases, the media can institute or attempt to institute a moral panic (see the case study of the Oakland Ebonics debate in Chapter 16 for an example of how this process works).

Bad is stronger than good

Research in psychology and sociology has established beyond a doubt that negative and positive evaluations are not symmetrical (Baumeister et al. 2001). That is, it seems to be human nature to assign more weight and importance or validity to bad news than to good news.

It is important to keep this in mind when considering the impact the media have on political campaigns and candidates. Bad news is far more interesting to the public than good news, from which follows the fact that bad news sells more papers and gets more broadcast coverage. However, there are many cases where a media outlet prefers to overlook the bad in favor of the good for a wide variety of reasons, few of which are neutral.

Two examples at either extreme: during the Reagan presidency, there were multiple opportunities for the news media to show the administration and the president in a very unflattering light. They declined to do, and instead began referring to Reagan as "the Teflon president." There's an irony to that pronouncement – a sort of self-fulfilling prophecy – that was largely lost on the public. At the other extreme, it was the print news media that initiated a string of events that culminated in President Nixon's impeachment trial and resignation. Woodward and Bernstein's reports about break-ins at the Watergate Hotel and their refusal to give up the chase got the attention of the public and Congress, which was eventually compelled to act (Sigleman and Tuch 1997).

Here I look more closely at the 2008 presidential election; first, at issues of language ideology, social class, and media gatekeeping as reflected in the media coverage of former governor Sarah Palin, followed by a similar study of the Obama campaign and rhetorical framing.

The 2008 presidential election

In the 2008 presidential election – and in all elections to come – the mainstream media outlets found themselves competing with cable television offerings and, more significantly, the internet. An unprecedented wealth and variety of information, analysis and opinion became – and continues to become – available. This has both complicated and amplified the framing process.

There was a striking and unprecedented contrast between candidates in 2008. Some mainstream news outlets capitalized more extensively on these contrasts than others. On one extreme (the conservatively oriented Fox news programs) news reporters and commentators were very positive about Governor Palin and negative about Senator Obama; MSNBC News reporters and commentators took the opposite stance.[10] When rhetoric got out of hand, responsible media and watchdog organizations that set out to correct the public record were usually lost in the roar of the crowd.

To establish one point very clearly at the outset: every politician, every public speaker, every individual adjusts style and language to suit their audience and elicit desired reactions.[11] We adjust without thinking about it, for the most part. In politics, however, there is a performance aspect to public speaking, and thus the way in which politicians shift can be very deliberately planned. Whether spontaneous or planned, some individuals are more successful than others at shifting in style to engage the audience.

Framing Palin

> We believe that the best of America is not all in Washington, D.C. . . . We believe that the best of America is in these small towns that we get to visit, and in these wonderful little pockets of what I call the real America, being here with all of you hard working very patriotic, um, very, um, pro-America areas of this great nation.
> Sarah Palin, public address, Greensboro, NC, October 16, 2008)

As is the case with every politician who comes into national focus, as soon as former Governor Sarah Palin had accepted the Republican vice-presidential candidacy in the 2008 presidential election, the media outlets began their investigations. Broadcast, print and internet news sources reported on the Governor's history, her performance as a politician and a government official, and her positions on topics relevant to the role she sought. In Palin's case, additional subjects were added: her appearance, the nature of her religious beliefs, and her children and family circumstances were also brought into play.[12] That is, much of the debate around Palin's candidacy was gendered, and as such, overtly sexist.[13] Beyond sexism was the issue of socioeconomic class.

In the course of an election campaign, political parties focus on specific groups within the population where they need support. Palin was presented as a small-town, working-class American mother with a no-nonsense approach to politics. At the same time, she accused her Democratic opponents of being too removed from "real Americans" to know what was needed. She emphasized the difference (as she saw it) between city and country, secular and non-secular, and the classes.

Palin speaks a regional variety of American English specific to the Matanuska-Susitna Valley of Alaska, which is unfamiliar to most Americans in the Lower Forty-Eight. In her public appearances, the Governor chose to emphasize her regional features, which was one way to underscore her origins and claim a certain kind of authority.[14] Sarah Palin's stylistic choices got the immediate attention of the media and the public, in large part because her public speaking style was remarkably informal (Purnell *et al.* 2009).

An open and frank discussion of socioeconomic class is not the usual way of things in a national campaign. Instead Palin used language features to set her own frame. This policy provided a way for detractors to zero in on what some saw as a serious lack of education and world knowledge. The Governor's folksy style was apparently designed to establish her authenticity, and so in challenging her linguistic choices, observers were also challenging her sincerity and the authenticity of the frame she established for herself.

Questions about the origins of Palin's regional variety of American English,[15] the way she sometimes "dropped the g sound" in words like *going* (Liberman 2004); her pronunciation of the word *nuclear*;[16] and her use of euphemistic forms such as *heck*, *darn*, and *doggone* (Evans Davies 2009; Purnell *et al.* 2009) all became the focus of negative attention.

Note that I am distinguishing between the content, logic and quality of Palin's statements (which I will not evaluate here), on the one hand, and, on the other, the sociolinguistic markers in her speech.

It is likely that everyone who ever ran for higher office has had detractors who focused on their variety of English and specific language traits. The difference in Palin's case was the extent to which the news media chose to be a part of the process. A few words about the nature of satire and parody will help in understanding the media's role in the linguistic subordination of Sarah Palin.

Satire uses humor to make an emotion-laden subject easier to approach, while in parody, the humor is an end unto itself. Those who employ parody aim in the first line to entertain with extreme portrayals of established ideas or characters. Satire is less dependent on mimicry, and has a larger underlying purpose that arises out of anger and frustration.

It is possible to achieve both at one time. Currently the most popular example is The Comedy Network's *The Colbert Report*. Colbert's parody of a conservative talk-show host is humorous on the surface, but his purpose is more than humor. The entire show is an elaborate satire that is meant to throw light on what Colbert believes is wrong and what needs to change in the American government.

In the time running up to a presidential election, all candidates are open targets for parody and satire. Political cartoonists, comedians, commentators all take part in this ritual. In parody, the performer begins by studying a candidate in order to identify his or her most distinctive characteristics. In the first line these are often linguistic features (phonology, lexical items, grammar), gestures, mannerisms, and other distinctive aspects of communication. There may be an attempt to look and dress like the object of the parody, while the content of the communication originates in the subject's ideas, beliefs and actions. By contrast, the comedian reproduces the subject's language and style, emphasizing certain aspects for humor's sake. Mockery of this kind is meant to expose what is silly or ridiculous (in the opinion of the performer), and to open the object up for criticism and ridicule.

In its extreme form, mockery provides a shortcut to language-focused subordination. Sociolinguists, critical language theorists and anthropological linguists are interested in mocking as an overt gesture of gatekeeping, one clearly intended to pass on a negative message about the person being mocked. In the study of linguistic and stylistic mocking, the emphasis has been primarily linked to race and ethnicity. There is a great deal of work on Mock Spanish (Hill 1995; 1998; 2008); African American English (Ronkin and Karn 1999) and the accents of Asians who learn English as a second language (Huebner and Uyechi 2004; Klein and Shiffman 2006; Lo 1999), among others. Less work has been done when the underlying motivator is not racism or xenophobia, but socioeconomic class distinctions.

In the case of Palin's candidacy for vice-president, it is precisely such socioeconomic class distinctions which were brought into play. The campaigners took a carefully calculated stand when they presented Palin to the electorate using associations that come along with her constant references to small-town, Joe Six-Pack, hockey-mom, and the working class. Darling (2009: 16) contends that terms like these "represent a set of conflations which link whiteness, rurality and poverty to backwardness and conservatism."

In the months before a presidential election, there is an upswing in parody and mockery that no major candidate escapes. In the 2008 election campaign, one of the most watched sources for this kind of parody was NBC's *Saturday Night Live* (SNL), a television sketch comedy show which has provided parody and satire of presidential candidates since the 1970s.

In the 2008 election, SNL's Tina Fey (a former cast member who returned in order to take on this role) performed several parodies of Sarah Palin to great acclaim. Critics and commentators drew attention, repeatedly, to the facility with which Fey recreated Palin's dialect or accent.

In "The Linguistic Mocking of Sarah Palin," Davies (2009) compares the SNL parodies of all four candidates (McCain, Palin, Obama, Biden) and finds that in three cases, idiosyncratic traits were amplified for the sake of humor, but in Palin's case the underlying message was distinctly different. Davies proposes that those who wrote the skits about Palin meant to expose the candidate's faults and make them available for ridicule, in order to demonstrate her unsuitability for office.

In fact, there was nothing unusual or inappropriate in this; parody and satire are protected rights, and SNL has a proud history of taking a political stand. But with every new parody of Palin, the tone intensified. Finally, the information industry got involved. Rather than simply observing and reporting news from the campaign, news media began to fold information and reports about Fey's parody of Palin into their coverage, obscuring the line between satire and news. Clips of the skits began to show up on major news broadcasts, sometimes paired with clips of Palin herself. On a CNN news broadcast, Wolf Blitzer took pains to point out how Fey's parody had further solidified the general impression that Palin had performed very badly in a televised interview (CNN's *Late Edition*, September 28, 2008).

This phenomenon did not elude the Republican campaign organizers or Palin's supporters. Writing for *The Rocky Mountain News* after Fey's parody of Palin's interview with Katie Couric had aired, Littwin noted that "Palin needed to be perceived as semi-credible again, meaning that when people looked at her, they didn't see Tina Fey. In other words, she needed a debate that didn't provide a late-night TV punch line" (2008).

Darling posits that when mocking has reached this stage, the object has lost all credibility and cannot be taken seriously, something borne out by the commentary of the time in news reports of all kinds:

> Communication is critical for Palin, since she mangles the English language so consistently that she's become the subject of ridicule.
>
> (Zirin 2008)

> But Palin is also alarmingly unskilled when it comes to a more indigenous matter: speaking the English language.
>
> (Maura Kelly, an American freelance journalist writing for *The Guardian*)

There is a broader perspective to take into account when looking at the variety of media commentary. Thinking in terms of the linguistic marketplace, mockery and parody are not all powerful and do not transcend every social barrier. Many observers dismissed out of hand the recasting and parody of Palin's language and ideas. For such persons, the parody may not have discredited Palin, but it certainly further cemented sky-high social class animosities. Commentators who ridiculed Palin's accent or pronunciation of certain words were offending a large part of their audience, because the features of Palin's speech that were mocked were features prominent in a wide variety of regional accents closely allied to working class communities and individuals.

CNN commentators and Keith Olberman (MSNBC) drew attention to Palin's pronunciation of *nuclear* (4 October 2008) and openly mocked her informal style (7 October 2008); writing in *The New York Times*, Maureen Dowd went into detail about what she saw as Palin's grammatical errors:

> She dangles gerunds, mangles prepositions, randomly exiles nouns and verbs and also
> – "also" is her favorite vamping word – uses verbs better left as nouns, as in, "If
> Americans so bless us and privilege us with the opportunity of serving them," or how
> she tried to "progress the agenda."
>
> (October 4)

Robert Schlesinger of *U.S. News and World Report* went so far as to point out a typo in one of Palin's mailings.

Commentators and news reporters who were openly critical of the way Palin expressed herself (instead of, or in addition to, commentary on the ideas she was trying to communicate) were gatekeeping. That is, they drew attention to Palin's pronunciation or style in order to bolster the argument *she is not one of us*. This is a common strategy in political campaigns. But in Palin's case, that approach added credibility to Palin's frame for herself; rather than be embarrassed about the faults held up for public ridicule, she embraced the associations made. Her linguistic choices seemed to telegraph her dislike and distrust of what she characterized as the liberal mindset and intellectualism.[17] The goal, it seemed, was to reach those who identified with her and "the overall theme that Ms. Palin and Senator John McCain have been trying to advance: that expertise is overrated, homespun sincerity is better than sophistication, conviction is more important than analysis" (Pinker 2008). Palin's anti-intellectualism has been compared to class warfare, both by her critics and those who supported the Republican Party and its candidates in the 2008 campaign:

> Palin is smart, politically skilled, courageous and likable. Her convention and debate
> performances were impressive. But no American politician plays the class-warfare
> card as constantly as Palin. Nobody so relentlessly divides the world between the
> "normal Joe Sixpack American" and the coastal elite
>
> (Brooks 2008).

It would be a mistake to generalize on the basis of observations about Palin to conservatives more generally. *The National Review*, founded by William F. Buckley, Jr., is generally seen as a cradle of conservative intellectualism and a home "for erudite and well-mannered debate" (Arango 2008). In this conservative setting, intellectualism and education are highly valued; those conservative elites who trained in Buckley's model (such as David Frum and David Brooks, quoted here) did not seem so focused on Palin's intelligence or lack of intelligence in their public commentary during the campaign. Far more interesting was Palin's willingness and seemingly instinctive ability to take on the party strategy built on language ideology, confrontational rhetorical style and class conflicts:

> But over the past few decades, the Republican Party has driven away people who live in cities, in highly educated regions and on the coasts. This expulsion has had many causes. But the big one is this: Republican political tacticians decided to mobilize their coalition with a form of social class warfare . . . The nation is divided between the wholesome Joe Sixpacks in the heartland and the oversophisticated, overeducated, oversecularized denizens of the coasts. What had been a disdain for liberal intellectuals slipped into a disdain for the educated class as a whole
>
> (Brooks 2008)

Boxing Obama

> [O]ur most brilliant presidents often work hard to seem publicly dumb in order to avoid the stain of elitism.
>
> Lim, *The Anti-Intellectual Presidency: The Decline of Presidential Rhetoric from George Washington to George W. Bush*, 2008

Lim based the observation above on his study of presidential speech between 1913 and the end of the George W. Bush administration. His quantitative analysis of the presidential speeches provided some surprising observations:

- Between 1913 and 2008, the length of the average presidential sentence fell from 35 words to 22.
- Between the advent of broadcast media and George W. Bush's last day in office, sound bites declined in length from 42 seconds to 7.
- In the first decade of the 1900s, presidential speeches were pitched at a college reading level; by 2008, the level was closer to eighth grade.

Where and why the overt dislike and distrust of intellectualism originated is a question that requires more close study and thought than can be taken up in this volume. What can be said with certainty is that in the current day, politicians and media both employ anti-intellectualism to appeal to what may be the larger portion of the voting (and money-spending) population.

This was especially the case during the George W. Bush administration. "As he takes to the road to salvage his presidency, Bush is letting down his guard and playing up his anti-intellectual, regular-guy image" (Baker 2006). In a book that has seen multiple editions and reprintings, the conservative popular historian Paul Johnson makes no bones about his distrust of all things intellectual: "Beware intellectuals. Not merely should they be kept well away from the levers of power, they should also be objects of suspicion when they seek to offer collective advice" (1988: 342).[18]

With the election of Senator Barack Obama to the office of president, anti-intellectualism has continued to escalate at a rapid pace. In Obama's case, allusions to education and elitism are complicated by race.

The media – specifically Fox News commentators – have played a large role in framing Obama as an out-of-touch elite, an intellectual who doesn't understand and harbors disdain for the common man. Discussions of Obama as an elitist often skew toward the silly, as was the case when the president stopped to have lunch at an Arlington, Virginia, diner on May 5, 2009. Commentators and newscasters including Sean Hannity, Laura Ingraham, Mark Steyn, Rush Limbaugh along with dozens of bloggers and a Cornell law professor all joined forces in deriding Obama's preference for Dijon mustard. The implication was that American mustard wasn't good enough for the president. Six days later, the Dijon débâcle had reached the mainstream media and Jason Linkins of *The Huffington Post* declared that this attack on Obama's choice of condiments had become a full-blown right-wing talking point (see Media Matters for America, 7 May 2009, for a summary of Dijon-gate commentary).

At first, many saw the election of an African American to the highest office in the country as a huge step forward in race relations. But racism in the United States did not go away with the Emancipation Proclamation or the Civil Rights Act, and it did not disappear with Obama's election. Those who think in racist terms – at least those who depend on public opinion for their jobs – know better than to voice racist opinions openly. On the surface at least, overt racism is rejected by all institutions, including the mainstream media. Nevertheless, prejudiced sentiments are still voiced, but by use of code words or euphemisms. During the 2008 campaign and the first year of Obama's presidency there was ample opportunity to watch such rhetorical strategies develop.

Code words can be used to a politician's advantage in reaching a specific audience within an audience. One African American journalist drew attention to the way that [Obama's] "language, mannerisms and symbols resonate deeply with his Black supporters, even as the references largely sail over the heads of white audiences."

In a similar way, George W. Bush used certain phrases that were meant to be understood by conservative Christians. This targeting of one audience is sometimes referred to as "dog-whistle rhetoric," a reference to the way that it is possible to get a dog's attention by blowing a whistle that humans cannot hear. The use of code words permits public mention of otherwise taboo topics. Terms such as "equal opportunity" or "quota" are clear signals that can be read as follows: "I can't say this aloud because it will get me in trouble, but I don't like affirmative action, and I think quotas reward those who don't deserve it."

Public comments about Senator Obama during the campaign and after ranged from highly charged to subtle code words. The comments in Table 8.1 all come from politicians, government officials and media representatives.

In the examples provided, the most startling and openly racist is the use of the word "boy" to refer to President Obama. In Ash v. Tyson Foods (2006) the Supreme Court ruled that under certain circumstances, calling an African American male "boy" was indeed evidence of discriminatory intent. Not every use of the word could be considered racist or discriminatory, but "it does not follow that the term, standing alone, is always benign. The speaker's meaning may depend on various factors including context, inflection, tone of voice, local custom, and historical usage" (Ash v. Tyson Foods 2006).

Almost as evocative and offensive as "boy" is the word "uppity." In the South especially, the use of "uppity" to describe an African American is a strong expression of condemnation. It is a way of chastising someone who aspires to more than is his or her place in life, in terms of education or lifestyle. A person who didn't show subservience – specifically an African American who insisted on living a full life – was "uppity."

In the wake of criticism of Representative Lynn Westmoreland's use of the word (*The Washington Post*, September 4, 2008), he steadfastly claimed he didn't know that "uppity" had racist connotations, an assertion that did not fall into the realm of plausible deniability.[19] So outrageous was Westmoreland's assertion of ignorance that other prominent Republicans from the South spoke openly and critically of the incident:

Table 8.1 Public comments made during the 2008 presidential election cycle

Quote	Origin	Citation
"That boy's finger does not need to be on the [nuclear war] button."	Representative Geoff Davis, Republican of Kentucky	2008. "Barack Obama, John McCain and the Language of Race." *The New York Times.* September 22
"Just from what little I've seen of her and Mister Obama, Senator Obama, they're a member of an elitist class individual that thinks that they're uppity."	Representative Lynn Westmoreland, Republican of Georgia	2008. Georgia GOP Congressman Calls Obama "Uppity." *The Washington Post.* September 4
"On the one side you have the concern of being viewed as the angry Black man, then on the other side you run the risk of looking like someone who's uppity. And I think the concern I have for Senator Obama is that he's bumping up against that uppity line . . . [he is] unbelievably presumptuous, egomaniacal."	Jonathan Capehart of *The Washington Post*	Commentary on *The Morning Joe.* MSNBC. July 30, 2008
"I forgot he was Black tonight, for an hour. You know he's gone a long way to become a leader of this country . . . wait a minute, he's an African American guy in front of a bunch of white people and there he is, president of the United States and we've forgotten that [he's African American] tonight."	Chris Matthews, political commentator	Live broadcast after the Presidential State of the Union Address. MSNBC. January 27, 2010
"If President George W. Bush got slapped around for being inarticulate, is Obama obnoxiously articulate?"	Liz Sidoti, Associated Press	2009. "In a Skeptical Age, Obama Is Government's Face." *AP News.* October 13
"He's charismatic, he's articulate, he's a very strong figure on the national stage. But something tells me that people are going to say [they want] experience and depth. As a result it's going to be, 'Can he live up to the standards?'"	Karl Rove, Republican Advisor	2007. "Rove: Obama 'Articulate' but Inexperienced." *Politics.* CNN.com. March 9
"I mean, you got the first mainstream African-American who is articulate and bright and clean and a nice-looking guy. I mean, that's a storybook, man."	Senator Joe Biden Democrat of Delaware	2007. "Biden's Description of Obama Draws Scrutiny." *Politics.* CNN.com. February 9
"But his biggest advantage could be his persona – young, attractive, articulate, a fresh face."	Anonymous editorial	2007. *Christian Science Monitor.* January 17
"Look at the health care bill. It was his number one priority. It took him forever to get it through and he had to compromise it to death." And a version of, "Listen he's a nice person, he's very articulate," this is what's been used against him, "but he couldn't sell watermelons if it, you gave him the state troopers to flag down the traffic."	Dan Rather, news anchor and commentator	2010. Commentary made on *The Chris Matthews Show.* MSNBC. March 8
"You know who voted for it? You might never know. That one. [inclining head toward Senator Obama] You know who voted against it? Me."	Senator John McCain Republican of Arizona	Second debate between the candidates, October 7, 2008
"[Obama's] an attractive guy. He's articulate. I have been impressed with him when I have seen him in person. But he's got a long way to go to be president."	George W. Bush	From an interview on *Your World with Neil Cavuto,* Fox News. January 31, 2007
Mr. Obama and his well practiced, articulate diction seem to be more of a focus of attention than the prime time line-up.	David Brezler	Examiner.com, January 26, 2011

There has been a very intentional effort to paint [Obama] as somebody outside the mainstream, other, "he's not one of us." I think the McCain campaign has been scrupulous about not directly saying it, but it's the subtext of this campaign. Everybody knows that. There are certain kinds of signals. As a native of the South, I can tell you, when you see this Charlton Heston ad, "The One," that's code for, "he's uppity, he ought to stay in his place." Everybody gets that who is from a Southern background. We all understand that. When McCain comes out and starts talking about affirmative action, "I'm against quotas," we get what that's about.

(August 3, 2008)

During the campaign detractors often used "arrogant" and "elite" in their criticisms of Obama. This was not entirely a matter of chance, as was made clear in an anonymous Republican campaign strategy memo that was came into the public domain shortly before the election:

The tactics that got [the Republican Party] to mid-September in a tie are not going to get them to 50 percent plus one in November. They need . . . an eye toward driving out the range of contrast that makes McCain different from Obama (action-oriented rhetoric v. grand prose; accessible v. uppity; humble servant of country v. arrogant.

(Allen 2008)

Of the terms discussed here (there are many others deserving examination), "articulate" may be the most opaque to those who are not African American (Robinson 2007; Clementson 2007). In her article "The racial politics of speaking well," Clementson interviewed successful African Americans to get their reactions to the word "articulate," with some interesting results: "Al Sharpton is incredibly articulate. But because he speaks with a cadence and style that is firmly rooted in black rhetorical tradition you will rarely hear white people refer to him as articulate" (Trisha Rose, as quoted in Clementson 2007).[20]

To call any person of color "articulate" is to express surprise at the high quality of that person's rhetorical skills. A similar but less direct pseudo-compliment sounds something like "you speak so well," which is usually taken as "you speak so well for an African American," or "you speak so well in comparison to other Asians." John McWhorter, a sociolinguist, conservative commentator and an African American, reports one such experience, in which someone wrote a letter to praise him for speaking *SAE "confidently," which he found to be insulting: "as if I have to take a deep breath and 'wield' [*SAE] and feel like I'm a pretty special fella for being able to, with my 'native' ghetto inflections and expressions turning up in my speech when I'm tired" (McWhorter, January 9, 2010).

Senator Harry Reid, a Democrat, was widely criticized when his comments on Obama were made public. Reportedly Reid talked about the fact that the Senator was "light skinned" and that he spoke "with no Negro dialect, unless he wanted to have one" (Heilemann and Halperin 2010: 37).

Obama accepted Reid's public apology with good grace. Part of the reason for that easy acceptance may well have had to do with the fact that Obama is indeed bidialectal, something he acknowledges himself. In his audiobook recording of his biographical *Dreams of my Father*, long passages are written in scene, with dialog reconstructed from remembered conversations. Obama shows a real talent for voicing people from many different cultures and language communities. He voices himself as an 18-year-old in conversation with other Black men, switching back and forth between *SAE and AAVE easily: "I learned to slip back and forth between my Black and white worlds, understanding that each possessed its own language and customs and structures of meaning" (Obama 2004: 82).

During the campaign Obama demonstrated his ability to shift into AAVE intonation and style on occasion. When Obama was paying the tab after lunch at a diner, the African American cashier asked him whether he wanted change, to which Obama said, "Nah, we straight." This small example of his ability to shift into AAVE was caught on tape, and reported on in a very limited way (March 10, 2009).

It is interesting to note that conservative commentators would try to drum up negative feelings for President Obama on the basis of his preferred mustard, but fail to draw attention to the fact that he can – and does – speak a highly stigmatized variety of English in some situations. Did the news media simply not notice these events when they happened, or did they choose not to comment because the topic was too sensitive? They had no such reservations when commenting on Sarah Palin's variety of English. So why the disparate treatment?

After the 2008 election, the conservative news media commentary about Obama intensified. The most extreme public commentary originated from people like Bill O'Reilly, Rush Limbaugh and Glenn Beck, who did not hesitate to use words like "bloodsucker," "socialism," and "fascism" in reference to the president. Radio news commentator Lee Rodgers claimed Obama "clearly is more sympathetic with the long-term goals of world communism, and let's be blunt about it, Muslim terrorists, than with any legitimate American goals" (*The Lee Rodgers Show*, March 11, 2009).

Joe Scarborough is a MSNBC cable news commentator and former member of the House of Representatives, a native of Florida and a prominent Republican with a large following. In commenting on Obama's policies, he lamented that under Obama the country is "moving closer toward European-style socialism . . . That's not a right-wing claim, it's the truth" (*Morning Joe*, MSNBC, March 4, 2009).

People may consider such outbursts nothing more than overblown rhetoric designed to draw a larger audience or sell more newspapers, but constant repetition of misleading, frightening images will take hold, regardless of the original intent.

The media played a significant role in the 2008 election, one that reached far beyond objective reporting. For both Palin and Obama, the variety of English spoken by the candidate became the focus, a way to draw attention to facts or events which could not be raised otherwise within the confines of what is socially acceptable. Potential concern about Palin's working-class, rural connections (real or embellished) was subverted into a discussion of her syntax and "g-dropping." In Obama's case, the unvoiced questions were more complex and touched on highly explosive topics, such as "Can we trust an African American man who sounds like Obama?"

The questions raised by the media may be sensible or silly, constructive or disruptive, but the importance or relevance of those questions does not determine how successfully they will take root in the public's mind. The media can make things come true by simple repetition, or proof by assertion. A demonstrably false claim that is constantly repeated will gain a foothold. This is a tactic that doesn't always work, but it seems to be particularly successful in political contexts. When it does work, the constant repetition may wear down the opposition so that they retreat or surrender, at which point the proof by assentation is complete.

The power of the media in the political process can hardly be underestimated, and one of the most important tools to this end is the language subordination process.

DISCUSSION QUESTIONS AND EXERCISES

- This chapter opened with a quote from Mark Crispin Miller who is associated with *The Project on Media Ownership* at Johns Hopkins University. Use the internet to learn about the project, its goals and approaches, and consider Miller's comment in that context before discussing it. In your first reaction, did you feel Miller's position was polemic and exaggerated, or did you accept the concepts more easily? What factors in your own life and experience inform your reactions to such statements?
- Consider the statement made above on p. 131 by a National Public Radio representative. Note the use of passive construction "NPR is considered by many" and ambiguous "people say" claims. What does the speaker mean specifically by the words "cleanest" and "crisp"? What is the unstated opposite?
- The following excerpt from *The Providence Journal Bulletin* is presented as news. How does it incorporate stages in the underlying language subordination process?

  No matter how qualified a person is, a voice twisted by regional or ethnic influences can be a stumbling block socially and professionally. If others can't understand you or your words are too richly flavored with down-home spice, you could find all your skill and intelligence thwarted by a telltale tongue.

  ("Voice of success silences dialect."
  The Providence Journal Bulletin, April 1994)

- What is the role of the news media in today's society? What rights and responsibilities do the media have? How have those things changed over the past 50 years? Consider this newspaper excerpt from a short report on the front page of *The Evening Record* (Ellensburg, Washington) of November 22, 1937 in your reply:

  President Roosevelt refused today to concede he used bad grammar. Shown an open letter by Professor Janet R. Aiken of Columbia University questioning his grammar in recent speeches, the president smilingly blamed newsmen who reported his extemporaneous remarks. . . . In her letter, Dr. Aiken wanted to know: "Did you learn how to [talk] that way at Groton or Harvard or where?"

- What does "manufactured authority" or "manufacturing authority" mean? What would be its opposite?
- Consider the following quotes from newspaper reports on accent reduction or elimination classes. What kind of imagery is used? Are logical fallacies evident?

January 1989

"Speak English, Troops"

Speech pathologists trained to combat foreign accents are doing big business in multi-ethnic California . . .

The influx of Asian and Hispanic immigrants has created strong demand for English-language training and accent-modification courses. Many foreign-born professionals believe that their accents impede their careers, and they are prepared to pay hundreds of dollars to free their English from traces of their homelands . . . A person with a heavy accent may start his or her career in a technical job where few speaking skills are required, but advancement usually brings a greater emphasis on communication. An employee who is difficult to understand may be shrugged off as stupid or simply passed over in favor of someone who speaks clear English.

- Read John McWhorter's editorial response to the public controversy around Senator Reid's "no Negro dialect" comment (McWhorter 2010) at http://xrl.in/500k. McWhorter is a sociolinguist and an African-American. Does anything surprise you about his position? In what points might you agree?
- How has the meaning of the word "spin" changed over the past 20 years? What do you understand it to be? Why do people choose to say "That's just spin," rather than explain the beliefs that cause them to reject the message?
- Imagine you walk into a meeting room and somebody comes up to you, looks you up and down, and smiling broadly, says, "Congratulations! You buttoned your shirt correctly!" How is this like (or not like) African American objections to being called articulate?
- Consider this idea from Tim Wise's *Between Barack and a Hard Place: Racism and White Denial in the Age of Obama* (2009). Wise proposes that racism has evolved to look like "enlightened exceptionalism . . . that allows for and even celebrates the achievements of individual persons of color . . . because they are seen as different from a less appealing, even pathological Black or brown rule" (ibid.: 9). Beyond the use of the word "articulate" in describing President Obama, is there other evidence of this kind of enlightened exceptionalism in the media's commentary on Obama's language, or more generally?

Notes

1 Here the terms "mass media" and "public media" are used interchangeably to mean communication formats designed to reach a large audience, for example, as in a nation-wide broadcast of a presidential speech. Traditionally "mass media" is understood to include nationwide radio, large circulation newspapers and magazines, and television. "News media," by contrast, refers to the communication of information about current events, at least in part, and encompasses broadcast, print, and internet sources.

2 The issue of bilingualism and discrimination in the workplace linked to bilingualism is relevant here, but for the moment the discussion is restricted to native speakers of English.

3 Other broadcasters have been described as *voices of authority*, as well. For example, the phrase was heard in connection with Walter Cronkite especially at the time of his death in 2009.

4 The broadcast news data cited here originates from the Television News Archives at Vanderbilt University. The archive has tape of ABC, NBC and CBS national news

broadcasts for every day since the mid-1960s; all of these are indexed. The archive also includes MacNeil-Lehrer and CNN Headline News reports since those services began, but those broadcasts are not indexed. All of the reports I was able to find were from the big three networks, which have been supplemented with other reports from my own daily viewing notes. The sources, in order of presentation: *CBS Evening News*, 1984; *San Jose Mercury News*, October 18, 1984; *The Providence Journal Bulletin*, April 1994; *NBC Evening News*, April 1993.

5 Language as a social tool is a human trait and not specific to any country. The process whereby authority in matters of language is seized has been widely institutionalized. In France, L'Académie française publishes an official French dictionary and is probably the best known institution of its kind. However, many countries and nation-states have institutions to promote what is believed to be the "right" or "proper" variety of language. Hindi, Korean, Foroese, Danish, Wolof are just a few examples.

6 Hermann and Chomsky's *Manufacturing Consent: The Political Economy of the Mass Media* was first published in 1988 with a second edition dated 2002. This collection of case studies provides a propaganda model composed of a number of news filters, which expose, for example, the way *The New York Times* took on the government's official position and thus promoted militarism and the Vietnam War. This is a seminal work for anyone interested in critical language studies.

7 There is a class of popular newspapers which takes a markedly different approach, which seems to be: anything that will sell a paper, no matter how outrageous or misleading, goes up front and center. The rest of this chapter excludes discussion of tabloids.

8 For example, in December 2005, Congress passed the Defense Authorization Act which granted exemption from the Freedom of Information Act to the Pentagon and the Department of Defense. This story was absent from almost all broadcast and newspaper news reports, despite its relevance to the freedom of the press.

9 See, for example, Jane Hill's analysis of the incident that led to former Senator Trent Lott's resignation as Majority Leader of the Senate, in which the mainstream media attempted to ignore an unambiguously racist statement until it was brought to public attention by prominent bloggers.

10 Fox News and MSNBC are perhaps the most openly partisan television news outlets. This is not to say that all media representatives from other outlets were strictly objective; there is plenty of evidence to show that this is not the case.

11 When a politician tries and fails to style shift to be more in line with the audience, the media can be merciless. Such an event happened during the 2008 campaign, when Hillary Clinton allegedly attempted to sound African American or Southern when addressing a primarily African American audience in Selma, Alabama. See Media Matters for America (http://mediamatters.org/research/200709130001).

12 See Heflick and Goldenberg (2009) on the objectification of Sarah Palin.

13 Overt sexism in the media was not restricted to male commentators: "Kristan, we've talked this morning about whether a mother of five can handle being the vice president. Who looks after the kids when she's working? Do you know?" (Maggie Rodriguez, CBS, *Early Show*). Nor was Palin the only woman to experience sexism – both overt and covert – in the 2008 election cycle. Such incidents (as in the example of men shouting "Iron my shirt!" at a Hillary Clinton rally) were rarely covered in any depth.

14 Purnell, Raimy and Salmons conducted an extensive study of Palin's speech; among other avenues of inquiry, they examined historical settlement patterns and how movement of ethnic groups contributed to Wasillian English. They examined the way certain phonetic features contribute to the national perception of Palin's English as Upper Midwestern.

15 These and similar subjects became hot topics for discussion online. For example, see
    http://xrl.in/4xcm where blogger Sisyphusshrugged presents evidence of what he has
    called Palin's Intermittent Gunderson Syndrome. The term is a reference in a
    character in the movie *Fargo*. Marge Gunderson is a Minnesotan with strong regional
    language features; the intermittent syndrome is a reference to the fact that Sarah Palin
    allegedly slips in and out of this accent in a way that is inauthentic. See also this post:
    http://xrl.in/4xdn from Shots in the Dark which explains very clearly how the author
    connects certain language uses with intelligence, or lack of intelligence, in the case of
    Sarah Palin.

16 The word "nuclear" became a focus of debate among linguists as well as media com-
    mentators. Nunberg provides an objective look at the debate, the variable pronun-
    ciation, and the social significance of the word. ("Going nucular: Language, politics,
    and culture in confrontational times," Nunberg 2006.)

17 In addition to Lim's work on anti-intellectualism discussed briefly in this chapter, there
    is a great deal of work on the complex links between ideology, rhetoric and anti-
    intellectualism that began with the 1963 publication of Hofstadter's *Anti-intellectualism
    in American Life*. See also Gonzalez (2009), Brooks (2008), Savage (2008) and Gitlin
    (2000).

18 I must point out that this statement, blunt and uncompromising as it may be, can be
    adapted to discussion of any group. "Beware religious conservatives . . ."

19 Westmoreland issued this statement on September 8, 2008: "I've never heard that
    term [uppity] used in a racially derogatory sense. It is important to note that the
    dictionary definition of 'uppity' is 'affecting an air of inflated self-esteem – snobbish.'
    That's what we meant by uppity when we used it in the mill village where I grew up."

20 At the same time Clementson is pointing out the bigotry implicit in calling an African
    American "articulate," she points out:

> With the ballooning size of the black middle and upper class, qualities in
> blacks like intelligence, eloquence – *the mere ability to string sentences together
> with tenses intact* – must at some point become as unremarkable to whites
> as they are to blacks.
>
> (Clementson 2007; emphasis added)

This narrow definition of acceptable English (with tenses intact) is one that is echoed
by other prominent African Americans and undercuts the primary argument, though
the writer seems unaware of this.

Suggested further reading

Gitlin, T. (1980) *The Whole World Is Watching: Mass Media in the Making and Unmaking
of the New Left*. Berkeley, CA: University of California Press.

Herman, E.S. and Chomsky, N. (2002) *Manufacturing Consent: The Political Economy of the
Mass Media*. New York: Pantheon Books.

Media Matters for America (2009) Emerging Culture of Paranoia. April 13. Available at:
http://xrl.in/567u.

Popp, R.K. (2006) Mass Media and the Linguistic Marketplace: Media, Language, and
Distinction. *Journal of Communication Inquiry* 30(1): 5–20.

Real people with a real language 9

The workplace and the judicial system

I am from India. Now a US citizen and live in USA for about 24 years. I had my University education in USA. After my PhD and 6 years of employment now I am unemployed and unable to secure a job. Recently I applied for a job . . . The employer called, told me that it was a prescreening interview. She told me she likes everything about me, but she does not like my accent. She said, as a part of the job I need to do telephone interviews . . . She also said she called me first, because she does not want to waste time . . . when it comes to hiring and promotion, my opportunity for advancement is clearly based on my accent.

> Anonymous commenter, http://www.theworkbuzz.com, October 27, 2010

I never thought about my accent much while I was living in Mississippi. My family had been there over 200 years . . . I moved to Texas and once again, my accent came under fire. I even overheard my boss talking to a coworker one day; she said, "If I'd known how bad her accent was, I never would have hired her."

> Anonymous commenter, http://www.antimoon.com/, December 18, 2005

The nutshell

Title VII of the Civil Rights Act was designed (in part) to protect workers from discrimination on the basis of race, ethnicity, national origin, sex, age and other protected categories, or traits directly linked to those categories. The Equal Employment Opportunity Commission (EEOC) provides directives on national origin discrimination with multiple examples of what does, and does not constitute discriminatory behavior (Equal Employment Opportunity Commission 2002).

While employers will often go to great lengths to cloak discrimination, sometimes there is direct evidence as in the case of Sergio Fonseca, a native of Guatemala and a native speaker of English, who sued his employer for discrimination on the basis of national origin. In 2004, the United States Court of Appeals, Ninth Circuit found Fonseca's case had merit, in part because of evidence like this:

> Fonseca went to tell [his supervisor] Peterson about a problem with the new computer system. Peterson was familiar with the problem, and Fonseca spoke clearly, but Peterson pretended not to understand Fonseca. Fonseca repeated himself more than once while Peterson laughed at him and mocked his accent and repetition.
>
> (Fonseca v. Sysco 2004)

More often employers who are actually guilty of discriminatory practices will try to prove to the court that they had a legal and reasonable motivation for their actions. This is where the courts become complicit.

The Civil Rights Act

With the passage of the 1964 Civil Rights Act (Pub. L. 88-352, 78 Stat. 241), some types of discrimination in the workplace have been illegal under Title VII. In broad terms, Title VII makes it illegal to deny a person employment, promotion or workplace advantages (benefits, use of facilities). The scope of the law is limited to protected categories (also referred to as classes) which are: race, color, national origin, sex, or religion. This protection extends to associations, which means simply this: You cannot refuse to hire Asians, nor can you refuse to hire someone who is married or otherwise interacts with Asians.

Title VII also acknowledges those characteristics or traits that are inextricably linked to protected categories. For example, an employer cannot fire an employee for wearing a head covering that is required by his or her religion. This would apply to a Muslim female who wears a hijab, or a Jewish male who wears a yarmulke.[1] Nor can an employer discriminate against an employee or applicant on the basis of stereotypes and assumptions, even if they are not factually true.

In the case of racial discrimination,[2] "It is clearly forbidden by Title VII to refuse on racial grounds to hire someone because your customers or clients do not like his race" (Matsuda 1991: 1376).[3] Similarly, a qualified person may not be rejected on the basis of linguistic traits linked to a protected category. In contrast to racial discrimination, however, an employer has some latitude in matters of language: "[a]n adverse employment decision may be predicated upon an individual's accent when – but only when – it interferes materially with job performance" (Civil Rights Act of 1964, §701 et seq., 42 U.S.C.A. §2000e et seq.). The problem, as we'll see, is the lack of parameters. For example, what does "materially" mean in this context?

The EEOC released updated Compliance Manual for national origin discrimination in 2002, which addresses the issue of accent directly:

> Linguistic characteristics are closely related to national origin, and basing employment decisions on a qualified individual's foreign accent or limited ability to speak English may constitute national origin discrimination. Not all employment decisions based on linguistic characteristics will violate Title VII, however. The EEOC guidelines state, for example, that a business with a diverse clientele may lawfully assign work based on an employee's ability to speak a foreign language. In addition, an employment decision based on a foreign accent will not violate Title VII if the individual's accent materially interferes with his or her ability to perform a job. For example, if effective communication in English is required to perform a job and an individual's accent materially interferes with the ability to communicate in English, rejecting the individual for the job because of the accent would not violate Title VII.
>
> (Equal Employment Opportunity Commission 2002)

District courts have sometimes "shown some deference to the EEOC guidelines or have at least used the guidelines to help inform their analyses" but at the same time the courts are free to ignore the guidelines and have sometimes simply denied their relevance (Robinson 2008: 1528). A court that takes such a stance is making it easier for an employer to defend his or her decision not to hire or promote. The employer is required to convince the court that the decisions made were not discriminatory:

- By demonstrating that the individual's English language skills were insufficient to meet the employer's needs (Cutler 1985; Matsuda 1991; Oppenheimer 2010; Robinson 2008; The Legal Aid Society 2009; Vertreace 2010).
- By establishing a bona fide occupational qualification (BFOQ). The BFOQ is the more difficult case for the employer. The path taken depends on which of two different theories of liability is used. Disparate treatment, in which proof of discriminatory intent is crucial, requires a BFOQ defense; for disparate impact, in which such proof is not required, the employer must establish only business necessity:

> The Plaintiff makes out a prima facie case by showing that the employer's selection device has a substantially adverse impact on his protected group [. . .] it remains open to the plaintiff to show that "other . . . selection devices, without a similarly undesirable . . . effect, would also serve the employer's legitimate interest[s]."
>
> (Cutler 1985: 1169)

The employer must convince the court that there was a legitimate business necessity that precluded hiring the person in question. The trick is to find and document what legal scholars call "second generation discrimination" because "Trait discrimination of this sort is increasingly at the core of Title VII litigation" (Yuracko 2006).

> Unequal treatment may result from cognitive or unconscious bias, rather than deliberate, intentional exclusion. "Second generation" claims involve social practices and patterns of interaction among groups within the workplace that, over time, exclude no dominant groups. Exclusion is frequently difficult to trace directly to intentional, discrete actions of particular actors, and may sometimes be visible only in the aggregate.
>
> (Sturm 2001: 460)[4]

In terms of language-focused discrimination, Title VII has one large limitation: Under the law as it currently stands, only those language traits tied to a national origin outside the U.S. are covered. If a person from Sweden, Thailand or South Africa believes he or she has been discriminated against on the basis of accent, the EEOC provides advice and legal assistance. A person from Appalachia, on the other hand, would have no recourse under Title VII. Appalachian English cannot be identified as originating outside the U.S. in any way that would satisfy the courts.

There is little consistency in the way the courts approach issues of communication and accent. One assumes that the legal system is unbiased, and sometimes there is evidence of that. Just as often, however, the courts are willing to put their own beliefs and language ideologies first, even when those beliefs are directly contradicted by expert testimony (see especially Fragante, below).

In the current day it is hard to imagine a judge or jury simply refusing to believe testimony from a geneticist, biochemist, or DNA expert. But language is deceptively approachable, and everyone who has reached a certain level of education feels empowered. As we will see in the Kahakua case, a judge may choose to believe one expert over another simply because one of them provides an opinion that very closely matches his own personal opinions.

Rarely do the courts explore the meaning of the word "communication," nor are there any widely accepted and used methodologies to assess the communication demands of a given job in a non-prejudicial way.

The legal process[5]

Alleged language-focused national origin discrimination cases usually begin when an individual files a complaint with the EEOC (or a similar agency on a state or local level). The employee may then file a civil action in the trial courts, in which he or she claims that civil liberties (as set out in the federal statutes known as the Civil Rights Act of 1964) have been violated.

In some instances, these cases are brought to the courts not by the individual or group of individuals with the same complaint, but by a private agency acting for the injured party, such as the ACLU, or by a government agency, such as the EEOC. This action may be initiated at the state level, as many states have adopted civil liberties legislation patterned on the federal statutes.[6]

An individual claiming language-focused discrimination must first prove a prima facie case of disparate treatment in four steps:

1   establishment of identifiable national origin;
2   proof of application for a job for which he or she was qualified, and for which the employer was seeking applicants;
3   that he or she was rejected in spite of adequate qualifications; and
4   that after such rejection, the job remained open and the employer continued to seek applicants with the Plaintiff's qualifications.

After a *prima facie* case has been established, the burden of proof shifts to the employer, who must convince the court that there was a legitimate reason to fire or turn away the person with the accent. If the employer does this, the burden shifts back to the Plaintiff to show that the purported reason for the action was pretext (that is, an excuse) for invidious discrimination. The Plaintiff must prove that the employer was motivated by discriminatory reasons, or otherwise prove that the reason given by the employer is simply not believable (Civil Rights Act of 1964, €701 et seq., 42 U.S.C.A. 2000e et seq.). Figure 9.1 shows the number of Title VII language focused complaints tried in the period 1972–1994.

Discrimination in the workplace

In an excellent study of language and discrimination in the workplace in Great Britain, Roberts, Davies and Jupp (1992) provide numerous examples of discrimination focused on language, and directed toward ethnic and racial minorities. No such systematic and well-documented study exists for workers in the United States. The evidence of discrimination provided here is limited to specific instances which have found their way into the legal system and represents what is most likely a very small fraction of the whole.

Here the discussion is based on 25 language-focused national origin discrimination cases that were heard in the federal and state courts and by the EEOC between 1972 and 1993, with exceptions as noted.[7] More recent cases are brought into the discussion, but they are not included in any statistics seen here. In some of the cases included, both racial and

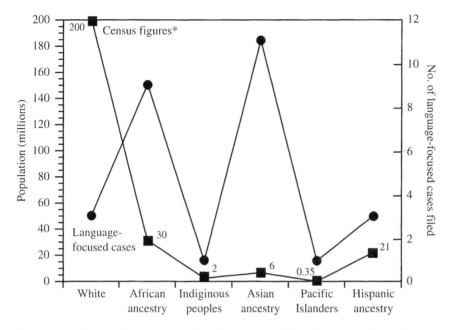

Figure 9.1 U.S. population by race and relative number of Title VII language-focused complaints tried, 1972–1994. (Figures rounded. "Hispanic" may be any race)

Source: U.S. Census 1990

national origin discrimination were at issue. In most of the cases, accent, language use and communication figured prominently in the testimony, argumentation, discussion and final opinion.[8] Table 9.1 provides an overview.

How widespread is language-focused discrimination? The General Accounting Office of the United States Government (GAO GGD 90-62 Employer Sanctions: 27) conducted a carefully designed statistical study of a stratified random sample of employers nationwide, and reported that 10 percent of their sample, or 461,000 companies employing millions of persons, openly, if naively admit that they "discriminated on the basis of a person's foreign appearance or accent" (ibid.: 38). In hiring audits specifically designed to detect discrimination on the basis of accent (telephone inquiries about advertised jobs), such discrimination was found to be prevalent (ibid.).[9] This behavior was documented again in Carroll v. Elliott Personnel Services (1985), when an employment agency receptionist was directed by her manager to screen all persons inquiring over the telephone: to those who did not "speak right," the job was closed. Carroll was also told to make notations about the caller's speech and accent. Carroll sued on the grounds that her employer was compelling her to break the law, and she won her case.

There are a number of possible reasons for the low number of documented cases, some of which include:

● employers who discriminate may do so in a sophisticated and subtle way;
● the persons discriminated against are so accustomed to this treatment that they no longer react;
● if they are aware of the treatment, they may not know that they have legal recourse, or how to pursue it;

Table 9.1 Distribution of 25 language-focused discrimination cases in the courts/ EEOC hearings by plaintiff's national origin

Plaintiff's national origin	No. cases filed	Court found for	
		Plaintiff	Defendant
ASIA, PACIFIC RIM			
The Philippines: Lubitz, Fragante, Carino	3	1	2
Vietnam: Tran	1	0	1
China: Ang, Hou	2	0	2
India: Duddey, Mandhare, Patel	3	1	1
Cambodia: Xieng	1	1	0
Korea: Park	1	1	0
	11	4	6
CARIBBEAN/WEST INDIES			
Dominican Republic: Meijia	1	0	1
Haiti: Stephen	1	0	1
Cuba: Rodriquez	1	0	1
	3	0	3
CENTRAL/SOUTH AMERICA			
Venezuela: Dercach	1	0	1
Bolivia: Ipina	1	0	1
	2	0	2
EASTERN EUROPE			
Armenia: Vartivarian	1	0	1
Poland: Berke	1	1	0
Ukraine: Staruch	1	0	1
	3	1	2
AFRICA			
Nigeria: Dabor	1	0	1
Liberia: Andrews	1	0	0
Ghana: Kpodo	1	0	0
	3	0	1
OTHER			
African-American: Sparks, Edwards	2	2	0
Hawaiian-Creole: Kahakua	1	0	1
	3	2	1
Total	25	7	15

● complaints are handled internally or mediated by an outside party, and resolved before litigation becomes necessary.

Of course, many discriminated against on the basis of language may not find anything surprising or wrong about that fact. This is, after all, not the only society in the world that promotes a standard language ideology.

The bulk of the burden seems to fall, predictably, on the disenfranchised and the unassimilated. Cutler claims that the manner of enforcement of Title VII "permits an employer to reject qualified applicants of a particular national origin as long as he hires more assimilated applicants of the same origin instead" (Cutler 1985: 1164).

Once on the stand in a courtroom, what do the employers offer in the way of excuse? The approaches taken by defendants range from the naively and openly discriminatory to the understated:

Sophia Poskocil, originally of Colombia and a native Spanish speaker, was repeatedly passed over for a position in the Roanoke, Virginia, school system. This despite the fact that she had an excellent education at a U.S. college, solid experience and outstanding letters of reference. Poskocil sued under Title VII:

> During the trial, evidence was introduced that the school district based its decision not to hire Poskocil on student evaluations. Students in Poskocil's Northside High School class complained that Poskocil was difficult to understand because of her foreign accent. In their evaluations, students wrote, among other things, that the "instructor [Sophia Poskocil] *barely spoke English*, [and] was hard to understand." Ultimately, the district court granted summary judgment in favor of the school district, stating that the plaintiff failed to demonstrate that the county discriminated against her. What is disturbing about the case is that Poskocil was not applying to teach a high school English class, which might have made the students' complaints more relevant, but rather Poskocil was applying to teach Spanish classes. Moreover, it appears that no one at her trial had a difficult time understanding her.
>
> (Smith 2005: 253)

In Willamina, Oregon, the postmaster was harassed and threatened with physical violence:

> Galdamez began to receive hostile comments from customers and other residents based on her race, accent, and national origin almost immediately upon taking the job [of postmaster] in Willamina. Several customers, including the mayor, expressed displeasure with having a Hispanic postmaster or criticized her accented English. One local newspaper referred to Galdamez's "thick accent from her native Honduras" in explaining that she had not "made friends in some quarters" and was the object of an ouster campaign.
>
> (Galdamez v. John Potter, Postmaster General 2004)

In Indiana:

> [I]n offering examples of Mr. Dercach's communication problems, Mr. M. explained that workers would ask Mr. Dercach what he wanted them to do, and then simply walk away, unable to understand. Mr. M. refused to attribute such incidents to Mr. Dercach's accent, but offered no other explanation. He said they just couldn't understand him "like normal people with normal language."
>
> (Dercach v. Indiana Department of Highways 1987)

Florida:

> After listening to the transmission described by Dispatcher M. as jargon, ... Rodriguez claims that during [a telephone] conversation Sgt. M. told him to "speak English like in Queens, New Jersey, not Little Havana." Sgt. M. testified that he could not recall ever having talked to Rodriguez.
>
> (Rodriguez v. City of Hialeah 1989)

Washington State:

> Managerial level employee LS told Xieng he was not being promoted because he could not speak "American."
>
> (Xieng v. Peoples National Bank of Washington 1993)

Hawai'i:

> The ability to speak clearly is one of the most important skills . . . we felt the applicants selected would be better able to work in our office because of their communication skills.
>
> (Fragante v. Honolulu 1989)

So the court has before it a Plaintiff who claims that his or her basic civil liberties have been violated, and a Defendant – an employer – who claims the right to make appropriate business decisions. How do courts handle this conflict? What factors, legal and otherwise, play a role in the decision making process?

In some cases one must assume that sometimes a Plaintiff will claim language-focused discrimination when in fact none has taken place – or there is insufficient evidence to persuade the court that there has been discrimination. It also happens that a Plaintiff establishes that she has been discriminated against, but the laws and court system are complicated, and what looks like a minor slip could result in an early dismissal or the lack of remedy for the Plaintiff. Sometimes it is hard to determine, on the basis of case summaries available from legal databases, whether the failure was factual, technical or ideological.

There may be clear evidence of language-focused discrimination which the court overlooks because there is, in addition, a bona fide reason to deny employment. However, as Cutler points out, employers are favorably predisposed to potential employees who are "like" them, and less disposed toward potential employees who are "unlike" them. Because the courts fail to recognize this fact, and refuse to reject the validity of the personal preference rationale, "Title VII becomes a statute which, at best, coerces job applicants to assimilate and, at worst, keeps them jobless" (Cutler 1985: 1166).

I proceed from the point at which the Plaintiff and the Defendant have made their cases, and the court must now decide whose argumentation better fulfills the requirements set forth by the law. It is possible to trace the influence of the standard ideology through much of the court's deliberations.

In the case summaries below, there are examples of successful and unsuccessful Title VII language trait-based complaints. The chapter concludes with an overview of the cases and the way ideology has interfered (or failed to interfere) in the legal process.

Selected court cases[10]

Kahakua v. Friday

James Kahakua's story is a good place to start, for reasons that will be clear shortly. In Chapter 12, the sociolinguistic complexities of living in Hawai'i will be discussed in more depth. For the moment, the fact that James Kahakua is a native of Hawai'i and bilingual speaker of English and Hawai'ian Creole English (HC) is not as simple a statement as it might seem on the surface. Even the phrase "a native of Hawai'i" is fraught with ambiguity, because it raises the sensitive subject of native Hawai'ian rights and self-determination. What it means to be Hawai'ian, who has the right to call themselves Hawai'ian, how to interpret terms like *haole*,[11] these are questions that are hotly debated. So we return to Mr. Kahakua, a university-trained meteorologist with 20 years of experience. Kahakua applied for a promotion which would have required him to read prepared weather reports on the radio. It is important to note that these reports would have been prepared ahead of time, so that editing could be undertaken as necessary.[12]

Likewise, it is important to remember that as a life-long native, Kahakua was absolutely prepared to use the longest and most difficult placenames (such as 'Alalā-keiki, 'Ale-nui-hāhā, Hanakāpī'ai) crucial to talking about the weather, and very difficult for a mainlander to learn.

Mr. Kahakua was not given this promotion. His employer found him unqualified to do so, not because he is incapable of reading, but because as a bilingual English–HC speaker, he has an Hawai'ian accent.

Subsequently, Mr. Kahakua sued his employer under Title VII of the Civil Rights Act, on the basis of language traits linked to national origin, and he lost. He lost because the judge, who was not a native of Hawai'i, believed that it was reasonable to require that radio announcers speak "Standard American English" (which was not defined explicitly) and furthermore, the judge added that "there is no race or physiological reason why Kahakua could not have used Standard American English pronunciations" (Matsuda 1991: 1345). The speech pathologist who testified on behalf of the employer gave the judge ammunition when she was questioned during the trial: "I urgently recommend [Mr. Kahakua] seek professional help in striving to lessen this *handicap* . . . Pidgin can be controlled. And if an individual is totally committed to improving, professional help on a long-term basis can produce results" (emphasis added) (ibid.).

This is a very good – if very disturbing – example of how people think about language: if we want to, if we try hard enough, we can acquire a perfect language, one which is clean, pure, free of variation and unpleasant social associations. Language which is not perfect is a handicap, and does not have to be accepted.

The judge and the speech therapist are sure of themselves: they stake their professional reputations on their opinions and pronouncements about language in general and Mr. Kahakua's language in particular. The court has decreed that Mr. Kahakua could, if he wished, comply with what they see as the reasonable request of his employer.

Kahakua's attorney disagreed, as any linguist would disagree: Mr. Kahakua can no more comply with the demand that he completely lose his native phonology – his accent – than he could comply with an order of the judge to grow four inches, or, and much more controversially, than it would be possible for him to change the color of his skin. The complexity of the relationship between language, ethnicity and ideology in Hawai'i has only been touched upon. The Fragante case, also in Hawai'i, will make some things clearer.

Fragante v. City & County of Honolulu[13]

One commonly heard myth or misconception about Hawai'i is that of the paradise without racism, where everyone is equal and visitors are welcomed and treated well. In fact, Hawai'i's history is rife with ethnic and race conflicts that continue to the present day (Okamura 2008; Roher 2005a, 2005b).

In April 1981, at the age of 60, Manuel Fragante emigrated from the Philippines to Hawaii. While Fragante speaks a number of the languages of the Philippines, his entire education had been conducted in English, including his university degree in law. For most of his adult life he was in the military; as a younger man he volunteered to serve on the American side in the Vietnam War. He continued his military training in the U.S. at various army installations and military schools, and his grades and evaluations were consistently excellent.

His daughter had settled in Hawai'i, and so Fragante moved, took up residence and eventually became a naturalized citizen. Because he wanted to stay busy and supplement his income, he began to look for work.

In late 1981 he replied to a newspaper ad and applied for an open entry level Civil Service Clerk position with the City of Honolulu's Division of Motor Vehicles and Licensing. Clerks at this level handle filing, process mail, act as cashier, provide information, and order supplies. Of the 721 applicants who took the written civil service examination, Fragante scored first in subjects that included vocabulary, grammar, and spelling. This ranking assured that he would move forward in the interview process.

A subset of the original applicants came in for an oral interview with two administrators. During the interview, the assistant licensing administrator repeatedly underscored the chaotic atmosphere of the DMV, how demanding the public could be, and how important communication was.

Both interviewers gave Fragante a negative evaluation, noting his very heavy accent. He was not offered employment. Later they would testify that they found Fragante hard to understand, and that his accent was the only reason he had been declined.

Fragante pursued administrative remedies without success, and then filed a claim under Title VII against the City and County of Honolulu. His complaint alleged that he had been discriminated against because of his accent. In a letter to his attorney, he expressed his surprise and outrage:

> I have traveled to Europe and South America and managed to communicate effectively in English with strangers who hardly spoke the tongue. How, then, could certain English-speaking interviewers of the City government claim, or pretend, I could not be understood?! Outside that interview office, I never encountered any communication problem with anybody in Hawai'i or on the mainland.
>
> (Matsuda 1991: 1335)

The district court did not question any of the decisions made by the defendant, and based on their own interview with Fragante, decided that he was "hampered by his accent or manner of speaking."

This is another example of how courts are willing to depend on their own often factually incorrect or biased understanding of language issues:

> Fragante argues the district court erred in considering "listener prejudice" as a legitimate, nondiscriminatory reason for failing to hire. We find, however, that the district court did not determine Defendants refused to hire Fragante on the basis that some listeners would "turn off" a Filipino accent. The district court after trial noted that: "Fragante, in fact, has a difficult manner of pronunciation."
>
> (Fragante v. Honolulu 1989)

The judge rejected the testimony of the linguist who testified about Hawai'ian Creole in support of the plaintiff. The linguist, the judge stated, was not an expert in speech (Matsuda 1991: 1345–1346).[14]

People in the judicial system do not leave their experiences or culture behind when they go to work. The guards at the door, the office clerks, the judges – everyone has a personal history through which all new information is filtered, no matter how dedicated each person is to doing their job well. In Fragante, the issue of racism might have been raised, but there is no trace of it in any of the published documents about the case. It seems as though the courts are unaware of racism within a particular group, as here, where one Asian group dominated and discriminated against other Asian ethnicities (Anheta 2006; Kim *et al.* 2008; Okamura 2010; Tiongson *et al.* 2006). In Hawai'i, there is a long history of discrimination toward Filipinos, particularly by other Asians.[15]

Fragante and Kahakua have something in common, beyond the fact that they both lost their court cases. Filipinos and native Hawaiians tend to be poor, and both groups are low in social prestige and (for the most part) political power. National origin discrimination linked to language trait is hard to prove, but in some contexts it would seem to be impossible.

The courts have stated that "[t]here is nothing improper about an employer making an honest assessment of the oral communications skills of a candidate for a job when such skills are reasonably related to job performance" (Fragante 1989). Matsuda calls this the *doctrinal puzzle of accent and antidiscrimination law*: Title VII disallows discrimination on the basis of accent when it correlates to national origin, but it allows employers to discriminate on the basis of job ability. Employers claim that "accent" impedes communication, and thereby poses a valid basis for rejection; the courts are especially receptive to this argument (Matsuda 1991:1348 ff.).

In an interesting twist to Fragante's story, he eventually did take a job as a statistician with the State of Hawai'i after he lost the Title VII case. Ironically his job involved conducting telephone interviews, further giving credence to the argument that the city misjudged the degree to which his accent would interfere with his performance (ibid.).

Akouri v. State of Florida Department of Transportation

George Akouri, a licensed engineer with many qualifications and years of experience, applied for and received a job as a maintenance contract engineer with the Florida Department of Transportation (DOT). During his six years with DOT, Akouri applied for three promotions to supervisory positions, and was turned down three times. In 2000 he filed a charge of discrimination on the basis of national origin with the EEOC. In 2001, he was fired.

Direct evidence of discrimination is increasingly rare as managers become more aware of how Title VII works. In this case, however, the administrators seemed to be completely unaware of Title VII, because when Akouri asked why he had not been promoted, the supervisor answered candidly. He explained that the position involved supervising a crew of men who were Anglo, and that white men would not take orders from him, a foreigner, particularly as he had an accent.

The jury found that Akouri had been discriminated against and awarded him back pay and damages. DOT filed an appeal with the district court and lost – Akouri's claim of discrimination stood fast. However, the court then reduced the award of $700,000 to nominal damages, and denied Akouri's motion for a new trial.

Often at this point in the appeals process, the issues have to do not with the original charges, but with procedure. In this case, two appeals courts decided that Akouri had not provided enough documentation to warrant the back-pay award: "the record is devoid of any evidence of [Akouri's] actual salary at the time he was employed by the DOT. Thus, there was no figure from which the jury could have reasonably calculated net lost wages."

Note that in this case, evidence was enough to validate Akouri's claims, but not enough to convince the court that he was entitled to back pay. More generally important: the court did not direct the Defendant to take any action to correct or improve their procedures for hiring and promoting.

Kyomugisha v. Clowney and the University of Wisconsin, Milwaukee[16]

In the early 1990s, Florence Kyomugisha left her native Uganda for the U.S., where she enrolled at the University of Wisconsin, Milwaukee as a graduate student in political science.

Ms. Kyomugisha was a native speaker of Runyankole and Luganda, indigenous languages of Uganda, as well as of English.[17] She attended Makerere University in Kampala before applying to the graduate program at the University of Wisconsin.

As a student, Kyomugisha began employment in UW-M's Office of Affirmative Action and Equal Opportunity. Over the course of the next four years, three different supervisors were so satisfied with her performance that she was promoted to Administrative Program Specialist. Then a new Assistant Chancellor for Equal Opportunity was hired.

In the next few months, Assistant Chancellor Charmaine Clowney made numerous and documented demeaning and hostile remarks about Kyomugisha's Ugandan accent, excluded her from making oral presentations that she had been making successfully for four years, and restricted her responsibilities in other ways.

After complaints and counter-complaints to the Chancellor and to the federal Equal Employment Opportunity Commission, Clowney issued notice that Kyomugisha's employment contract would not be renewed.

Florence Kyomugisha lost her job at the University of Wisconsin in part because of alleged communication difficulties with her supervisor, Ms. Clowney[18] and so Kyomugisha filed charges against Clowney and the university under Title VII of the Civil Rights Act. The official complaint filed with the court asserted that "the defendant Charmaine P. Clowney was intentionally motivated by prohibited animus based on national origin and acted in bad faith and with malice and in derogation of her duties and contrary to the [laws].[19]

Kyomugisha believed that Clowney was claiming accent as a communicative hindrance as an excuse (or in legal terms, as *pretext*) to fire her, because Clowney disliked African nationals and did not want to work with somebody from Uganda.

The attorney representing Kyomugisha questioned Clowney in a deposition (testimony taken under oath as part of the preparation for a trial). While Clowney is herself an attorney, she was also represented by counsel from the university, who was present.

In the following excerpt from the deposition, "attorney" refers Kyomugisha's lawyer. Please note that he uses the word *animus* rather than *prejudice*, *racism*, or some other more incendiary term.

> *Attorney*: You know about discriminatory animus from your professional preparation in the field of affirmative action and discrimination law; isn't that correct? You were responsible for doing the investigations of discrimination at the university, and you need to know what the laws about that, correct?
>
> *Clowney*: Yes, sir.
>
> *Attorney*: And you know about the sociology of discrimination, right?
>
> *Clowney*: Yes.

Attorney: And you would agree that the process of communication between two individuals involves a degree of burden sharing between the two individuals for purposes of making each other understood, correct?

Clowney: Sometimes. It depends on the nature of the two individuals. I would agree that the burden is more on an investigator to be understood in a university community than employees. The burden is more so on the professional than the nonprofessional.

Attorney: Now, I'm speaking of two people who speak with each other, who have divergent accents. You agree that you have an accent, correct?

Clowney: At times I might. I don't know if I do or not; you tell me.

Attorney: Well, isn't it true that all people have an accent of one kind or another?

Clowney: Not all people, some people. My mother is a schoolteacher and she doesn't necessarily have an accent.

Attorney: Well, do you think somebody from another part of the country who speaks with a different intonation would say that that person in fact has an accent?

Clowney: Possibly, yes.

Attorney: And communication between two such people involves the acceptance of a certain responsibility for burden sharing between each other in order to effectuate communication; isn't that correct?

Clowney: It can. It depends on the relationship between the two individuals.

Attorney: One of the factors in that relationship that could make the communication difficult is when one individual refuses to accept burden, a burden in connection with effectuating comprehensibility; isn't that correct?

Clowney: How about the burden on the other person to go and take courses and study and to be understood as well. What about – why should the burden – I also understand diversity, but why should the burden be on the recipient rather than, I mean, if you look at modern-day diversity studies, we'd be here all day. There's a double burden; there's a dual burden. I'll – I'll say there's a dual burden.

Attorney: Isn't it true that in some conversations where one person has a racial animus of one type or a national origin animus of one type that person refuses to accept a burden, any burden for effectuating the communication and thereby make – makes the allegation that the person is incomprehensible?

Clowney: I'm not going to answer that. I'm not an expert on communications skills. I've written papers on communication skills and racial animus. I can't say that. You're – you're asking me to draw inferences here and I can't say that. There are people I know that are trained who don't have any kind of animus; and if they can't understand someone, they get frustrated, and then have nothing to do with race, sex, religion, whatever. But the bottom line is that, you know, it's – you have to listen a little bit carefully, but, you know.

Attorney: Do you feel like you accepted your portion of the burden in trying to understand Florence's oral communications?

Clowney: Yes.

Attorney: Whether you feel that you accepted your portion of the burden to comprehend what Florence was saying to you when she was orally communicating with you?

Clowney: Yes, I do.

Attorney: Do you feel that you made a reasonable good faith effort to understand Florence?

Clowney: Yes, I do.

Attorney: Is it your testimony that notwithstanding that effort that was not enough
   and you still had oral communication problems with Florence?

Clowney: Yes, I do.

The fact that Clowney was both an attorney and the Assistant Chancellor for Equal
Opportunity in charge of the office investigating claims of discrimination might seem to
be ironic. It is also a sobering example of the reach of standard language ideology.

   Subsequent to this deposition, the university decided to settle this case and so it never
came to trial. Ms. Kyomugisha received compensatory damages, back pay, and the
attorney's costs she had incurred. The university's lawyers did not disclose the reasons the
university decided to offer a settlement.

   Ms. Kyomugisha was knowledgeable about the law, and she had the strength of will and
resources necessary to pursue her legal rights. Her story ends well, but many others – most
others, I would claim – do not. Everyday individuals are reminded that the language they
speak marks them as less-than-good-enough. Most don't realize that they have rights, or
that there are organizations who will help making sure those rights are protected. Some
might know that they have a legal claim, but be afraid to risk retribution.

   Then there are those whose claims are bound to fail, because the ideology of the
workplace and that of the court work together to make sure that they do.

Dercach v. Indiana Department of Highways

Anthony Dercach was born in the Ukraine and raised in Venezuela where he attended
Spanish-speaking schools. He moved to the United States at age 19, and had at that point
no English language skills.

   Dercach was hired by the highway department as a maintenance worker, and after three
years was promoted to crew leader at the recommendation of his foreman, because of his
ability to drive a Mack truck. Two years later, after a series of resignations, Dercach served
as acting, temporary unit foreman. The department then advertised the unit foreman
position, received 12 applications, and set up interviews. The person given the unit
foreman position had also been a crew leader, but had less seniority than Dercach.

   Two people on the interview committee testified that they chose not to recommend
Dercach for promotion to unit foreman because he had had problems with paperwork
and because he had had problems communicating with others. One of the interviewers
testified that workers would ask Mr. Dercach what he wanted them to do, and then simply
walk away, unable to understand. Mr. Moser refused to attribute such incidents to Mr.
Dercach's accent, but offered no other explanation. He said they just couldn't understand
him "like normal people with normal language."

   The plaintiff repeatedly denied that Dercach's accent was an issue in their promotion
decision; the court did not find those denials to be credible. The court recognized that
Dercach had indeed been discriminated against on the basis of national origin, but they
still found for the plaintiff, because there was one credible reason: Dercach had a very
limited ability to read and write English, skills that were necessary for the job.

   During [Dercach's] cross-examination, he was shown several of his requests for vacation
leave; those requests had been filled out by Mr. Dercach's wife or foreman. Asked to locate
the request for vacation for a trip to Hawai'i, he was unable to do so. Asked to read aloud

a story in *USA Today*, he was unable to do so. Asked to read aloud a headline from the same newspaper, he was unable to do so. Asked to read aloud an exhibit critical of his paperwork, he was unable to do so.

All witnesses testified that the highway department Field Operations Handbook for Foremen was an essential manual for unit foremen; Dercach himself testified that it was "the Bible" for unit foremen. While he was being questioned by the Defendant's attorneys he was asked to find the performance standard for "full-width litter pickup." After several minutes of searching, he then pointed to the performance standard for "flushing bridges."

In Dercach, the court felt that blatant discrimination could not mitigate the fact that the Plaintiff, while hard working and knowledgeable, was unable to read or write English and because the job required close work with a written code book and the ability to write multiple reports on a weekly basis, the court found for the defendant. It was not in the court's power to penalize the employer for blatant national origin discrimination, and in fact, the highway department got away with violating the Civil Rights Act.

Two years after Dercach's trial, the Supreme Court provided guidelines on how to rule on mixed-motive Title VII cases. Supreme Court held that in such cases the employer/defendant can sidestep liability by proving that even if the illegitimate reason for the employer's action were eliminated, the employer would have made the same decision on the basis of the non-discriminatory reason alone. Congress stepped in on this ruling, and changed the law so that it is enough for the Plaintiff to prove that the discriminatory reason was a motivating factor. In such cases, the Plaintiff could sue for attorney's fees, and an injunction on the employer which demanded a change in policy and discriminatory practice (Smith 2005: 242).

Hasan v. Contra Costa County

Saed Hasan came to the U.S. from Palestine to study engineering. At the University of South Dakota he maintained a 4.0 GPA for both his undergraduate and graduate degrees. After three years working as a civil engineer on a variety of projects, he applied for the position of entry-level engineer with Contra Costa County, California.

Hasan went through the interview process, and in the verbal portion ranked second in a field of 344 applicants. There were four openings at the time, but Hasan was not offered work. He applied again in 1998, and this time ranked first in the verbal portion of the interview. Again, he was not offered work. Over two years the county advertised a total of 12 openings for civil engineers with Hasan's background and experience. One of those positions was never filled because the county interviewers were not satisfied with the candidates. The other 11 were filled with people who spoke English without a foreign accent. The Defendants admitted that, with one or two exceptions, Hasan appeared to be "demonstrably better qualified" than the engineers who were hired.

After Hasan complained to Human Resources he met with Clifford Hansen, Deputy Director of Public Works. Hansen had been on both hiring committees, and in fact, hiring decisions were his responsibility alone. Hansen was quite straightforward in listing his reasons for rejecting Hasan. He stated that, "when it comes to choosing between a person who has an accent and a person who has no accent, he will choose the person who has no accent." Hasan filed a lawsuit.

During discovery – the period before a case goes to trial in which both sides assemble evidence and work on strategy – Hasan's attorneys requested access to the interview committee's written notes from the verbal interviews. The Defendants turned over only one set of notes, and claimed that notes of the other two people on the October 1997 interview panel had been lost. Defendants also lost the envelope in which the notes were kept, and finally, they destroyed the tape recording of Hasan's 1998 oral interview.

Hasan's attorneys hired a forensic documents examiner to look at the notes they did have. In the examiner's professional opinion, a number of remarks had been written at a different time than the rest of the notes. All the notes added at a later time were negative, including "very difficult to understand," and "He talks way too much!" Hasan won his case; he was awarded back pay, damages and court costs.

In some cases, the behavior of the Defendant and Defendant's council damages whatever reasonable claims they might have had. In this case, the employer's hiring and promotion practices were so blatantly discriminatory and their attitude so disdainful that they made it easier for the court to find for the Plaintiff. The Defendants indulged in excessive delay tactics, which resulted in increased legal costs for Hasan and might have forced him to drop his suit, which he did not. The County then went on to appeal the award of court and legal costs, and was firmly slapped down by the appeals court.

The trial court observed both parties over the course of the litigation, and specifically found that much of Hasan's fee award could be attributed to the tactics of the County. The district court correctly applied the relevant law and was well within its discretion in determining both Hasan's entitlement to the attorney's fees and the amount ultimately awarded (Hasan, Decision of the Appeal from the United States District Court for the Northern District).

Mandhare v. W.S. LaFargue Elementary School

In 1965, at the age of 29, Sulochana Mandhare left her home in the Maharashtra region of India and came to the United States. At that point in her life, Ms. Mandhare – a native speaker of Marathi – had been studying English for almost 20 years.[20]

Ms. Mandhare speaks in a soft voice and an English which is characterized by full vowels in unstressed syllables, distinctive intonation patterns, aspirated fricatives and stops, and a lack of distinction between initial /v/ and /w/. She is an intelligent and articulate woman, and she tells her story in a clear and completely comprehensible accented English (1994, personal communication).

After some time in the U.S., Ms. Mandhare relates, she decided to continue her education. She had arrived with undergraduate degrees in both liberal arts and education, but she returned to school and in 1972 completed a Master's Degree in Education at New Orleans's Loyola University; in 1979 she was certified as a school librarian after completing a program at Nichols State University. After working for one year as an elementary school librarian, Ms. Mandhare applied for and was given a job as a librarian at a school serving kindergarten through second grade in the Lafargue, Louisiana school district, for the 1980–1981 school year.

Ms. Mandhare talks about that year as happy and successful. Her responsibilities were to oversee the small library, read stories to the children and introduce them to using the resources, and she enjoyed this work. Therefore, when in April 1981 she was told that her contract would not be renewed because of her "heavy accent, speech patterns and grammar problems," and in spite of her excellent skills as a librarian, she was stunned and angry. She investigated her options, and because she understood that the Civil Rights Act prohibits national origin discrimination in the workplace, she filed suit. This civil action was decided in Ms. Mandhare's favor; the decision was reversed by the U.S. Court of Appeals in favor of the School Board.

The official published summary of the case indicates that Ms. Mandhare then met with the Superintendent of Schools and on the advice of her supervisor requested a transfer to Thibodaux Junior High School, as a librarian.[21] The School Board refused to reappoint Ms. Mandhare to this requested new position; testimony revealed that in their private and public deliberations, Ms. Mandhare's foreignness and accent had been discussed.

The trial court was very firm in this case: Ms. Mandhare had been discriminated against, and must prevail. However, the school's initial decision that the Plaintiff could not teach young children because of her "heavy accent and speech patterns and grammar problems [which] prevented her from effectively communicating with primary school students" (Mandhare v. W.S. LaFargue Elementary School) was never questioned. The court took this claim on faith, and instead stated:

> Defendant's contention that its legitimate reason for plaintiff's termination or non-appointment was that she had a communication problem because of her accent which prevented her from effectively communicating with primary school students is a feigned contention. Plaintiff was not being considered for a position which would require such communication. She was to be appointed librarian at a Junior High School, a position for which it was established that she was eminently qualified.
>
> (ibid.)

It is important to remember that in this case, as in every other case discussed, no effort was made to make an objective assessment of the communication skills required for the job, the Plaintiff's speech, the quality of her interaction with children or her intelligibility. The administrators found the Plaintiff's accent difficult; they decided not to reappoint her to her job in the grade school. This alone would have made them the focus of the court's scrutiny (although not necessarily to the Plaintiff's favor), but they redeemed themselves in the court's eyes: They praised the Plaintiff's industry and skill, and they went out of their way to locate a position in a school where her accent would neither offend nor inconvenience. The court could then focus on the School Board, which refused to give the Plaintiff this new job. The validity of the initial firing was never challenged. Thus everyone (except the School Board) was happy: the administrators were left intact as arbiters of the standard language ideology and lionized for their largesse; the court was not forced to challenge those educators on the factual basis for their decisions about appropriate language; Ms. Mandhare was to be reinstated as a librarian, in a junior high school.

The question remains: were Ms. Mandhare's civil rights protected? Were her best interests really served? Put more controversially, if Ms. Mandhare had been forbidden to ride public transportation, and challenged that restriction, should she then have been pleased to be offered alternate transportation, in the form of a bicycle, a Mercedes Benz, or another, different but equally functioning, bus?

Ms. Mandhare did not really want the transfer to another school in a school district which had treated her so badly; she wanted back pay, which she did not get. Whether or not she would have been satisfied with the new position was never established, because the trial court decision was reversed by the U.S. Court of Appeals for the Fifth Circuit:

> The district court's determination that the Board had intentionally discriminated against Mandhare is clearly erroneous. The court focused on the wrong issue. It premised its conclusion on the Board's refusal to follow LeBlanc's recommendation that Mandhare be transferred to a junior high librarian position. That was not the issue as framed by the unamended pleadings and pre-trial order. Mandhare's action asserted discrimination in the Board's refusal to reemploy her as elementary school librarian, not their failure to create and transfer her to a junior high position.
>
> (Mandhare v. Lafargue Elementary School 1986: 5)

The terrible irony of this reversal should be clear: Ms. Mandhare was originally protesting her dismissal on the basis of language-focused national origin discrimination; the judge in that first case chose not to deal with that delicate issue, but to bypass it completely by focusing on the possibility of a position in another school. This gave the Appeal Court an out, which it took. The Appeal Court accused the Trial Court of focusing on the wrong issue and on that basis, it reversed the decision.

In the end, both courts were satisfied to let the school administrators and School Board exclude on the basis of accent. In the analogy above, the first court offered Ms. Mandhare a Mercedes-Benz when all she wanted to do was ride the bus. The Appeal Court said that the court had been wrong to offer Ms. Mandhare a Mercedes-Benz that didn't exist and that no one was obliged to buy for her; it did not even question why she had been forced off the bus in the first place, and it certainly didn't offer her the opportunity to get back on, or compensate her for her trouble.

The Appeal Court filed the reversal on May 2, 1986, six years after Ms. Mandhare was denied renewal. The failure of the American judicial system caused her untold emotional anguish, financial difficulty, and was detrimental to her health. Today, she works as librarian for a private school in her home town of Thibodaux, but she will carry this experience with her for the rest of her life.

Hou v. Pennsylvania, Department of Education, Slippery Rock State College

Roger Hou, a native of China, is a naturalized citizen of the U.S. He came to the States to study in the early 1960s, became a citizen in 1965, and received a Ph.D. from the University of Indiana at Bloomington the next year.

Hou was hired by Slippery Rock State College as an Associate Professor of Mathematics in 1969, and achieved tenure in the 1973–1974 school year. From 1972 to 1976, Hou applied for promotion to full professor. All six of his applications were denied. After his last unsuccessful application, Hou filed a discrimination suit against the college.[22]

If you recall, the first stage in a case like this is for the Plaintiff (Hou) to establish *prima facie*. Hou did reach that standard by showing that: (1) he is Asian, and thus a member of protected minority; (2) he was qualified for promotion in the years in question; (3) he was not promoted; and (4) Anglo faculty members had been promoted in the same period.

At that point, the burden of proof shifted to the college, who had to prove that there were legitimate, non-discriminatory reasons not to promote Hou. The college did this by presenting evidence that Hou was a mediocre teacher, and further, that his mediocrity was due, at least in part, to his heavy accent.

Higher educational institutions were meant to be included within the scope of Title VII; nevertheless, the "trend in many courts has been to exercise minimal scrutiny of college and university employment practices, due, in large part, to the subjective factors on which many academic employment decision are based" (Hou 1983). There is considerable forbearance for the opinions put forth by school administration. In addition, the courts have shown reluctance to reverse higher education administrative decisions (ibid.).

This deference for academic decision worked to Hou's detriment. The judge pointed out that: "The issue of accent in a foreign-born person of another race is a concededly delicate subject when it becomes part of peer or student evaluations, since many people are prejudiced against those with accents" (Hou v. Pennsylvania Department of Education and Slippery Rock College 1983).

The court then went on to approve the loophole used by the institution:

> We find that comments about Dr. Hou's accent, when made, were directed toward the legitimate issue of his teaching effectiveness. Teaching effectiveness, as the testimony at trial indicated, is an elusive concept [citations omitted] (evaluation of teaching ability [is] necessarily [a] matter of judgment). Teaching effectiveness does, however, include the ability to communicate the content of a discipline, a quality which should be carefully evaluated at any college or university.
>
> (ibid.)

There was never any discussion of factual, non-prejudicial assessment of Dr. Hou's communicative competence or intelligibility. The defense depended exclusively on anecdotal evidence provided by the defendant, and this satisfied the court.

No steps were taken to isolate potentially legitimate reasons from the discriminatory ones. In an earlier chapter we looked at the studies which examined the way foreign accents are heard in an educational setting (Atagi 2003; Gluszek and Dovidio 2010; Kang and Rubin 2009; Katz et al. 2009).[23] In a thorough review of studies on accent discrimination in education, Fought (2006) assembles the evidence to establish that the mind is capable of manufacturing accents where none exist, a phenomenon she calls accent hallucination. Her conclusion was that it is "possible for expectations about language and ethnicity to override the actual linguistic nature of an individual speech in the minds of hearers" (ibid.: Chapter 9.6).

Kang and Rubin (2009) look at this from a slightly different but complementary angle.

If Hou's attorney had been aware of this academic work and presented it to the court, there might have been a closer examination of Hou's situation. In the end it is possible that his lecture style was the problem, but the tone of some of the student evaluations of his performance makes it clear that without further research, there was no way to be sure Hou wasn't being discriminated against on the basis of his national origin.

Lawyers interested in Title VII language-focused cases have been debating how to ameliorate the kind of questionable evidence that was used by Hou's employers:

> [T]he first step in remedying this injustice and making it easier for plaintiffs to win foreign accent discrimination cases is to have courts vigilantly exclude customer preference arguments – such as the student evaluations in Poskocil – that operate as a partial defense to foreign accent discrimination and do nothing more than detract from a sound inquiry of whether the plaintiff's English skills are sufficient to perform his or her job satisfactorily.
>
> (Smith 2005: 234)

Sparks v. Griffin and Edwards v. Gladewater Independent School District

In some cases, language and accent are an issue and do stand in for a protected category, but there is more than one kind of discrimination going on.

The Sparks and Edwards cases both had to do with the variety of English they spoke in the classroom, and in both cases the court focused primarily on racial discrimination. In many pages of correspondence on the matter of Ms. Sparks' dismissal, the school administrator (Mr. Griffin) commented only once on the language issue: "Mrs. Sparks has a language problem. She cannot help the negro dialect, but it is certainly bad for the children to be subjected to it all day" (Sparks v. Griffin 1972).

In Edwards v. Gladewater Independent School District (1978), the discussion of language use is limited to general comments: "The plaintiff's contract was not renewed allegedly because of complaints received from parents and students . . . Several complaints concerned students' alleged inability to understand the plaintiff's 'Black accent.'"

If the accent issue had never been raised in Sparks or Edwards, these Plaintiffs would still have won. This was fortunate for the courts, as it relieved them of the trouble of dealing with questions of language, dialect and accent and still more controversially, with the question of AAVE. In discussing the language-focused discrimination portion of Sparks, the court limited its comments to one short footnote: "With no disposition to be unkind, we question, based on the spelling and composition of the two letters . . . the ability of Mr. Griffin to diagnose a 'language-problem'" (Sparks v. Griffin 442).[24]

The letters written by Mr. Griffin regarding the dismissal of Ms. Sparks and referred to by the court were, in fact, poorly written and contained many spelling and/or typographical errors; nevertheless, the court is clearly uncomfortable chiding an educator, in this case, an administrator with advanced degrees, in matters of language use: "with no disposition to be unkind." More importantly, the court never addressed the content of Mr. Griffin's complaint (Ms. Sparks' "negro dialect" and its appropriateness for the classroom); it addressed only the superintendent's qualifications to make judgments on that dialect, given his poor letter writing skills.

Would the court have thought seriously about this criticism if Mr. Griffin had written elegant, grammatically appropriate prose? If the attorney had argued that Ms. Sparks' teaching effectiveness was compromised by her language use? It seems likely that the school systems could have found a line of argumentation which would have pleased the courts; they just failed to do so in this case. The court neatly sidestepped the "concededly delicate subject" of language-focused discrimination for Edwards as well: "The district court stated in its opinion that it was 'apparent' that the plaintiff could be easily understood and that there was no evidence the plaintiff made grammatical errors rendering her speech difficult to understand" (ibid.).

In these two cases, the schools were deservedly punished for racial discrimination; for language-focused discrimination, they were slapped on the wrist.

It is worthwhile looking at how race and national origin intersect in cases involving persons of African origin. Figure 9.2 breaks down the nine examined language-focused cases which were filed by such persons.

The two successful cases were brought by African Americans, native speakers of English who also speak AAVE. The others were brought by persons who speak English as a second language. This is some indication that there are more negative feelings about persons who have recently immigrated from Africa than there is about U.S. residents who are native

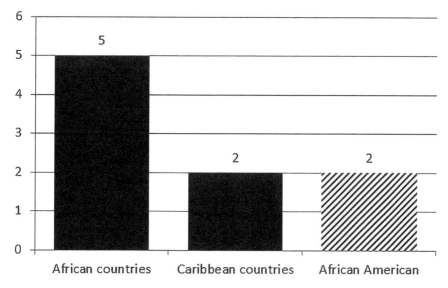

Figure 9.2   Title VII cases won and lost by persons of African ancestry, by area of geographic origin, between 1975 and 1995

speakers of English, even if the variety of English in question is stigmatized (see Kyomigusha v. Clowney). There is little work done on the way ethnic and national origin differences may cause strife within the African American community, but that such problems exist is a matter of record.

Xieng v. Peoples National Bank of Washington

How do some plaintiffs manage to avoid settlement, make it to court, and to win? Xieng provides the ultimate example of a successful case.

Phanna Xieng is a Cambodian-American who worked for Peoples National Bank of Washington. Mr. Xieng was repeatedly denied a promotion although he had an excellent work history, high marks in his reviews, and had been filling in on the very position he applied for over an extended period of time. There were documented comments from his superiors concerning his accent as the primary stumbling block to his promotion. In this case, the court could not overlook the fact that Mr. Xieng could carry out the job he claimed he could do, in spite of his accent, precisely because he had already been performing well at the job. It might seem that being on the inside – already employed by the Defendant – provides an employee with a valid language-focused discrimination complaint with some strong evidence, but there are many similar cases in which promotion is denied.

Is it the case, then, that the Plaintiff's chances of winning a language-focused dis-crimination case depend to the greatest degree on the integrity and objectivity of the judge hearing the trial? Unfortunately, it is not as easy as this. Below it will become clear that for some areas of employment, even the most open-minded of courts still are subject to the unwritten laws of a standard language ideology.

Context

In civil rights violations of the kind discussed here, courts are disposed to favor the employer, which makes it very difficult for the Plaintiff to build a successful case. These cases fail for all kinds of reasons in a variety of combinations, five of which we have seen here:

1   Kahakua: Court declared Kahakua's accent a handicap that he could overcome if he wanted to, and found he had not been discriminated against.
2   Fragante: Court refused to recognize the connection between foreign accent and national origin discrimination.
3   Dercach: Blatant language-focused national origin discrimination established, but the presence of a valid reason for non-promotion caused the court to rule for the employer.
4   Mandhare: Discrimination established, but faulty legal procedure resulted in a lack of remedy.
5   Hou: Court found no evidence of discrimination, but there was no independent or impartial evaluation of Hou's communication skills.

Employers point out that the decision-making process in business hiring and promotion is often unavoidably subjective in nature. The courts have supported them in this:

> It does not follow, though, that ethnic discrimination is the only explanation why Plaintiff was not promoted. Other plausible explanations may exist. For instance, Nasser may not have chosen to promote Plaintiff simply because he personally did not like her.
>
> (Vartivarian v. Golden Rule Insurance 1992)

But how can the courts distinguish between an admissible business judgment based on business necessity or personal preference and inadmissible considerations based on race or national origin? Is it simply a matter of presentation of the right arguments by the employer? The language we've seen so far shows:

1   *Refusal to acknowledge accent as an immutable characteristic of national origin (mis-recognition).* The court added, "There is no race or physiological reason why Kahakua could not have used Standard American English pronunciations" (Matsuda 1991: 1345).
2   *Allowing direct and non-factual association of negative social values with stigmatized linguistic variants (disinformation)*: "The agency contended that the appellant's accent was undesirable . . . found to lack authority, friendliness, clarity and other qualities desired in a broadcasted voice" (Staruch, EEOC Hearing Opinion).
    [The judge said] "The white candidate was selected because he had 'better diction, better enunciation, better pronunciation, better cadence, better intonation, better voice clarity, and better understandability'" (Matsuda 1991:1345, citing from Kahakua, Findings of Fact).
3   *Willingness to allow the media to set its own standards on the basis of personal preferences, even when those preferences necessarily involve language focused discrimination (claiming authority)*: "the judge credited the testimony of speech experts that . . .

Standard American English should be used by radio broadcasters" (Kahakua, ibid.).

"The agency stated that the appellant's voice was not suitable for broadcast purposes . . . Appellant's voice was described as having a definite Western Ukrainian accent. As in the United States, where national network news is broadcast in 'television accent' rather than the regional accents sometimes heard on local broadcasts" (Staruch, ibid.).

4   *Lack of concern with established facts about language structure and use, or with consistent, non-prejudicial evaluation of language skills (disinformation)*: "[An external review found him] . . . 'not persuasive'; his pronunciation as 'often incorrect', delivery 'dull' and 'sounding strange to the listener'" (ibid.).

"I [expert witness, a 'speech consultant'] urgently recommend he seek professional help in *striving to lessen this handicap* . . . Pidgin can be controlled. And if an individual is totally committed to improving, professional help on a long-term basis can produce results" (Kahakua 1989: Excerpts of the Record: 31, as cited by Matsuda 1991:1366, original emphasis).

There must be a better way to approach these cases, and in fact, Matsuda proposed a process that would be fair to employers and employees both, one by which every position can be evaluated in four steps (Matsuda 1991: 1369). My recasting of Matsuda's four-step process takes more linguistic factors into consideration:

1   In a typical interaction, the consequences of miscommunication are grave.
2   Oral communication is the sole or primary way in which information is exchanged.
3   The speech interactions are under high stress where time is of the essence.
4   The interactions are typically the first and only exchange, so that neither person has time to adjust in listening and comprehension patterns.
5   There is no face-to-face contact.
6   There is "noise in the channels," such as a bad telephone connection, lots of background noise, cross-talk.

Matsuda suggests that there are some jobs that fit all of her points, such as a 911 operator. On the other end of the scale would be a computer programmer who worked alone. Most jobs would fall some place between the two extremes, and there is still room for loopholes. Consider, for example, a retired police officer applying for a 911 position in a large city. The police officer is a native speaker of Spanish, and has a strong Spanish accent in his oral communication. Would the hiring committee be acting within reason if they rejected him on that basis? Under what circumstances would they be wrong?

If ideology is most effective when its workings are least visible, then the first step must be to make visible the link between the enforcement of standard language ideology and social domination. Given the way the schools, media and employers work together to promote language ideology, the education of the public is both a lonely and a difficult – but certainly not an impossible – task.

Linguists have hard-won knowledge to offer which would be of some assistance in the difficult questions faced in matters of language policy, but that knowledge is often not sought; if sought, it may be summarily rejected; in either case, it is often hotly resented. Nevertheless, there are good reasons to persevere. This type of behavior causes real harm to real individuals, and it deserves attention.

In the judicial system there may be some lessons for linguists to learn from psychologists and psychiatrists, whose contributions to trial law are better established, although the effectiveness and value of those contributions are often challenged, see Vartivarian v. Golden Rule Insurance (Faust and Ziskin 1988).

While the overall quality of contribution of psychologists in legal cases is still being debated, some issues have been clarified as a result of that body of testimony. The law now defines and takes seriously such human conditions as battered woman syndrome, clinical depression and post-traumatic stress syndrome. Conversely, while the courts have called on linguists to address technical matters of authorship and identification to be used as evidence, they are less interested in a linguist's definition of communicative competence or assessment of intelligibility, as was seen in Kahakua and Fragante; these are areas where the courts are satisfied with their own powers of reasoning and expertise.

Xieng provides an interesting illustration of the status of linguistics in the courts: there was no expert testimony at all on the pivotal matter, which was the employer's claim that Mr. Xieng's accent was too strong and impeded communication. However, a psychiatrist was called, who then argued and convinced the court that there did exist a "causal relationship between the [employer's] national origin discrimination and Xieng's severe emotional distress and depression" (Xieng v. Peoples National Bank of Washington 1991: A13).

Psychologists ask themselves a two-part question to determine the quality of their forensic contribution:

1   Can we answer questions with reasonable accuracy?
2   Can we help the judge and jury reach a more accurate conclusion than would otherwise be possible (Faust and Ziskin 1988: 31)? That is, does the subject lie beyond the knowledge and experience of the average layman, and can the expert inform without invading the province of the jury by expressing a conclusion as to the ultimate issue?

For most of the cases presented here, a list of questions could have been presented to linguists which would have met both of these basic criteria. Questions about the process of standardization, differences between spoken and written language varieties, cultural differences in discourse style and structure which may cause processing difficulties, second language acquisition and accent, subconscious social evaluation of active variation, and change over time and space could be answered with reasonable accuracy. We could provide the judge and the jury with information and knowledge beyond that of the average layman, but the issue is this: we cannot make them want that information, no matter how factually correct or how strongly supported by empirical evidence.

Linguistic contributions to the legal process are not valued because ideology intervenes in a way that it does not in matters of mental health. A judge may have no personal investment in accepting evidence linking systematic, long-term physical abuse and violent behavior; she is more likely to have a strong personal reaction when asked to reconsider the assumptions underlying the standard language ideology.

Fairclough, who acknowledges this somewhat depressing state of affairs, also points out that "resistance and change are not only possible, but are continuously happening. But the effectiveness of resistance and the realization of change depend on people developing a critical consciousness of domination and its modalities, rather than just experiencing them" (1989 [2001]: 4).

Some of the discussion around language standards is so emotional in tone that parallels can be drawn to disagreements between scientists and theologians over the centuries. In our own time, in the courts, science and rational inquiry have come up against public opinion based on personal preferences and intuition:

> [T]he real problem faced is not legal but sociological. In the centers of population men have gone on assuming certain bodies of knowledge and certain points of view without realizing that they were living in a different world from that inhabited by a considerable portion of their fellow-citizens, and they have been unconscious of the danger which threatened them at the inevitable moment when the two worlds should come in.
>
> (*The Nation*, July 22, 1925: 28, cited in Caudill 1989)

This editorial was written at the height of Scopes trial, in which fundamentalists and empiricists argued the very definition of truth. It was a trial surrounded by sensational journalism and followed with great interest by many people. Scopes, a science teacher who taught the theory of evolution in a state which forbade him to do so, lost his case and was fined one hundred dollars.

But something else, something perhaps more important, was won. Before the trial, one might gather that the majority of American citizens had never come in contact with evolutionary theory. After the trial, many of those people were thinking about their own beliefs, about science, and about the nature of authority and its relationship to knowledge. Whatever an individual's personal beliefs, after the Scopes trial it became increasingly difficult for anyone to dismiss out of hand the facts put forth by scientists. Today, more than 70 years later, evolution is taught in all public schools and most private ones. And today fundamentalists still fight to have evolutionary science displaced by biblical narratives.

The Scopes trial involved free speech, educational policy, and a range of sociological issues. When the topic is discrimination on the basis of language, the stakes are very different. Mandhare, Hou, Xieng, Kahakua and the other cases like them test an even more basic freedom: the individual's right to be different:

> The way we talk, whether it is a life choice or an immutable characteristic, is akin to other attributes of the self that the law protects. In privacy law, due process law, protection against cruel and unusual punishment, and freedom from inquisition, we say the state cannot intrude upon the core of you, cannot take away your sacred places of the self. A citizen's accent, I would argue, resides in one of those places.
>
> (Matsuda 1991: 1391–1392)

It would seem that linguistics and language-focused discrimination have yet to meet their Scopes trial.

Appendix: the U.S. civil court structure

Before we leave the thorny discussion of linguistics and language-focused discrimination, let us look closely at the civil court structure in the U.S (Table 9.2). The first level is the trial courts.

If any party is dissatisfied with the outcome of a trial, they may appeal to the intermediate courts of appeal (Table 9.3).

Table 9.2 First level of trial courts in the U.S.

State trial courts	U.S. District Courts
Almost all cases involving state civil and criminal laws are initially filed in state or local trial courts. They are typically called Municipal, County, District, Circuit, or Superior Courts. Appeals from the state trial court usually go to the state intermediate court of appeals. About 95% of all court cases in the U.S. come through the state trial courts.	There are 94 federal district courts, which handle criminal and civil cases involving: (a) Federal statutes (b) The U.S. Constitution (c) Civil cases between citizens from different states where the amount of money at stake is more than $75,000 (most District Court cases fall into this group). Most appeals from here go to the U.S. Circuit Court of Appeals.

Table 9.3 Intermediate Courts of Appeal

State intermediate Courts of Appeal	U.S. Circuit Courts of Appeal
40 states have intermediate courts of appeal. These courts are the first court of appeal for most state cases. In 10 states the State Supreme Court is the only court of appeal.	There are 12 Circuit Courts. Each state and U.S. District Court is assigned to one of the 12 circuits.

If any party is dissatisfied with the outcome of the trial, they may appeal to the State Supreme Courts of Appeal (the final court of appeal for all but a small number of cases).

The U.S. Supreme Court is free to accept or reject the cases it will hear. It must, however, hear certain rare mandatory appeals and cases within its original jurisdiction as specified by the Constitution.

Civil action flowchart

The sequence of events is:

- Attempt to find an in-house resolution.
- If this fails, Plaintiff files complaint with the EEOC.
- EEOC finds cause and *prima facie* is established (if not, the plaintiff may proceed independently).
- Plaintiff and/or EEOC files and serves Complaint on the Defendant.
- Defendant returns an Answer.
- Discovery (depositions, etc.).
- Trial.
- Judgment.
- Appeal or Judgment Execution.

Relevant court cases

The relevant court cases discussed in this chapter are shown in Table 9.4 and the list of all court cases studied but not cited is given in Table 9.5. These latter cases are included, however, in the statistics cited in this chapter. Some of these cases settled out of court or were otherwise resolved at an early stage.

Table 9.4 Relevant court cases

Name	Date	Court reference
GOLD v. FEDEX FREIGHT EAST, INC.	2007	*In re Rodriguez*, 487 F.3d 1001 (6th Cir. 2007)
SALEM v. HERITAGE SQUARE	2007	2007 U.S. Dist. LEXIS 67493 (N.D. Cal. Sept. 4, 2007)
AKOURI v. FLORIDA DEPT OF TRANSPORTATION	2005	408 F.3d 1338 (11th Cir. 2005)
GALDAMEZ v. POTTER	2005	415 F.3d 1015 (4th Cir. 2005)
RAAD v. ALASKA STATE COMMISSION FOR HUMAN RIGHTS	2004	86 P.3d 899; 2004 Alas. LEXIS 5; 93 Fair Empl. Prac. Cas. (BNA) 178; 85 Empl. Prac. Dec. (CCH) P41,629
ELGAGHIL v. TARRANT COUNTY JUNIOR COLLEGE	2000	45 S.W.3d 133 (Tex. App. 2000)
FLORES v. ARIZONA	2000	160 F. Supp. 2d 1043 (D. Ariz. 2000)
HASAN v. CONTRA COSTA COUNTY	2000	45 Fed. Appx. 795 (9th Cir. 2000)
HASHAM v. CALIFORNIA STATE BOARD OF EQUALIZATION	2000	200 F.3d 1035 (7th Cir. 2000)
POSKOCIL v. ROANOKE COUNTY SCHOOLS	1999	1999 U.S. Dist. LEXIS 259 (W.D. Va. Jan. 11, 1999)
RIVERA v. BACCARAT	1998	10 F.Supp.2d 318 (S.D.N.Y. 1998)
KYOMUGISHA v. CLOWNEY AND THE U OF WISCONSIN	1997	Civil case filed; depositions followed by settlement
PRADO V. L. LURIA & SON, INC.	1997	975 F.Supp. 1349 (S.D. Fla. 1997)
HOU v. PENNSYLVANIA, DEPARTMENT OF EDUCATION	1993	573 F. Supp. 1539 (W.D. Penn. 1993)
LUBITZ v. GARRETT	1992	962 F.2d 7; 1992 U.S. App. LEXIS 17272 (4th Cir. 1992)
STARUCH v. U.S. BUREAU OF INFORMATION.	1992	*EEOC Opinion*
VARTIVARIAN v. GOLDEN RULE INSURANCE COMPANY	1992	1992 U.S. App. LEXIS 12458 (7th Cir. June 3, 1992)
ANG v. PROCTER & GAMBLE CO.,	1991	932 F.2d 540, 546 (6th Cir. 1991)
DABOR v. DAYTON POWER & LIGHT COMPANY	1991	888 F. 2d 127 (6th Cir. 1991)
XIENG v. PEOPLES NATIONAL BANK OF WASHINGTON	1991	120 Wn.2d 512, 844 P.2d 389, 1993 Wash. LEXIS 24, 65 Fair Empl. Prac. Cas. (BNA) 1090 (1993)

Table 9.4 Continued

Name	Date	Court reference
CARROLL v. ELLIOTT PERSONNEL SERVICES	1989	51 FEP 1173, 1175, 1989 WL 167678 (D.Md.1989)
FRAGANTE v. HONOLULU	1989	888 F.2d 591 (9th Cir. 1989)
KAHAKUA v. FRIDAY	1989	876 F.2d 896 (9th Cir. 1989)
RODRIGUEZ v. CITY OF HIALEAH	1989	716 F. Supp. 1425 (S.D. Fla. 1989)
STEPHEN v. PGA SHERATON RESORT, LTD.	1989	873 F.2d 276, 279 (11th Cir. 1989)
GUTIERREZ v. MUNICIPAL COURT OF THE SOUTHEAST JUDICIAL DISTRICT, COUNTY OF LOS ANGELES	1988	838 F.2d 1031 (9th Cir. 1988)
IPINA v. MICHIGAN, DEPARTMENT OF MANAGEMENT & BUDGET	1988	699 F. Supp. 132 (W.D. Mich. 1988)
DERCACH v. INDIANA DEPARTMENT OF HIGHWAYS	1987	1987 U.S. Dist. LEXIS 13413; 45 Fair Empl. Prac. Cas. (BNA) 899 (N.D.Ind.1987)
GOMEZ v. ILLINOIS STATE BOARD OF EDUCATION	1987	811 F.2d 1030 (7th Cir. 1987)
MANDHARE v. LAFARGUE ELEMENTARY SCHOOL	1985	605 F. Supp. 238 (E.D. La. 1985)
BELL v. HOME LIFE INSURANCE	1984	596 F. Supp. 1549 (9th Cir. 1984)
CARINO v. U OF OKLAHOMA BOARD OF REGENTS	1984	750 F.2d 815 (10th Cir. 1984)
TRAN v. CITY OF HOUSTON	1983	1983 U.S. Dist. LEXIS 18958, 31 Empl. Prac. Dec. (CCH) P33412, 35 Fair Empl. Prac. Cas. (BNA) 471 (S.D. Tex. Feb. 28, 1983)
BERKE v. OHIO DEPARTMENT OF PUBLIC WELFARE	1980	628 F.2d 980 (6th Cir. 1980)
EDWARDS v. GLADEWATER INDEPENDENT SCHOOL DISTRICT	1978	572 F.2d 496 (5th Cir. 1978)
GARCIA v. VICTORIA INDEPENDENT SCHOOL DISTRICT	1978	1978 U.S. Dist. LEXIS 16423; 17 Empl. Prac. Dec. (CCH) P8544 (S.D. Tex 1978)
MARTIN LUTHER KING JUNIOR ELEMENTARY SCHOOL v. MICHIGAN BOARD OF EDUCATION	1978	463 F. Supp. 1027 (E.D. Mich. 1978)
MEJIA v. NEW YORK SHERATON HOTEL	1978	459 F. Supp. 375, 376 (S.D.N.Y. 1978)
LAU v. NICHOLS	1974	414 U.S. 563; 94 S. Ct. 786; 39 L. Ed. 2d 1; 1974 U.S. LEXIS 151
SPARKS v. GRIFFIN	1972	460 F.2d 433 (5th Cir.1972)
PARK v. JAMES A. BAKER III, SECRETARY OF THE TREASURY	1990	EEOC No. 05870646.

Table 9.5 Cases studied

Reference	Full legal title
Andrews 1992	George W. Andrews v. Cartex Corporation. Civil Action No. 91-7109. 1992 U.S. District Court
Ang 1991	Ang v. Procter & Gamble Co., 932 F.2d 540, 546 (6th Cir. 1991)
Bell 1984	Bell v. Home Life Insurance Co., 596 F. Supp. 1549, 1554-55 (M.D.N.C. 1984)
Berke 1980	Berke v. Ohio Department of Public Welfare, 30 FEP Cases 387 (S.D. Ohio 1978), aff'd, 628 F.2d 980 (8th Cir. 1980)
Carino 1984	Carino v. University of Okla., 25 F.E.P. 1332, 1336-37 (W.D. Okla. 1981), aff'd, 750 F.2d 815 (10th Cir. 1984)
Carroll 1989	Carroll v. Elliott Personnel Services, 1989 U.S. Dist. LEXIS 16676, 51 Fair Empl. Prac. Cas. (BNA) 1173, 1175 (D.Md. 1989)
Casas 1983	Casas v. First Am. Bank, 31 Fair Empl. Prac. Cas. 1479, 1480-82 (D.D.C. 1983)
Dabor 1991	Dabor v. Dayton Power & Light Co., 925 F.2d 1462, 1991 U.S. App. LEXIS 16912 (6th Cir. Ohio 1991)
Edwards 1981	Edwards v. Gladewater Independent School District, 572 F. 2d 496 – Court of Appeals, (5th Circuit 1981)
Dercach 1987	Dercach v. Indiana Dep't of Highways, 1987 U.S. Dist. LEXIS 13413
Fragante 1989	Fragante v. City & County of Honolulu, 888 F.2d 591 (9th Cir. 1989)
Duddey 1989	John Duddey v. David S. Ruder, Chairman Securities & Exchange Commission, EEOC No. 05890115
Garcia 1978	Garcia v. Victoria Independent School Dist., 1978 U.S. Dist. LEXIS 16423, 17 Empl. Prac. Dec. (CCH) P8544 (S.D. Tex. 1978)
Hou 1983	Hou v. Pennsylvania, Dep't of Education, Slippery Rock State College, 573 F. Supp. 1539, 1983 U.S. Dist. LEXIS 11939, 33 Fair Empl. Prac. Cas. (BNA) 513 (W.D. Pa. 1983)
Ipina 1998	Ipina v. Michigan , 1998 U.S. Dist. LEXIS 10996 (W.D. Mich. June 30, 1998)
Kahakua 1989	Kahakua v. Friday, 876 F.2d 896, 1989 U.S. App. LEXIS 8253 (9th Cir. Haw. 1989)
King 1979	Martin Luther King Elementary School Children v. Ann Arbor School District, 473 F. Supp. 1371 (E.D.Mich.1979)
Kpodo (resolution unclear)	Kpodo and EEOC v. Madison Hotel Corporation, Civil Action No. 92-718 A. Eastern District Virginia, Alexandria Divison.
Lubitz 1992	Lubitz v. Garrett, 962 F.2d 7, 1992 U.S. App. LEXIS 17272 (4th Cir. Va. 1992)
Mandhare 1985	Mandhare v. W.S. LaFargue Elementary School, 605 F. Supp. 238, 241 (E.D.La. 1985). Unpublished opinion of Chief Judge Clark, U.S. Court of Appeals, Fifth Circuit, No. 85-3212.
Mejia 1978	Mejia v. New York Sheraton Hotel, 459 F. Supp. 375, 376 (S.D.N.Y. 1978)
Park 1995	Kee Y. Park v. James A. Baker III, Secretary of the Treasury, EEOC No. 05870646. http://goo.gl/hJlqZ
Patel 1997	Patel and Equal Employment Commission v. Eiki International, Inc. U.S. District Court for the Central District of California.
Rodriguez 1989	Rodriguez v. Hialeah , 716 F. Supp. 1425, (U.S. Dist. 1989)
Sparks 1972	Sparks v. Griffin, 460 F.2d 433, 443 (5th Cir. 1972)
Stephen 1989	Stephen v. PGA Sheraton Resort, Ltd., 873 F.2d 276, 279 (11th Cir. 1989)

Table 9.5 Continued

Reference	Full legal title
Tran 1983	Duong Nhat Tran v. City of Houston, 35 Fair Empl. Prac. Cas. (BNA) 471, 472 (S.D. Tex. 1983)
Vartivarian 1992	Vartivarian v. Golden Rule Ins. Co., 1992 U.S. App. LEXIS 11632 (7th Cir. May 13, 1992)
Xieng 1993	Phanna K. Xieng v. Peoples Nat'l Bank of Wash., 120 Wn.2d 512, 531, 844 P.2d 389 (Supreme Court WA1993)

DISCUSSION QUESTIONS AND EXERCISES

- In Kyomugisha v. Clowney and the University of Wisconsin, Clowney asked the following question during her deposition: "How about the burden on the other person to go and take courses and study and to be understood as well why should the burden be on the recipient?" How would you characterize Clowney's position? How do you think someone in her position might fail to see the flaws in her arguments?
- Matsuda talks about positive reactions to accents, which may "charm, surprise, intrigue." Which accents do you perceive positively? Pick one, and think about what underlies your positive evaluation. Is there any more substance to this positive evaluation than there is to a negative evaluation?
- One of Matsuda's students once wrote: "What would be the point of being a citizen if non-citizens had equal rights?" How would you answer that question?
- The courts have sometimes disagreed with the claim that accent is immutable. There is generally agreement that skin color is immutable, but language features are not. How do technological advances change our understanding of "immutability?" As it becomes possible to change skin color and gender, does that mean race and sex should no longer be protected?
- Where does religion – another protected category – fit into the question of immutability? See if you can come up with an interpretation that justifies the use of "immutability" in some cases and not others, and decide where language features fit into the bigger picture.
- Of the cases presented in this chapter, which is most reminiscent of the language subordination model? Which is least?

Notes

1 As will become clear, there are exceptions. For example, if the employer could show that the environment poses a physical danger to someone wearing a headscarf, the court would likely agree with the employer. In addition, companies employing less than 15 workers are not bound by these statutes.

2 Discrimination is a matter of law: "the effect of a statute or established practice which confers particular privileges on a class arbitrarily selected from a large number of persons, all of whom stand in the same relation to the privileges granted and between whom and those not favored no reasonable distinction can be found" (*Black's Law Dictionary* 1991: 323).

3 Some courts have ruled that the customer-preference argument does not apply to language-focused Title VII discrimination. This is a matter of some debate, and Smith argues persuasively that customer preference should be excluded in these cases as they are in other protected categories.

4 See also Cutler (1985).

5 You will find flow charts for the court system and the progression of civil actions in the Appendix at the end of this chapter.

6 The EEOC reviews complaints and if they find a violation has taken place, they may take on the case and file suit for the employee against the employer. Raj Gupta, formerly of the EEOC, estimates that the EEOC prosecutes 70 percent of such cases; in the other 30 percent, they may or may not grant a Notice of Right to Sue. Lack of such Notice does not prohibit the employee from proceeding; the right to pursue such matters in the courts is sacrosanct. Thus the Notice of Right to Sue is primarily an indication to the employee of the strength of the case. For employees of federal government agencies, the EEOC conducts the hearing, which is empowered by Title VII to hear discrimination cases; if they find for the plaintiff, they can order remedies. The federal agencies can appeal only to the EEOC.

7 Further excluded or missing are: cases which primarily concerned the English-Only question and cases in which language-focused discrimination played a minimal role in the Plaintiff's arguments.

8 There are no summary statistics kept by the EEOC and no central logging system for such cases, and even if proceedings were begun, many cases are not summarized for publication. All statistics are based on the court cases that took place prior to May, 1993.

9 This study was conducted in response to a series of inquiries from Congress on the effect of the 1986 immigration laws. Not all the GAO's findings were clear or interpretable, especially in the matter of specifically accent-based discrimination. The report in question outlines a number of reasons for this having to do with sampling and design questions.

10 A table of all cases mentioned is provided in Table 9.4. All quotes are taken from court documents and summaries of court findings, opinions, and complaints. Table 9.5 provides a list of all the cases studied for this chapter but not cited expressly but included in the statistics quoted.

11 *Haole* is a reference to both skin color (white) and geographic origins (someplace other than Hawai'i). It is often used and understood in a negative way.

12 According to Clark and Wilkes-Gibbs:

> In many circumstances, as in literary forms, lectures, and radio broadcasts, writers and speakers are distant from their addressees in place, time, or both. They might be assumed to adhere to a weakened version of mutual responsibility . . . speakers still monitor what they say . . . It is just that they do all this without feedback from listeners.
>
> (1990: 35–36)

The radio broadcasters, of course, are reading from prepared texts and so the distribution of communicative burden does not apply in the way it does in discourse.

13 Most of the details of this case originate in Matsuda's seminal 1991 article on language-focused discrimination in the courts (Matsuda 1991: 1902).

14 It seems that three distinct kinds of expert witnesses testify in these trials: linguists (for example, Charlene Sato of the University of Hawaii testified in the Kahakua case); speech pathologists; and "speech consultants." The last group is often composed

of those who teach "accent reduction" classes, or otherwise have a vested interest in the official commendation of a *SAE. Some judges, especially the judge who heard the Kahakua case, are very receptive to arguments made by accent reduction witnesses.

15 Fragante is Filipino, a fact that might seem trivial most people outside Hawai'i, but it is not. Japanese-Filipino relations are considered in more depth in Chapter 12.

16 I was contacted by the Plaintiff's attorney and asked to consult on this case, should it come to trial. The case was settled after early depositions, and thus my services were not required, and I took no compensation for initial consultations.

17 English is the official language of instruction from first grade onwards in Uganda; the University of Makerere's language of instruction is also English. English is the language of government and commerce and the primary medium of education; official publications and most major newspapers appear in English, and English is often employed in radio and television broadcasts. There are other languages which serve as *lingua francas*, including Swahili and French. Which is dominant at any one time is dependent on a wide range of political and social variables.

18 As the Chancellor of the University acknowledged in 1996, while Ms. Kyomugisha does not speak "Wisconsin English, she nevertheless speaks perfectly fine English" (Kyomugisha v. Clowney, complaint filed October 16, 1997).

19 There were no charges of racism filed against Clowney, perhaps because she was also African American. Racism and animosity between African Americans and African nationals is a larger topic, one that is relevant to this and other cases.

20 I conducted two phone interviews with Ms. Mandhare in 1994. Those interviews are the source of much of the detail provided here.

21 Ms. Mandhare tells a very different story. In interview, she alleged that her first year at the K-2 school was also the principal's first year, and that he openly admitted that he had promised her job as librarian to someone else. She reports that he asked her to request a transfer, which she did not wish to do. After this episode, he told her in a one-to-one meeting that she had a "very heavy accent."

22 For a more recent but very similar case, see Poskocil v. Roanoke County. Poskocil, a native of Columbia who speaks Spanish as her first language, had repeatedly applied for a teaching position and was repeatedly rejected on the basis of her accent, to which the students objected. Poskocil was applying to teach Spanish.

23 In another study, Kavas and Kavas (2008) found much less animosity toward teachers with accents at Southeastern University. However, their data originated in a self-administered solicitation of student opinions. This provides us with an idea of what students believe they believe, or what they know they are supposed to believe, but it reveals nothing about the actual nature of the relationship between foreign-accented faculty and the student.

24 Hill (2008) examines the predisposition to make excuses for and rationalize evidence of racism when the person in question is a white male in a position of power.

Suggested further reading

Legal scholarship

Del Valle, S. (2003) *Language Rights and the Law in the United States: Finding Our Voices.* Buffalo, NY: Multilingual Matters.

Smith, G. (2005) "I Want to Speak Like a Native Speaker": The Case for Lowering the Plaintiff's Burden of Proof in Title VII Accent Discrimination Cases. *Ohio State Law Journal* 66: 231–267.

Sturm, S. (2001) Second Generation Employment Discrimination: A Structural Approach. *Columbia Law Review* 101: 458–568.

U.S. Equal Employment Opportunity Commission (1996) *National Origin Discrimination: Employment Discrimination Prohibited by Title VII of the Civil Rights Act of 1964, as Amended.* Washington, D.C.: U.S. Equal Employment Opportunity Commission, Technical Assistance Program.

Wyld, D.C. (1996) Managing in a Nuevo Mundo: Accommodating Linguistic and Cultural Diversity under Title VII. *Employee Responsibilities and Rights Journal* 9: 285–302.

Yuracko, K.A. (2006) Trait Discrimination as Race Discrimination: An Argument about Assimilation. *George Washington Law Review* 74: 365–71.

Legal cases

The quickest and easiest way to get information about a court case is to use Google's "legal opinions and journals" search which is a category within the "scholarly search" page. Type the information you have about the case you're looking up (the names of plaintiffs and defendants are a good place to start).

Language

Derwing, T.M. and Munro, M.J. (2009) Putting Accent in Its Place: Rethinking Obstacles to Communication. *Language Teaching* 42: 476–490.

Southern Poverty Law Center (n.d.) Speak up to Bigotry. In *Handbook*, available at: http://www.splcenter.org/get-informed/publications/speak-up-responding-to-everyday-bigotry.

Law reference

FindLaw News, cases and codes; a resource for students, legal professionals and the public, available at: http://www.findlaw.com/.

Glossary published by the U.S. Court System, available at: http://www.uscourts.gov/common/glossary.aspx.

Lawsource.com is a comprehensive, uniform, and useful compilation of links to freely accessible on-line sources of law for the United States and Canada, available at: http://www.lawsource.com.

Legal terms and definitions at Law. com, available at: http://dictionary.law.com/Default.aspx?selected=199.

The real trouble with Black language[1]   10

It is not the Black child's language which is despised: It is his experience.

James Baldwin, "Nobody knows my name" (1985b)

A white face goes with a white mind. Occasionally a Black face goes with a white mind. Very seldom a white face will have a Black mind.

Nikki Giovanni, attributed

Grammar: resistance is futile

AAVE has been the focus of formal study for some 40 years, so that there is no lack of material available for anyone who is interested in learning about it. While there is not space to look into that wealth of information in this chapter, a short summary of crucial features of Black language (referred to here primarily as African American Vernacular English, AAVE) will be helpful when considering the speech communities that use these languages in a larger context.[2]

The features of AAVE that distinguish it from other varieties of American English have to do with phonology and the grammatical or syntactic structures, as seen in Table 10.1. However, there are other aspects which are more markedly different. Most important are AAVE's prosodic and rhetorical features (Alim 2004b; Alim and Baugh 2007; Baugh 1983; Green 2002a; Rickford and Rickford 2000; Smitherman 2000, 2003a, 2003b, 2006), in particular, concepts (such as *style*) which do not lend themselves to the quantitative analysis of traditional sociolinguistics.

In *Spoken Soul*, Rickford and Rickford point to more than three decades of research as solid evidence "that listeners are able to identify accurately the ethnicity of Black and white speakers on the basis of tape-recorded samples of their speech, some less than 2.5 seconds long" (2000: 101–102, 241n).[3] Green (2002) provides a detailed look at AAVE pitch range, tone, intonation and syllable structure, all contributing to the understanding of AAVE as a language with a unique rhythm.[4] Work in linguistic profiling adds weight to the common belief that it is usually possible to identify a person's race (and sometimes, ethnicity) on the basis of the spoken word without visual cues (Anderson 2007; Baugh 2003; Chin 2010; Smalls 2004).

Middle-class African Americans may seldom or never use grammatical features of AAVE, but such persons can still signal solidarity with the greater African American community by careful engagement of discourse strategies, intonation contour, and pitch. These strategies are what Smitherman calls the African American Verbal Tradition, which further encompasses speech acts specific to the community such as signification, call-and-response, tonal semantics and sermonic tone (Smitherman 1995b).[5] Smitherman elaborates on this in other publications.

Table 10.1 Some features of African American English

Feature	*SAE written form	AAVE
Voiced stops /b/ /d/ and /g/ are often devoiced or dropped at the end of words	cab, hand talked	cap, han talk
Final consonant cluster reduction, for example, in word-final position /sp/, /st/, and /sk/ are reduced	test, list	tes, lis
Postvocalic /r/ sounds are deleted	store, fourth	sto, foth
/l/ is often vocalized in word final position, resulting in homonyms	tool : too	too : too
/ai/ > /a/ monophthongization, (found in all Southern varieties of English)	I think I've got something in my eye.	Ah think ah've got somethin in ma ah. (cited in Rickford and Rickford 2000: 99)
Merging of simple and past participle forms.	So what we've done is, we have come together	So what we have done is we've came together (Weldon 2004)
Existential it	There's some coffee in the kitchen Sometimes there wasn't any chalk, any book or any teacher	It's some coffee in the kitchen Sometimes it didn't have no chalk, no book, no teacher (Green 2002: 81)
Copula deletion (primarily where other varieties of English can contract is or are	People're going to look at you like you're funny. She's my sister	People gon' look at you like you funny (Weldon 2004) She my sister
Verb marker for perpetual action	The coffee is cold The coffee is always cold	The coffee cold The coffee bees cold (Smitherman 1988 [1999]: 83)
Perfect particle "done" before a verb referring to something completed in the recent past	I have had enough.	I done had enough. (Rickford and Rickford 2000: 120)
Future tense marked for aspect Future tense "fixing to" + non-finite verb	I am going to eat you, Shine Are you (plural) getting ready/about to eat?	I'ma eat you, Shine (Dundes 1990: 147) Y'all finna eat? (Green 2002: 70)
Negation strategies	He didn't go any further than third or fourth grade No game lasts all night	He ain't go no further than third or fourth grade (Rickford and Rickford 2000: 122) Don't no game last all night long (Green 2002: 78)[1]
Possessive marker ('s) deleted	That's the church's responsibility	That's the church responsibility (Green 2002: 102)
Syntax – uninverted questions inverted	I asked Alvin if he could go	I as Alvin could he go (Labov 1972a)

Note: [1] Smitherman cites "I cain't kill nothin and won't nothin die," as an example of an idiom that originated in the AAVE oral tradition. It is an excellent example of multiple negation, but it also is not easy to translate. The speaker is referring to his or her own bad luck.

The African American verbal tradition clashes with the European American tradition because there are different – and, yes, contradictory – cultural assumptions about what constitutes appropriate discourse, rhetorical strategies, and styles of speaking. While the African American linguistic style has been described as passionate, emotional, and "hot" and the European as objective, detached, and "cold," we are seriously oversimplifying if we assert that one tradition is superior. What is not an oversimplification, however, is that African and European Americans have different attitudes about and responses to a speaker depending on whether she uses one style or the other.

(Smitherman 2000: 254)

Since the first edition of this book, serious study of Hip Hop culture has produced a body of interdisciplinary work relevant to this discussion. In terms of language, discourse and communication, much of this work has occurred at the cross-section of linguistics and cultural anthropology (Bucholtz 2003). While the term was first used to reference a musical movement, Hip Hop Studies have expanded beyond the local to the global. In the States, Hip Hop is a reference to an urban, youth-focused culture which has evolved from its origins in African American and Latino communities on both coasts in the 1970s, and which values creativity, color and style.

This is a very large topic and one that cannot be seriously addressed in this chapter, but the relevance of the complex relationship between the languages of African American communities and evolving Hip Hop Nation can hardly be overestimated. What is especially interesting is the way this approach has made it possible to bring almost intangible issues into clearer focus. In his 2004b study and elsewhere, Alim addresses the importance of creativity of "Style. Steelo. Steez. The fact that there are at least three different lexical items to describe the concept of style in Hip Hop Nation Language . . . underscores its importance to the community" (2004b: 2–3). There are suggestions for further readings in this area at the end of the chapter.

Style, authenticity, and race

Smitherman looked closely at the distinctive style and rhetorical features of AAVE in her analysis of the African American community's differing responses to the Anita Hill and Clarence Thomas controversy.

In 1991, George Bush nominated Clarence Thomas, an African American jurist, to the Supreme Court. In the course of confirmation hearings in the Senate a witness rose to lodge a protest. Anita Hill, an African American law professor who had worked under Thomas at the EEOC, came forward to charge Thomas with sexual harassment in the workplace. She provided ample detail and answered the Senate's questions with dignity and calm. A media frenzy arose around Hill's testimony and Thomas's responses; the matter was debated fiercely across the country.

Thomas was confirmed by a 52–48 vote. Many who supported Hill suggested that in a Senate that was 98 percent male, Hill's charges were never taken seriously (Smitherman 1995a). In her study of reactions to the case, Smitherman found cultural differences in discourse style: Hill's rhetorical devices were distinctly Anglo, while Thomas capitalized on and ruthlessly exploited the African American Verbal Tradition for all it was worth. He seized the rhetorical advantage, swaying Black opinion by use of the touchstones of the Oral Tradition and sociolinguistically constructing an image of himself as culturally Black and at one with the Folk.

(ibid.: 238–239)

Approaching this same issue from another angle, Weldon's (2008) study of middle-class African Americans again underscores the importance of African American verbal traditions in establishing a linguistic connection to the great African American community. In analyzing a video recording of African Americans talking together during a televised symposium she found that some participants moved back and forth between AAVE and *SAE by means of phonology and grammar, but the most usual strategy was to employ AAVE rhetorical devices.

Spears, a native speaker of AAVE, provides a more personal view of the rhetorical contrasts between his native variety of English and *SAE. It is a very useful illustration, and so I quote it in full:

> The radical difference between the discursive toolkit of African Americans and other Americans, whites in particular, is revealed by an observation I have made numerous times. Often at social gatherings of blacks and whites (or other nonblacks), everyone begins the evening talking together. The talk is effortless, natural, and unmonitored. There arrives, however, a point late in the evening when many of the black guests in integrated conversation groups begin shifting into black ways of speaking. As this continues, the whites (and other nonblacks) increasingly fall silent, no longer able to fully understand or participate in the conversation that the blacks are carrying on. Their confusion must result from listening to remarks made in English, the common language, whose meaning, intent, and relevance cannot be interpreted, for the simple reason that those remarks require a different communicative competence. These occurrences are instructive for highlighting the difference between linguistic (grammatical) competence and communicative (discourse) competence. They also reinforce the idea that the principal differences between African American speech and that of other American English speakers lie in communicative practices. This is one of several reasons why African American communicative practices require more attention.
>
> (Spears 2007: 100)

This analysis of culturally specific rhetorical styles makes one thing very clear: even when no grammatical, phonological or lexical features of AAVE are used, a person can, in effect, still be speaking AAVE. Thus, while the core grammatical features of AAVE may be heard most consistently in poorer Black communities where there are strong social and communication networks, AAVE prosody, intonation and rhetorical style are heard, on occasion, from prominent and successful African Americans in public forums. These may be individuals who grew up in AAVE-speaking communities but who are bidialectal, or others who grew up with a different variety of English altogether, and still chose to try to acquire AAVE (with differing degrees of success, as seen in Baugh's (1992) examination of the mistakes made by adults who are acquiring AAVE as a second language.

So some subset of AAVE speakers have learned how to shift toward *SAE in terms of grammar in order to evade the overt discrimination that comes along with their mother tongue. Most of these people will still signal their allegiance to the community by means of intonation and other prosodic features. This is almost certainly not a conscious decision, but an element of language performance – an attempt to satisfy the expectations of the listeners – that is a common feature of human communication.

Defying the definition

The 1990 census reported that the U.S. African American population grew about 10 percent between 1980 and 1990, for a count of 29,427,000, or about 12 percent of the country's total population. In 2007, the estimated population figures saw some change (Figure 10.1). How many Americans of African descent speak African American Vernacular English is a relevant but difficult question, in part because there is no definition of AAE or AAVE that has wide consensus.[6]

Various authors have put the number of AAVE speakers between 80 and 90 percent of the African American population (Baugh 1983; Rickford 2000). What can be said with more certainty is that AAVE speakers come from all socioeconomic backgrounds and circumstances. Further, while not all persons of African ancestry speak AAVE, the language is spoken by people who are not African American. Children and adolescents learn the language they hear around them, regardless of race or ethnicity. A blond, blue-eyed child raised with African American playmates in an African American community where AAVE predominates will in fact, learn AAVE – though she may also learn other varieties of English at the same time.

Stereotypes about AAVE speakers (for example, that it is primarily the language of the poor who live in large cities) originate primarily through the information and entertain-

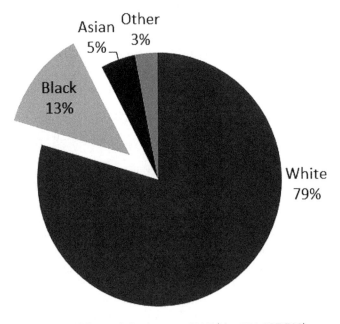

Figure 10.1 U.S. population by race, 2007 (N = 301,237,703)

Source: U.S. Census Bureau

ment industries which have "conveyed the impression that Black speech was the lingo of criminals, dope pushers, teenage hoodlums, and various and sundry hustlers, who spoke in 'muthafuckas' and 'pussy-copping raps'" (Smitherman 1988: 84).

There are dozens of websites that exist only to mock African American English (often referred to as Ebonics).[7] On some of these sites, classic literature has been translated into what is supposed to be Ebonics; on others you will find quizzes to test how Black you are or how well you "speak Ebonics," as seen in Figure 10.2.

Many of these sites have been closely studied – not to document errors (of which there are many) – but to look at the way an anti-Ebonics ideology is constructed (Hill 1995, 1998; Rickford and Rickford 2000; Ronkin and Karn 1999). For example, the so-called translation of the nursery rhyme "Jack and Jill went up the hill" into Ebonics includes the line "Jack be felt down," which Ronkin and Karn (1999: 366) cite as a case of the misuse of the passive voice, as well as the hyper-use of habitual "be." That is, non-AAVE speakers who set out to mock the language show a fondness for adding superfluous instances of "be" in places it does not belong. "Jack be felt down," is as ill formed in AAVE as the sentence "Jack down were fallen" is ill formed in any variety of American English. Ronkin and Karn provide many similar examples of AAVE that has been mangled (out of ignorance or an attempt at humor) with the apparent purpose of highlighting how very different AAVE is from "good" or "proper" English.

It has been established that AAVE has a rule-governed grammar. As this is the case for all living languages, it could be said that grammar is inevitable, and resistance is futile. To ignore this fact about AAVE is to demonstrate ignorance, condescension and disrespect.

You are 70% black

sometimes you can be ghetto, but you know how to have good manners when needed

Figure 10.2 How black are you?

Source: Adapted from an on-line poll

Linguists do bear some responsibility for language-focused stereotypes, for the simple reason that for some 40 years, most of the scholarly work on AAVE has focused on the inner-city poor. There were many reasons for this, some of them practical, as in Rickford's observation that the most segregated and poorest African Americans are the most persistent speakers of AAVE and thus provide a great deal of useful data (Rickford 2010: 28). There are also ideological and practical motivations evident in the earliest work on the African American language community:

> [S]ociolinguists' validation of [AAVE] as a legitimate linguistic variety [was] a revolu-tionary viewpoint that challenged generations of racism, linguistic and otherwise . . . Thus the most useful conceptualization of the AAVE speech community at the time, both politically and theoretically, was one in which those speakers whose speech was mislabeled as substandard or even as not really language at all were placed at the very center, as the most competent and systematic speakers of a complete and systematic variety.
>
> (Bucholtz 2003: 402)

To make up for what is, in retrospect, a lop-sided picture of AAVE, linguists have been looking more closely at the wider African American community, most specifically at the middle classes (Anderson and Middleton 2005; Kautzsch 2002; Kendall and Wolfram 2009; Wassink 2004; Weldon 2008). Kendall and Wolfram (2009) lay out a comprehensive blueprint for a more inclusive sampling across the full range of speech acts that compose what might be called the African American linguistic marketplace (Wolfram, forthcoming). This reasonable and perhaps too-long-put-off shift of focus takes into account the growth of an African American middle class and in parallel, the evolution of what has been called African American Standard English (AASE) (Spears 2009: 3), African American English (AAE) or Black Standard English (BSE) (Taylor 1983). Given the tendency to focus too closely on one aspect of the larger picture, Wolfram cautions against absolute dichotomies:

> Weldon's study exposes spurious dichotomies such as the nominal distinction between standard and vernacular African American English; it also raises questions about the role of personal presentation and audience in public speeches, including the extent of stylistic shift, performative code-switching, and the persistence of vernacular variants in the speech of some prominent African Americans in more formal public settings with mainstream, public audiences.
>
> (Wolfram 2011)

There is a great deal of regional and social variation in AAVE. The language of African Americans living in the rural South is different from that of the Latino- and Anglo Americans who live alongside them, but it is also different from the AAVE spoken in urban centers in the South (Cukor-Avila 2001, 2003; Green 2002; Rickford 2010; Wolfram 2007). With increasing wealth and the growth of the Black middle class, the community becomes more socially complex, and AAVE keeps pace.

Of these grammatical features (which are not exclusive to the African American language community, please keep this in mind), only the use of what as a relative pronoun seems to be disappearing from both urban and rural AAVE. Other features (negative inversion, regularized past form) seem solid regardless of the setting. More relevant still, Wolfram (2004c) identifies a number of features which are new or intensifying in urban AAVE.

Table 10.2 Some of the differences between urban and rural AAVE, by feature

Feature	Example	Urban AAVE	Rural AAVE
1. Habitual *be + v-ing*	I always be playing ball	+	In decline
2. Resultative *be done*	She be done had her baby	+	Not in evidence
3 *ain't* for *didn't*	I ain't go yesterday	+	In decline
4 3rd person singular *-s* absence:	She run everyday	+	+
5 Remote *been*	I been ate it	In decline	+
6 *For* to complement	I want for to bring it	Not in evidence	+
7 Negative inversion	Didn't nobody like it	+	+
8 Regularized past form	I knowed it	+	+
9 *what* as a relative pronoun	The man what took it	Not in evidence	In decline

Source: Adapted from Wolfram (2004c)

There is a growing body of research which focuses on what Morgan and DeBerry (1995) claim is another dimension of variation within and between AAVE communities by looking at the way that African American youth active in Urban Hip Hop culture must choose among grammatical, lexical and phonological variables which identify them as aligned with either the West or East coast. In a similar way, Wolfram and his students (2007: 8) have looked at features such as /r/ deletion in postvocalic word final position (mother, manager) to establish that supra-regional features of AAVE are subject to regional influences.

Baugh draws attention to wider implications of terminology and labels:

> Ebonics suffers from several definitional detriments that can no longer be dismissed . . . I therefore hope that these remarks expose some of the scholarly and educational perils of attempting to adopt Ebonics as either a technical linguistic term or as an educational philosophy, at least as long as multiple and contradictory definitions [exist]. Just as a house that is divided cannot stand, linguistic terminology that alleges to have scientific validity cannot survive with multiple definitions.
>
> (Baugh 2000: 86)

Anglo attitudes toward AAVE[8]

African Americans who speak American English without any grammatical or stylistic features of AAVE – for example, those who grow up with no contact of any kind to an African American family or community – certainly do exist, although their number would be very hard to estimate.

It's important to remember that for most Anglos, the primary and sometimes sole experience of African Americans comes through mass media, where Black men and women in power suits sound Anglo or very close to it, for as Smitherman (1997) explains: "Blacks have believed that the price of the ticket for Black education and survival and success in White America is eradication of Black Talk." In the information industry, those who do speak AAVE are seen primarily when someone – usually somebody poor, possibly victimized and/or suspected of a criminal offence – is interviewed. It is hardly a surprise that most Anglos have a skewed impression of AAVE and AAVE speakers (see also the earlier Smitherman quote on stereotypes in the media).[9]

These practices do not go unnoticed by African American media professionals:

> A few years ago most of the blacks at CNN lodged a protest about the material we were using on the air. They complained that every time we did a story on poverty, we rolled out "b-roll" showing blacks, and every time we did a story on crime, we rolled out "b-roll" with blacks in it. We went back and looked at our file tape and, in fact, it was all black.
>
> (Westin 2000: 24, as cited in Abraham and Appiah 2006)

We take in ideas and pictures – Black men being arrested, a stockpile of guns – like a daily dose of medicine lest we forget the way the world works: More evidence of a gulf between them and us, African ancestry and Anglo, criminal and victim.

In a parallel way, Anglos rarely hesitate when they are asked their opinions on AAVE. Without pause, individuals will tell you what is wrong with the language and the people who speak it. Complaints tend to fall into two categories: (1) targeted lexical items or grammatical features which cause immediate reaction; and (2) general issues of language purity and authority. The purpose is the same, however, no matter the packaging: this kind of criticism is the tool of choice when it comes to silencing the peripheralized.

In their criticisms of AAVE, Anglos tend to focus on morphological markers (for example, third person singular verb endings as in she sit, he go, she say, he yell) and the pronunciation of specific words. One of the most salient points of phonological variation which is strongly stigmatized from outside the Black community might be called the great ask–aks controversy.

The verb "to ask" is commonly defined as meaning to call for information, to request a desired thing, or to inquire. There are two pronunciations heard commonly in the U.S.: [æsk] and [æks]. In rapid speech, a third pronunciation [æst] is often heard, derived from [æsk]. The *Oxford English Dictionary* establishes this variation between [æsk] and [æks] as very old, a result of the Old English metathesis[10] asc-, acs-. From this, followed Middle English variation with many possible forms: ox, ax, ex, ask, esk, ash, esh, ass, ess. Finally, ax or aks survived to almost 1600 as the regular literary form, when ask became the literary preference.

Most people know nothing of the history of this form, and believe the *aks* variant to be an innovation of AAVE speakers. In fact, it is found in Appalachian speech, in some urban dialects in the New York metropolitan area, and outside the U.S. in some regional varieties of British English.[11] I have heard it from friends and Italian-American relatives in the Hudson Valley. However, if I had pointed the usage out, there would have been broad and angry denial.

Anglo-English speakers are eager and willing to point out this usage in others which is characterized as the most horrendous of errors:

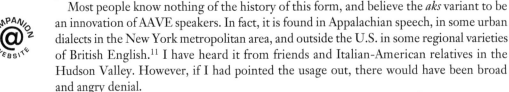

> On the last day that I met with my adopt-a-class last year, I told the students that they will have to learn to read, write, do math, and speak English properly if they are going to get a first-rate job and be a success. I told them there was one word that will mark them as uneducated . . . A young girl raised her hand and said, "The word is ax." . . .

I asked her if she could pronounce the word properly. She said, "Yes, it is ask." . . . I felt terrific. By simply raising that one word on an earlier occasion, I had focused their attention on something that I think is important, and I am sure you do as well . . . You were present at Martin Luther King, Jr. High School last week when the opening ceremony was conducted regarding the High School Institute for Law and Justice. A young girl in the class was asked to read her essay. The content of her essay was excellent, but at one point she pronounced the word "ask" as "ax." I believe that every-one in the room recognizing the mis-pronunciation was distressed and, regrettably, the substance of her essay was [thus made] less important.

(Edward I. Koch, Mayor of New York city, to the
Chancellor of Education, cited in Koch 1989: 21–22)

I guess what I'd like to say is that what makes me feel that Blacks tend to be ignorant is that they fail to see that the word is spelled A-S-K, not A-X. And when they say aksed, it gives the sentence an entirely different meaning. And that is what I feel holds Blacks back.

(Female call-in viewer, *Oprah Winfrey Show*, 1989)

My husband came here from Germany and he learned how to say a-s-k, so why can't you?

(Overheard)

All of these criticisms of the stigmatized *aks* variant assume that its use is the result of ignorance or stupidity following from lack of education or laziness. Why else, this rea-soning goes, would someone hold on willfully to such an ugly, contemptuous usage? Most disturbing is the cheerful, almost gleeful acceptance of a single variable as a suitable basis for judging the speaker's character and intelligence, and from there, to reject the content completely. Former New York Mayor Koch dismisses a presentation which he otherwise finds well done and convincing on the basis of a single sociolinguistic variant; Harper's prints his letter to the Chancellor of Education without comment.

The authority cited here is the written language: *aks* is wrong because we write *ask*. This kind of criticism is particularly illogical, given the large-scale lack of correspondence between sound and symbol in English. The call-in viewer, citing the authority of the written language, provided excellent proof of this. She spoke what is commonly considered *SAE (albeit with a strong Chicago accent), and like others who speak unstigmatized varieties of American English, she did not aspirate the /h/ in "what"; she pronounced spelled /spelt/, and she left out the /n/ and /t/ in "sentence," and substituted a glottal stop.

Uninformed or less than factual criticisms are troublesome, but they are overshadowed by other more explicit and unapologetic condemnations of AAVE which extend to unfounded criticisms of African American culture and values. Such criticisms are often openly made, in particular by newspaper columnists, as in a sports column:

Ungrammatical street talk by Black professional athletes, and other Blacks in public professions such as the music industry, has come to be accepted. Indeed, "Moses, you is a baaad damn shootin' individual" comes a lot closer to proper English usage than many public sentences uttered by Black athletes . . . But there's a problem here. Black athletes – and Black musicians and TV performers, etc. – are role models for young Black children. We in the media have begun to pass on the street language of Black "superstars" verbatim . . . and what this is doing is passing the message to a whole new generation of Black children that it's OK to talk that way; more than OK, it's terrific to talk that way . . . the situation is compounded by leading Black characters in several network television shows, who use street grammar to advance the feeling that they are young and cool.

The dilemma is that it doesn't make much difference for the Black professional athletes, etc., who talk this way – they're wealthy men who are going to live well off their bodily skills no matter if they can talk at all, much less correctly . . . if a Black child emulates one of the dumb-talking Black athletes he sees being interviewed on TV, he is not going to be thought of as a superstar. He is going to be thought of as a stupid kid, and later, as a stupid adult . . . They probably aren't talking that way because they think it's right; they're talking that way because it's a signal that they reject the white, middle-class world that they have started to live in the midst of.
(Bob Greene's Sports Column, *Chicago Tribune*, December 3, 1979)[12]

While censure of AAVE is not hard to find, it is not often that such criticisms and the underlying assumptions are so openly and unapologetically voiced.

Greene identifies two professions which he associates with successful African Americans: sports and entertainment. What these people have in common, in his estimation, is the fact that they speak AAVE, that they are in the public eye, and that they have the power to lead the Black youth of America astray. His point, and it is factually true, is that with the exception of these two groups, very few African Americans who achieve mainstream economic and social success are able to do it without the necessity of linguistic and to some degree, cultural assimilation.

What seems to bother Greene so much is the fact that the gatekeeping mechanism is not perfect: it does not extend to all African Americans. Some have successfully evaded the language of what he freely identifies as that of the Anglo middle class. It is irritating to him that these people have managed to become successful without good language, but there is something even more upsetting. As a sports journalist, he finds himself compelled to pass on the language he hears from athletes, thus becoming complicit in letting the secret out to Black children: not all African Americans give in linguistically, and yet they still get to the top.

Greene makes a series of factually incorrect assumptions. Black children learn AAVE not from television actors and sports figures (as Greene surmises), but in their homes, as their first and native variety of U.S. English. More importantly, Greene assumes that the only role models that African American children have are these sports and entertainment individuals, and further, that a good role model will not sound Black. For him, the two are mutually exclusive. His message is clearly stated:

If you're a Black child, and you're not one of the 100 or so best slam-dunkers or wide receivers in the world, you can go ahead and emulate the way you hear your heroes talk. But the chances are that you'll wind up as the hippest dude passing out towels in the men's washroom.

(ibid.)

The stereotypes that underlie Greene's assumptions are of course very disturbing, but there are other issues here which are more subtle and perhaps more damaging.

This is a good example of both explicit threat and unfounded promise in one statement. The threat is real enough: Black children who don't learn white English will have limited choices; what he claims is demonstrably true. But the inverse of this situation, the implied promise, is not equally true: Black children who learn *SAE will not be given automatic access to the rewards and possibilities of the Anglo middle-class world. Greene actually touches upon the fallacy underlying this promise when he acknowledges (later in his column) that successful Blacks who wear uniforms (airline pilots, army officers) are often taken for service personnel in public places.

Anglo discomfort with AAVE is often externalized in this paternalistic voice. It can be seen to work in a variety of forums, including popular fiction.[13] The novel is one of the most interesting points of access to current language ideology, in that the way that characters in novels use language and talk about language can be revealing. The following excerpt from a romance novel entitled *Family Blessings* provides a typical social construction of an idealized relationship between an *SAE speaker and an AAVE speaker. Here the hero, a young Anglo police officer, has taken on the job of setting an African American child straight:

"Yo."

"What you talkin' like a Black boy for?"

"I be Black."

"You might be, but no sense talking like a dumb one if you ever want to get anywhere in this world . . ."

. . .

"I could turn you in for dat, you know. Teachers in school can't even make us change how we talk. It's the rules. We got our culture to preserve."

"I'm not your teacher, and if you ask me, you're preserving the wrong side of your culture . . . listen to you, talking like a dummy! I told you, if you want to get out someday and make something of yourself and have a truck like this and a job where you can wear decent clothes and people will respect you, you start by talking like a smart person, which you are. I could hack that oreo talk if it was real, but the first time I picked you up for doing the five-finger discount over at the SA station, you talked like every other kid in your neighborhood . . ."

"I'm twelve years old. You not supposed to talk to me like dat."

"Tell you what – I'll make you a deal. I'll talk to you nicer if you'll talk to me nicer. And the first thing you do is stop using that F word. And the second thing you do is start pronouncing words the way your first-grade teacher taught you to. The word is that, not dat."

(Spencer 1993)

Like Greene's sports column, the hero in this novel has both threats and promises for the African American child. The kind of authority cited is different: Greene draws on his own mastery of middle-class written English, as exemplified in his profession as a writer; in contrast, this fictional character has nothing more to underscore his pronouncements about language than his own observations and the trappings of his own success. This is what you can have, he says, if you start sounding like me. If you do not, you do so out of stubbornness and stupidity, and there is no hope for you. This character is otherwise portrayed as an honest, trustworthy, caring and intelligent individual, to which the author adds this dose of linguicism without apparent second thought.

Occasionally there is a public outpouring of pure emotion, without any of the common sense arguments, complex rationalizations, or threats and promises which are such an integral part of more organized institutionalized subordination tactics. Such outpourings are useful, because they get right to the heart of the matter:

> I am sitting here just burning . . . the ones that want to speak or care to speak that way, *they want to be different. I believe they put themselves that way to be separate.*
> (European American call-in viewer, *Oprah Winfrey Show*, 1987, emphasis added)

AAVE seems to symbolize African American resistance to a cultural mainstreaming process which is seen as the logical and reasonable cost of equality – and following from that, success – in other realms. Alternately, AAVE evokes a kind of panic, a realization that desegregation has not done its job. The reasoning seems to be that the logical conclusion to a successful civil rights movement is the end of racism not because we have come to accept difference, but because we have eliminated difference. There will be no need for a distinct African American (or Honduran, or Vietnamese) culture (or language), because those people will have full access to, and control of, the superior European American one.

When an African American woman tells a reporter about the unifying function of AAVE in her community, his response first acknowledges that language as viable, but then he rejects her construction of the language as one with a positive function. Instead, he recasts AAVE as a willful act of political resistance:

> *Woman*: So we gotta have our survival mechanism within our community. And our language is it. It lets us know that we all in this thing together.
> *Reporter*: Black English is not Standard English spoken badly – Black English is revenge.
> (*CBS Evening News*, December 5, 1985)

The *Oxford English Dictionary* defines "revenge" as "The act of doing hurt or harm to another in return for wrong or injury suffered; satisfaction obtained by repayment of injuries." Thus AAVE is not seen as first and foremost a positive feature of a vibrant Black community. Instead it is willful act of rebellion: destructive, hurtful, and primitive in its motivations. The reporter attempts to construct an objective picture and definition of AAVE, but then falls back on more traditional views of the excluded and resentful outsider.

This kind of reasoning is seen even from linguists on occasion. The ongoing convergence–divergence controversy (is AAVE becoming more or less distinct? closer or farther away from *SAE?) might be understood as the unease some have with the idea that the African American community has a healthy, thriving, naturally evolving culture of its own which resists assimilation despite the near inevitability that disadvantage will follow.

Such discussions and tendencies seem to come to the surface most often when the subject at hand is African American school performance and reading scores. The underlying ideological conflict can be seen very clearly in scholarly work on AAVE in the classroom and school system.[14]

William Labov's extensive work on how to improve the lot of African American students demonstrates the disconnect between what he knows to be true (AAVE is a fully functional language) and the common-sense arguments put forth by those who practice linguistic separatism. Two examples from his published work illustrate this tendency.

Labov and Harris's study of language use in Philadelphia produced a lot of important data on the basis of vocalic and verbal system changes and went on to conclude that the city is "separating into two distinct speech communities: white and Black" (Labov and Harris 1986: 20). The data was laboriously gathered and carefully analyzed, but the conclusions drawn are less than neutral. Labov's stance on the convergence–divergence controversy leans clearly toward assimilation. Consider the suggestions here:

> [I]t should be possible to *bring children closer to the systems used by other dialects* without changing their personalities and their friendship patterns. From everything we have seen so far, this kind of deep-seated change can happen if white and Black youth are in contact in the early years. The way will then be open for the group to shift as a whole, with the convergence that is the result of mutual influence. If the contact is a friendly one, and we achieve true integration in the schools, the two groups may actually exchange socially significant symbols, and Black children will begin to use the local vernacular of the white community. But even without such a thorough integration, we can expect that the children will learn from each other, and the present trend towards separation may be reversed.
>
> (ibid.: 21; emphasis added)

Let's take this apart.

1   Labov proposes that AAVE-speaking children shift toward other varieties of English as a first step toward better performance in school and an improvement in reading scores for the disempowered. He sees this as an important and even primary goal.
2   What is needed to make this shift happen is early contact between AAVE speakers and speakers of other (unnamed) varieties of English.
3   The result of early contact – handled correctly – would be true integration, in which the two groups really interact.
4   True integration will bring about linguistic convergence and the shift away from AAVE, which would be better than what is now happening (the two varieties are becoming less alike).

In a talk Labov gave at a conference in 2006 called "Unendangered Dialects, Endangered People," he is more specific about some of his points: "[AAVE] is [the AA community's] great resource, an elegant form of expression which they use when they reflect most thoughtfully on the oppression and misery of daily life" (Labov 2010b: 24). He goes on to propose a causal relationship between segregation and the existence of AAVE: "AAVE has developed its present form in the framework of the most extreme racial segregation that the world has ever known" (ibid.). Labov anticipates criticism, and makes a statement designed to forestall any more objections or suggestions that he is denigrating the language of the AAVE speaking community: "In no way have I suggested that AAVE is a cause of the problems of African American people" (ibid.).

Labov's position is that in the broadest sense, segregation is responsible for the current troubles in the African American community. Many would agree with this general statement. But he moves beyond this observation to draw other conclusions. Desegregation is crucially important; from desegregation will follow linguistic assimilation and the gradual disappearance of AAVE:

> If the mixed populations of our Philadelphia schools should actually be integrated, we may even reach a time when young black children use elements of the white vernacular . . . At that point, AAVE as a whole might be in danger of losing its own distinct and characteristic forms of speech. I expect that some among us would regret the loss of the eloquent syntactic and semantic options that I have presented here. But we might also reflect at that time that the loss of a dialect is a lesser evil than the current condition of an endangered people.
>
> (ibid.: 25)

Consider the way AAVE is seen here. It is not the language of a vibrant, active community; it is the product of segregation. Labov uses words like *resource* and *elegant*, but he seems to be seeing its use as restricted to those times when African Americans "reflect most thoughtfully on the oppression and misery of daily life" – a very narrow and pessimistic view of AAVE (for a closer reading and rebuttal of many of the points in Labov's 2007 paper, see Rickford 2010.)[15] Labov equates regressive and discriminatory practices with the existence, persistence and spread of AAVE. The end to segregation brings – in Labov's view of the world – linguist assimilation, loss of AAVE, improved reading scores and generally a happier, more congenial U.S. Each of those points has been challenged multiple times in this book. It is hard to imagine a better example of the insidious nature of language ideology and the way it digs itself into otherwise open minds.

Anglo attitudes toward AAVE are complex, because AAVE taps into the most difficult and contentious issues around race. AAVE makes Americans uncomfortable because it is persistent, and because it will not go away, no matter how extreme the measures to denigrate and exclude. Official policies around this (and other) stigmatized varieties of language are policies of patronage and tolerance rather than acceptance. The irony is that AAVE is the distinctive language of a cultural community we don't want to acknowledge as separate; at the same time, the only way we know how to deal with our discomfort about AAVE is to set it apart.

African American attitudes toward AAVE

Within the African American community, discussions around AAVE seem to embody some of the most difficult and painful issues of identity and solidarity. To begin with, it must be stated that it is hard to find any African American, regardless of profession, politics or personal belief, who would deny the practical necessity of bidialectalism and selective assimilation to *SAE norms. The fact that African American children with aspirations outside their own communities must learn a language of wider communication (Smitherman 1995b) is acknowledged as a fact of life. Opinions on this range from sober utilitarianism and resignation to righteous anger:[16]

> Pragmatic reality forces the burden of adjustment on groups who are outside positions of influence and power. It does little good to claim that street speech is a valid dialect – which it is – when the social cost of linguistic and other differences can be so high.
>
> (John Baugh, linguist)

[O]ur position is quite clear. We believe that for people to excel they must acquire and use to their advantage the language of power and the language of finance. Standard American English is that. I admit it is not fair, but I did not create those rules. We only assist people in working their way up through them.

(Dr. Bernadette Anderson, accent reduction therapist)

The worst of all possible things that could happen would be to lose that language. There are certain things I cannot say without recourse to my language. It's terrible to think that a child with five different present tenses comes to school to be faced with those books that are less than his own language. And then to be told things about his language, which is him, that are sometimes permanently damaging . . . This is a really cruel fallout of racism. I know the Standard English. I want to use it to help restore the other language, the lingua franca.

(Toni Morrison, author, poet, Nobel Prize winner)

Language is political. That's why you and me, my Brother and Sister, that's why we sposed to choke our natural self into the weird, lying, barbarous, unreal, white speech and writing habits that the schools lay down like holy law. Because, in other words, the powerful don't play; they mean to keep that power, and those who are the power-less (you and me) better shape up mimic/ape/suck-in the very image of the powerful, or the powerful will destroy you – you and our children.

(June Jordan, poet, writer, political activist)

Studies and interviews with African Americans indicate that while anger is rarely openly voiced, arguments for bidialectalism based on personal experience are quite common:

I have some associates that find it very difficult to work and maintain any kind of decent job, because of the fact that they cannot adequately speak, so to speak, the normal language.

(Man on the street, *CBS National News*, December 5, 1985)

But my opinion always has been that you have to learn to survive in the real world, and if you speak Black English, there's no way you're going to survive. There's no way you're going to get a job that you really want. There's no way that you're going to make an income that's going to make you live right.

(Female university staff, interviewed for Speicher and McMahon 1992: 399)

Clear and logical arguments for bidialectalism are made regularly, and still this issue does not rest its head. But this cannot be surprising. To make two statements: *I acknowledge that my home language is viable and adequate* and *I acknowledge that my home language will never be accepted* is to set up an irresolvable conflict.

   Alice Walker, who in her novels about African Americans often uses language issues to illustrate the emotional cost of assimilation, has put it more succinctly: "It seems our fate to be incorrect," she said in a 1973 interview. ". . . And in our incorrectness we stand" (O'Brien 1973: 207). The day-to-day pressure to give up the home language is something that most non-AAVE speakers cannot imagine, and it is here that novelists provide insight into a cultural phenomenon which is otherwise inaccessible to Anglos:

Darlene tryin to teach me how to talk. She say US not so hot . . . peoples think you dumb. What I care? I ast. I'm happy. But she say I feel more happier talkin like she talk . . . Every time I say something the way I say it, she correct me until I say it some other way. Pretty soon it feel like I can't think. My mind run up on a thought, git confuse, run back and sort of lay down . . . Look like to me only a fool would want you to talk in a way that feel peculiar to your mind.

(Walker 1982)

"I done my homework. You already seen it," Shoni said.

"I did my homework. You already saw it," LaKeesha said.

"That too," Shoni said. Both sisters laughed. "Why you all the time be trying to get me to talk white?"

"It's not white; it's correct." She didn't feel as sure as Esther and Mrs. Clark were when they said it. Sometimes she was a little afraid that she was talking white, that she could lose herself in the land where enunciation was crisp and all verbs agreed. And at home, especially on weekends, it was hard to hold on to that language of success and power . . . "When you go to work, you have to know the right way to speak," she added, looking in Shoni's eyes as if she was sure of what she was saying, even though she wasn't.

(Campbell 1994)

Pressure to assimilate to *SAE norms originates from outside and from inside the African American community. In both of these excerpts, Black girls and women encourage each other to acquire the white language, a language, they are told, which will bring them not only success and power, but happiness ("But she say I feel more happier talkin like she talk"). To accept this proposition in the face of direct personal evidence to the contrary is the challenge that these fictional characters, like all AAVE speakers, must somehow meet.

Evidence of real resistance to linguistic assimilation is hard to find outside of fiction. The most cited example is surely James Baldwin's moving editorial "If Black English Isn't a Language, Then Tell Me, What Is?" (*New York Times*, July 29, 1979). The writings of June Jordan call clearly for the recognition of the validity of AAVE. Another rare instance is found in the highly autobiographical account of the Simpson murder trial by the African American prosecutor, Christopher Darden:

[It] isn't to say all Black people sound alike; of course not. But who can deny that we have our own dialect and our own accent? . . . It seemed to me that by the time I got to college, we were given a choice. We could learn to speak more mainstream, to sound more white, or we could be proud of our heritage and acknowledge that culture extends to language as well as paintings and books. I was proficient in English. I could read it and write it expertly, and I knew the rules for speaking it. And so I felt no need to change the way I spoke, to ignore the heritage and the background that formed my diction, my speech patterns, and the phrases I used.

(Darden and Walter 1996: 77)

The push–pull AAVE speakers must reconcile comes into real focus with the first day of school, where the dominant philosophy is one that promotes code-switching. Children are not to be deprived of their home language (in theory); instead they learn an additional language (which might be called Standard English or academic English or "the language of wider communication") which is to be used outside the home and community. On the surface this looks to be a balanced and fair approach, but it does not bear up to close examination. Stanley Fish's series of essays on higher education, his description and rationalization of this approach reveal it for the separate-but-equal policy it is:

> If students infected with the facile egalitarianism of soft multiculturalism declare, "I have a right to my own language," reply, "Yes, you do, and I am not here to take that language from you; I'm here to teach you another one." (Who could object to learning a second language?) And then get on with it.
>
> (Fish 2009)

A growing body of work challenges the institutionalized belief that giving up AAVE is necessary for African American students to succeed in traditional academic settings (Young 2007; Young and Martinez 2011). Quite to the contrary, Young *et al.* believe that a reliance on code-switching is counterproductive:

> [Code-switching] actually facilitates the illiteracy and failure that educators seek to eliminate, promotes resistance to standard English rather than encourage its use, and further stifles the expression of lucid prose from people whose first language is something other than English.

Young and Martinez propose that the reasoning behind code switching represents "acceptance, advocacy, and teaching of an outmoded view of literacy that stems from dominant language ideology, a belief that places a colonial vision/version of language above all others, if not ideologically, definitely practically" (ibid.). Code-meshing, in contrast, does not set up artificial boundaries between varieties of English,[17] nor does it try to reconcile a policy of affirming a child's right to his or her own language[18] with a policy that devalues AAVE (for example) and privileges *SAE.

Most efforts to seek public validation of AAVE are less visible, and still are met with a great deal of resistance. An African American journalist responds in an opinion piece to such a group organized in the Midwest:

> In Madison, Wisconsin, for example, some Blacks are trying to push the value of BEV, according to a recent report in the *Wisconsin State Journal*. They want to change the way professionals, teachers and the government view the lazy verbiage of the ghetto.
>
> The group argues that Black English is merely different, not a disability.
>
> I disagree with that. I think it is dysfunctional to promote BEV – or even legitimate it with an acronym. And the dysfunction exists not so much among the students as with their ill-equipped African American "leaders" and educators.
>
> (Hamblin 1995)

Some successful African Americans (for example, John Baugh and Bernadette Anderson, above) acknowledge the schism between promises and threats, but are resigned to the fact that there is nothing practical to be done about it. Others rationalize linguistic subordination in a number of ways. Denial – the simple refusal to admit to the existence of AAVE – is not uncommon: "There is no such thing as Black English. The concept of

Black English is a myth. It is basically speaking English and violating the correct rules of grammar" (Male audience member, *Oprah Winfrey Show*, 1987).

We have seen that AAVE is not accepted, and may never be accepted as a socially viable language by the majority of U.S. English speakers. Thus, for AAVE speakers one of the two statements (I acknowledge that my home language is viable and expressive and sufficient to all my needs and I acknowledge that my home language will never be accepted) cannot stand. One of these positions must be challenged or amended if the conflict is to be resolved.[19] Extreme examples of this are available, even in print:

> Although we were surrounded in New York by a number of poorly spoken and frequently stereotypical Black and poor Southern dialects, my siblings and I soon learned to hear it for what it was – the language of the street, the language of Black trash. The language that went right along with Saturday-night knife fights to settle a grudge.
>
> (Hamblin 1995)

Rachel Jones (1990) does not deny the existence of AAVE, but she does refuse to admit that any successful African American might speak it. In her view, Malcolm X, Martin Luther King, Jr., Toni Morrison, Alice Walker, James Baldwin, Andrew Young, Tom Bradley and Barbara Jordan do not talk Black or not Black; they "talk right." For Jones, the fact that most of these African Americans depend on AAVE intonation, phonology, and rhetorical features to mark their spoken language for solidarity with the Black community is irrelevant. In this way, the definition of AAVE becomes very narrow: it encompasses only the grammar of the language in so far as syntactical and morphological rules are distinct from *SAE.

The rationalizations found here and elsewhere are well-established steps in the language subordination process. Note the appeal to written language norms as a source of authority, the mystification of grammar and disinformation in the following:

> What Black children need is an end to this malarkey that tells them they can fail to learn grammar, fail to develop vocabularies, ignore syntax and embrace the mumbo-jumbo of ignorance – and dismiss it in the name of "Black pride."
>
> (Rowan 1979: 36)

Here Rowan, a journalist, has stated his belief that AAVE speakers must be taught grammar because, apparently, they do not acquire any to start with; that they have insufficient lexicons; and that their language functions without syntax. These statements are misinformed, and lean primarily on that part of the mystification process which would have native speakers of a language hand over authority:

> I'm a Northwestern student presently, and I got to be a Northwestern student because of my grammar and because of the way I can speak. Black English may have had its place back in the times of slavery, back in the times when we had no way of educating ourselves . . . now we do have a way of educating ourselves, and I think by speaking the way [an AAVE speaker] speaks, you are downgrading society. You are saying that you don't want to educate yourself. We have a different way to educate ourselves today.
>
> (Female audience member, *Oprah Winfrey Show*, 1987)

There is an interesting equation in this young woman's statement. She tells the audience that she was able to study at a prestigious university because of the variety of English she speaks; that is, because she does not speak AAVE. From this we might conclude that any *SAE speaker can gain admittance to Northwestern on that basis alone, which is an obvious error. People are admitted to a university on the basis of grades, test scores, and essays, among other things; performance in school and on standardized tests follows in great part from a command of the written language, a skill not acquired equally well by all *SAE speakers. The audience member has moved from spoken language to written language without even making note, and she then moves on to the assumption that education, if effective, will negate language differences, which must equal poor language, which in turn "downgrades society."

It is worth noting that another young African American woman in the audience, an AAVE speaker, points out to this Northwestern student that there is a material difference between written and spoken languages, but her statement is ignored.

The association of AAVE with slavery is not an uncommon one, and it is perhaps the most difficult one to address. The exact origins of AAVE are unclear, and the source of great debate among linguists. That the African American diaspora was crucial in the development of the language is undeniable, but it does not follow from this historical fact that the language is now dysfunctional or has no good purpose. Later in the *Winfrey* taping, Smitherman points out that the language developed as a vehicle of solidarity in a time of oppression.

This excerpt is a particularly interesting one in ideological terms:

> I do not approve of Black English. In the first place, I do not understand it; in the second place, I think the objective of education is to lead out. I think that in our society – though we ought to take advantage of the cultural differences that really make Americans American – we ought to eliminate those differences which are either the basis or result of divisiveness in our society.
>
> (Donald McHenry, former U.S. Ambassador to the United Nations, in *Jet* 1980: 57(25): 40, cited in Starks 1983: 99–100)

The statement is interesting in the way it is similar to the criticisms of Anglos. First, this is the only time I have been able to document an African American citing communication difficulties as a reason to reject AAVE. Even those most vehemently negative about the language generally admit that it is comprehensible, or do not touch on this issue at all. McHenry also draws in arguments often heard in the debate on bilingualism and the English-Only movement. These include questions about what it means to be an American citizen, and the often-stated fear that the nation-state cannot survive willful refusal to assimilate to supra-regional norms. This is not a new complaint; in 1966 the Superintendent of Public Instruction of California went on record with his prediction of complete breakdown of communication: "Correct English just has to be taught to the next generation unless we want a reply of the Tower of Babel bit around 1984" (cited in Drake 1977: 91).

McHenry restates the common belief that the only way to achieve the ideal society is to become a homogenous one, and to this end we must eliminate not all differences, but those which are unacceptable and divisive. The conflict between the wants of peripheralized groups and the needs of the majority are raised here quite clearly. But there is a question which is not addressed: the connection between language and those basic human rights which are protected by law from the tyranny of majority rule.

There is no doubt that there is great internal conflict in the African American community centered around AAVE. Those who are bidialectal feel the need to justify their choice to be so; Blacks who are not comfortable speaking AAVE are often defensive about their language, and protective of their status as members of the Black community. The greater African American community seems to accept the inevitability of linguistic assimilation to *SAE in certain settings, but there is also evidence of mistrust of Blacks who assimilate too well:

> Suspicion and skepticism are common Black reactions to Black users of LWC [the language of wider communication, or *SAE] rhetorical styles. These perceptions exist simultaneously with the belief that one needs to master LWC in order to "get ahead." I call it "linguistic push–pull"; Du Bois calls it "double consciousness." The farther removed one is from mainstream "success," the greater the degree of cynicism about this ethnolinguistic, cultural ambivalence. Jesse Jackson knows about this; so did Malcolm X and Martin Luther King; so does Louis Farrakhan. The oratory of each is LWC in its grammar but AVT in its rhetorical style.
>
> (Smitherman 1995b: 238)

On occasion, African Americans have gone on record with their own experiences as bidialectal speakers. Those experiences are seldom benign:

> Hearing the laughter . . . and being the butt of "proper" and "oreo" jokes hurt me. Being criticized made me feel marginal – and verbally impotent in the sense that I had little ammunition to stop the frequent lunchtime attacks. So I did what was necessary to fit in, whether that meant cursing excessively or signifying. Ultimately I somehow learned to be polylingual and to become sensitive linguistically in the way that animals are able to sense the danger of bad weather.
>
> The need to defend myself led me to use language as a weapon to deflect jokes about the "whiteness" of my spoken English and to launch harsh verbal counter-attacks. Simultaneously language served as a mask to hide the hurt I often felt in the process. Though over time my ability to "talk that talk" – slang – gained me a new respect from my peers, I didn't want to go through life using slang to prove I am Black. So I decided "I yam what I yam," and to take pride in myself. I am my speaking self, but this doesn't mean that I'm turning my back on Black people. There are various shades of Blackness; I don't have to talk like Paul Laurence Dunbar's dialect poems to prove I'm Black. I don't appreciate anyone's trying to take away the range of person I can be.
>
> (Aponte 1989)

It seems that African Americans who speak *SAE are not immune from a different kind of trouble: Aponte's experiences and reactions to those experiences are perhaps the best possible illustration of push–pull, and his story seems to be a common one. Blacks who speak primarily AAVE are subject to ongoing pressure to assimilate to *SAE norms in a number of settings outside their communities; in fact, they are threatened with exclusion if they do not. Blacks who do not speak AAVE may be treated with skepticism and distrust by other African Americans. Language ideology becomes a double-edged sword for those who are monodialectal – threats originate from inside and outside the home language community.

At this point it is necessary to consider that there are many persons of African descent resident in the U.S. who are immigrants from the Caribbean and from Africa, and who come to this country speaking another language entirely. Within the indigenous African American community there is a complicated set of reactions to these immigrants which can be overtly negative, in ways which are not always visible to outsiders. Edwidge Danticat's (1994) novel, *Breath, Eyes, Memory* brought these issues into the consciousness of the public. Her story of the Haitian experience in the U.S. makes clear how important a role language plays in the negotiations between African Americans and immigrants of African descent:

> My mother said it was important that I learn English quickly. Otherwise the American students would make fun of me or, even worse, beat me. A lot of other mothers from the nursing home where she worked had told her that their children were getting into fights in school because they were accused of having "HBO" – Haitian Body Odor. Many of the American kids even accused Haitians of having AIDS because they had heard on television that only the four H's got AIDS – heroin addicts, hemophiliacs, homosexuals and Haitians. I wanted to tell my mother that I didn't want to go to school. Frankly, I was afraid.
>
> (NPR, *All Things Considered*, September 30, 1994)

Her experiences (as well as documented experiences of other Haitian immigrants) indicate that there is a hierarchy among immigrants who come into the African American community, and the Haitians are very low in the pecking order. How AAVE fits into the complex issue of acquisition of English for native speakers of Haitian Creole and other Caribbean and African languages is something which has not yet been explored in depth, but which deserves to be studied both as a linguistic issue and a social one.

It would be useful, in this context, to look at the way prominent African Americans deal with the conflict inherent to the choice between languages. In the first edition of this book I provided a close reading of a 1987 *Oprah Winfrey* taping entitled "Black English." Much of that discussion had to be left out of this second edition, because Harpo Productions (Winfrey's production company) decided to no longer allow me to use extended examples. I have edited that discussion to stay within the bounds of fair use, but for anyone who would like to read it in its entirety, I suggest locating a copy of the first edition.

The second example I include here is an episode related by Shelby Steele in his 1991 book *The Content of Our Characters*.[20] The *Oprah Winfrey* taping was live, with an audience that was primarily African American. The experts invited to contribute to the conversation were two black women (Dr. Geneva Smithermann, a linguist specializing in AAVE) and Dr. Bernadette Anderson, a professional accent reduction specialist. The third guest was a white male, a professional radio news broadcaster.

It is important to remember that Oprah is not impartial on this subject. She has demonstrated her comfort speaking AAVE in a number of contexts, while she uses a more formal English in most public situations. During this filming she acted as a host to her invited guests, a facilitator to the audience discussion, and simultaneously as a participant with opinions of her own. The introductions she reads from cue cards are perhaps not entirely her own formulations; her statements may sometimes be made in a spirit of fostering discussion. But in general, it is clear that she is willing to give her opinion on the questions at hand: on occasion she claims the floor when audience members want to speak. Her comments are peppered with formulations such as *I know, to me, I think, I don't understand*. She also uses constructions like *if you don't know, you must know, don't you know*, in those instances where she puts her own opinions forth. Her tone is not coercive, but it does border on the frustrated and pleading at times.

At the time the segment in question was filmed, Winfrey's stance on AAVE was a complex and conflicted one. At first glance, it might seem that she stands firmly on the side of standardization and linguistic assimilation. As has been seen with other African Americans, she does not directly deny the existence of AAVE (which she consistently calls "so-called" Black English, perhaps because she is uncomfortable with the term rather than the language itself), but she challenges AAVE using many of the strategies seen earlier in this book.

She first attempts to relegate AAVE to the realm of the secondary: "Are we talking about correct English or are we talking about dialect?"; when audience members protest this, she regroups by defining for them the difference between Black English and *SAE, a difference which turns out to rest exclusively on subject–verb agreement. She defines *SAE very simply: in *SAE, verbs and subjects agree. She asks the audience if a person should feel ashamed for speaking *SAE, for choosing "to speak correctly."

Winfrey seems to have a definition of AAVE which focuses only on grammatical agreement and excludes phonology and rhetorical devices. She identifies Martin Luther King, Jr., Whitney Young, Mary McCleod Bethune as speakers not of Black English, but of *SAE. Once again, Jesse Jackson is raised as an example of someone who speaks AAVE but knows how to shift in his public discourse to a style appropriate for the most formal settings. The fact that Jesse Jackson strongly marks his public discourse with AAVE rhetorical devices, and sometimes uses AAVE grammatical strategies regardless of his audience, does not come up.

She quotes Jackson's famous statement that "excellence is the best deterrent to racism" but fails to discuss her equation between lack of excellence and the primary language of the African American community.

Winfrey focuses the discussion of Black English on the social repercussions this language brings with it in the world outside the African American community. She seems truly distraught and dismayed when young African Americans in the audience tell her that they want to use their own functional language and reject pressure to assimilate. Here, Winfrey's own status as a successful business woman and employer of many seems to push to the forefront. Given her own position, she does not understand young Blacks who still voice their resistance to assimilation. In fact, she challenges a white panelist on this count: "Let me ask you, why would you want to tell Black people or make Black people believe that corporate America is going to change for them?"

Winfrey justifies her rejection of AAVE based on the documented history of its reception. However, when call-in viewers or audience members who agree with this basic premise move on to openly deride AAVE, she momentarily switches allegiance. In four cases there are comments from whites which cause her to pause and come to the defense of AAVE or AAVE speakers. She sometimes does this with humor, but there is also tangible uneasiness when the discussion moves beyond grammar to statements which are at the very least intolerant, and in some cases tip over the line into racism.

The arguments put forth by those who call in (none of whom are AAVE speakers) to the show fall into four categories:

1   African Americans choose to set themselves aside; if they are excluded, it's because they want to be.

2   African Americans are ignorant because they can say the word "ask," because to say "aks" is to confuse the listener. Here Winfrey points out that if the caller understands the word "aks" in context, what exactly is the problem?

3   African Americans are ungrateful. If they don't want to speak proper English, they should go back to Africa. Winfrey's objection here is quick and to the point when she repeats a point made by Dr. Smithermann: What country do Black people go to?

4   African Americans have a right to speak incorrectly if they want to, but other people shouldn't be forced to suffer and listen to it. Winfrey asks for clarification: how does AAVE cause the speaker to suffer?

Overall, Winfrey's stance is complicated by her own place in corporate institutions, where there are gatekeeping mechanisms she subscribes to and openly promotes. For example, she asserts that employers (of which she is one) have the right to demand that employees represent employers as they wish to be represented, a right which she believes extends to language. When audience and panel members point out her fallacies in common-sense arguments, or present counter-arguments, Winfrey has one of three strategies:

1   She appeals to the authority of those panel or audience members who support her position, primarily to Dr. Anderson, the accent reduction specialist.

2   She counters with more common-sense but factually fragile arguments.

3   Or she cuts away completely, as when an audience member stands to admonish other African Americans to reject the idea that they are ignorant or don't speak right.

Winfrey's discomfort with the underlying conflict reaches its peak when audience members attempt to use her and her language as an example of the necessity of assimilation and the rewards which follow. It is interesting that the African American guests who hold up Winfrey's language as a model never point out that Winfrey herself, like so many other African Americans prominent in the public eye, is often heard to use AAVE intonation when speaking with Black guests, and that she relies on AAVE rhetorical devices on many occasions.

Winfrey would like the issue to be a simple one of grammatical relations, which would allow her to make decisions as an employer which would be free of racial implications. Ideally, she believes, education should neutralize language distinctions stemming from differences in race and class. She has the best interest of her community and people in mind, and a clear picture of the steps necessary for African Americans to achieve economic and social equality. She seems to see a role for herself here, in educating those who come after as a part of the process called dropping knowledge within the African American community. She has traveled this road herself, after all. She has made choices, some of which raise hard questions: "Does it mean that you are ashamed because you choose to speak correctly, you choose to have your verbs agree with your subject?"

When she is confronted with evidence that there is a connection between identity and language choice, that negative reactions against AAVE have not to do with the message, but the messenger, her ability to rationalize her choices and the reality of linguistic assimilation is challenged.

Shelby Steele provides very different insights into the conflicts which face African Americans. Steele is one of a group of prominent scholars and writers who form the core of an African American conservative think tank, who have been public in their criticism of the civil rights establishment. Some of the central ideas of this body of work include the supposition that human nature is more important than race, and that national interest is more important than ethnic affiliation. His *The Content of Our Characters* is interesting here because he addresses, in a limited way, the issue of language. His discussion illustrates the way that rationalization works in the language subordination process. Steele's current position on AAVE, although never clearly stated, seems to be assimilationist. What he relates in his essay is the logic which allows him to make the transition from accepting his own language as viable and functional to rejecting it.

As a teenager, Steele was a speaker of AAVE in public situations which included non-AAVE speakers. The story he tells here is probably a fairly typical experience for young Blacks when they establish social contacts outside the African American community. Here, an older white woman continually and repeatedly corrects both AAVE grammatical and phonological features in his speech:

> When I was fourteen the mother of a white teammate on the YMCA swimming team would – in a nice but insistent way – correct my grammar when I lapsed into the Black English I'd grown up speaking in the neighborhood. She would require that my verbs and pronouns agree, that I put the "g" on my "ings," and that I say "that" instead of "dat." She absolutely abhorred double negatives, and her face would screw up in pain at the sound of one. But her corrections also tapped my racial vulnerability. I felt racial shame at this white woman's fastidious concern with my language. It was as though she was saying that the Black part of me was not good enough, would not do, and this is where my denial went to work.

Steele's initial reaction is anger at the woman's rejection of "the Black part of me [as] not good enough." This episode seems to have been his first direct experience with language-focused discrimination. Thus he confronts the conflict between the experience of being discriminated against and his experiences with AAVE as a viable and functional language. As a 14-year-old, then, Steele was not yet convinced that AAVE was an inappropriate or bad language. Corresponding to his anger toward the woman is a recognition of the link between it and his race ("the Black part of me"). On this basis, his early conclusion is that the woman who has corrected him is racist.

Now, he does something perhaps unusual. He confronts the woman through her son, and she seeks him out angrily to have a conversation about her motives in correcting his language:

> A few days later she marched into the YMCA rec room, took me away from a Ping-Pong game, and sat me down in a corner. It was the late fifties, when certain women painted their faces as though they were canvases . . . it was the distraction of this mask, my wonderment at it, that allowed me to keep my equilibrium.

> She told me about herself, that she had grown up poor, had never finished high school, and would never be more than a secretary. She said she didn't give a "good goddamn" about my race, but that if I wanted to do more than "sweat my life away in a steel mill," I better learn to speak correctly. As she continued to talk I was shocked to realize that my comment had genuinely hurt her and that her motive in correcting my English has been no more than simple human kindness. If she had been Black, I might have seen this more easily. But she was white, and this fact alone set off a very specific response pattern in which vulnerability to a racial shame was the trigger, denial and recomposition the reaction, and a distorted view of the situation the result. This was

the sequence by which I converted kindness into harassment and my racial shame into her racism.

First note that his original position has reversed on a number of levels:

PRIOR TO CONFRONTATION	AFTER CONFRONTATION
her racism	her simple human kindness
his anger, resentment	his racism
wrongdoing denied	acceptance of wrongdoing
acknowledges AAVE	rejects AAVE
draws a link between	denies a link between
race and language	race and language

This is an interesting example of how ideology functions to cloak the truth. Steele is recounting the way in which he was made aware of his position as subordinate, and chose to change his allegiance to the dominant group. There is no doubt that he is sincere about the story that he tells, or that he truly believes the common-sense arguments he puts forth. But he uses a number of coercive strategies to manufacture consent from his audience, and they bear consideration. One is the way that Steele attempts to make his readers believe that there is a commonality of opinion regarding language. He knows, as they surely do, that AAVE is an inadequate language:

> If she had been Black, I might have seen [the truth] more easily. But she was white, and this fact alone set off a very specific response pattern in which vulnerability to a racial shame was the trigger, denial and recomposition the reaction, and a distorted view of the situation the result.

Steele assumes that his readers will share some basic beliefs:

- that there is a right and a wrong way to use English;
- that it is appropriate for more established and knowledgeable persons to direct younger ones to that better language;
- that questions of right and wrong in language move beyond race.

Further, Steele explains his inability to see these facts as a function of his immature view of the world and his unwillingness to accept personal responsibility ("If she had been Black, I might have seen this more easily"). His youthful AAVE speaking self relies on denial of the basic truth about language; his mature and reasonable self (the one who is like his readers) knows the truth of the matter. Thus, by linking the last logical proposition (questions of right and wrong move beyond race) to the first two (there is a good and a bad language, and it is appropriate to censure users of bad language), he coerces a certain degree of acceptance of his language ideology.

    Steele relates this conversation with the mother of a friend as a kind of epiphany, in which he becomes aware of truths not just about himself, but about people in general. In this way Steele himself and this woman function as imaginary formations (Haidar and Rodríguez 1995). Imaginary formations are understood as the way the subject (Steele), his interlocutor (the readers), and the object of their discourse (the woman who corrected him, and her motivations) are represented not as individuals, but as symbols of larger groups or types. In this analytical approach, a person perceives and projects him or herself primarily as a representative of their specific place in the social structure. Thus, Steele represents himself as a successful African American who has moved beyond denial and racism to take responsibility for his own life.

More interesting, perhaps, is the imaginary formation of the white woman who leads him to accept the necessity of rejecting his home language. This woman is by her own account (and one he obviously does not disagree with) someone with little to recommend her: she has never finished high school and will never achieve a great deal of economic success; she even looks clownish. She has not accepted or recognized sources of authority or knowledge, beyond a history of personal difficulty and sacrifice. But because she is an *SAE speaker, she feels authorized to correct his language because if she does not do so, he is doomed to a life "in a steel mill." She tells him these things not because she has any investment in him (she denies such a motivation), but out of some greater urge to do good, an urge which is sufficient authority for Steele. This woman represents the hard-working, well-meaning middle American *SAE speaker who knows best, and whose authority is not to be questioned. She was the mother of a friend, but she has transcended that role to become an imaginary formation.

There are various ways individuals attempt to neutralize Smitherman's "linguistic push–pull" and Du Bois' "double consciousness" (Du Bois 1897 [2007]), but Steele takes a step which moves beyond denying or limiting AAVE. Whereas Winfrey was clearly unable to go along with criticisms of AAVE which devalued the messenger rather than the message, Steele accepts the criticism of the messenger as appropriate, along with rationalizations and beyond that, safeguards which anticipate challenges. If you question or reject the common-sense arguments which underlie his position, you are practicing denial and recomposition. The rejection of arguments for linguistic assimilation is thus projected as racist.

What do Oprah Winfrey and Shelby Steele – along with all the other African Americans who have spoken out on the matter of the languages of the African American community – have in common? Perhaps only two things can be pinpointed with any surety: the need to resolve the conflict, and the complexity of their responses. It seems that in every case, opinions are formed by personal experiences outside the African American community which are often overtly negative. It cannot be denied that some of the most scornful and negative criticism of AAVE speakers comes from other African Americans.

Consider Oprah Winfrey, who insists on the necessity of *SAE verb paradigms, for example. Despite her firm stand on these issues, she does not advocate for the abandon-ment of all AAVE rhetorical features, intonation or lexical choice, as she herself uses these on occasion and she points to other African Americans who do the same as good language models. *SAE speakers, on the other hand, in particular Anglo *SAE speakers, have a much lower tolerance for non-grammatical features of AAVE than some seem to realize, something that needs to be examined in the larger context of linguistic profiling. This is an area which requires further study and research, because it is not until speakers become aware of differences in perceptions that the underlying conflicts can be addressed.

Where we at

The observations and conclusions in this chapter will make many people unhappy and others mad. Our common culture tells us constantly that to fulfill democratic ideals the nation must be homogeneous and indivisible. In the 1960s, the courts put an official end to racial segregation in schooling, housing, public places, and the workplace. What does it mean then to say that there is an African American culture distinct enough from other American cultures to have its own variety of English, a variety that persists in spite of stigmatization of the most demeaning and caustic kind, and despite repercussions in the form of real disadvantage and discrimination?

AAVE is a source of controversy between the African American community and the rest of the country, and within the African American community itself, because it throws a bright light on issues that are too difficult or uncomfortable to deal with. Equal rights and equal access are good and important goals, but the cost is high. Perhaps it is too high. Clearly, AAVE speakers get something from their communities and from each other that is missing in the world which is held up to them as superior and better. But the conflict remains. "We're not wrong," says an exasperated AAVE speaker in response to criticism. "I'm tired of living in a country where we're always wrong."

The real trouble with Black English is not the verbal aspect system which distinguishes it from other varieties of U.S. English, or the rhetorical strategies which draw such a vivid contrast, it is simply this: AAVE is tangible and irrefutable evidence that there is a distinct, healthy, functioning African American culture which is not white, and which does not want to be white. James Baldwin, who wrote and spoke so eloquently of the issues at the heart of the racial divide in this country, put it quite simply: "the value [of] a Black man is proven by one thing only – his devotion to white people" (Baldwin 1985b: 5).

The real problem with AAVE is a general unwillingness to accept the speakers of that language and the social choices they have made as viable and functional. Instead we relegate their experiences and capabilities and most damaging, their potential to spheres which are secondary and out of the public eye. We are ashamed of them and because they are part of us, we are ashamed of ourselves.

DISCUSSION QUESTIONS AND EXERCISES

- This chapter does not include a discussion of the AAVE speech or expressive language features which are so distinctive. Examples include verbal routines and rituals such as preaching, signifying, boasting, toasting, and call-and-response. Pick one of these and consult the works cited here to compose a brief description with examples.
- What misconceptions did you have about AAVE before you began reading this chapter and/or any additional reading? Do you think these readings and discussions will have any long-term effect on your own beliefs and reactions?
- If you are a native speaker of AAVE and you are comfortable doing so, take questions from your classmates who are unfamiliar with that language. You must be the one to offer this possibility to the class, so that there is no hint of coercion.
- Discuss the concept of Hip Hop Nation and the role of language as a tool in that social movement (Smitherman 1999 provides a good starting place).
- Read Jordan's (1995b) "Nobody Mean More to Me Than You and the Future Life of Willie Jordan" and prepare to discuss the following issues: (a) How does Jordan's classroom method compare to Young's code-meshing approach? How similar or different are her methods and philosophy compared to code-meshing? (b) Do you think her position on

AAVE in the classroom is visionary, self-deceptive, naïve, bellicose, ethically sound, unrealistic, all/some/none of the above?

● What would it take to implement a code-meshing approach in public school classrooms? Can you anticipate criticisms or objections and respond to them before the fact?

● Compare Price's (2009) sports column to the excerpts from Greene's sports column discussed in this chapter. In both cases, professional sports broadcasters are expressing negative, even racist opinions about professional athletes who are also native AAVE speakers. The journalists who are quoted in Price's column are African American; Greene is not:

> Let's be honest. Many of these guys are just flat-out uneducated, which just speaks to the hypocrisy of the "student-athlete" system. If they tried to go up there and speak properly – without major training – some would be too uncomfortable, nervous and self-conscious to say anything worthwhile . . . this problem has to be fixed before they get to college – or they've got to undergo some training once they get there. I suspect, though, that some whites are sometimes too scared to correct them for fear of being called racists for "criticizing the way Blacks talk."

(a) How is it that these African American journalists feel entitled or obligated to criticize the athletes' language?

(b) Do you think it's correct to say that Anglos don't voice similar criticisms because they are afraid of being called racist?

(c) If Greene's column is racist, as suggested in this chapter, are the African American journalists also being racist?

● Consider the central question of critical language theory: *How do people come to invest in their own unhappiness*? Or, as Woodson puts it more emphatically (and perhaps, controversially): "Here we find that the Negro has failed to recover from his slavish habit of berating his own and worshipping others as perfect beings" (Woodson 1933: 84). How do these statements relate (a) to each other; and (b) to Greene's and Price's columns?

● Read Toni Cade Bambara's short story "My Man Bovanne," which is told from the point of view of a middle-aged African American woman in conflict with her adult children. Note how AAVE is used for the dialog of some characters but not others. Bambara is a native AAVE speaker, and made those decisions consciously.

(a) Given the overall theme of the story, how does the variable use of AAVE serve to illustrate the conflict?

(b) How many features of AAVE described in this chapter can you identify in "My Man Bovanne?" Are there other features that are not described here?

Notes

1 African American scholars who study AAVE across types of language communities tend to use the term "Black Language" rather than "Black English" (the term used in the first edition of this chapter). Alim (2004a: 17) uses the term Black Language "to denote both language structure and language use. Viewing Language this way allows us to conceptualize BL as a distinct set of structural features and communicative norms and practices."

2 Suggestions on where to start if you are interested in learning more about the history and grammar of AAVE follow at the end of the chapter.

3 This subject will come up again in a later chapter with the discussion of Baugh's work on linguistic profiling in the housing industry (2000).

4 Other varieties of American English have distinct intonation patterns. See Dumas (1999) on stress patterns in Southern Mountain English.

5 There is a complicated relationship between AAVE and other varieties of U.S. English, few aspects of which can be explored here. One important and divisive issue is the selective appropriation of AAVE lexical items into other varieties of English. Appropriation and its counterpart, supportive assimilation, are subjects which need to be explored systematically and objectively. This subject was raised also in the discussion of African Americans and linguistic profiling in animated film.

6 Linguists tend to use the term African American Vernacular English (AAVE) or African American English (AAE), but there are many other variants that are widely used; Black English Vernacular (BEV) is probably one of the most common.

7 For further reading on Mock Spanish, see the recommendations at the end of this chapter.

8 As far as I am aware, there is no body of work on how Latino or Asian communities hear or interpret AAVE, or what values are attached to AAVE speakers. As I cannot extrapolate that information from the available data, I have to restrict my analysis to Anglos.

9 The representation of African Americans in entertainment was touched upon in Chapter 6, but the subject is a very large and complex one. Any real examination would have to include consideration of age-grading.

10 Metathesis is the process by which letters, sounds or symbols are transposed, as in the change of Old English *brid* to Modern English *bird*.

11 The movie *My Cousin Vinnie* is set in the South, with two main characters who are Italian American New Yorkers with very strong accents. This is one of the few fictional treatments that purposefully draws attention to stigmatized features of Anglo English that I'm aware of, and well worth watching.

12 At the end of this chapter you will find another news column on the subject of athletes' use of AAVE.

13 Eagleton has argued that literature has a singular relationship to the ideological process. He finds it to be:

> the most revealing mode of experiential access to ideology that we possess. It is in literature, above all, that we observe in a peculiarly complex, coherent, intensive and immediate fashion the working of ideology in the textures of lived experience of class-societies.
>
> (1976: 101)

The representation of spoken dialect in written fiction is a very large and complex topic. See especially the work of Dennis Preston on this issue.

14 Labov has produced a tremendous body of work on AAVE, from multiple angles. He has been deeply involved in attempts to improve AAVE speakers' academic achievement and reading scores by means of individualized reading programs. His concern for the well-being of the students and their community is genuine and deeply felt, but it is also rife with SLI potholes.

15 Academics in a dozen different disciplines have taken up the question of explaining and proposing solutions for solving the reading-related problems of the African American children. Language and grammar are rarely mentioned, but poverty plays

a central role (Cavanaugh 2007; Hochschild 2003; Hodgkinson 2002; Ludwig *et al.* 2001; Taylor *et al.* 2003).

16 See Baugh (1983: 122); *Oprah Winfrey Show* (1989: 2); LeClaire (1994: 123–124); Jordan (1989).

17 This is relevant not just to speakers of stigmatized varieties of English, but also to those who would generally be said to speak *SAE. Graff notes that his middle-class, middle-American students' attempts to write formally resulted in awkward, turgid prose because they were forced to abandon the language they knew for one that was foreign to them (Graff forthcoming).

18 Both academics and educators have written widely on the subject of affirming the home language of students (Freeman 1975; Kinloch 2005; Parks 2000; Scott and National Council of Teachers of English 2009; Sledd 1983; Smitherman 1995b).

19 There is a third option for individuals who speak stigmatized language varieties, and that is simple avoidance and isolation. Rather than subject themselves to mockery or rejection, sometimes speakers of such languages will simply refuse to engage. This is true in all language communities.

20 I am thankful to John Baugh for directing my attention to Shelby Steele's writings, which he also analyzed in part in his 1994 NWAVE presentation at Stanford.

Suggested further reading

Alim, H.S. (2006) *Roc the Mic Right: The Language of Hip Hop Culture*. London and New York: Routledge.

Alim, H.S. (2009) Hip Hop Nation Language. In A. Duranti (ed.) *Linguistic Anthropology: A Reader*. New York: John Wiley and Sons.

Alim, H.S. and Baugh, J. (eds.) (2007) *Talkin Black Talk: Language, Education, and Social Change*. Multicultural Education Series. New York: Teachers College Press.

Dyson, A. (2009) The Right (Write) Start: African American Language and the Discourse of Sounding Right. *Teachers College Record* 111(4): 973–998.

Green, L. (2002) *African American English: A Linguistic Introduction*. New York: Cambridge University Press.

Jordan, J. (1995) Nobody Mean More to Me Than You and the Future Life of Willie Jordan. In P. Elbow (ed.) *Landmark Essays on Voice and Writing*. Mahwah, NJ: Lawrence Erlbaum.

McWhorter, J.H. (1998) *The Word on the Street: Fact and Fable about American English*. New York: Plenum Trade.

Perry, T. and Delpit, L.D. (eds.) (1998) *The Real Ebonics Debate: Power, Language, and the Education of African American Children*. Boston: Beacon Press.

Rickford, J.R. (2010) Geographical Diversity, Residential Segregation, and the Vitality of African American Vernacular English and Its Speakers. *Transforming Anthropology* 18(1): 28–34.

Rickford, J.R. and Rickford, R.J. (2000) *Spoken Soul: The Story of Black English*. New York: John Wiley and Sons, Inc.

Smitherman, G. (1997) The Chain Remain the Same: Communicative Practices in the Hip Hop Nation. *Journal of Black Studies* 28(1): 3–25.

Smitherman, G. (2006) *Word from the Mother: Language and African Americans*. New York: Routledge.

Winford, D. (2003) Ideologies of Language and Socially Realistic Linguistics. In S. Makoni *et al.* (eds.) *Black Linguistics: Language, Society, and Politics in Africa and the Americas*. London: Routledge.

Wolfram, W. (2002) *The Development of African American English*. Malden, MA: Blackwell Publishers.

Wolfram, W. (2004) The Grammar of Urban African American Vernacular English. In E.W. Schneider and B. Kortmann (eds.) *A Handbook of Varieties of English: A Multimedia Reference Tool*. Berlin: Mouton de Gruyter.

Young, V.A. (2007) *Your Average Nigga: Performing Race, Literacy, and Masculinity*. Detroit: Wayne State University Press.

Hillbillies, hicks, and Southern belles **11**

The language rebels[1]

> The South eagerly defines itself against the North, advertising itself as more earthy, more devoted to family values, more spiritual, and then is furious to have things turned around, to hear itself called hick, phony, and superstitious. The South feeds the sense of difference and then resists the consequences.
>
> Ayers *et al.* (1996: 63–64)[2]

Defining the South

Drawing a map of any kind is not a neutral exercise. Every mapmaker brings a set of goals, presumptions and generalizations to the task. The purpose may be simply to gather data for others to use in their work, as was the case with traditional dialectology; these days it is more likely that a linguist takes an interest in mapping variation over space as one step in a larger investigation (Figure 11.1).

Regional variation shown on dialect maps is usually based one or more kinds of data: linguistic perception, linguistic production, and listener perception. Not even the most ambitious language atlases attempt to map all three of these dimensions. Any attempt to draw the geographic, cultural, political or linguistic boundaries of what we call the Southern United States would have to take in all these theoretical and practical considerations, and it would still be impossible to put a line on the map and declare it absolute (Table 11.1).[3]

However, there are a few features that almost all the Southern varieties of American English have in common, salient and distinct markers of the South. These are three of many features that outsiders will try to use when imitating someone from the South. That is, this is what most Northerners expect to hear when venturing South of the Mason–Dixon line:

1. the merger of /i/ and /e/ before nasal sounds (so that "pin" and "pen" are both "pin," "hem" and "him" are both "him," etc. Figure 11.2);
2. the monophthongization of /ai/ to /a/ as in the words tie, rice, dime which will sound something like tah, rahs, dahm.
3. you all or y'all for the second person plural pronoun.

The monophthongization of /ai/ to /a/ is the first stage in the Southern Shift, a series of changes in the vowel system. The shift from /ai/ to /a/ has been called the most distinctive feature of the Southern U.S. English (Baranowski 2007: 149). The distribution of this shift away from the older form /a/ to /ai/ shows distinct patterns. In Charleston, for example, Baranowski found that the wealthiest are more likely to use the newer variant /ai/, while

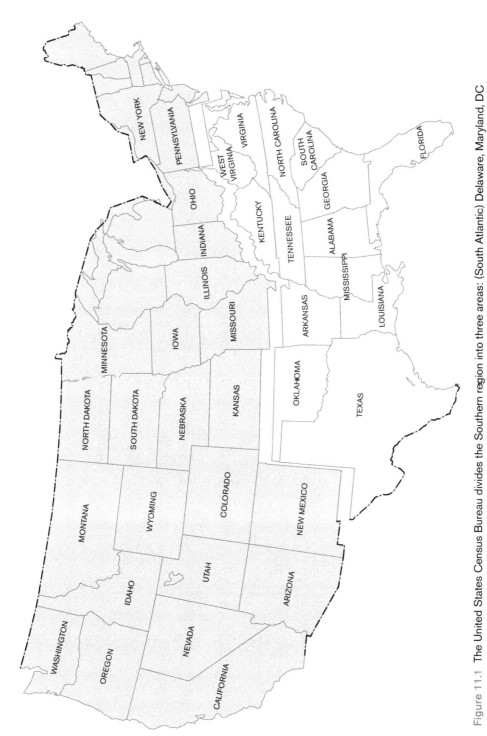

Figure 11.1 The United States Census Bureau divides the Southern region into three areas: (South Atlantic) Delaware, Maryland, DC

Source: U.S. Census Bureau

Table 11.1 Estimated population in the Southern States, 2009

State	Population
Alabama	4,625,354
Arkansas	2,830,047
Florida	18,182,321
Georgia	9,509,254
Kentucky	4,234,999
Louisiana	4,342,582
Mississippi	2,918,790
North Carolina	9,036,449
Oklahoma	3,606,200
South Carolina	4,403,175
Tennessee	6,144,104
Texas	23,845,989
Virginia	7,698,738
West Virginia	1,810,358
The South, Total	103,188,360
US total	307,006,550

Source: U.S. American Community Survey 2009

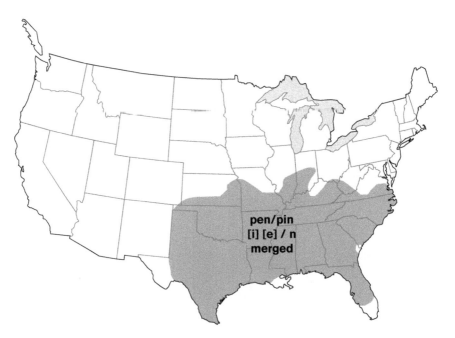

Figure 11.2 Approximate geographic area where words with an /i/ or /e/ before /n/ are realized as homonyms

the lower economic classes are more persistent in the use of the more traditional /a/ before obstruents and in a word final position (ibid.: 154).

The individual's understanding of boundaries is something of great interest to geographers, who have studied what has been called the maps in the mind. Ayers' body of work confirms that non-Southerners do have a consistent sense of a Southern core, which is referred to as the Deep South or Southern Trough.

The Southern Trough

[This] cuts across Mississippi and Alabama, embracing parts of Arkansas, Louisiana, and Georgia at the edges. This trough appears to most Americans as the least desirable place in the United States to live . . . The whole South appears to be a vast saucer of unpleasant associations.

(Ayers *et al.* 1996: 69)

The concept of an undesirable South moves in concentric rings outward from the Southern Trough, as seen in a composite "mental map" constructed from a study of environmental preferences voiced by students (Gould and White 1992: 97). In Minnesota, the students found the most desirable areas of the country to be their own native Minnesota as well as California, with other favored points in the Colorado High region. In contrast, they see the Southern Trough as the least desirable place to live (Figure 11.3).

The composite map for the Alabama students looks much like a mirror image of the Minnesota map, although the Southerners, too, tend to see California as highly desirable (Figure 11.4).

What a person expects to hear is tied very closely to what he or she expects to experience. As a child I never spoke face to face with anyone with a Southern accent. Everything I knew about the South I learned by watching *Gomer Pyle*, *Green Acres* and *The Andy Griffith Show*. I have a clear memory of my fourth grade teacher telling the class we should not watch *The Beverley Hillbillies* because of the "ungrammatical and ignorant" way of speaking. And of course, everybody watched anyway. This means that for me, a Southern accent came to symbolize a very limited and peculiar set of characters, which went on until I was old enough to read *To Kill a Mockingbird* and developed a real interest in a culture and place so different from urban Chicago. In time I came to understand, slowly, that the

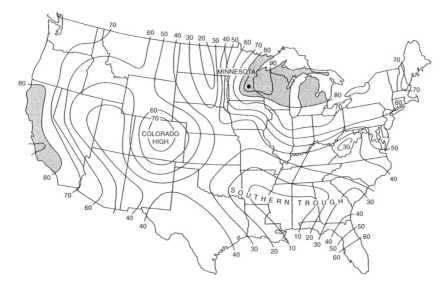

Figure 11.3 Negative evaluation of the "Southern Trough" as a place to live by University of Minnesota students

Source: Reproduced by permission of the authors from P. Gould and R. White (1974) *Mental Maps*. Baltimore, MD: Penguin, p. 98

Figure 11.4 Positive evaluation of the "Southern Trough" as a place to live by University of Alabama students

Source: Reproduced by permission of the authors from P. Gould and R. White (1974) *Mental Maps*. Baltimore, MD: Penguin, p. 101

South was a big and complex place, though to this day I sometimes find myself reacting to certain Southern accents in a negative way, and once again I realize how strong a hold the standard language ideology has everyone.

Large numbers of people growing up in circumstances similar to mine have never had any reason to reexamine their preconceptions. Instead the early stereotypes have been reinforced by *The Dukes of Hazzard County*, a general public disdain for things that sound Southern, and very specific criticisms from people in positions of power, some subtle and some not so.

In addition to television comedies, Southern stereotypes originated in syndicated comic strips (*Kudzu, Lil' Abner, Gasoline Alley*) and films (*Sweet Home Alabama, Ma and Pa Kettle, Forrest Gump, Deliverance*). The *Encyclopedia of Southern Culture* lists a range of stereotypes, including sadistic overseers, chivalrous men, good old boys, cheerleaders, beauty pageant mothers, Pentecostals, poor white trash and drunken backwoods predators (Wilson and Ferris 1989). In this artificial view of the South, English has an indiscriminate "twang" or a "drawl" and is peppered with funny and clever idioms.

This might be thought of as a North–South mental divide, a here/there that renders details of linguistic differentiation unimportant. It is certainly true that by and large, outsiders cannot distinguish an Appalachian accent from a Charleston accent, or Texas from Virginia. Of course, the reverse is also true: for the most part, Southerners are unable to tell one Northern accent from another.

Sounds like home to me

How Southerners evaluate themselves and their speech is an important part of understanding the role of language as a marker of regional loyalties, and the resistance to leveling across space.

In a survey of 798 adult residents of Georgia, individuals answered questions about what it means to "have a Southern accent," and were subsequently asked to evaluate their own language (the results presented as "heavy" Southern or "no" accent as seen in Figure 11.5).

In any such direct inquiry, some people will underreport their own usage (claim to have no accent when in fact they do) and others will claim an accent when they are not local to an area and have not successfully acquired a new phonology. Thus this poll is not one which can tell us who actually has a Southern accent, or how "heavy" accents really are, but it can tell us that people attach bundles of social markers to degrees of Southern accent.

For that reason, such polls are useful in ways perhaps not anticipated by the persons who constructed them. In the selection of questions to be asked, the pollsters reveal much of the preconceived notions about connections between certain ways of life and language markers embodied in accent. But do these questions comprise a set of sociocultural distinctions truly relevant to the construction of definitions of "North" and "South"? Between real Southern and half-hearted or make-believe Southern?

In this questionnaire, most stereotypes about the South are represented one or more times. The pollster is looking for Southern/Non-Southern distinctions based on religious and cultural practices and beliefs, so that real Southerners – those who will admit to having "strong" accents – are the ones who eat chitlins and moon pies, drive an American car to church on Sunday mornings while other, less Southern types are at home eating bagels and lox.

Something to note: In comparing the polls in Figures 11.5 and 11.6, it becomes clear that perceptions differ very little in matters having to do with stereotype. About 50 percent of both groups find *Gone with the Wind* relevant to a definition of the South (but what if they factored race into the analysis? Would the preference hold true?). This is a clear demonstration of the strength and durability of stereotypes in defining both self and other.

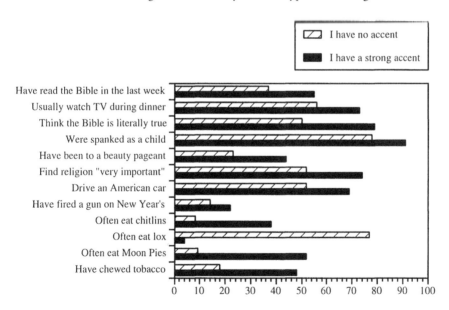

Figure 11.5 Responses of adults residing in Georgia to the yes/no question "Being Southern means that you . . ."

Source: Survey conducted April 12–24, 1995 by the Applied Research Center, Georgia State University. Margin of error +/– 3.4 points

For the most part, variation in language is active below the level of consciousness. In the South, distinctive language features are cultivated by many. The term once used to describe such situations is covert prestige as in this example (Riddle 1993):

> Joe is proud of the fact that he has a strong Piedmont accent, even knowing that it may well cost him in a job interview. If he tried to sound Yankee, his friends would laugh at him. Here the values of home and community are more important than the economic or social promises that are attached to "sounding Yankee."

Covert and overt prestige are relative concepts and highly dependent on a speaker's point of view. On an internet chat site, when asked what accents he likes and which ones he hates, someone like Joe says:[4] "There's an accent from the part of the Piedmont of NC where I am from – slow, deliberate, thoughtful and very country. Sounds like home to me." The fact that language variation lies at the heart of much of everyone's construction of the South can be documented in a variety of ways.

A survey undertaken by the Center for the Study of the American South in 2001 further speaks to the fact that Southerners see language distinctions as important. Respondents were first asked to describe themselves along the familiar parameters (sex, race, age) as well as less common ones (church attendance, political leanings, regional allegiances). Those who consider themselves Southerners were far more likely to claim a strong or noticeable accent (74.8 percent acknowledged an accent of some degree; 25.2 percent denied having one at all) (Table 11.2).

It is hard to imagine constructing a similar survey for Northerners. For such a survey to be conducted in Cincinnati, for example, what would be the equivalent of *Gone with the Wind* or moon pies?

The map in the mind

In a range of studies focusing on linguistic perceptions, Preston (1989a, 1989b, 1993a, 1993b; Preston and Long, 1999, and elsewhere) also found that in linguistic terms, non-Southerners tend to draw rough distinctions between the Southern Trough and the rest of the Southern states: Tennessee and Kentucky are the "Outer South;" Texas is its own kind of South, whereas Florida is hardly South at all in the minds of most Northerners. The "Southwest" may include Texas, but may also exclude New Mexico and Arizona, which are often grouped with those states which are perceived as prototypically West.[5] Figure 11.6 shows the results of a *Journal-Constitution Southern Life* poll in 1995.

Table 11.2 Do you have a Southern accent?

Do you consider yourself a Southerner?	Do you have a Southern accent?		
	Yes, strong	*Noticeable*	*No*
Yes, a Southerner	29.8	45.0 (74.8 combined)	25.2
No, not a Southerner	8.1	17.0 (25.1 combined)	74.9

Source: Center for the Study of the American South, 2001, "Southern Focus Poll, Spring 2001," Odum Institute for Research in Social Science, University of North Carolina at Chapel Hill. N = 605.

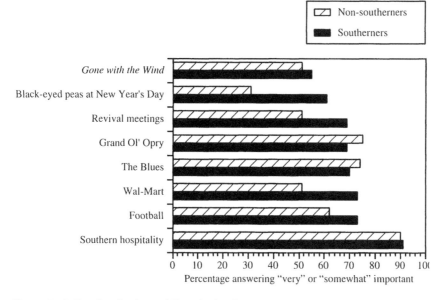

Figure 11.6 Results of a *Journal-Constitution Southern Life* poll in which 1078 Southerners and 507 non-Southerners answered the question "How important are the following to your definition of today's South?"

Source: Poll conducted in February and March 1995 by the Institute for Research in Social Science, University of North Carolina at Chapel Hill. Margin of error +/− 3 points for Southerners and 5 points for non-Southerners

In spite of these perceived differentiations, Northerners remain very unaware of what distinguishes one Southern variety of English from another, thus producing the one-size-fits-all accent when attempting to "sound Southern."

Students from Hawai'i have a very particular perspective on mainland regional dialects, one that casts some light on the schism between mental maps and linguistic evaluation.

Preston compares a traditional composite construction of Southern (roughly the Trough) first to the Hawai'ian perceptual boundary of the South (which adds Texas, Kentucky, Tennessee, North Carolina, and the Virginias). The students were then asked to evaluate tape-recorded samples of speech from a much wider geographical range, resulting in the third boundary seen on the map (Figure 11.7). Clearly, what Hawai'ian students hear as a Southern accent moves far beyond the boundary of what they identify as the South.

Thus, if we were to isolate those states which seem consistently to be marked as some kind of Southern in cultural and linguistic terms (Table 11.2), we are then talking about almost 103 million people, or just over 34 percent of the total population of the United States in the first decade of the twenty-first century.

This number might be too small, because it excludes those parts of Missouri, Illinois, Indiana and the Southwest where English is perceived as clearly Southern in accent. On the other hand, the figure is clearly too large; to assume that all 103 million people in the 12 named states are natives and speakers of the indigenous variety of English is a generalization that cannot bear close examination.

Beyond race, there are other dimensions which are not taken into consideration here. For example, there are many Native American language communities in the South

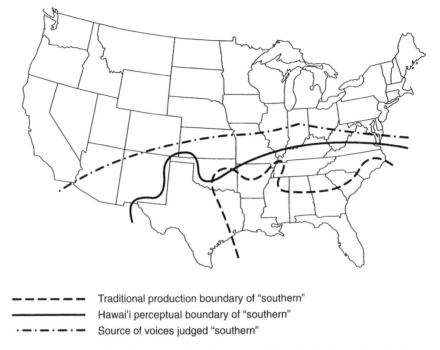

— — — — — Traditional production boundary of "southern"

———————— Hawai'i perceptual boundary of "southern"

· — · — · — · — Source of voices judged "southern"

Figure 11.7 Comparison of perceptual, production, and identification boundaries for the area
"Southern," from the point of view of Hawai'i respondents

Source: Preston (1989a: 129). Reprinted with permission of the publisher, De Gruyter

(Scancarelli and Hardy 2005), large enclaves of Spanish speakers (Bankston 2007), and smaller ones of Louisiana Creole and Gullah, among others. Thus it is only a very rough estimate to say that somewhere around 30 percent of the population speaks U.S. English with an accent which is heard as "Southern."

There seems to be a strong urge to synthesize the South into a single population united primarily in the fact that it is distinct from the North. This is a process Southerners themselves both promote and reject, according to Ayers *et al.*:

> The South plays a key role in the nation's self-image: the role of evil tendencies overcome, mistakes atoned for, progress yet to be made. Before it can play that role effectively, the South has to be set apart as a distinct place that has certain fundamental characteristics. As a result, Southern difference is continually being recreated and reinforced . . . The South eagerly defines itself against the North, advertising itself as more earthy, more devoted to family values, more spiritual, and then is furious to have things turned around, to hear itself called hick, phony, and superstitious. The South feeds the sense of difference and then resists the consequences.
>
> (Ayers *et al.* 1996: 63–64)

Hostility with a smile

Nora Norules, a young attorney, worked for a law firm in a large city. With hair like spun gold and eyes like wild violets, she favored traditional business suits.

One day Ms. Merry Erudite, a client, said to Bob, a senior law partner, "When your new attorney speaks, her looks fall off her. In fact, your firm begins to look shabby after she utters a few sentences. Bob, she wouldn't know an irregular verb if it bit her on the elbow. She says, for example, 'I have went,' and she doesn't know she's made a glaring mistake."

"I know, but what can we do? She is, after all, a brilliant attorney," said Bob.

Merry said, "She also says 'have ran' and 'has broke.' I suggest that each time one of your employees says, 'I have went,' you pull out a stun gun, and let 'em have it. Then stress proper usage by repeating, 'I have gone. I had gone. He has gone. They have gone.' Maybe they'll get the idea and remember to replace went with gone when using helping verbs."

Dolly Withrow, *Charleston Daily Mail*, July 27, 2009.[6]
Reproduced with permission.

I start with an excerpt from Withrow's newspaper column to establish one clear fact: there are Southerners who participate – gleefully – in the language-focused subordination not just of strangers, but of their neighbors and co-workers. Note that the characters in Withrow's fictional scenario are not poor or uneducated; the person who is getting the brunt of the criticism is beautiful and accomplished.

Perhaps this column was meant to be humorous, but in fact the author has provided an excellent example of Bourdieu's strategies of condescension (Bourdieu and Thompson 1991: 68–71). Strategies of condescension is a reference to a tactic whereby an empowered individual (someone with social legitimacy in terms of employment or education or language or other kinds of authority) – appropriates the subordinated language for a short period of time in order to exploit it. In this case, the author repeats the verb constructions which offend her in order to mock them, and the person who uses them.

Withrow is a former college professor of English, someone who writes for newspapers and has written a book about grammar and usage. Those accomplishments are enough for her to claim the advantage over someone she describes as a brilliant lawyer. Withrow claims authority in matters of language with some particularly harsh and hostile imagery which reduces speakers of the unnamed dialect to creatures in need of violence to be kept in line. The strategy of condescension is in fact a part of a larger strategy of subversion, or within the framework set up for this study, part of the overall language subordination model.

There are many Southerners who are known to a wider audience: politicians Bill Clinton and Al Gore; writers Elmore Leonard, Roy Blount and Dorothy Allison; journalists Katie Couric and Kokie Roberts; actors Matthew McConaughey and Channing Tatum. And still, the Southerners who seem to come most quickly to the minds of Northerners are the fictional ones, and more than that, the stereotypical fictional ones: Gomer, Pa and Ellie Mae and the rest of the Beverly Hillbillies, murderous backwoodsmen, vapid beauty queens, spoiled young women and wise old ones.

One of the primary characteristics of the stereotyped Southerner is ignorance, but it is a specific kind of ignorance – one disassociated from education and literacy:

A. [William Natcher, a member of the House of Representatives from Kentucky] "mumbled in a Mississippi drawl nobody understands."

(NPR, March 23, 1994, Reporter: Kokie Roberts)

B. *Anchor*: Don't ask me why, but you know and I know the rest of the country tends to snicker when they hear a strong Southern accent, which can make the speaker feel a little self-conscious. So what do you do about it? Well you can ignore it or get annoyed, or like some Greenville, South Carolina students, if you can't beat 'em, you can join 'em.

(*ABC Evening News*, December 15, 1991)

C. I got an interview with an extremely elite undergraduate college in the Northeast. They conducted the first substantial part of the interview in [another language] and it went well. When they switched to a question in English, my first answer completely interrupted the interview . . . they broke out laughing for quite a while. I asked what was wrong and they said they "never would have expected" me to have such an accent. They made a big deal about me having a [prestigious accent in the second language] and such a strong Southern accent. Of course, I had been aiming for bland Standard American English. After that, I got a number of questions about whether I'd "be comfortable" at their institution. Subtle, but to me it was not ambiguous.

(University foreign language professor, native of the South)

D. For 37 years, Charles Kuralt has shown us what network news can be – calm, thoughtful, perceptive. Beneath that deceptive North Carolina drawl, there's a crisp intelligence.

(*Lansing State Journal*, "Daily Guide", April 3, 1994, p. 1)

Together, these comments on the relationship between language, intelligence and communication demonstrate the ways in which language barriers are built and rationalized. In Example (A), the reporter (notably herself from New Orleans, and the child of life-long politicians) projects to her listeners an unwillingness to understand the Southern accent in question. Although she is clearly in a position to ascertain Representative Natcher's place of origin, she is content to misrepresent this, lumping all Southerners together into a group of drawling and incomprehensible non-conformers who deserve to be pointed out and mocked.

While (A) demonstrates an irritability and condescension which is at odds with journalistic objectivity, (B) resorts to trivialization and mockery. In a nation-wide broadcast, the newscaster uses the first person plural, we. This is a coercive gesture, one that forces an alliance.

Example (C) – this one anecdotal – demonstrates Northern discomfort when a link is drawn between intellectual authority and the South. A new PhD, a native speaker of English, interviews for a faculty position in a foreign language department. He speaks that language fluently, and with a prestigious accent. His experience, demeanor and education have earned him an interview at an Ivy League school, which goes well. Until the interview switches to English. Whatever advantages he brought into the room are forgotten and he is summarily rejected. He remains the same person, expressing the same range and quality of ideas, but his currency is devalued by language features which link him to the South.

In (A) the reporter was irritable about the accent which she found out-of-place and inappropriate (and hence worthy of rejection); the search committee members in (B) have nothing to do with their discomfort but to externalize it as humor. This group behavior they find socially acceptable, regardless of the way it affected the job candidate.

In (D), the author does not deny that a Southerner has used language in a clear and perceptive way. Instead, she specifically draws attention to the fact that Kuralt's language is not what she expected it to be. Humor, which can be loosely defined in just this way – how people react when reality and expectations clash – often focuses on a juxtaposition:

> Gov. Clinton, you attended Oxford University in England and Yale Law School in the Ivy League, two of the finest institutions of learning in the world. So how come you still talk like a hillbilly?
>
> (Mike Royko, "Opinion", *Chicago Tribune*, October 11, 1992)

> Federal law requires commercial airliners to carry infants trained to squall at altitudes above two hundred feet. This keeps the passengers calm, because they're all thinking, "I wish somebody would stuff a towel into that infant's mouth," which prevents them from thinking, "I am thirty-five thousand feet up in the air riding in an extremely sophisticated and complex piece of machinery controlled by a person with a Southern accent."
>
> (The Dave Barry 1995 Calendar, Tuesday, April 4 1995)

In contrast to the Northern construction of intelligence which is closely linked to a high level of education, there is a construction of Southern intelligence that has more to do with common sense and life experience. Typified by the character of Sheriff Andy Taylor in the popular television series *Mayberry RFD* and *The Andy Griffith Show*, this is the Southerner whose intelligence is native rather than acquired. Many plots and comic situations in Mayberry depended on the construction of Southern mother-wit and its contrast to the less instinctual, acquired Northern intelligence.

As was the case with Disney animated stories, in this situation comedy Southern accents are restricted to those who fit the stereotype: while Andy has a North Carolina accent, his son, aunt, and cousins do not. Nor do the philosophizing barber or the mild-mannered town accountant, or the teacher (a serious love interest of the main character, and – in line with the patterns noted earlier in the Disney films – a speaker of *SAE) or the pharmacist. The only Southern accents in this rural Southern town are the deceptively clever Andy, the dimwitted but good-hearted car mechanics (Gomer and Goober), and the occasional rural characters who come into town to make music or straighten out legal problems resulting from clan feuds, illegal stills, or excessive violence (Ernest T. Bass). There are no regularly appearing African American characters in this particular corner of the South.

It is primarily on the basis of intellect linked to education that Northerners try hardest to convince Southerners that their language is deficient. People with unacceptable accents are encouraged to get rid of them by enrolling in a class. The people who show their allegiance to home and region by means of language are expected to understand that they are subordinate, intellectually and culturally, to their neighbors. The fact that the stereotypes which underlie this reasoning are imaginary formations is irrelevant; their power is still real, and they are effective.

As Withrow's column excerpt at the beginning of this chapter demonstrates, the subordination process is most successful when the targets of these efforts become actively complicit.

What is so particularly interesting about subordination tactics in this case is that the object of subordination is a whole nation of people, united in terms of history and culture rather than in terms of race or ethnicity. It is fairly easy to conceive of the strategies and processes by which African Americans – 12 percent of the population living in communities across the country – are rendered susceptible to language subordination, and come to embrace and propagate a language ideology which works to their own disadvantage. But the process is a bigger challenge when the targeted group is as large and as internally diverse as the Southern U.S.

Many persons born and raised in the South have no desire to live anywhere else, and thus it would seem that threats of exclusion and gatekeeping would be less effective. To someone living in the heart of Georgia or North Carolina or Tennessee, the idea that they need to acquire an "accentless" variety of Midwestern English to succeed might seem ludicrous. Nevertheless, personal anecdotes indicate that Northern bias and standard language ideology have an increasingly long reach:

> "It's ironic," says [Judith] Ivey [actor], who is from the Lone Star State, "that probably the one project that will give me the most exposure [a movie set in the South] . . . is one that requires my Texas accent. Particularly since I was told that if I didn't get rid of it, I would have a very limited career."
>
> (Liebman 1993:14)

> School official . . . said the [accent reduction] course began when she heard people complain that their accents interfered with business. "Instead of listening to what you're saying, they're passing the phone around the office saying, 'Listen to this little honey from South Carolina.' It's self-defeating. It's annoying. It's humiliating."
>
> (Riddle 1993: A5)

> Soon after Atlanta was awarded the 1996 Olympics a year ago, a column appeared in the *Atlanta Business Chronicle* exhorting people to "get the South out of our mouth" to impress all the expected visitors. The author . . . a communications consultant from New Jersey, wrote: "By cleaning up our speech, maybe we can finally convince the world that we're not just a bunch of cow-tipping morons down here."
>
> (Pearl 1991)

> [A] human resources worker at Southern Bell, [X] is trying her best not to sound like a Southern belle . . . she is up for a promotion, and she is worried the decision will be made by Northerners . . . She is also taking night speech classes at a community college. Unless she can drop the accent, she fears, the promotion committee "might not think I'm so sharp."
>
> (ibid.)

In all of these cases, Southerners exhibit insecurity about their language and a willingness to accept responsibility for poor communication. In the third case above, the person voicing the criticism and calling for acceptance of responsibility and change toward Northern norms is, in fact, from New Jersey. But she still claims the right to speak for all the people in that region where she lives and works: she wants the world to see her as something other than a "cow-tipping moron" in spite of the fact that she lives in the South.

It is unclear whether she rejects the "cow-tipping moron" stereotype as unfair and untrue, or subscribes to it and wishes not to be included in that group. In either case, she believes that the way to accomplish such a goal is to convince the rest of the South to talk as she does. But here she takes on a Herculean task, for the South provides, more than any single ethnic, racial, or national origin group, strong resistance to language subordination.

The news media has been shown to be particularly enamored of stories having to do with accent reduction, and those reports always include a discussion of such efforts in the South. "Hush Mah Mouth! Some in the South Try to Lose the Drawl" (Pearl 1991) is not an unusual headline or introductory comment in these kinds of reports. They often contain some small commentary from dissenting Southerners: "Somebody was going to judge me on the way I spoke, then I would judge him as being close-minded" (*ABC Evening News*, December 15, 1991).

The news media does not often report on Southern resistance to language subordination. When doing so, however, journalists still manage to put a decidedly ideological spin on the rejection of subordination. In a newspaper report on the death of an accent reduction course in South Carolina due to lack of interest, the reporter summarizes various reasons why interest might have died out: "With tongue firmly in cheek, [the instructor] offered three possible reasons: Everybody's cured. Everybody thinks the rest of the world talks funny. Or, in a country that now has a Southern President and vice president, maybe nobody much cares anymore" (Riddle 1993: A5).

The tone here is humorous. Clearly it is difficult for those who consider themselves *SAE speakers to take seriously the idea that the South could be content with itself in terms of language. It is equally difficult to imagine, in spite of professed wishes to this effect, that Southerners would somehow magically lose their accents, and could be "cured" of this language which is so uniquely their own.

Another reporter writes of a "Pro-Drawl Movement" in which the resistance is trivialized, and once again the strategy of condescension extends to the representation of Southern U.S. English in quasi-phonetic terms:

> Ludlow Porch's radio talk show is at the center of Atlanta's Southern resistance. Mr. Porch, whose voice is as slow and sweet as molasses in January, gets a steady stream of female callers who call him "sweet thang" and male callers who call him "mah friend." When complimented, Mr. Porch is apt to say, "Well, ah'm tickled" or "Bless your heart."

> But even Mr. Porch concedes that things are changing. He lives in a suburb where he goes for weeks without hearing a Southern accent. And he admits that, sometimes, he even catches himself "doin' silly things – like pronouncin' mah 'g's."
>
> (Pearl 1991)

Filtered through the reporter's standard language ideology condescension, resistance is stripped of much of its power. Here Mr. Porch's concern about the fate of his culture and language are made into humorous objects. He is then made to testify against himself, in that he admits that language changes, even as he watches. The journalist's only conclusion can be that language is changing away from Southern norms, and toward Northern ones. Thus once again, resistance is demonstrated to be useless.

When Southern voices are heard uncensored, it almost always appears within Southern boundaries, as in this column from the *Dallas Morning News*:

> The [Southern League] encourages Southerners in the exercise of their indefeasible right to be Southern, never mind Northern reproaches and sneers . . . The language of the older South is the language of the small towns in which most Southerners grew up. Gone with the wind! The culture of the towns, and sometimes the towns themselves, have disappeared . . . The old way of speaking has charm and value.

> Language is a part of being . . . The more such threads we break heedlessly, the more isolated we become in a society seemingly bent on annihilating memory itself. We're not supposed to love the past, we're supposed to hate it. Modernity drums this message into us relentlessly.
>
> (Murchison 1996)

There is no doubt that in the delineation of the nation, we use accent as a cultural shorthand to talk about bundles of properties which we would rather not mention directly. When a Northerner appropriates a pan-Southern accent to make a joke or a point, he or she is drawing on a strategy of condescension and trivialization that cues into those stereotypes so carefully structured and nurtured: Southerners who do not assimilate to Northern norms are backward but friendly, racist but polite, obsessed with the past and unenamored of the finer points of higher education. If they are women, they are sweet, pretty and not very bright.

Focusing on language difference allows us to package the South this way, and to escape criticism for what would otherwise be seen as narrow-mindedness. Accent makes it possible to draw the nation's attention to the South's need for redemption without specifically raising those topics which make us nervous. If white Southerners are not distinguishable by other ethnic markers, by characteristic physical features, or religion, language is one simple and effective way of distinguishing between self and other. Because in this case differences are historical and cultural, there is less footing for an ideology which subordinates and trivializes the language and the cultures attached to it.

Nevertheless, the process continues. Accent reduction courses taught by Northerners spring up, find some uneasy response in communities with strong Northern ties, and then die away. Movies are made in which the lazy and narrow-minded twang and drawl. Southern students who come North are taken aside and told that their native language phonology will be an impediment to true success. Job applicants are laughed at, and on the floor of Congress, reporters smirk and report not on the Representative's position, but on his or her language.

The South has resources to call on, ways to deflect subordination tactics and it seems that at the writing of this book, many Southerners are willing to take a stand:

> Notwithstanding the debate over [the South's] regional boundaries and the definition of its cultural ethos, it is safe to conclude that no region in the United States has a stronger sense of its identity. The increasing commodification of things Southern – from kudzu to speech – is ample testament of this persistent and intensifying awareness.
>
> (Wolfram 2003: 124)

Thus the institutions which are most responsible for the subordination process coax and wheedle toward the ultimate goal of cultural and linguistic assimilation, and are met with suspicion and defiance.

The seduction of accent reduction

The news media has topics which seem to be of steady and ongoing interest to them, and these are brought to the public's attention on a regular basis. One such topic is the area of accent reduction, or a concentrated effort to take a person who speaks English with a stigmatized regional, social, or foreign accent, and (supposedly) replace it with one which is favored.

Accent reduction is marketed and sold by individuals who own their own businesses, or more rarely, in courses organized by local schools and colleges. College courses to reduce accent are found primarily in areas with high levels of immigration. There are also a multitude of private coaches who will take on students, but speech or accent reduction provided privately is expensive.

The New York Times ran a news article that reads like an advertisement about an accent reduction institute, in which prices were stated plainly: group training, $40 per hour per individual; $100 an hour for individual training (not including materials); or the owner will instruct privately "at a fee of $150 an hour, or $210 for an hour and a half session, plus material and travel time, though most clients visit him" (Luongo 2007).

There are legitimate reasons to offer this kind of instruction. People who have acquired English as a second language and who would simply like to come closer to a native pronunciation of U.S. English may want and pursue such training. Actors often need to learn how to simulate another accent, in a contrived setting and for short periods of time. These are not unreasonable goals, and they are often pursued by well-meaning individuals:[7]

> It is the position of ASHA [American Speech-Language-Hearing Association] that no dialectal variety of English is a disorder or a pathological form of speech or language. Each social dialect is adequate as a functional and effective variety of English. Each serves a communication function as well as a social solidarity function. It maintains the communication network and the social construct of the community of speakers who use it. Furthermore, each is a symbolic representation of the historical, social and cultural background of the speakers. ASHA also recognizes that standard English has been adopted by society as the linguistic archetype used by the government, the mass media, business, education, science, and the arts.
>
> (Prepared statement of Charlena M. Seymour, President, American
> Speech-Language-Hearing Association before the
> Congressional Hearings on Ebonics, January 23, 1997)[8]

And yet a large proportion of those advertising accent reduction or elimination draw in students with false promises and under false pretenses.

In any city of average size, there will be a few people who have hung out a shingle and sought clients with the claim that they can teach them to lose one accent and acquire another. There is no regulation or licensing for such businesses, in the same way that an individual can claim to have developed a miracle diet and charge money for it.[9]

The providers of these services are often quite willing to take a public stance on issues of multilingualism and accent:

> It is absolutely wrong to discriminate on the basis of accent. However, I think this country would be much better off if everybody spoke the same language and if communication was as clear as possible . . . If we were all clearly communicating – this doesn't mean behaving the same – we'd be much better off as a society. I'm not denying heritage, but I think that speech impediments make a person feel bad about him or herself. Speech differences [can foster] misinterpretations. Accents divide people.
>
> (*New York Newsday*, June 29, 1993)

When asked by the reporter "Is this another step in the homogenization of America?" an accent reduction teacher in New York answers: "I'm not on a search and destroy mission to eradicate accents. You know most of the country speaks General American, and we want to fit in" (*CBS Evening News*, October 10, 1984).

Having asked the difficult question which addresses individual freedoms and the relationship of language and accent to identity, the reporter has also solicited the standard response, which is quite simply, that homogenization is a good thing. The issue of whether or not the goal is realistic or attainable has never been raised, but the ideal – linguistic assimilation to *SAE norms – is seen as an appropriate price to pay in order to succeed.

The media like accent reduction, and they do not seem to distinguish between reasonable claims about language and more outrageous ones. In fact, they seem to be so clearly enamored of the idea of accent reduction and assimilation to a homogenous *SAE, that they are willing to write and broadcast stories about these efforts on a regular basis.

Disinformation is easily documented across media outlets, and it is the nature of the disinformation which is revealing. The story we hear again and again from news media representatives is that their own language is the national aesthetic and that those in the broadcast media speak a homogeneous English which does not betray (and one notes the value-laden nature of that particular lexical choice) their regional origin. In fact, broadcast news journalists do speak U.S. English with the same range of social, regional and stylistic variation that every other speaker uses. What this means, then, is that not all variation is unacceptable or forbidden or stigmatized: it is only those variants associated with groups out of favor which must be addressed. Asian, Indian and Middle Eastern accents and Spanish accents are not acceptable; apparently French, German, British, Swedish, accents are, regardless of the communication difficulties those languages may cause in the learning and communication of English.

In New York, the accent reduction teacher tells the reporter that they want "to fit in"; but the fact is, those speakers do fit into their settings, in linguistic terms. What she seems to be saying is that a language which signals a New York or Puerto Rican origin is a liability, whereas one which indicates the Midwest is not. The subtle argument is not for overall linguistic assimilation to a perfectly static U.S. English, but to a language which is generally Midwest, middle-class, and colorless.

The individuals who provide us with information and news on a daily basis in print and broadcast forums have an unusual amount of power and control in the lives of the public. They are given free admittance to our homes, to bring to us their factual knowledge about the workings of the world. This process involves choosing among those pieces of information to share, and presenting them in a form which is accessible and understandable. The translation process from raw material to finished news report involves filters of all kinds, many of which we are not immediately aware of when we take in the information over our dinners. The politics and cultural preconceptions which shape the news and the presentation of the news include ideas about language, and the importance of language. The process of language standardization is one which is implicitly and explicitly supported by the information industry, for practical reasons. In practical terms, it is useful for them to have authority in issues of language, which is their primary tool. The assumption of this authority happened long ago, but it is necessary in this social contract as in others to remind all parties of the terms. Consider the ABC piece on accent reduction designed for those who have a Southern accent.

ABC Evening News, December 15, 1991

Anchor: Don't ask me why, but you know and I know the rest of the country tends to snicker when they hear a strong Southern accent, which can make the speaker feel a little self-conscious. So what do you do about it? Well you can ignore it or get annoyed, or like some Greenville, South Carolina students, if you can't beat 'em, you can join 'em. Here's Al Dale.

[film clip*: My Fair Lady*, "The Rain in Spain Stays Mainly in the Plain"]

Al Dale: Henry Higgins had Eliza Doolittle and Dave F. has Mary M.

Student: "There is a tall willow outside my window" [pause, due to dissatisfaction with her pronunciation. Repeats:] "Maaa."

Teacher: OK, try it again.

Al Dale: At South Carolina's Greenville Tech, F. teaches a popular course called "How to Control your Southern Accent". Not how to lose it, just how to bring it under control.

Teacher: A communication problem is when someone starts paying more attention to how you're saying something than what you're saying.

[film clip *Cool Hand Luke*, "What we've got here is failure to communicate."]

Al Dale: In movies and on television, Southern accents are often used to indicate villainy or dim wittedness.

[television clip, *Andy Griffith Show*. Man fooled into believing that dog can talk.]

Al Dale: That attitude irritates Bill J. who signed up for the course because he does business on the phone with Northerners.

Student: They will make fun of you, and "listen to this guy," you know, "put him on the loudspeaker."

Al Dale: In the offices?

Student: Yeah, you know they want everybody to hear.

Student: The more you get into it, to me, the more I realize you know not how bad I sound but how much better I could sound.

Al Dale: Other students on campus say sounding Southern is just fine.

Student: Don't see any reason changing it now.

Student: Somebody was going to judge me on the way I spoke then I would judge him as being close-minded.

Al Dale: Students in the class say they're not trying to deny their heritage.

Student: I don't feel comfortable with the way I speak. I feel like I should do better.

[Film clip: *My Fair Lady*, "The Rain in Spain"]

Al Dale: Just as it did for Eliza Doolittle, what worked for these students is practice . . .

Students: "Pepper . . . hanger," "sister, remember," "I can't follow the minnow in the shallow water."

DISCUSSION QUESTIONS AND EXERCISES

● In this chapter, the popular entertainment examples that contribute to Southern stereotypes are dated. You may not know who Lil' Abner is, and you may never have seen an episode of *The Beverley Hillbillies*. Does this indicate to you a decline in Southern stereotypes? If not, where are the current-day stereotypes to be found? How were your beliefs and opinions about the South (or the North) formed? If you are interested in pursuing this question, you may want to start with Cooke-Jackson and Hansen (2008) "Appalachian Culture and Reality TV: The Ethical Dilemma of Stereotyping Others."

● Read the following article: Knight, D. (2000) Standards. In R. Dal Vera (ed.) *Standard Speech and Other Contemporary Issues in Professional Voice and Speech Training.* New York: Applause, pp. 61–78.

  Summarize Knight's main points and his arguments. Which ones do you find credible, and why?

● If you are a Southerner, how many different Southern accents do you recognize? Do you consider yourself good at telling accents apart? What features do you take note of when people talk? Which accents do you dislike, and can you figure out why, objectively?

● If you know a child of 10 years or so and have that child's parent's permission, see if you can elicit opinions about the South (or North, depending on where you live) without leading. If this isn't possible, try someone of your grandparent's generation. Compare your findings in class.

● Without thinking or preparation, write down as many non-fictional Southerners you can think of. These can be personal acquaintances or public figures. When you're finished, go back and try to be specific about what part of the South each person comes from. Check your answers for accuracy. What results do you draw from this exercise? (If you are a Southerner, reverse this process and make a list of Northerners or Westerners.) If you are a Southerner, how much do you know about, for example, North Dakota as compared to Michigan, or Kansas compared to Idaho? Do you notice any linguistic differentiation? Is there differentiation that you just don't hear?

● Read the entire column by Withrow quoted at the beginning of the section called "Hostility with a Southern Accent." Consider that you have been engaged by the same newspaper to write a column that represents a different point of view. In what ways might it be possible to approach Withrow to have a calm and rational discussion about the subject of grammar? She clearly feels very strongly about this subject, and she will need to be approached carefully, with solid arguments.

● A woman writes to Dear Abby to say that she has moved to the Boston area after living her whole life in Jackson, Mississippi. It has been two years, but she is still not used to people laughing in her face and mocking her accent. She doesn't understand why people find this not only acceptable, but amusing. She wants to know how best to respond when she comes across this behavior. How do you think Miss Abby will respond, and why?

● In an article called "The Nationalization of a Southernism," Tillery *et al.* (2000) present evidence that one feature of Southern U.S. English is actually spreading into the North, at a good pace. What feature do you think this might be? Read the article and discuss how and why this might be happening. If you would like to look at this issue more closely, read Hyman (2006).

Notes

1   In this chapter I am leaving aside African American Vernacular English as it is spoken in the South. The similarities and differences between Southern AAVE and Southern White Vernacular English (SWVE) are a matter of disagreement among linguists, one that cannot be addressed here in sufficient detail. See especially Cukor-Avila (2003) for a concise overview of what is called the divergence–convergence debate.

2   Ayers is a life-long resident of the South and an expert on Southern history. Those interested in language variation over space and most especially the concept of the South will find *All over the Map: Rethinking America's Regions*, a book Ayers co-wrote and co-edited, to be of great use and interest.

3   Kretzschmar provides a concise but thorough discussion of the technological and theoretical challenges of mapping Southern English (Kretzschmar 2003, 2004, 2008a, 2008b).

4   November 2008. URL on file.

5   Similar studies have been conducted in Germany (Dailey-O'Cain 2000); and for Garo, a language spoken in rural India and Bangladesh. The willingness of individuals to make such judgments is well documented.

6   An abbreviated biographical sketch of the author from the *Hamilton Stone Review*, Fall 2008:

> Dolly Withrow, a retired English professor, taught at West Virginia State University for 16 years . . . She is the author of four books, including *The Confident Writer*, a grammar-based writing textbook for college students and writers in general. A columnist for *The Charleston Daily Mail* and *The Jackson Herald*, Dolly has won national writing awards . . . West Virginia Public Radio broadcast her essays for three years. She is a public speaker and grammar workshop presenter.

7   The business of accent reduction is to be kept clearly distinct from speech pathology, in which professionals are trained to work with those who have difficulty speaking for reasons beyond their control. The majority of speech pathologists work, for example, with children with cleft palates, stuttering, central auditory processing deficit, dysphagia, speech aphasia after a stroke, and other serious conditions.

8   The transcript of the entire hearing is available online at: http://goo.gl/ZAJkX.

9   In a review of the first edition of this book, Knight (2000) alternately bashed and then reluctantly acknowledged points made in this text and in the writings of other linguists about those who sell their services as accent specialists. Specifically he admitted that there is no regulation or licensing for such businesses, but pointed out that neither were there such requirements for linguists.

   In fact, every academic linguist attends graduate school, passes masters and/or doctoral exams, and defends a theses or dissertation. Any linguist on a college faculty has had to apply and compete for that position. In short, academic linguists do not just hang up a shingle.

Suggested further reading

Bailey, G. and Tillery, J. (1996) The Persistence of Southern American English. *Journal of English Linguistics* 24: 308–321.

Cobb, J.C. (2005) *Away Down South: A History of Southern Identity.* Oxford: Oxford University Press.

Cooke-Jackson, A. (2008) Appalachian Culture and Reality TV: The Ethical Dilemma of Stereotyping Others. *Journal of Mass Media Ethics* 23(3): 183–200.

Griffin, L. J. and Thompson, A.B. (2003) Enough About the Disappearing South: What About the Disappearing Southerner? *Southern Cultures* 9: 51–65.

Hyman, E. (2006) The All of You-All. *American Speech* 81.

The Language Samples Project (n.d.) Varieties of English. Available at: http://www.ic.arizona.edu/~lsp/.

Wolfram, W. and Beckett, D. (2003) Language Variation in the American South: An Introduction. *American Speech* 78(2): 123–129.

Wolfram, W. and Ward, B. (2006) *American Voices: How Dialects Differ from Coast to Coast.* Oxford: Blackwell.

Defying paradise

12

Hawai'i[1]

He aha ka hala i kapuhia ai ka leo, i ho'okuli mai ai?
What was the wrong that silenced the voice?

Hawai'ian traditional[2]

But I can't talk the way he wants me to. I cannot make it sound his way, unless I'm playing pretend-talk haole. I can make my words straight, that's pretty easy if I concentrate real hard. But the sound, the sound from my mouth, if I let it rip right out the lips, my words will always come out like home.

Lois-Ann Yamanaka, *Wild Meat and the Bully Burgers* (1996: 13)

Mainland Americans tend to have a romanticized and unrealistic impression of Hawai'i, one that goes no farther than images gained from advertisements aimed at tourists: luaus, pristine beaches, and an easy-going *aloha* spirit that makes everyone welcome and equal. In fact Hawai'i has the same range of problems found everywhere in the U.S.: poverty, racial and ethnic conflict and discrimination in the workplace and educational system (Southern Poverty Law Center 2010). It also has an indigenous population of native Hawai'ians and all the issues that follow from annexation and colonization (McGowan 1995; Okamura 2008; Takagi 2004; Trask 1992, 1999).

In Hawai'i, racial, ethnic and socioeconomic conflicts are played out – in part – in terms of language ideology, at a level of complexity unmatched anywhere in the mainland. Matters that would seem uncontroversial to mainlanders are anything but in the Islands. Issues of authenticity and authority have everything to do with who may call themselves Hawai'ian and who can claim to be *Kanaka 'Oiwi* or *Kanaka Maoli*; that is, native Hawai'ian (Pennybacker 1999).[3]

The significance of this – and of all the ethnic distinctions that are so carefully delineated in Hawai'i – might be best understood by listening to what Hawai'ians say about themselves. What follows are anonymous excerpts from discussion boards where people who live or have lived in Hawai'i for long periods talk about how they see themselves, and about the difficulty of navigating the complex relationships between ethnicity, race, class, language and privilege. These excerpts are from exchanges that took place on discussion boards in 2004–2005. All punctuation, spelling and capitalization are reproduced exactly. Note that *Haole* is a reference both to pale skin color and origins outside of the islands:

1   While living in Hawaii, people would regularly ask me "What are you?" and when I
    simply told them "Filipino" that was never enough. I couldn't be "just" Filipino. Only

when I gave them my complete ethnic breakdown of Filipino, Chinese and Spanish was the average local satiated by my answer. So, from my experience, a rigorous breakdown of one's ethnicity is not a matter of trying to fashion an "improvement" but rather, that's the status quo in Hawaii.

2   I'm absolutely LOCAL – but I'm not *kanaka maoli*. I have lived in Hawaii most of my life and would NEVER PRESUME to call myself Hawaiian just because I live here. That would be incredibly disrespectful to my friends and others who have blood quantum (any percentage).

3   Anyone in California can be a Californian, but there's a difference between a Hawaiian and a Hawaii resident.

4   I think Hawaii (my home) has way too much Asians to be even called Hawaii now. It is a known fact that an estimated 80% of Hawaii's population are Asians. So the saying "Hawaiian land in Filipino hands" should be revised to . . . "Hawaiian land in Asian hands."

5   I've run into a lot of racist people during my life living here. Even though I was born here in Kealakekua some people can't get past that I'm fair-skinned (thanks to being 50% Norwegian, 25% Finnish, 12.5% German and British) and can't tan at all. Thus when I was younger, and to an extent today, I run into people who treat me poorly because I'm haole.

Hawai'ians talk

The aboriginal Polynesian language of Hawai'i ('Olelo Hawai'i) was the only language spoken in the islands until they were colonized, when Hawai'i was annexed by the U.S. and her government forcibly disbanded. As is usually the case in when a country is colonized, 'Olelo Hawai'i was systematically suppressed and finally outlawed. It wasn't until 1978 the native language regained its status as one of the official languages of the state.[4]

Even before colonization, a trade language – a pidgin – took root and then evolved into Hawai'i Creole. There is still a good deal of controversy about the nature, origin and development of pidgins into creoles, but a few things have been established. First and foremost: A pidgin is nobody's native language.

Pidgins arise in a restricted social context, where people speaking two or more different languages must communicate with each other for short periods of time, in specific ways. The classic example is that of a seaport, where ships from near and far come and go, and unloading or loading cargo. For these very specific and limited situations, communication is accomplished by means of a pidgin, a language cobbled together from three or four languages in contact. The structure of a pidgin is reduced and simplified. For example, pidgins don't have subordinate clauses or copulas and they use a reduced pronoun system. These kinds of simplifications are true of pidgins no matter where they arise.

If the conditions are right, and children are born into a setting where a pidgin is actively used, the pidgin may evolve into a creole. The children take in the raw data of the pidgin and in the process of language acquisition, they expand it into a fully functioning language (Grimes 1994; Grimes 1994; Marlow and Giles 2008; Tamura 2008).

One way of thinking about this is that a pidgin must acquire native speakers in order to become a creole (Nichols 2004; Ohama *et al.* 2000; Sakoda and Siegel 2003; Siegel 2008).

Hawai'i Creole (HC) lexical items come primarily – but not exclusively – from English. However, the structure of the language draws heavily on Hawai'ian, Portuguese and Chinese. Sakoda and Siegel's *Introduction to Hawai'i Creole* (2003) provides a concise yet thorough overview of the language's history and structure, along with examples of most grammatical strategies. For instance, this example of an infinitive clause structure that doesn't occur in English:

> *Hr fo tawk enikine.*
> (She's the kind who'd say anything)

(ibid.: 101)

While 'Olelo Hawai'i was in danger of extinction at several points and its ultimate fate is not yet clear, HC is a healthy language spoken by some 600,000 people. Of these, 100,000 to 200,000 do not speak any other variety of English. This means that of the almost 1.3 million inhabitants of Hawai'i as of 1990, almost half of the inhabitants speak HC to some degree, and somewhere between 10 and 30 percent speak it as a primary language (Grimes 1994).[5]

Beyond HC, 'Olelo Hawai'i and English, Hawai'i is as multilingual a place as one could find in the United States. There are Hakka, Cantonese, Japanese, Korean, Tagalog, Ilocano, Cebuano, Hiligaynon, Portuguese, Spanish, and Samoan language communities which have been flourishing for many generations. There are also populations of more recent immigrant workers.

In Figure 12.1, a pie chart displays the 2009 statistics published by the United States Census Bureau about languages other than English spoken at home. On the basis of these numbers, one might conclude that HC is a dying or dead language, when exactly the

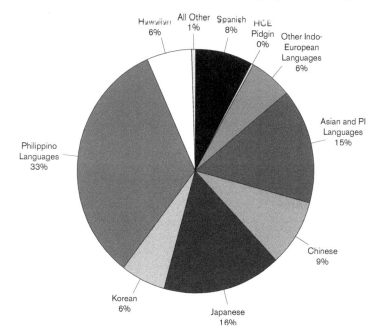

Figure 12.1 Languages spoken in Hawai'i

Source: U.S. Census Bureau 2009

opposite is true. Figure 12.2 shows the U.S. Census Bureau (2009) figures for foreign-born residents of Hawai'i by place of origin.

As is the case with all creoles, HC exists in various forms along a continuum of most to least similar to the base language – in this case, English. On that end of the continuum where HC has more in common with English, it is used in a wide variety of public settings; Grimes (1994) reports that it is commonly heard in the judicial system and is used there by officers, jurors, plaintiffs, and defendants, that it is used by some on radio and TV in public service announcements, and that there is a "growing body of serious literature, including poetry" (ibid.). In its basilectal form (where there is the least mutual intelligibility with English), HC is spoken widely by persons of all ages and races, but it is more common among the poor and working class, which accounts in part for its stigmatization. This is an area where U.S. Census Bureau methodology cannot cope with the complexities of language use. This is a larger issue that needs to be addressed, as government funding for all kinds of services is dependent on these statistics.

Marlow and Giles (2008) look closely at the complex interplay of social forces behind choices Hawai'ians make between HC and *SAE. They found that all of their subjects believed in the primacy of *SAE and its use in business and formal situations. Wording used to get this idea across was very similar to that heard from native speakers of AAVE when interviewed about parallel language issues (Eades *et al.* 2006; Ohama *et al.* 2000; Tamura 2002). As is usually the case, the HC speakers are willing to give back the

Africa, 0.5
Oceania, 6.3
Latin America, 3.2
Northern America, 1.8
Europe, 4.9
Asia, 83.3

Europe	10,479	4.9
Asia	176,707	83.3
Africa	1,040	0.5
Oceania	13,452	6.3
Latin America	6,788	3.2
Northern America	3,763	1.8
Total (excluding born at sea)	212,229	100.0

Figure 12.2 Foreign-born residents of Hawai'i by place of origin

Source: U.S. Census Bureau (2004)

ideological constructions they have learned which allow them to rationalize rejection of the home language:

> *M*: So, you said that "to get through life" you have to learn Standard English. What do you mean by that?
> *Ch*: Well, like when you go for a job, you cannot talk Pidgin, because they won't hire you.
>
> (Marlow and Giles 2008: 61)

At the same time, the subjects declared that they were more comfortable speaking HC, and that the language was important to them despite stigmatization:

> I think it's important for the kids, growing up here in the Islands to learn Pidgin, because it's reminiscent of how it was back in the days of the plantation . . . different cultures, different ethnic groups. It's really important to know that and to embrace it because that's our own culture. That's the culture of the Islands . . . it allows us to remember where we came from and how it got us to where we are today.

Finally, Marlow and Giles find evidence of what anyone would guess on the basis of day-to-day experience in the world: even in formal situations, sometimes the vernacular is called for in order to establish solidarity.

> *C*: [Pidgin] definitely helps now, well now with my job. The oddest thing is that I can turn it off and on. I can be with a client that is very local and I can flip it in a second and just start talking broken English.
> *M*: So that's what you do then?
> *C*: Yes. It really helps me to connect with my clients.

Hawai'i is also subject to the same social forces that make an L2 accent a handy excuse to discriminate. In this case, the discrimination is not so much racial as it is ethnic in character. It is impossible to understand the situations considered in Chapter 9 (Kahakua, Fragante) outside of this cultural context.

If you recall, Manuel Fragante sued the Department of Motor Vehicles for language-focused discrimination in hiring; Fragante is a native of the Philippines, and the DMV cited his accent as part of their decision to deny him employment. An important element of the Fragante case is the fact that when he applied for the position, his interview was conducted by Hawai'ians of Japanese descent. Okamura (2008: 155–186) outlines the systematic degradation of Filipinos in Hawai'i throughout the twentieth century, during which time Filipino men were seen (and treated) as emotionally volatile, primitive, sexually aggressive and violent. This historical animosity is directly relevant to the language-focused discrimination in Fragante's case.

At one time the largest and certainly most established immigrant group, the Japanese in Hawai'i had marked advantages in terms of political and cultural clout, all of which came to an abrupt end with World War II, when anyone of Japanese heritage suffered extreme discrimination. Soon after the war, the Japanese community began to rebuild and by the1960s, Japanese political dominance had been firmly established. Under Haole rule, institutional racism had functioned to hold back people of color; under Japanese dominance, other Asians and some Anglos suffered the same disadvantage (Okamura 2008). This solidification of Japanese political dominance culminated in 1974 with the election of George Ariyoshi as governor.[6]

Under the Ariyoshi administration extreme measures were taken to cement Nisei control.[7] Laws were introduced which capped immigration; and access to state employment and welfare were subject to length of residence. Institutionalized exclusion of both Haoles and Filipinos was rampant in education especially, where the administration was dominated by ethnic Japanese interests.

As power shifts from one group to another, deep resentments are formed between those groups. Filipinos, Japanese, Pacific Islanders, Chinese, Haole, each group has a mindset about the others but there is one subject on which all groups seem to agree: HC, and the people who speak it (Figure 12.3).

Hawai'ians at school

In 1987, the Board of Education of the State of Hawai'i made a policy decision they called "Standard English and Oral Communication":

> Standard English [shall] be the mode of oral communication for students and staff in the classroom setting and all other school related settings except when the objectives cover native Hawai'ian or foreign language instruction and practice.
>
> (Sato 1991: 653)

The issue was not whether English should be the language of instruction, or the target of language instruction; the Hawai'ian school board takes that as given. The issue is, instead,

Figure 12.3 Sound American! Accent reduction in Hawai'i

Source: Photo by Patrick Cates. Reproduced by permission

which language is proper in an educational setting. Not surprisingly, "Standard English" is evoked, but not defined. Neither is there any explicit definition of the vernacular language that has brought about this policy statement to begin with. Multiple newspaper accounts of the controversy which ensued from this proposal did not hesitate to name it:

> Panel wants pidgin kept out of schools
>
> Panel urges pidgin ban in schools
>
> Board votes 7–4 to keep pidgin out of classroom[8]

Thus this proposal would have had the effect of outlawing HC in the schoolroom. It would also have barred the language from playgrounds at recess, gymnasiums during basketball practice and cafeterias during lunch.

The 1987 proposal by the School Board, then, would have taken this well-established language spoken natively by more than half a million people and banned it from the school system. Why was this language, of all the many languages spoken in Hawai'i, singled out for exclusion? While in Arizona legislatures debate bilingual education for native speakers of Apache and Spanish, in Hawai'i it occurs to the School Board to ban a language which, on one end of the continuum, is mutually intelligible with English. Why?

During extensive public debate of this issue, a Honolulu newspaper conducted a survey of 986 graduating high school seniors on this topic, and that report reveals how socially complex HC is, and how closely tied it is to issues of economics and class. Whereas only 26 percent of the private school students surveyed felt that HC use should be allowed in school, 54 percent of the public school students supported its use. Comments ranged from "Pidgin English fosters illiteracy," "Pidgin is a lazy way to talk; it promotes backward thinking," and "Correct English will get you anywhere" to the polar opposites of "Banning pidgin would violate our freedom of speech," "Pidgin is a natural language," and "It's our way to make Hawai'i different from anywhere else in the United States" (Verploegen, June 1, 1988, cited by Sato 1991: 654).

Hawai'i's Waianae Coast is the home of the greatest concentration of *Kanaka Maoli* and not coincidentally, of HC speakers; it is also one of the poorest areas, with the largest proportion of homeless (Magin 2006). An elementary school teacher who is a native speaker of HC further clarifies the connection between language, identity, authenticity and race:

> What we're finding is that children who appear to be pidgin speakers to the max, meaning it appears they can't speak anything else, those same children are sitting in front of the TV set every night or reading standard English, right? They are surrounded by it. These kids are bilingual. We'll never give pidgin up. We won't give it up because it means something to us. It means we're not holy, we're not standard English – we are people of color. We won't give up pidgin because we love it.
>
> (12 September 1990, Drummond 1990, broadcast).

By legislating language in the schoolroom – a subject that comes up regularly over the years – the School Board hopes also to legislate world view, and a choice for status over solidarity.

Once again it becomes clear that the process of standardization and language sub-ordination is not so much concerned with an overall homogeneity of language, but with excluding only those languages linked to the social differences and it is this which make us uncomfortable. By the simple expedient of substituting one language for another, we hope to neutralize social conflicts grounded in race, ethnicity, and economics. If this could be achieved, "Nothing then would [be] left but the antipathy of race, and that, too, is always softened in the beams of a higher civilization," hypothesized the Commissioner of Indian Affairs. While his methods would be seen as unacceptable today, the underlying sentiment remains.[9]

It is worthwhile to consider the mindset that allowed the question to be raised at all. We want the children of the United States to have a thorough command of English, but it is more than that. We are not satisfied with English as it lives and breathes, English with a Cuban accent, the English spoken off the coast of South Carolina, or Hawai'i Creole English. We want the right English, the one correct English. In the face of huge amounts of factual evidence that a homogenous and monolithic variety of perfect English does not and cannot exist, we still pursue this mythical beast as if it were the solution to all of our societal ills. One Good English, we feel, is the right of our school children, and the responsibility of their teachers.

Talk story: "Without Pidgin, I would cease to be whole"

Wala'au or "talk story" is a phrase which means something like "let's sit down and talk a while" or "to start a conversation" as in the Hawai'i Creole (HC) sentence *We go make one time fo wala'au den* (Why don't we set a time to talk?).[10] The 'Olelo Hawai'i (native Hawai'ian) word *wala'au* is often used interchangeably with HC "talk story" in ways that conflate the morphology of both languages, as in "Wala'au-ing with the baby" or "She's talkin story with daddy."[11] As a cultural activity, talk story is not restricted to one language or language variety and while it is primarily a spoken language act, it is also used in print, as in the online 'Olelo Hawai'i newspaper column "Hala'au Sessions with Makela" at Big Island Weekly (bigislandweekly.com).

HC is primarily a spoken language and as such, anyone and everyone local can and does "talk story." Moreover, in language communities such as these where spoken language is primary, good storytelling is especially highly valued.

Broadcast news outlets also know the value of good storytelling, and for many years television news programs have used the last few minutes of airtime to present what they refer to as human interest stories. These reports often deal with topics which are meant to be amusing or inspiring, or have an obvious and unapologetic lesson in citizenship and morals. Commentaries on language often come in this packaging. One such report aired on July 3, 1983 on ABC under the title "Pidgin language fad is used as defense against tourists in Hawaii."[12] This is not a neutral or simply informative news piece; in fact, the ABC report employs many of the steps in the language subordination process outlined earlier. The title is enough to establish trivialization as the primary subordination tool: Hawai'i Creole is a fad, something insubstantial that cannot last for any length of time. There is an element of marginalization as well, which portrays Hawai'ians as willfully different from, and hostile to, tourists.

The report is factually wrong even in the essentials, using misinformation to establish a tone: "Pidgin is a decades old blend of oriental languages and teen slang." Not only is this statement factually incorrect, it is also phrased to combine mystification ("the orient") and marginalization of the non-compliant ("teen slang"). Every element of the story is designed to reinforce the theme that pidgin is laughable, and pidgin speakers are not to be taken seriously. The only uses for HC are trivial, humorous, or, in the case of tourists, obstructionist.

There is more here than blatant mockery. There is a subtle tone in the way the reporter talks about speakers of this language, further underscored by inclusion of clearly staged conversations. We see three dialogues in HC, each of them between two persons. First two men are interviewed while they lie in the sun; we next see two staged dialogues: another pair of young men looking into the surf, evaluating the conditions for surfing, and a young couple arguing in a parking lot.

Here HC is the language of the young, the unemployed, the over-wrought and emotive, the fun-seeking, the beach boy and the teenager: people who are believed to have no serious purpose in life. As there are no adults speaking HC, we must assume it is a language of youth and will pass with maturity, like pimples or an obsession with loud music. As a language which typifies "good grammar gone to grief," it can have no serious purpose. Having established all of this, the report now turns to the popular books which are selling well, and which have engendered positive reaction or attention to pidgin from the mainstream. There is no way to know if the reporter is unaware of the range and use of HC by a large proportion of the Hawai'ian population, from judges to beach boys, around dinner tables and in classrooms, or of the fact that it has been carefully studied by linguists. Perhaps he is ignorant of these basic facts; perhaps he is purposefully choosing to undercount and under-represent the community of HC speakers, not an uncommon strategy. The only authority the reporter consults is a non-native HC speaker who is cast in a light as frivolous and trivial as the native speakers themselves.

Such public disavowals and criticisms of HC are not unusual; more than twenty years after this report aired, negative commentary still shows up regularly in letters to the editor, along with the simmering debate on the role of HC in the schools and classrooms. What has changed, however, is the way HC speakers have begun to assert themselves, reclaim authority in matters of language use, and publically promote HC as a valid and crucial element of Hawai'ian identity.

Lee Tonouchi – a forceful advocate for HC and its speakers – and someone who rejects both speaking and writing *SAE – has promoted the reappropriation of the term *Oriental*. Reappropriation is the process in which a stigmatized language community reinterprets a negative label by claiming its use for their own. Examples include the way the GLBT community has reclaimed *queer* and parts of the African American community *nigger*:

> Didn't used to boddah us, didn't used to boddah my faddah guys. Lotta people, da previous generation, dey all say "Oriental," dey no say "Asian American," eh? Just dat during our time, dea's a shift now, try be more PC. So I guess I like rebel against da movement on da continent, do our own thing.
>
> (*Honolulu Weekly*, November 13, 2002; http://goo.gl/fKNJm)

In an essay about her documentary "Pidgin: The Voice of Hawai'i"[13] producer/director Marlene Booth provides a striking example of resistance to the forces of subordination and assimilation. The University of Hawai'i requires that all undergraduates pass an oral English exam before graduating: "Speech 101, 102, and 103, three semester-long classes, were designed to de-Pidginize (my word) the speech of Hawai'i's university students" (ibid.). At least one native HC speaking faculty member teaching these courses ran into problems that the students were willing to talk about, perhaps because she was an HC speaker: "they did not want to sound like haoles. Succeeding by taking on the speech and mannerisms of Caucasians became too high a price to pay for many students. Talking like a haole implied turning your back on family, friends, ethnic group, and neighborhood, moving away from group identity and becoming instead a self-defined individual" (ibid.).

The links that follow provide a wide range of examples in which people talk or write in support of HC in direct or indirect ways. Some are in Hawai'ian accented English, some in HC.

Professor Kent Sakoda, a native speaker of HC, provides a short introduction in that language.	http://goo.gl/e6krm
"Low-class Hawaii Pidgin English" is a professionally produced dramatization of novelist Lois-Ann Yamanaka's portrayal of the way HC speakers have been demeaned and marginalized in the classroom.	http://goo.gl/ekP2B
Podcasts by Rochelle delaCruz for KBCS 91.3 FM *Hawai'i Ways*, "English" and "Language Gap."	http://goo.gl/tHT5p
Hawaii Pidgin: The Voice of Hawaii. Short video broadcast. An American Public Television and Hau Pana Films production.	http://goo.gl/vNeIa
Hour-length documentary on Hawai'i Pidgin, Marlene Booth, producer excerpts "Hawai'i's Reel Stories" gathered into a collection at YouTube.	http://goo.gl/KQ1O7 http://goo.gl/JtIiY
Recording of Lee Tonouchi giving a formal presentation.	http://goo.gl/1LPqh

DISCUSSION QUESTIONS AND EXERCISES

- Is Hawai'ian Creole a language? Be prepared to argue both sides.
- First, consider the short excerpt from Lois-Ann Yamanaka's novel, *Wild Meat and the Bully Burgers* (1996: 13) at the beginning of the chapter. Then read Pennybacker's article (March 1, 1999) on Lois-Ann Kamanaka's satirical novels set in the Hawai'ian Islands, and written in Pidgin:
    Pennybacker, Mindy. "What Boddah You?: The Authenticity Debate (Lois-Ann Yamanaka)." The Nation. http://goo.gl/0hVjx.
- Who objected to Yamanaka's books, and on what basis? Was censorship called for?
- Reconsider Lois-Ann Kamanaka's satirical novels set in the Hawai'ian Islands as well as Pennybacker's article on Kamanaka's work (March 1, 1999), Talmy (2010) and The Southern Poverty Law Center's report called "Prejudice in Paradise" which can be found at: http://goo.gl/IJU7T. With more context and historical background, do your opinions about Kamanaka's work change? In what way?

Notes

1 In the original language of the islands, the glottal stop (say "uh-oh" and you'll hear your voice stop or "pop" in your laryx) is a meaning-bearing sound which functions like a consonant. In writing, the 'okina – much like a backwards single quote – is the symbol for the glottal stop. Thus *Hawaii* is technically a misspelling. To make this clearer, a comparison: *Ameria* is to America as *Hawaii* is to Hawai'i. More information on the sounds and writing system can be found at: http://www.coralreefnetwork.com/network/hawaiian.htm.

2 *Hawaiian Dictionary* by Mary Kawena Pukui and Samuel H. Elbert. Honolulu: University of Hawai'i Press, 1986.

3 The Hawaiian Homes Commission Act of 1921 contained a controversial definition of "Native Hawai'ians" (*Kanaka Maoli*) as persons "with at least one-half blood quantum of individuals inhabiting the Hawai'ian Islands prior to 1778." The result is a declining number of people who can legally claim Native Hawai'ian status and the intensified peripheralization of Hawai'ians to racial minority status (42 U.S.C. § 3057k: US Code – Section 3057K: "Native Hawaiian" defined). The *Kanaka Maoli* have been petitioning the government for the same status as other indigenous Indian nations, which would give them a degree of sovereignty.

4 HC is the only aboriginal language to be thus recognized in the U.S. In 1990, the federal government recognized the right of Hawai'i to preserve, use, and support its indigenous language. The movement to support and nurture the language is growing and seems to be successful. Grimes (1992) reports that there are 2,000 mother tongue speakers out of 200,000 to 220,000 ethnic Hawai'ians (20 percent of the population), including 8,000 Hawai'ians and 81,000 at least half Hawai'ian.

5 More current demographic data should be available, given the fact that the U.S. Census Bureau gathers information on languages spoken at home in every state. However, the Census Bureau does not recognize HC as a real or full language, and so that choice was not offered to speakers answering the question "What language do you speak at home?" Any HC speaker who felt strongly enough about the importance of HC had to fill in the blank marked "other."

6 Ariyoshi and his contemporaries are sometimes referred to as the Nisei generation, a Japanese language term for the first generation of Japanese born outside of Japan to Issei (Japanese born).

7 This is not unique to the Japanese in Hawai'i, of course. Any group coming into political power will be concerned with how to keep and bolster that power. The Nisei's ascent is set apart, however, by their internment experiences during WWII, the result of "race prejudice, war hysteria, and a failure of political leadership." ((Personal Justice Denied: Report of the Commission on Wartime Relocation and Internment of Civilians, 1982.)

8 Headlines of a series of articles which appeared in *The Honolulu Advertiser* in September, 1987, by D. Reyes.

9 In another state, this one in the Southwest where native speakers of Spanish and a number of Native American languages attend schools, a proposal was put forward at a State Board of Education meeting in 1987 which echoes in many ways the actions of the Hawai'ian school board. In this proposal, a new competency standard was proposed which, had it been implemented, would have required that seventh graders "speak expressively through appropriate articulation, pronunciation, volume, rate, and intonation" before they were promoted to the eighth grade. In this case, the professional educators and administers approached the issue by posing a number of

thoughtful questions for themselves, questioning first the parameters of what would constitute "appropriate" accents:

- Can we establish an acceptable standard for children in all school districts in [the state]?
- Can we be assured that Hispanic, Native American, and Asian students will not be retained because of what may be considered an "unacceptable" pronunciation?
- What happens to children who do not master this competency?
- When will they receive needed attention to academic skills and conceptual development?

Administrators consulted a range of specialists in language and linguistics as well as education, and came to the conclusion that this proposed policy was ill conceived, summarizing their position quite simply: Accent is a minimal type of competency in relation to conceptual development and language use. "Rather, let us teach children to use language to expand intellectual development, to appreciate the richness of expression, and enrich lives by knowing what words to choose and use rather than how to pronounce them."

While this case took a reasonable ending, similar legislation and policies continue to be debated in other states. Stalker (1990: 64) reports that in the 1980s, bills requiring school systems "to determine which students do not use [*SAE], and to provide remedial work for them" were submitted multiple times and rejected each time, but only because funding for testing and remedial work was not available.

10 One online resource for HC can be found at http://www.e-hawaii.com/pidgin.

11 YouTube provides an opportunity to experience languages as they are spoken in spontaneous exchanges. Searching the terms "wal'au" or "talking story" will bring up examples of Hawai'ians speaking to each other without violating privacy.

12 The first edition of this book included a transcript of this broadcast, but ABC declined to grant permission to use it in the new edition. Beyond consulting the first edition, it is possible to request a video copy of the news segment itself from the Vanderbilt Television News Archives at http://goo.gl/7RJLf (summary page). This is not a free service, but it is reasonably priced.

13 Available online in pdf format (http://Goo.Gl/kSpK4) or as a film clip (http://goo.gl/JtIiY).

Suggested further reading

Booth, M. (n.d.) Learning Da Kine: a Filmmaker Tackles Local Culture and Pidgin. http://Goo.Gl/kSpK4.

Furukawa, T. (2007) "No Flips in the Pool": Discursive Practice in Hawai'i Creole. *Pragmatics* 7(3): 371–385.

Galinsky, A.D. *et al.* (2003) The Reappropriation of Stigmatizing Labels: Implications for Social Identity. In Jeffrey Polzer (ed.) *Identity Issues in Groups*. Emerald Group Publishing.

Keller, L. (2009) Prejudice in Paradise: Hawai'i has a Racism Problem. *Intelligence Report* Issue 135, Southern Poverty Law Center, available at: http://goo.gl/lJU7T.

Marlow, M.L. and Giles, H. (2008) Who You Tink You, Talkin Propah? Hawaiian Pidgin Demarginalised. *Journal of Multicultural Discourses*, 3(1), 53–68.

Nichols, P. (2004) Creole Languages: Forging New Identities. In E. Finegan and J.R.

Rickford (eds.) *Language in the USA: Themes for the Twenty-first Century*. Cambridge: Cambridge University Press.

Okamura, J.Y. (2008) *Ethnicity and Inequality in Hawai'i*. Temple University Press.

Tonouchi, L.A. (2002) *Living Pidgin: Contemplations on Pidgin Culture*. Tinfish Press.

Watson-Gegeo, K.A. and Boggs, S.T. (1977) From Verbal Play to Talk Story: The role of routine in speech events among Hawaiian children. In S. Ervin-Tripp and C. Mitchel Kernan (eds.) *Child Discourse*. New York: Academic Press.

Winford, D. (2003) *An Introduction to Contact Linguistics*. Malden, MA: Blackwell. Contains chapters on pidgins and creoles and language contact.

The other in the mirror

13

Immigration is still the greatest form of flattery.

Jack Paar, comedian. attributed

Without *other*, there can be no *self*.

Wellman (1993: 244)

The price of admission

When fears about the upswing in immigration began to peak in the nineteenth century, the metaphor of the melting pot became popular with journalists. Perhaps the idea of a common, unified, united and unvarying American culture sold a lot of magazines; certainly it seems that people took comfort in the idea. All the odd, disruptive, unsettling cultures filing through Ellis Island and San Francisco would soon be stripped down and remade into something American. This is the goal of assimilation, where the less powerful group loses the traits that make it different, including its language (Dicker 2008: 53). A comparison of political cartoons over space indicates that regardless of the stigmatized immigrant group, whether Irish, Guatamalan or Kenyan, the imagery and discourse strategies are remarkably similar.

Who were these immigrants who held on to their own cultures and languages so stubbornly? Figure 13.1 is derived from census figures for the year 1900, and it indicates that the new immigrants – primarily from Italy, Germany, Great Britain, and Scandinavian – settled primarily in the cities of the Northeast. More than a hundred years later, many still consider this concept of one America – an assimilated Anglo-Saxon America and a linguistic Utopia – as possible and desirable.

In 2010, the U.S. Census Bureau[1] estimated that the United States is a nation of some 310 million people, of whom about 3.2 million are Native American and about half a million Hawai'ian. To this number we might add the population we think of as Mexican American or Chicano/a, who are descendants of Europeans but also of the aboriginal peoples of Central America and the Western U.S. Thus it is an obvious and inescapable truth that the majority of people residing in the U.S. are immigrants or the descendants of immigrants. Most came of their own free will, while others came in chains. We are a nation of immigrants, but having made the transition and established ourselves, there is a strong urge to be protective of what is here; we talk at great length about closing the door behind us. At times, we have acted on this impulse:

- In the 1840s, during a depression, mobs hostile to immigrant Irish Catholics burned down a convent in Boston.
- Congress passed the Chinese Exclusion Act in 1882, one of the first U.S. immigration laws, to exclude all people of Chinese origin.

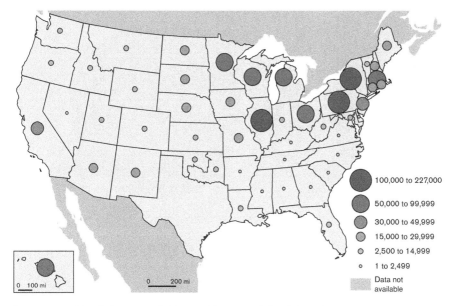

Figure 13.1 Population 10 and older unable to speak English well enough to be understood in ordinary conversation in the year 1900

Source: U.S. Census Bureau

- In 1942, 120,000 Americans of Japanese descent had their homes and other property confiscated, and were interned in camps until the end of World War II. At the same time, many Jews fleeing Nazi Germany during that war were excluded under regulations enacted in the 1920s.[2]
- In 2010, the Governor of Arizona signed a law that, if it is not struck down by higher courts, will have institutionalized overtly unconstitutional limitation of the rights of Mexican Americans, all in the name of border security.

With each immigration wave the focus of unease has shifted. Language often becomes the focus of debate when these complex issues of nationality, responsibility and privilege are raised. English, held up as the symbol of the successfully assimilated immigrant, is promoted as the one and the only possible language of a unified and healthy nation. Using rhetoric which is uncomfortably reminiscent of discussions of race in fascist regimes, a California Assemblyman notes the multilingual commerce in his home town with considerable trepidation: "you can go down and apply for a driver's license test entirely in Chinese. You can apply for welfare today entirely in Spanish. The supremacy of the English language is under attack."[3]

In fact, history has established again and again that language cannot be legislated. Grammar books may be written and taught, newspaper columnists may rant, but such things have no real effect. Figure 13.2 makes it clear just how multilingual a nation the U.S. is.

In considering the history of multilingualism and public fears around it, Heath *et al.* noted that "whenever speakers [of other languages] have been viewed as politically, socially, or economically threatening, their language has become a focus for arguments in favor of both restrictions of their use and imposition of Standard American English" (1981: 10).

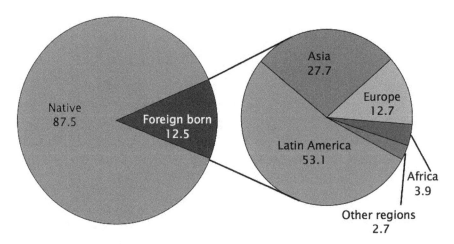

Figure 13.2 Total population by nativity and foreign region of birth for 2009, percent distribution

Source: U.S. Census Bureau, ACS, 2009

This is illustrated by the history of German use in the U.S., a language (and people) which particularly irritated Benjamin Franklin, who expressed his fears in a letter dated 1753: "Those [Germans] who come hither are generally the most ignorant Stupid Sort of their own Nation, and as Ignorance is often attended with Credulity when Knavery would mislead it, and with Suspicion with Honesty would set it right" (as cited in Crawford 1992b: 18–19).

The relationship between shifting power bases and the public's awareness of language use often focuses on legislation of one type or another, as in this news report on a vote to repeal an English-Only law in Florida:

> In reality, Miami has been a bilingual city for a long time. *The Miami Herald* is printed every day in both English and Spanish. Automatic teller machines here offer both languages. And whether you're at the airport . . . or on the streets, you constantly hear English and Spanish. But after the Mariel boatlift of 1980 brought thousands of Cubans here, voters overwhelmingly passed a law prohibiting the use of any language in official county business except English. For example, if you want to testify at a commission hearing, question your water bill, or make a formal complaint, it must be in English.
>
> (*ABC Evening News*, May 14, 1993)

While most of the public debate around language has to do with a deceptively simple question (which language?) the underlying conflict is far more complex and interesting. When immigrants become bilingual (as happened, for example, in the case of the German immigrant population, something that would have irritated Benjamin Franklin, no doubt), the question is no longer *which language*, but *which English* or more specifically in this chapter, *which accent* and ultimately, which race, ethnicity, religion, worldview.

Who has a foreign accent?

The Census Bureau estimates that in 2008 there were 37.5 million foreign-born residents in the U.S., but significantly more – about 54.5 million – who spoke a language other than English at home – an increase of a whopping 140.3 percent since 1980.[4] This does not mean, of course, that all 55.5 million speak English with an L2 accent; in fact, there is no reliable way to estimate how many people are vulnerable to this kind of discrimination.

One thing can be said with certainty: millions of people resident in the U.S. are not native speakers of English. Many speak a language other than English in their homes, neighborhoods, personal lives and sometimes also in their work. As discussed in Chapter 2, any individual who takes on the task of learning a second or third language in adulthood will have some degree of L2 accent, the degree of which is not readily predictable and will not correlate, over all, to education, intelligence or motivation. We do know, however, that 62.3 percent of the Spanish-speaking population speak Spanish at home.

Second, there are preconceived notions about non-native speakers of English which have repercussions even to the way we count individuals in their communities and refer to them. The U.S. Census Bureau distinguishes between Spanish, Asian, and Other Languages, a category that includes all of the continent of Africa (Table 13.1). It is from this departure point that we look at the way foreign language groups and the language stereotypes associated with those groups are used to classify – and often to dismiss – individual rights and freedoms.

The degree of accent is not necessarily relevant to these behaviors; where no accent exists, stereotype and discrimination can sometimes manufacture one in the mind of the listener.

A high degree of education does not bring with it any protection from discrimination based on foreign accent, as was seen in Chapter 9 in the case of Fragante v. City and County of Honolulu, and Hou v. Pennsylvania Department of Education. In fact, some people are willing to reject foreign accent in a public way when expectations about social prominence are affronted and stereotypes confounded. This was the case in a 1987–1988 search for a president at the University of Michigan, when a Regent told student reporters that his institution "would never hire a president with a foreign accent" (Wainess 1994) as an explanation of that Regent's opposition to a particular candidate, a native speaker of Greek. The Regent was voicing an illegal intent, but this statement – made public six years after the search when the rest of the documentation was released – still passed without public commentary. Indeed, this was proof of discrimination but by the time the papers were made public, there was nothing to be done about it.

A person who is a non-native speaker of English may want nothing more than to assimilate to the language and culture she sees around her; she may work very hard at it, and still sound distinctly like a native speaker of Farsi or Portuguese, simply because sincerity and application are not enough to replace one accent with another. Thus hard work toward a non-stigmatized variety of U.S. English will not necessarily protect anyone from discrimination. This is a lesson hard learned:

> One student in the [accent reduction] class, . . . a 22-year-old from Colombia, feels that the course is critical to his future. "To tell you the truth," he said during a break, "this class is my last hope. If it doesn't work out, I'm going back to my country."

> The problem, he said, is that he feels that his accent sets him apart from others, even though he has lived in this country for nine years. He graduated from Newton High School in Queens and is now a junior at Queens College.

Table 13.1 Population 5 years and older who spoke a language other than English at home, by language group and English-speaking ability, 2007

| Characteristic | Total people | English-speaking ability | | | |
		Very well	Well	Not well	Not at all
NUMBER					
Population 5 years and older	280,950,438	(X)	(X)	(X)	(X)
Spoke only English at home	225,505,953	(X)	(X)	(X)	(X)
Spoke a language other than English at home	55,444,485	30,975,474	10,962,722	9,011,298	4,494,991
Spoke a language other than English at home	55,444,485	30,975,474	10,962,722	9,011,298	4,494,991
Spanish or Spanish Creole	34,547,077	18,179,530	6,322,170	6,344,110	3,701,267
Other Indo-European languages	10,320,730	6,936,808	2,018,148	1,072,025	293,749
Asian and Pacific Island languages	8,316,426	4,274,794	2,176,180	1,412,264	453,188
Other languages	2,260,252	1,584,342	446,224	182,899	46,787
PERCENT					
Population 5 years and older	100.0	(X)	(X)	(X)	(X)
Spoke only English at home	80.3	(X)	(X)	(X)	(X)
Spoke a language other than English at home	19.7	55.9	19.8	16.3	8.1
Spoke a language other than English at home	100.0	55.9	19.8	16.3	8.1
Spanish or Spanish Creole	62.3	52.6	18.3	18.4	10.7
Other Indo-European languages	18.6	67.2	19.6	10.4	2.8
Asian and Pacific Island languages	15.0	51.4	26.2	17.0	5.4
Other languages	4.1	70.1	19.7	8.1	2.1

(For information on confidentiality protection, sampling error, nonsampling error, and cefinitions, see www.census.gov/acs/www/)

(X) Not applicable.

Note: Margins of error for all estimates can be found in Appendix Table 1 at www.census.gov/population/www/socdemo/language/appendix.html. For more information on the ACS, see www.census.gov/acs/www/.

Source: U.S. Census Bureau, 2007 American Community Survey

"I was practically raised in this country," he said, speaking in a soft lilting accent. "But I have this accent. Does that mean I'm not an American? I don't know."

(Hernandez 1993)

It is crucial to remember that it is not all foreign accents, but only accent linked to skin that isn't white, or which signals a third-world homeland, which evokes such negative reactions. There are no documented cases of native speakers of Swedish or Dutch or Gaelic being turned away from jobs because of communicative difficulties, although these adult speakers face the same challenge as native speakers of Spanish, Rumanian, Thai or Urdu.

Immigrants from the British Isles who speak varieties of English which cause significant communication challenges are not stigmatized: the differences are noted with great interest, and sometimes with laughter. A student asks to speak to a professor after class. "Fine," says the native of Scotland, a long-time resident of Ireland and England. "You can call tomorrow afternoon." The student is perplexed: having asked to see this professor, she is told to telephone. When the confusion is cleared up (in the Professor's variety of English "to call" means "to stop by"), they laugh about it. Another professor, a native of India and a bilingual, life-long speaker of English, is met with a colder reception when similar difficulties arise.

"Better get rid of your accent," sings an angry Puerto Rican youth in response to more hopeful dreams of a better life outside the fictional barrio of *West Side Story*.

There are many people who must cope, day by day, with the fact that the way they speak English is not acceptable. Some of them have other currencies – political and economic power, social pre-eminence, artistic excellence, other public achievements – with which to offset the disadvantages an accent brings with it and to disarm the prejudiced listener. In face-to-face conversation, most listeners, no matter how overtly negative and hostile, would be hard pressed to turn away and ignore Arnold Schwarzenegger (Austria), Penélope Cruz Sánchez (Spain), Christiane Amanpour (Iran), Gabriel García Márquez (Columbia), Arianna Huffington (Greece), Zbigniew Brzezinski (Poland), Nelson Mandela (South Africa), or Ang Lee (China).

But most do not have these resources. People have always come to the United States because in the imagination of the world, it is a place of real opportunity. The costs of democracy, of assimilation, are not spelled out in the papers they must file to live here, but in the stories of people like Henry Park. The narrator of the novel *Native Speaker* draws a vivid picture of himself and all immigrants: "They speak . . . not simply in new accents or notes but in the ancient untold music of a newcomer's heart, sonorous with longing and hope."

What the newcomer must learn for him or herself is the grim reality of limitations imposed by a standard language ideology. For most this will not be a surprise; we are not the only nation that promotes the idea of a standard, homogeneous language.

DISCUSSION QUESTIONS AND EXERCISES

- What is the connection between nationalism and language?
- The United States is not the only country which subscribes to a standard language ideology. How (if at all) would somebody studying Greek come to know and understand the sociolinguistic clues embedded in Greek?

- After six years of learning a foreign language exclusively in a classroom, what can the average student not know?
- Find a native speaker of a language other than English, someone who is willing to talk to you. Using the following examples, ask your informant these questions:
  - I understand you grew up in Italy. Where exactly?
  - How many native languages are there in Italy?
  - Where in Italy is the best (standard) Italian spoken? The worst?
  - What do you like or dislike about the best variety of Italian? The worst?
  - Did your own Italian accent cause you any discomfort when you were there? Did it provide you with any advantages?
- Report to the class on what you learned about the culture and language ideology of the country in question.
- Most Americans feel they know the basics about England. In class, discuss what you know about the use of English in Great Britain. Do you know where people believe the best English is spoken, or by whom? Which regional or social varieties of English are most likely to be made fun of?
- In so far as possible, repeat the third exercise with persons who are natives of Great Britain. Try to find a range of people from different parts of England, Wales or Scotland. In class, discuss how close (or far away) the class was in the estimation of prestigious and stigmatized varieties of British English.

Notes

1 http://goo.gl/WdkR0.
2 ACLU Briefing Paper at http://www.aclu.org/library/pbp20.html.
3 Report on pending English-Only legislation in California, CBS *Evening News*, October 1986.
4 http://goo.gl/dLFrt.

Suggested further reading

Edwards, J. (2009) Language and Nationalism. In *Language and Identity: An Introduction*. New York: Cambridge University Press.

Language and Nationalism in Nineteenth-century Europe (summary), available at: http://goo.gl/4Kh5i.

May, S. (2008) *Language and Minority Rights: Ethnicity, Nationalism and the Politics of Language*. 2nd edn. New York: Routledge.

McCarty, T. and Zepeda, O. (2010) Native Americans. In J.A. Fishman and O. Garcia (eds.) *Handbook of Language and Ethnic Identity: Disciplinary and Regional Perspectives*. 2nd edn. New York: Oxford University Press, pp. 324–339.

Wiley, T. (2010) The United States. In J.A. Fishman and O. Garcia (eds.) *Handbook of Language and Ethnic Identity: Disciplinary and Regional Perspectives*. 2nd edn. New York: Oxford University Press, pp. 302–323.

¡Ya basta!

14

The term Hispanic, coined by technomarketing experts and by the designers of political campaigns, homogenizes our cultural diversity (Chicanos, Cubans, and Puerto Ricans become indistinguishable), avoids our indigenous cultural heritage and links us directly with Spain. Worse yet, it possesses connotations of upward mobility and political obedience.

Guillermo Gómez-Peña

9.7 million Latino/a citizens reported voting in the 2008 presidential election. This was an increase of 47 percent from 2004.

Voting and Registration in the Election of 2008, http://goo.gl/5cJPN

Counting in Spanish

The U.S. Census Bureau reported an approximate 48.4 million persons of Latino/a origin in 2009, about 15.5 percent of the current total population. Figure 14.1 provides a view of immigration over time. On this basis it is quite easy to see how it is that the Census Bureau projects that people of Latino ancestry will make up almost 25 percent of the nation's population in 2050.[1]

The government uses "Hispanic" as an umbrella term for everyone who is of Spanish-speaking national or ethnic origins. Figure 14.1 draws attention to how broad this category is, how many different national identities, world views and cultures are subsumed into the idea of *Hispanic*.

Diversity over space[2]

One indication that Latinos/as retain strong ties to homeland and heritage can be seen in settlement patterns (Figure 14.2). For example, large-scale immigration from Cuba began with Castro's rise to power in 1959. Those immigrants formed communities in Southern Florida (such as "Little Havana" in Miami) and the metropolitan New York area. Cubans – especially those who feel strongly about returning to the homeland and regaining political power – maintain strong ties to Cuba, its culture, and to each other. There are neighborhoods in the cities and towns of Southern Florida where Spanish is the dominant – and sometimes the only – language (Figure 14.3).

On the West Coast, Spanish-speaking (largely Mestizo) communities were well established when the Treaty of Guadalupe Hidalgo was signed in 1848, formally transferring much of the West and Southwest territory from Mexico to the U.S. The treaty had many provisions that were meant to protect Mexicans' rights, most of which were

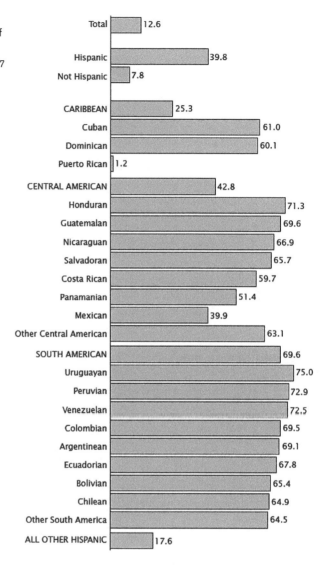

Figure 14.1
Latino population by country of origin

Source: U.S. Census Bureau, 2007 Community Survey

broken. Many historians see the Treaty of Guadalupe Hidalgo as the beginning of systematic racism and discrimination toward Mexicans and Spanish speakers more generally. The many bicultural and Spanish dominant communities along the border can document a long history of discrimination in every aspect of daily life. The Chicano movement of the 1960s and 1970s was an organized, large-scale effort to address such inequalities (Figure 14.4).

Currently the term *Chicano* is generally understood to be reserved for those of Mexican origin who were born and raised in the U.S., but who do not identify themselves in the first line as Americans. According to Rubén Salazar, "A Chicano is a Mexican-American with a non-Anglo image of himself" (June 2, 1970).[3] More recently Gustavo Arellano, author of the popular and often controversial *Ask a Mexican!* newspaper column for California's *Orange County Weekly* has written at length about intercultural tensions

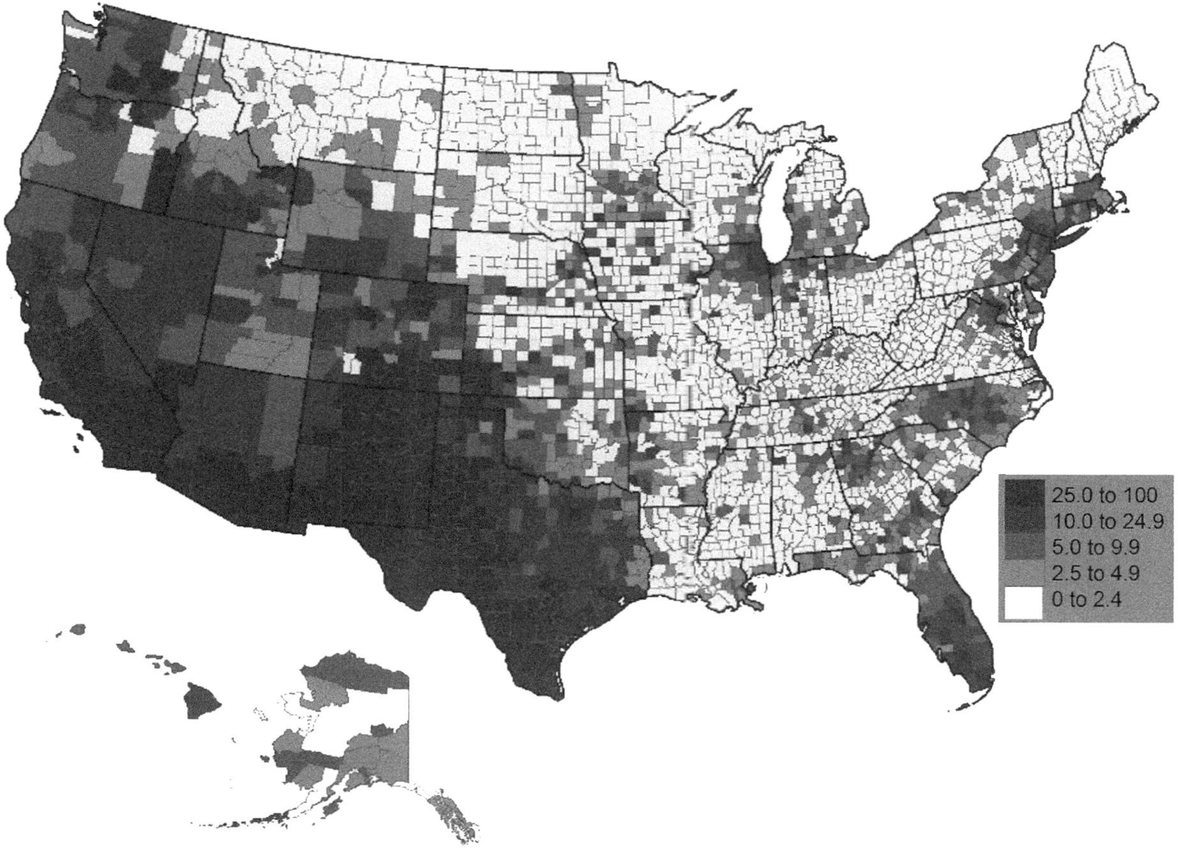

Figure 14.2
Latino/a communities over
space

Source: Adapted from 2009 U.S.
Census Bureau

25.0 to 100
10.0 to 24.9
5.0 to 9.9
2.5 to 4.9
0 to 2.4

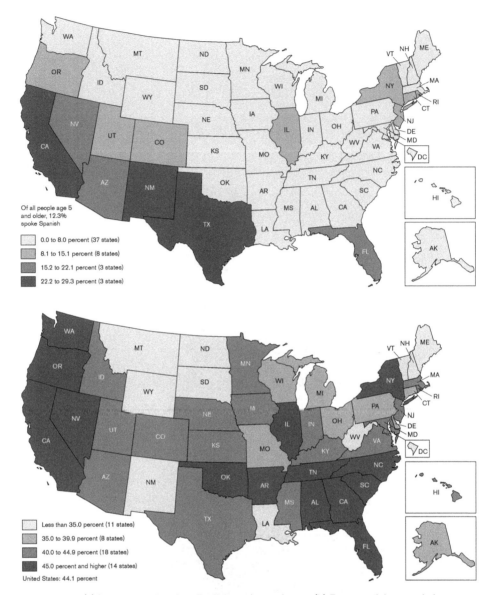

Figure 14.3 (a) Language other than English spoken at home; (b) Percent of the population speaking a language other than English at home who spoke English less than "very well"

Note: Population 5 years and older. For information on confidentiality protection, sampling error, nonsampling error, and definitions, see www.census.gov/acs/www/.

Source: U.S. Census Bureau, 2007 American Community Survey

between well-established Chicanos and those newly arrived from rural Mexico. Chicanos may refer to such Mexicans as *Chúntaro*, while the newly arrived use the term *Pocho* (rather than Chicano) for an Americanized Mexican (Arellano 2007).

The history of Puerto Ricans in the U.S. is very different. With the Jones–Shafroth Act of 1917, Puerto Ricans were granted U.S. citizenship,[4] so that there is no discussion of

Figure 14.4 Texas restaurant sign, 1949

Source: Photo by R. Lee, 1949. Reprinted by permission of The Dolph Briscoe Center for American History

immigration quotas, work visas or resident status. Puerto Ricans have no need for visas, but they have been the focus of discrimination for a long time in the Northeast. This is probably due, at least in part, to the strong ties between Stateside Puerto Ricans and Puerto Rico and the fact that many of the communities in the U.S. prefer their own culture and language to assimilation. The largest wave of Puerto Rican immigrants (often referred to as "the Great Migration") began with the Depression and lasted through World War II and into the 1950s. Puerto Rican communities settled in East Harlem, on the Lower East Side, Upper West Side, in Chelsea, and Hell's Kitchen, as well as in Brooklyn and the Bronx.

Despite differences in their history and culture Mexicans, Puerto Ricans and Cubans have all been identified by the U.S. Census Bureau as *Hispanic*. What unites them and the other countries in that group is a strong allegiance to the homeland and family, a common religion (primarily Roman Catholic) and an inclination to hold onto Spanish as a primary language.[5] Oboler's work with Spanish-speaking immigrants from nine countries (all ages, both genders) employed as garment workers in New York also establishes the importance of solidarity within national origin groups (the wish to be identified as Cuban or Puerto Rican or Dominican), while at the same time, workers take pride in the commonality of language (Oboler 1995, 2006). Others have made similar observations:

> Latinos in the United States predominately self-identify as "Hispanic" and/or "Latino" *in addition to* their national origin, but they do not self-identify as "American." Undergoing a process of "racialized assimilation," Latinos are not viewed by other U.S. citizens as "unhyphenated Americans" but as, specifically, "Latino and Latina Americans."
>
> (Vasquez 2010: 48 original emphasis; citations excluded)

There is a twist to this discussion of labels, however, and it is an instructive one. In 1970, the U.S. Census Bureau wanted to develop better methods to identify Spanish-speaking people before the next (1980) census. The 19 committee members were predominantly of Mexican ancestry and included the leaders of civil rights organizations. It was this group that recommended use of the term *Hispanic* as one that would embrace all persons of Latin American origin (Gómez 2007: 150–151). Today the term is contested for a variety of reasons, but the Census Bureau shows no interest in re-evaluating its usefulness.

Zentella (1996) provides another perspective on the matter of labels imposed on peripheralized populations. She speaks and writes of what it was like for her as a child to have had a singing and dancing Chiquita Banana as a solitary Latina figure in the public eye. She uses the term *chiquitafication* to describe public policies and practices which homogenize Latino/a cultures and languages into a tidy and digestible package for the rest of the nation, identifying three specific misconceptions arising from this practice: (1) the idea of a homogeneous "Hispanic community" that refuses to learn English; (2) the belittling of non-Castilian varieties of Spanish; and (3) the labeling of second-generation bilinguals as semi- or alinguals (ibid.: 1).

As seen in Figure 14.5, the individual's allegiance to national origin patterns quite strongly to that person's language preference. That is, a person who speaks primarily Spanish is far more likely to name a specific national origin, such as "Mexican" or "Guatemalan" or "Peruvian" rather than the less specific *Latino/a* or *Hispanic*. The group that is most likely to self-identify as American is composed of those who report that they speak primarily English.

There is reason to be wary about attempts to demonize immigrant populations. John Tanton, the founder of many different extreme anti-immigration groups and periodicals, has been vocal about his belief that Mexican immigrants pose a real threat to Americans: Tanton has warned of a coming "Latin onslaught" and proposed that high Latino birth rates would lead "the present majority to hand over its political power to a group that is

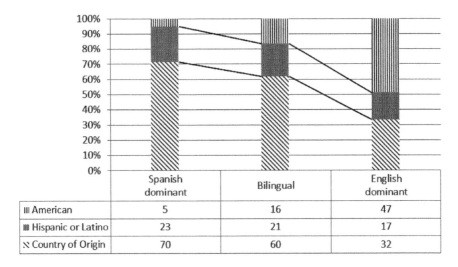

	Spanish dominant	Bilingual	English dominant
▥ American	5	16	47
▦ Hispanic or Latino	23	21	17
▨ Country of Origin	70	60	32

Figure 14.5 How individuals self-identify national origin, by language preference and use in answer to the question "In general, which of the terms that you use to describe yourself is the term you use first?"

Source: Adapted from data provided by the Pew Hispanic Research Center, 2010

simply more fertile." Tanton repeatedly demeaned Latinos in the memos, asking whether they would "bring with them the tradition of the *mordida* [bribe], the lack of involvement in public affairs" and also questioning Latinos' "educability" (Beirich 2009).

In their study of the representation of Latino/as in the media, Penfield and Ornstein-Galicia (1985) note general trends: Latino/as are almost always portrayed as violent and with explosive tempers; Chicanos/as in California's large cities are drug-pushers, gang-members, pimps. In rural areas they are migrant farm workers. Just as Disney never thought to give the character of a carpenter (or a fire fighter, or a street sweeper) a French accent, film makers find it difficult to imagine Latinos/as as accountants, copy shop owners, engineers or veterinarians.

The Spanish universe

Some Latinos live in communities of monolingual English speakers, where a Spanish accent stands out. Others live in communities where multiple varieties of English co-exist in relative harmony, in which Spanish, English, and Chicano or other varieties of Latino English each have a place. Chicano English, Puerto Rican English and Cuban English in Los Angeles, New York and Miami are distinct from each other, with distinctive syntactical, morphological and discourse markers (Jenkins 2009; Villa and Rivera-Mills 2009, García and Otheguy 1988; Penfield and Ornstein-Galicia 1985; Valdés 1988; Zentella 1988).

When Zentella protests the labeling of second-generation Spanish-language immigrants as *semi-lingual* or *alingual*, she is referring to code switching, the orderly (grammatically structured) alternation between two or more languages, a subject of great interest to linguists and one which is widely studied.[6] This complicates the picture of the Spanish-speaking universe considerably. We have distinct languages, each with its own stylistic repertoires: Spanish and English. To these we add more recently developed but distinct varieties of English, for example, Chicano English and Chicano Spanish as they are spoken in the Southwest and West. Now we have also the phenomenon of living and working with three languages, and switching among them as determined by language-internal (syntactical and morphological) rules as well as social ones. In comparison, style switching may seem to an unsympathetic outsider nothing more than a language hodge-podge, one often labeled *Spanglish*.

I would argue that whether the object of subordination is the *act* of style switching, or pressure to use one specific language rather than another, the ultimate goal remains the same: to devalue and suppress everything Spanish. To call code-switching *Spanglish* in a dismissive way is just another subordination method with a long history: to deny a language and its people a distinct name is to refuse to acknowledge them. There is a shorthand at work here, and that is, there is only one acceptable choice: it is not enough for 44 million Spanish speakers to become bilingual: they must learn the right English – and following from that, the right U.S. culture, into which they must assimilate completely. Certainly Spanish speakers feel that discrimination toward them has more to do with language than with immigration status, skin color or economics (Figure 14.6).

On rare occasion, there will be public commentary which makes clear that the offer we make to immigrants is contingent on a certain kind of English, as in this radio broadcast (May 23, 1994) which begins with images of confusion and bloodshed in a multiethnic urban setting:

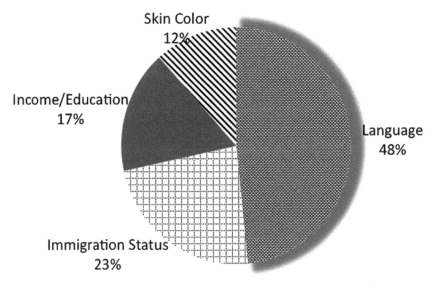

Figure 14.6 Percent of Spanish speakers who identified each category as primary source of discrimination

Source: Adapted from Hakimzadeh and Cohn (2007)

Los Angles has cosmopolitan eyes and ears. We know a Korean billboard from a Chinese one even though we may not read either language. Those bloody names that spill out of the television every night – Gorazde, San Cristobal, They don't sound so foreign here as they might in the Dakotas. So, why are we frustrated at the sound of our own voices?

Note the blunt tactic of a straightforward demand for cooperation: *We are frustrated by ourselves, by the multilingualism of Los Angeles.* By coercing participation in this way, the commentator makes his frustration everyone's frustration. Thus, a great deal of latitude can be assumed in matters where he might not otherwise feel entitled to impose his opinion:

It's because over the counters in our banks, over the tables in our restaurants, and over the phones in our offices, in job interviews and in meeting rooms, Los Angeles speaks not just with dozens of foreign languages, but with dozens of variations of English, not to mention our own native accent, from Ice-T to Beverly Hills 90210. It's all English, we're all speaking the same language, but that doesn't mean we're communicating. How do you bring up something that's more personal than bad breath and more embarrassing than an unzipped fly? How do you tell people who are speaking English that it's a kind of English we can't understand? Mostly we don't even try. We say, "Thank you," and then we hang up the phone and call back a few minutes later, hoping that someone else will answer.

(ibid.)

Morrison first assumes that all immigrants want to be bilingual, but then shifts the focus of outrage from *no English* to the *wrong (accented) English*, or English that literally stinks of unwashed humanity. There are no excuses made for rejecting the communicative burden; it is acceptable just to "hang up the phone." He moves on to make some concessions: accent is immutable past a certain age, even when people would like to acquire a perfect English.

> The newcomers want to learn English . . . The cruelest thing about this is that learning the words is the easy part; learning the accent may never happen. An expert in these things says that after puberty, muscles that have formed one language for years just can't change very easily to a new one.

Finally, we come to the heart of the matter. Certain accents are frustrating and disturbing and worthy of reduction (he has already admitted that accent *elimination* is an impossibility). He wants to reduce these accents, but there's a complication: in so doing he is making a negative statement about the social identities to which they are attached.

In order to soften this blow and render accent reduction more palatable, Morrison employs another tactic: the concern with fairness is labeled "politically correct," a neat and very quick way to render an idea trivial, petty and worthy of rejection. *I know that this is wrong on some level*, the commentator is saying, *but it is done so much – why fight it?*[7]

The changing colors of Mexico

Before looking more closely at language-focused discrimination in the Southwest, it is important to consider how issues of race, ethnicity and language work together.

From the time of the first U.S. Census in 1790 to the 1850 Census, there were only two possible choices for race: *white* or *black*. After 1850 the Census Bureau started experimenting with different levels of classification, and included categories such as *Mulatto* and *Amerindians*. In 1930, for the first and last time, the Census Bureau included *Mexican* as a race. The protests of the Latino community were organized and persistent, with the result that in 1940 this practice was stopped (Gross 2007; Leeman 2004). The term *Mestizo* would likely have been acceptable to Mexican-Americans, but the Census Bureau chose not to pursue that possibility, and in 2010 that is still the case.

Mestizo is a category officially recognized in most of Central and South America as a reference to persons of mixed ancestry, descended from both the indigenous peoples of the southwestern U.S., Mexico and Central America, and the Europeans who colonized them. There are many communities of indigenous peoples in Mexico, but some large portion of the rest of the population could be seen as Mestizo. Miguel Barriento, an advocate for the Mestizo community in Nevada, summarized the situation: "We are not White. We are not Black. We are a mix of White and Indian, which is Mestizo" (March 23, 2010).

Latino/as may be any race, but "the general image of Latinos is that of the Mestizo. In other words, the supposed 'Latin look' is that of the Mestizo" (Baker 2009). Baker makes this point in support of the drive to add Mestizo to the choices for race offered by the Census. He also notes that because the Mestizo population outnumbers the Afro-Latin and other Spanish-speaking populations, the contributions of those groups are minimized as a result:

> [B]aseball star David "Big Papi" Ortiz (black) does not physically look like actress Cameron Diaz (white), and that soccer legend Pele (black) looks nothing like

funnyman George Lopez (Indio/Native American), and so on. Yet, they are all Latinos here in the U.S.

(ibid.)

While social scientists and politicians debate this issue of race, the public has come to its own conclusions. Anglos do see Mexicans as racially *other*: not white or black, but brown. Barrett (2006) took a job as wait staff at an Anglo-owned Mexican restaurant in California to study Anglo/Mexican language ideologies in a realistic, unarranged setting. The casualness with which staff and managers acknowledged the color line (wait staff is Anglo; kitchen staff is Latino) is seen in this example of an exchange between Barrett and a manager:

Manager: Oh, your check isn't in this pile, this is the brown pile.
Me: They're divided that way?
Manager: Well, you know, kitchen and wait staff.

(Barrett 2006: 176)

A comparison of the official stance (Mexicans are *white*, according to the U.S. Census Bureau) and the reality documented by Barrett and many others (Cobas and Feagin 2008; Gómez 2007; Hill 2008; Niemann *et al.* 1999; Rinderle and Montoya 2008; Santa Ana 2002, among others) suggests that Mexican-Americans occupy an ambiguous position in the social order that has rendered them *off-white* (Gómez 2007).[8] This is what Foley (1998) calls, quite aptly, "a parallel universe of whiteness" (as cited in Powers 2008: 62).

The relevance of these complex issues of race will become clearer in the following sections on specific kinds of discrimination.

We're not going anywhere: performing race

In teaching an annual course on language and discrimination, I found that arguments rarely escalated past the usual soft-voiced and apologetic differences of opinion. One exception came during a class discussion on English-Only. A Mexicana student raised the subject of the growing Latino population in California and what that meant to a majority-rule-based electoral system and language rights. The tension in the room was immediate.

Another student said to her, quite defensively, "WE settled California" to which she responded with a short, concise history of Spanish settlements in the Southwest that predated Anglo settlements by a good margin. There was an awkward silence.

Then the other student said, "We're still the majority."

To which she said, "We were there first, and we're still there and we're not going anywhere." She might have added, *and it won't be so long before we're the majority, bucko*, but she withheld, quite sensibly, that obvious fact.

Another student, quiet until that point, raised the question of individual liberties, the Bill of Rights, and language, and the conversation veered away. It is my practice to allow such conversations to run their natural course without interruption or manipulation, though in this case I was sorry the discussion ended so quickly

This kind of exchange repeats itself daily, in all kinds of communication acts in every possible setting and tone. One way to look at such interactions is by means of performance theory.

Human beings are by nature performers; we project our identities again and again to ourselves and everyone else, in an act that that provides a kind of psychological cultural grounding. In our everyday lives we "simultaneously recognize, substantiate, and (re)create ourselves as well as Others through performance . . . performance becomes a ubiquitous force in our social and discursive universe" (Madison 2005: 73–74).

In a classroom where societal racism is discussed and confronted, the performance of race and ethnicity can become emotionally extreme. In such situations there is more than factual knowledge at stake, there is also the individual's sense and understanding of self. The exchange in my classroom was immediately fraught, because by asserting herself, the Mexicana student was challenging the conventionally taught history of the United States, among other things. At that, some or all of the Anglo students felt the need to reassert their own identities, preferring their own narratives to hers.

There are commonalities in such situations that have been widely studied. In this kind of classroom situation:

> [Anglo student responses] range from overt racism, to entrenchment in white supremacy, to refusing to listen to others, to actively denying the importance of racism and student complicity in it. Furthermore, students typically present themselves as moral and responsible social actors who would rather not be identified as racist and subsequently attempt to persuade others that they support equality and justice.
>
> (Johnson *et al*. 2008: 114)

The discussion in my classroom was an excellent example of how individuals perform race and ethnicity. That is, the Mexicana student presented or performed herself to herself and to the class as a confident, knowledgeable, assured woman of color who knew exactly where the flaws in the other student's arguments were. She would not be intimidated. The student who challenged her responded by *performing whiteness*. Johnson *et al.* provide another example, from their own work with college students in Southern California. From a student essay:

> I am "white," but at my high school "white" people were the minority. Quite frequently I would be walking in the halls, unable to understand anything being said around me. At one of my jobs, my co-workers would talk about me and my friends, right in front of our face, in a different language.
>
> (ibid.: 126)

There is a structured racism here that is so deeply embedded that it becomes normative and invisible to the privileged. The student is sharing information about an experience he or she found hurtful and unsettling. On the surface many reading her short statement will nod in agreement, thinking *yes, it is rude for people to speak Spanish in front of me, as I can't understand them*. One way to challenge this mindset is to ask a simple question: Is it equally rude to speak English in front of a Spanish speaker with limited or no English skills?

The answer to that question gets to the heart of the matter: as an English speaker, the student who complained about being excluded believed she or he was reasonable in expecting everyone to accommodate to her/him.

It can certainly feel uncomfortable to not understand languages being spoken in one's presence, and yet: "*Discomfort is not oppression*. It is a sign of privilege when white students believe they should be able to understand everything going on around them or never have their racial embodiment questioned publicly" (ibid.: 126–127; emphasis added).

This mindset is at the very heart of long-standing conflicts between the U.S. and Mexico. Our common history is very old and checkered, and most of it is unknown to those people who are most adamant about halting immigration from Mexico. This might be seen as a failure of our education system, but that kind of policy is not made in a vacuum; the impetus was born out of a communal agreement that may have been founded in apathy or jingoism. Grand narratives (also called meta narratives) may be flawed, but many feel a strong allegiance to the stories which provide a comforting cultural buffer zone.

The everyday language of white racism[9]

The importance of language to identity and to ethnicity has been well established by sociolinguists and anthropological linguists. For people of Mexican heritage living in California, there is a lot of data to suggest that for these Latinos/as, language is perhaps the primary marker of allegiance (Arellano 2007; Fought 2002a; Gómez 2007; Hidalgo 1986; Mendoza-Denton 1999; 2008; Salazar 1970; Santa Ana 1993).

In studying the connection between language and ethnicity, Fought interviewed adolescent Latinos/as to explore how language choices reflect life choices (Fought 2002a, 2006). The relationship between language choice and assimilation/solidarity may seem like simple common sense, but as we have seen, many common-sense beliefs about language are not factual. In this case, the use of language features to signal solidarity with one community over another was only theory until Labov's groundbreaking work on the island of Martha's Vineyard off the coast of Massachusetts. Using quantitative methods and statistical analysis, he examined the diphthong /ai/ and found that the first element was raised in the speech of fisherman and others who showed a dislike of or resistance to the many summer visitors to the island, and a high degree of pride in local heritage. In the course of his fieldwork he also established that adolescents who intended to move off the island as adults and live on the mainland began to give up local language markers well before that day came, while those who intended to stay and take up traditional employment were far more likely to retain local language markers such as the raised first vowel in /ai/.

It is this kind of pattern that Fought found among Chicanos/as in California. People who grew up speaking Spanish and who speak it fluently sometimes choose not to speak it at all; at the other extreme are those who never learned Spanish and who see this as a lack in themselves, because it is seen that way by the rest of their community or peer group.

Consider Fought's interview with Veronica, a 17-year-old from Los Angeles who identifies herself as Mexican, but (as she relates) is then corrected by other Chicanos/as. She is told that she can't be Mexican, because she doesn't speak Spanish. In a similar way, another student, Amanda, is often told that she's a disgrace because she doesn't speak Spanish at all, a statement that will be delivered with differing degrees of disapproval (Fought 2002b: 201).[10]

The link between nation and language is so strong that the terms for the two are often used interchangeably. For example, it is not uncommon to hear one person ask another, "Do you speak American?" *Mexican* and *Spanish* are also used interchangeably:

> CF: Even if they're Mexicans, some people don't speak Spanish.
> E: No! Some people are like that. I hate people like that, that are Mexican, and they try to act like if they don't know Mexican. So – but some of my friends that are Mexican, and – they don't know how to speak Mexican.

(ibid.: 202)

Another example from a study conducted in Texas by Achugar and Pessoa indicates that this mindset is not exclusive to California:

> [T]here you know I have met some Chicanos here that don't speak any Spanish but that seems to be because their parents came from some other part of the country where they try to be white or something and so they don't speak any Spanish, but hopefully . . . I've met some white people that have lived here all their life and they don't know any Spanish, like none. And I'm like, "How can you not know any?", I mean, don't you hear people talking ever? Like, I don't understand that. So, yeah, they just must be very, like, secluded, like all their friends are white.
>
> (Tania, English-dominant, cited in Achugar and Pessoa 2009)

For the rest of this chapter the discussion will focus primarily on the experiences of Mexicans, Mexican Americans, Chicanos/as and Latinos/as in the Southwest. It is important to note that there are large populations of Cubans, Salvadorans and other Spanish-speaking individuals in Southern California; however, the nature of the data does not allow me to separate these groups when discussing, for example, housing discrimination.

A sampling of discriminatory language-focused practices against Latinos/as

1   San Jose, CA: A 58-year-old Latino speaking on his cell phone in Spanish was punched in the face by a 28-year-old Anglo male, who shouted "Speak English!" (Dee 2009).
2   Pennsylvania, 2008: In hearing a criminal case on conspiracy to commit robbery, a judge offered four Spanish-speaking defendants a choice: learn English or go to jail for two years (Weiss 2008).
3   "[A professor] in college refused to believe that I had written an essay . . . because she assumed that Mexicans don't write very well and so therefore I couldn't have written this paper" (Cobas and Feagin 2008).
4   In Beaufort County, North Carolina, a county commissioner asked the health and social services departments to keep count of the number of clients with Spanish surnames. He wanted to determine how many undocumented immigrants were using city services (Collins 2008).
5   Texas, 2009: Over at least a three-year period police officers wrote citations for "non-English-speaking driver," a law that does not exist. In every case the person ticketed was a native speaker of Spanish. As soon as this practice came to light, the police department began an investigation of all involved officers for dereliction of duty. Fines collected from drivers ($209 each) were refunded and charges dropped. A representative of the League of United Latin American Citizens drew attention to the fact that there were active police officers who believed that it was a crime not to speak English (Goldstein 2009).
6   Connecticut, 2010: A study of traffic tickets issued by the East Haven police department over an 8-month period established that while Latinos/as make up less than 6 percent of the population, they accounted for more than 50 percent of tickets issued. In addition, the study found that police officers routinely misrepresented the race of the person receiving the ticket in their reports (Macmillan 2010).
7   Tennessee, 2005: A family court judge tells a mother from Mexico she must learn English and use birth control. That same judge threatens to terminate parental rights

of a mother if she could not speak English at a fourth grade level when she appeared before him in sixth months (Barry 2005).

8   Texas, 1995: A judge scolds a mother who speaks only Spanish to her 5-year-old daughter: "You're abusing that child and you're relegating her to the position of housemaid. Now, get this straight. You start speaking English to this child because if she doesn't do good in school, then I can remove her because it's not in her best interest to be ignorant. The child will only hear English" (Verhovek 1995).

The most vulnerable

Cirila Baltazar Cruz is a native of the Oaxaca region in isolated Southern Mexico, one known for its anthropological riches and for its extreme poverty.[11] Cruz is a member of the indigenous *Kitse Cha'tño*, or Chatino tribe, which speaks a language which falls under the Zapotecan branch of the Oto-Manguean family. Chatino is nothing like Spanish; there is no mutual intelligibility. For example, here is a sentence in Chatino compared to Mexican Spanish and English:

CHATINO: N-da nu xni' ndaha ska ha xtlya ʔi nu 'o.

N-da	nu	xni'	ndaha	ska	ha	xtlya	ʔi	nu	'o
give	the	dog	lazy	one	tortilla	Spanish	to	the	coyote

SPANISH: El perro flojo le dió un pan dulce al coyote.

ENGLISH: The lazy dog gave a sweetbread to the coyote.[12]

Cruz is a native speaker of Chatino; she speaks very little Spanish and no other language. As is common in her village, she never learned to read and write. Nevertheless, she left her children in her mother's care and came to the U.S. to find work that would allow her to send money home to Oaxaca. She took employment at a Chinese restaurant in Pascagoula, Mississippi, and was supplied housing by her employer (Abierta 2009; Byrd 2010a, 2010b; Cruz 2010; Macedo and Gounari 2006; Padgett and Mascareñas 2009; Southern Poverty Law Center 2010).

In November of 2008, Cruz went to the Singing River Hospital and gave birth to a healthy daughter. Subsequently a Spanish-speaking patient advocate of Puerto Rican heritage and a social services representative came into Cruz's room and questioned her. Cruz understood very little, but the social worker and patient advocate kept asking questions. At some point Cruz's cousin, a fluent speaker of Spanish and Chatino came to visit, and offered to translate. One of the social workers told him "that she was talking to [Cruz] and to keep his mouth shut."[13] The social workers insisted he wait in the hall.

Rather than call in a Chatino translator, the social services representatives constructed a set of reasons to remove the child from her mother's custody, including the charge that she traded sex for housing, that she had stated an intention to put the child up for adoption, that she was unprepared to care for the child and had not even purchased formula or a bassinet. Reporters from Mississippi's *Clarion Ledger* were allowed to review documents outlining these charges and others, which included language-related charges:

Cruz was charged with neglecting her child, in part, because "she has failed to learn the English language" and "was unable to call for assistance for transportation to the hospital" to give birth. Her inability to speak English "placed her unborn child in danger and will place the baby in danger in the future."

(Byrd 2010b)

Without investigating or documenting any of these charges or presenting any evidence, the Mississippi Department of Human Services' representatives used this narrative when they went before a judge, first to gain permission to remove the child from her mother's care, and later, to request termination of Cruz's parental rights.

Cruz was discharged from the hospital and told she could not take her daughter with her. When she returned the next day with her cousin to ask for her baby, she was told the child was no longer there. That day, two different social workers associated with the hospital contacted state and federal immigration authorities to report Cruz as an illegal alien (Padgett and Mascareñas 2009).

The official complaint filed by the attorneys representing Cruz outlined the charges:

> The individual defendants conspired to remove [Cruz's newborn daughter] from her mother in order to place the infant child in the custody of a white local attorney couple who were seeking to adopt and who frequently practiced before the same judge who sanctioned the removal. In doing so, the individual Defendants deliberately took advantage of Plaintiff Baltazar Cruz's indigence, inability to speak or understand English, and lack of familiarity with the U.S. legal system in order to attempt to remove [the child] permanently from her mother.

As of this writing, the case has not yet gone to court, but the defendants have been charged with conspiring to violate Cruz's constitutionally protected rights (due process, equal treatment, unreasonable seizure) and further, to deny Cruz and her daughter their constitutional rights to family integrity. The charges are based on the accusation that these actions were taken on the basis of race and/or national origin.

It wasn't until the child was a year old that she was returned to Cruz, who then took her daughter home to Mexico. This very tardy reunion came about not because Mississippi took any steps to rectify the situation, but because of an investigation by the U.S. Department of Health and Human Service's Office for Civil Rights and Administration for Children and Families. The letter written by the last agency to executive director of the Mississippi office listed a number of infractions and violations of procedures. HHS expressed concerns about this case not just because of the nature of the violations, but because "The MDHS staff interviewed did not see these issues as problematic. This leads us to conclude that this may be how business is conducted and that this is not an isolated incident" (Byrd 2010b).

The workplace

As was seen in Chapter 9, Latinos/as are actively discriminated against in the workplace. Earlier in this chapter Barrett's study of language ideology in an Anglo-owned Mexican restaurant provided another example in the form of a linguist's first-person account. Two generalizations might be made at this point: first, Barrett's study shows how deeply rationalizations for discriminatory behaviors are engrained, and, second, that the systematic, almost obligatory use of racist language and racist treatment toward Latinos/as is just obscure enough to keep such practices out of the courtroom.

Stepping back, it is clear that all employers, good, bad or indifferent, take a number of features into account to make initial, sometimes very hasty, yes/no hiring decisions. This happens as a matter of course, and for the most part, below the level of consciousness. Markley's study of employers in Texas established that individuals were willing to make judgments on such things as intelligence and diligence on the basis of a recorded voice alone (Markley 2000).

Such preconceptions mold the employers' expectations for workers before they begin employment, and extend to strategic decisions with long-term impact (which individuals are suited for which positions, assumptions about skill sets and intelligence, who to train further).

Maldonado (2009) set out to interview "forty employers from twenty-six farm operations and firms (packers/shippers, equipment and input suppliers, warehouses) representing the various sizes and types of agricultural operations in Washington" to gather data on Anglo/Latino relations in such settings. Of the 40 employers interviewed, 28 were Anglo, and each described without hesitation a division of labor based on race. Employers sometimes reacted with irritation or direct anger when asked about race or ethnicity; all had a set of arguments to rationalize or neutralize the inherent racism in their employment practices. Here is one example of an employer who has so naturalized racism in his view of the workplace that he doesn't hesitate to provide answers that are clearly illogical:

> [T]he workers are one hundred percent Hispanic . . . [O]n all the ranches that I run . . . we have no Caucasian people at all . . . And the reason being is that we don't get anybody applying for it. It's mostly been just Hispanic people were applying. (Interviewer: How do you think it became that way?) Supply and demand, you know. Basic economics.
>
> (ibid.: 1024)

The role of language in the racialization process comes out in an almost matter-of-fact way in another interview with an employer who rejects the necessity of talking about ethnicity or race at all:

> I, it just [laughs] I could, I could go into a whole soapbox in my opinion . . . Race, race is an issue in this country mainly because those populations want to keep it an issue in this country. When you really get to the hiring and, and firing and who's on your team type situation . . . it's based, as far as I'm concerned, on performance. I don't care if you're from Mars; if you can do the job and you can communicate with me . . . and do it effectively, hey, you're hired.
>
> (ibid.: 1023)

The employer begins a sentence "If you can do the job and communicate with me" and then pauses. That pause signals the speaker's reaching for a phrase that will qualify and restrict the first part of the sentence. "If you can communicate with me and do it effectively" could be read thus: *There are two necessary qualifications if you want to work with me. You have to be able to do the job, and you have to be able to make me understand you.* Thus the employer is anticipating communication breakdown and handing the responsibility for successful communication to the worker alone. This is, in itself, not a violation of any law; an employer may reasonably require that an employee be able to communicate with him or her. What is interesting about this exchange is the tone.

Racism is often expressed in this off-hand way, just as the rationalizations offered are usually pretextual, and the logic spurious. As in this case:

> He told me quite frankly that he would never hire anyone with a strong foreign accent, and especially not a Mexican accent. I asked him why. His only response was, "That's smart business. I have to think of the customers. I wouldn't buy anything from a guy with a Mexican accent."
>
> (Spicher 1992: 3–4)

Whether or not it is actually smart business to willfully ignore the needs and wants of a population of many millions of consumers is doubtful. Nevertheless, this anecdote is more useful than any number of statistics, because it makes some things painfully clear: the degree of accent is irrelevant when the focus is not on content, but form. The businessman cannot conceive of a middle-class, Spanish-speaking population with money to spend, and therefore the entire Mexican American population is worthy of rejection.

Education in the Southwest

There is a long and well-documented history of discrimination toward Spanish-speaking populations in the Southwest. Some of the most destructive policies have been practiced in education,[14] where Mexican children were routinely segregated into poorly staffed and overcrowded schools. Such practices ended – in theory – in 1954 with Brown v. Board of Education, when the Supreme Court struck down *separate but equal* policies. The most blatant forms of segregation lessened, but Latino/a children were – and are still – peripheralized, segregated, unfairly and incorrectly funneled into special education classrooms, denied opportunities readily available to Anglos, and forbidden to speak their own language even in one-on-one conversations on the playground.

Gandara and Orfield (2010) and Po (2010) present a stark picture of linguistic segregation in Arizona schools while Bratt's "Violence in the Curriculum: Compulsory Linguistic Discrimination in the Arizona-Sonora Borderlands" (2007) is a sobering look at the way institutionalized linguistic discrimination puts teachers and children on opposite sides of a great gulf, creating an antagonism that can, in extreme moments, end in physical violence. In Bratt's experience in Arizona, school districts create extreme English-Only policies tougher than the State guidelines, so that "teachers in more than one elementary district in rural Arizona are summarily fired if they are heard speaking Spanish, even to prevent an accident on the playground" (ibid.: 3).

Structured programs designed to help English language learners toward proficiency have had exactly the opposite result (Gandara and Orfield 2010), in large part because English speakers and English learners rarely interact, so that those with limited English proficiency are isolated from those situations where English is spoken:

> Our analysis of the hyper-segregation of Hispanic students, and particularly Spanish-speaking [English language learners], suggests that little or no attention has been given to the consequences of linguistic isolation for a population whose future depends on the acquisition of English . . . For ELLs, interaction with ordinary English-speaking peers is essential to their English language development and consequently to their acquisition of academic English.
>
> (Gifford and Valdés 2006: as cited in Gandara and Orfield 2010)

There have been periods when Arizona's policies emerged from the grip of moral panic to more inclusive approaches.[15] A broad bilingual-education program was put in place in the 1990s, which resulted in the hiring of several hundred native Spanish-speaking teachers, some from outside the U.S. (Gandara and Orfield 2010). Even in such open-minded and progressive periods, the underlying ideology has been anti-immigrant and anti-bilingual "serving to privilege the English-speaking Anglo majority and to marginalize and disenfranchise the Spanish-speaking Latino minority" (Cashman 2009: 45). And indeed, the progress of the 1990s was being reversed by 2000 when a ballot measure forbidding use of any language other than English in the classroom was passed.

Issues around language are tied to questions around immigration, arguably the most divisive topic in Arizona's post-colonial history. As is usually the case with immigration-focused extremism, anti-immigration rhetoric flares up in times of economic downturn. At the writing of the second edition of this book, the U.S. is "in the midst of the largest influx of immigrants in a century. . . a record in absolute numbers but still somewhat smaller proportion of the total population than was the case a century ago" (Hakimzadeh and Cohn 2007).

Certainly the country's fragile economy contributed to the fervor around two bills signed into law in April 2010 by Arizona governor Jan Brewer. State Bill 1070 aims to "identify, prosecute and deport illegal immigrants" (Archibold 2010a) in ways that opponents and critics find extreme to the point of violating basic human rights set forth in the U.S. Constitution. The targeting of the Mexican population has earned 1070 the nickname the *Breathing while Brown Bill* (Lemons 2010) an indication of the extreme anxiety the bill evokes among the Latino population, whether they are citizens, legal residents, or undocumented workers (Archibold 2010b). McKinley's report from Arizona quoted one bystander: "If they look at someone and they are of Mexican descent, they are going to be guilty until proven innocent," she said. "It makes you guilty for being brown" (McKinley 2010).

Challenges were quickly filed in the court by civil rights scholars and activists, professors of law and linguistics, the Mexican government, the ACLU and the U.S. Justice Department (McKinley 2010). Vivek Malhotra, the advocacy and policy council for the American Civil Liberties Union, summarized Arizona's new immigration laws quite neatly. "This law does nothing short of making all of its Latino residents, and other presumed immigrants, potential criminal suspects in the eyes of the law" (Archibold 2010d).

SB 1070 was written and publicized in a combative tone that caught the media's attention. HR 2083, also signed by the governor in April 2010, was launched more quietly. This newer bill was strikingly different in one important way. While SB 1070's focus was undocumented workers, HR 2083 focus shifts to the rest of the population, those who were born in the U.S. or came to the country through official routes, but who still self-identify as Mexican.

HR 2083 prohibits schools from offering courses at any grade level that advocate ethnic solidarity, promote overthrow of the U.S. government, or cater to specific ethnic groups. Observers posed many questions raised by the odd wording:

> Are Arizona schools in the habit of promoting the overthrow of the government? Is there an implicit accusation here?

> Does the school board mean ethnicity distinct from race? Would this include any ethnicity? So for example, a course offered to advanced students in high school on

the French Revolution, the Irish–English conflicts, the economics of the Middle East, these would all be prohibited?

Advocating ethnic solidarity – could that include discussion of our own Revolution?

In fact, the purpose of this law is very narrow: it was written to dismantle a popular and successful Mexican-American studies program in the Tucson school district.

(Calefati 2010; Kurowski 2010; Strauss 2010a, 2010b)

The law was written and promoted by Tom Horne, the state superintendent of public instruction, a man in a heated race for attorney general against an opponent known for his extreme stance on immigration. Khimm (2010) quotes Horne as he justifies the bill as a way to target specific courses in Tucson where Latino/a students are inculcated with "'ethnic chauvinism' . . . he skips straight to the inflammatory charge that [ethnic studies classes] could encourage students to revolt against U.S. government, effectively legitimizing fears of a Mexican 'reconquista'" (ibid.). In this view of ethnic studies, students and teachers are all seen as seditionists.

Horne's personal animosity toward a specific program attended by 3 percent of the 55,000 students in the Tucson school district has wide-reaching implications (Calefati 2010). Latinos may fill almost 50 percent of the classrooms in Arizona, but because Horne has a vested interest in the moral panic he is fostering, children of Latino/a, African or Asian backgrounds will be forbidden to learn about their heritage in school.

Finally, the State Education Office took the opportunity provided by the passage of these two bills to put new policies in place that target teachers who speak Spanish as a native language, or English with an accent. Reportedly based on the federal No Child Left Behind Act, the Arizona provision requires that teachers who teach English to English language learners (that is, Latinos/as who speak Spanish as a first language) must be "fluent in every aspect of the English language" (Calefati 2010). The person at the Arizona department of education who is charged with enforcing this new rule has been quite specific on the record:

> "The teacher obviously must be fluent in every aspect of the English language," said Adela Santa Cruz, director of the Arizona education-department office charged with enforcing standards in classes for students with limited English. The education department has dispatched evaluators to audit teachers across the state on things such as comprehensible pronunciation, correct grammar and good writing.
>
> Teachers that don't pass muster may take classes or other steps to improve their English; if fluency continues to be a problem, Ms. Santa Cruz said, it is up to school districts to decide whether to fire teachers or reassign them to mainstream classes not designated for students still learning to speak English.
>
> (Jordan 2010)

Very little information is publicly available on the details of this policy. Strauss (2010c) interviewed a spokesperson from the Department of Education, who provided a list of school districts that were being monitored, for example: "2009–10 school year – The education department monitored 61 districts and found 9 districts were cited for fluency" (ibid.). The school district stated that no teachers were dismissed or transferred on the basis of lack of fluency, but there was no further information or documentation.

Neither was there any background on the inspectors, what kind of training they had to qualify them, or whether there was any conflict of interest (for example, will any of them make a living in the accent reduction business?). There are no definitions of accent or grammar or even of the concept of fluency. Yet these inspectors hold the fate of hundreds of teachers in their hands.

As we have seen before, teachers are also protected under Title VII, and may not be dismissed or refused promotion on the basis of accent linked to national origin unless that accent makes it impossible for the employee to accomplish assigned work. Thus, if any teachers are reassigned or dismissed on this basis and they pursue a legal challenge, it would be up to Horne to prove that a native Spanish-speaking teacher is detrimental to the educational welfare of a Spanish-speaking child.

Aside from the question of civil rights and Title VII, the logic presented here is spurious. If only native English speakers should teach those who come to school with limited English proficiency, then by extension French classes must be taught by native French teachers, and Japanese by native Japanese speakers. The study of second language acquisition – and common sense – are enough to establish the fact that speaking a language is not sufficient training to teach it effectively.

Taken as a whole, these two new laws and the new educational policy present a disturbing picture of a state and population in the grip of a moral panic, where common sense and (some would argue) common decency have been sacrificed in order to assuage fears. As is usually the case in a moral panic, there is some rationale not very far in the background: demographics will continue to shift toward a Latino/a majority, so that sometime in the not too distant future, Anglos will no longer have numerical superiority. The question is, does it make sense to alienate and anger those people who will one day be the majority?

Hypothetically speaking

Consider this set of possibilities:

> The U.S. Census estimates that in the year 2030 Arizona will be only 30 percent Anglo or native English speakers. Another 58 percent will be Spanish speaking, and the remainder are Native American tribes who govern themselves and set their own policies.

> Imagine that in 2031, the State government of Arizona votes new legislation into place, which splits pretty much 30/65 percent along ethnicity and language lines. The governor vetoes the bill; the legislature overrides the veto. Spanish is now the official language of Arizona. The new bill includes the following sections:

>> Article I: Spanish is the official language of the state of Arizona.

>> Article II: The civil administration, the health services and social services, the public utility enterprises, the professional corporations, the associations of employees and all enterprises doing business in Arizona will institute Spanish-only policies.

>> Article III: All governmental offices and parliamentary structures will conduct business in Spanish.

>> Article IV: Workers will not be required or encouraged to speak any language other than Spanish.

Article V: All consumer information must be in Spanish.

Article VI: All public education at all levels is to be conducted exclusively in Spanish. English will not be used or heard in any Arizona school with the exception of classes in which the English language is being taught.

Article VII: Product labels, their instructions, manuals, warranty certificates as well as restaurant menus and wine lists must be in Spanish. All street signs, including shop signs, must be in Spanish. Violations will be heavily fined.

Article IX: Catalogues, brochures, folders, commercial directories and other such publications, must be in the official language. All software (for example, video games and operating systems) must be available in Spanish by the year 2035.

This will most likely strike you as absurd. It's too extreme in the way it simply nullifies the rights of native and/or monolingual English speakers. Such sweeping legislation must be challenged immediately in the courts.

But such things have happened, and there's a present-day example very close to home.

In 1763, the French withdrew from North America and at that point Canada became a British possession. The British colonial policy was to *make the world England*, and that process began immediately with a new English-speaking government and upper class dominating business and social circles. With the immigration of large numbers of British people, business trade shifted away from the traditional French merchants; the fate of the French who had been in Quebec since the first European settlements were made clear: you must assimilate.

French speakers were shut out of the most influential aspects of official life, and a tiered system developed in which Anglophones (English speakers, the British) constituted the governing classes; to be a Francophone was to be associated with the laboring classes. Francophones were at a marked disadvantage in every way; their children were segregated from Anglophone schoolchildren and had fewer possibilities in terms of education and training.

Of course, French did not die out. A large, healthy, well-established language community does not simply buckle under in the face of governmental decree. The Francophone population regrouped and began to find their way back.

In 1974, a new Francophone-dominant province government passed an Official Language Act with the intention of making French the normal, everyday language of work, instruction, communication, commerce and business. Another Bill (*Loi* 101) was passed in 1977 which went into much greater detail. In fact, all of the provisions suggested above were included, almost word for word in Bill 101.[16]

As is so often the tendency when power structures are concentrated in a small section of the community, the oppressed had become the oppressors (Freire 2000 [1970]).[17] The Francophone government asserted its right to exclude all things Anglophone, and they do so still. One example of many is Bob Rice's story.

A Québécois from birth and an Anglophone, Bob ran into trouble with an apostrophe, and it cost him dearly.

One day in 2004, Bob Rice received a ticket in the mail. Its intention wasn't very clear, but eventually he figured out that he was being fined by the *Office Québécois de la langue française* (Quebec Office of the French Language) because they had a complaint from a neighbor about the apostrophe on the sign for his plumbing company: Bob's (Figure 14.7).

Bob's Plumbing

Figure 14.7 Bob's Plumbing

The Quebec office of the French Language is responsible for enforcing the language legislation, which outlaws apostrophes in public signs. The reasoning here is that the province laws stipulate French-only on all public signs, and there is no apostrophe in the possessive form *Bobs*, in French.

Bob was given a $599 fine and a $187 delivery charge for the ticket. If he did not pay within the week, his pickup truck, farm tractor and car would be sold at an auction in his yard. Bob paid the fines, and solved the problem of the apostrophe by covering it up with a sticker of the Canadian flag.

Summary

Americans tend to think of monolingualism as the default. For whatever reason – educational gaps, ideology, mythology – most of us imagine that Spanish is spoken in Spain, Polish in Poland, and so on.

In fact, monolingualism is the exception across the world's populations, and that is the case even If you exclude consideration of immigrant languages. This is quite logical if you consider for a moment that national political boundaries change over time, usually as the result of war or its aftermath. The current boundaries of France include areas which were once Spain, Belgium, Italy, Switzerland and Germany. When the borders moved, the populations (for the most part) stayed put. For example, Occitan is a romance language closely related to Catalan. There are native speakers and small Occitan language communities in France, Monaco, Italy, and Spain. Occitan is just one example of the dozens of indigenous languages in Spain other than Spanish.

A government may make laws declaring one language to be the official language of the nation, but the facts indicate a different reality. This is true of every country in Europe and the world. It is true of the United States. Every few years a wave of protest washes over us, and a subset of the people demand that English be acknowledged as the country's one true language. In some cases it seems that people actually believe that such a thing is possible, and all it will take is a law to render us monolingual.

Such laws are primarily symbolic, of course. The demand for an English monolingual U.S. is akin to saying: *We're first. We're best. Everybody needs to acknowledge that, and unwillingness to do so is. . . un-American!* There are no rational arguments for this position. English-Only proponents can only appeal to majority rule, but even that can be challenged by invoking the Bill of Rights, and in any case, numerical superiority is slipping away in many places.

The U.S. is a multilingual nation, and our two most prevalent languages are English and Spanish. Whatever laws we pass, whatever language planning documents we write, those facts are undeniable. In the end, language will not be legislated.

DISCUSSION QUESTIONS AND EXERCISES

● Listen to Andre Codrescu's essay "Arizona Education Loses the Accent of America" (2010) on National Public Radio. Does his perspective change your thoughts about anything in this chapter? How is it relevant to the chapter – and book – in a broader sense? Radio link is available at: http://goo.gl/xGErO.

● Davila (Davila *et al.* 1993) undertook a preliminary, explorative statistical analysis of earnings by three groups of workers in the U.S.: Mexican Americans, German Americans and Italian Americans who speak their heritage language at home (and thus, Davila *et al.* postulated, spoke with an accent). In fact, the analysis indicated that those of Mexican ancestry earned significantly less than the other two groups. They suggest that Mexicans who have a closer affinity to their heritage culture pay a penalty for that preference, but they also list a number of other possible reasons for the discrepancy in earnings. Discuss what you think those reasons may be. Think in terms of immigration history and trends, geographic distribution, and legal considerations in addition to ethnicity and language.

● Consider the history of discriminatory practices taken against Native Americans as described briefly in Chapter 7, and compare that information (and any other research you might do on this topic) to Padgett's *Time Magazine* article about the Cruz case in Mississippi. What similarities do you see? How relevant are they to language-focused discrimination?

● Make a list of terms for people of Latino origin. (If you are yourself Latino/a, you can still undertake this exercise – but you should concentrate on non-Spanish speakers when collecting data. (If you are not comfortable with this, you could take a different approach, and make a similar list of Spanish language terms for non-Spanish speakers in the U.S.) Ask acquaintances, friends, family for help. In class, find a way to divide all the terms collected into groups. Are some terms purely derogatory and racist? Are there neutral terms which seem to be fairly safe; that is, they won't offend the majority of Latinos? How many of the terms do you use yourself, and which ones do you avoid? Can you reconstruct what goes through your mind if/when you use a term like "wetback"? This is not meant to be an exercise in blame; the purpose is to pinpoint the way you have learned to think about a particular ethnic group.

● Consider the Arizona School Board's intention to send out inspectors to decide whether a teacher speaks English fluently enough to work with Spanish-speaking children who are learning English. Can you imagine putting together a program (training the investigators, etc.) that would reach judicious, consistent evaluations? What would that look like?

● How is the language situation in Quebec relevant to the conflicts in the U.S. Southwest? Do you feel the Francophone laws in Quebec were well founded? Reasonable? Understandable? What do you think might happen if/when the Spanish-speaking population of Arizona reaches a strong majority?

● Explore the Pew Hispanic Center Web site by following the link to "Reports." Identify an issue that is (a) language related; and (b) could be addressed, at least in part, by "making the invisible visible" to Anglos.

● Consider the Census maps from the 2007 American Community Survey in this chapter. Note that those areas of the country which are most heavily bilingual Spanish/English are not necessarily the areas where English language facility is lowest. Why might that be, for example, in New Mexico?

● *"Discomfort is not oppression*. It is a sign of privilege when white students believe they should be able to understand everything going on around them or never have their racial embodiment questioned publicly." Discuss.

● Pursue the issue of the Mexican-American Ethnic Studies Program in the Tucson school district. A few places to start:

  ● Strauss, V. (2010) Why Arizona Targeted Ethnic Studies. *The Washington Post*, May 25. Available at: http://goo.gl/bpYnu.

  ● Arizona, in the Classroom [Editorial] (2011) *The New York Times*. January 17: A22. Available at: http://goo.gl/sXdvG.

  ● Tucson United School District Mexican American Studies Department Presentation to the TUSD Governing Board January 12, 2010 Director: Sean Arce, M.Ed. Available at: http://goo.gl/MpWO3.

  ● The full text of an e-mail exchange between Dr. Rodolfo Acuña and KGUN9 News director Forrest Carr. For ease of reading, Carr's questions are highlighted in yellow. The non-highlighted portions are Dr. Acuña's responses. Available at: http://goo.gl/yVnXx.

  ● May 24 (2010) What ethnic studies students are learning: an inside look. Available at: http://goo.gl/r8nez.

  ● June 3 (2010) Author Slams Arizona Education Boss over Ethnic Studies Ban. Available at: http://goo.gl/rwpB.

  ● October 19 (2010) Does TUSD's Ethnic Studies Program Violate Arizona's New Law? Available at: http://goo.gl/934G4.

Notes

1 All figures provided here originate from one of two primary sources: (1) the U.S. Census Bureau publications available online, and (2) the PEW Hispanic Center research reports and materials, unless otherwise noted.

2 Lipski (2008), Zentella (1997, 2004), and Silva-Corvalán (2004) are good resources to consult for detailed descriptions of Spanish as it is spoken in the U.S.

3 Salazar was a major figure in the Chicano movement. A respected journalist and writer for *The Los Angeles Times*, Salazar was killed by a sheriff's deputy while reporting on a Chicano protest of the Vietnam War. His death helped focus the country's attention on discrimination against Chicanos.

4 Originally the Treaty of Guadalupe-Hidalgo guaranteed that Mexican citizens who stayed a year in the territories newly ceded to the U.S. would be granted U.S. citizenship. Like other provisions of the treaty, Congress summarily deleted these promises before ratification.

5 It is important to note that Spanish is not the only language spoken in the countries identified as Hispanic. The Mexican population of more than 104 million includes more than 8 million speakers of indigenous Indian languages (about 8 percent of Mexico's total population), of whom almost half a million are monolingual and speak no Spanish at all (Lewis 2009). Guatemala's population of 9.3 million is approximately 55 percent Indian and 44 percent Mestizo. The Indian population includes

some 20,000 speakers of Kanjobal, 5,000 of whom are reported to be in Los Angeles (ibid.).

6 It is important to remember that the *study* of code-switching does not imply any kind of endorsement of code switching as the basis of language policy in educational setting.

7 In her (1995) book *Verbal Hygiene*, Cameron has an excellent discussion of the term "politically correct" that is well worth reading.

8 Gómez uses the term "off-white" but notes: "I might just as easily use the term 'off-black' to describe Mexican Americans' in-between status. Employing the term 'off-white,' however, invites focus on Mexicans' striving (but rarely succeeding) for white status and equality with whites" (2007: 163).

9 With apologies (and thanks) to Jane Hill, whose groundbreaking work in this area has been invaluable.

10 Fought's interviews with Latinos/as in Los Angeles also included discussions with bilingual speakers to explore the range of opinions on this subject.

11 Less than 4 percent of Mexico's population lives in Oaxaca, which contributes about 1 percent to the national economy. Over 60 percent of the population lives in poverty; only 6.4 percent of the population finishes grade school. Available at: http://goo.gl/76kMs.

12 The Chatino example originates from Pride (1965); subsequently I had help with it and its translation into Spanish. Thanks to Monica Macaulay, Joe Salmons, and George Aaron Broadwell. All imperfections are, of course, mine alone.

13 All direct quotations come from the complaint that was filed with the U.S. District Court for the Southern District of Mississippi, Jackson Division, naming the Mississippi Department of Human Services and Singing River Health System as defendants.

14 This was true also for African Americans and Native Americans. In the case of Native Americans (see "Good Enough English" in Chapter 7), children were often forcibly removed from their families to boarding schools in a last ditch attempt to break resistance to assimilation, in part by denying them their own languages. While Latino challenges to segregation in the schools had some success, the African American efforts in the courts did not (Powers 2008: 470).

15 If you are not familiar with the concept of "moral panic," you may want to read the first case study on moral panic in Oakland in Chapter 16 before continuing.

16 The current version of Bill 101 is available online in both English and French: http://www.oqlf.gouv.qc.ca/charte/reperes/Loi_22.pdf.

17 Paulo Freire is considered one of the founders of critical pedagogy; his most cited work is *Pedagogy of the Oppressed* (2000 [1970]). The irony is that Horne has banned that particular book in Arizona schools:

> Mr. Horne goes way overboard in trying to keep high school students from studying works like Paulo Freire's 'Pedagogy of the Oppressed,' a classic educational text, or any effort to deepen students' understanding of history, and their place in the world.
>
> (Arizona, in the Classroom, 2011)

Suggested further reading

Achugar, M. and Pessoa, S. (2009) Power and Place: Language Attitudes Towards Spanish in a Bilingual Academic Community in Southwest Texas. *Spanish in Context* 6: 199–223.

El Paso is possibly the most bilingual city in the U.S., and accordingly, attitudes toward

Spanish are markedly different than they are in other urban areas, such as San Diego or Chicago. Achugar and Passeo's 2009 article is a study of attitudes in El Paso, focusing on a particular social/educational group. The article itself includes extensive quotes from interviews, both in English and Spanish, with no translations of either language. What does this say about the author's own attitudes and opinions?

Cashman, H.R. (2009) The Dynamics of Spanish Maintenance and Shift in Arizona: Ethnolinguistic Vitality, Language Panic and Language Pride. *Spanish in Context* 6(1): 43–68.

This article provides interesting analysis of a language panic in Arizona, or the use of attitudes about language as a means to advance the social and political agendas of dominant groups. The author also looks at the opposite social force: the actions (or lack of actions in the form of passive resistance) that Spanish speakers take in order to resist external pressure to abandon Spanish for English.

Lipski, J. M. (2008) *Varieties of Spanish in the United States*. Washington, D.C.: Georgetown University Press.

For information on variation in Spanish in the U.S., this is a good source of information.

Mendoza-Denton, N. (2008) *Homegirls: Language and Cultural Practice among Latina Youth Gangs*. Malden, MA: Blackwell.

This is a linguistic/anthropological study of Mexican American girls of high school age. Anyone interested in Chicano culture, especially in Northern California, would find this a very worthwhile read.

A Class Apart:
Particularly worthwhile is this PBS American Experience documentary:

"From a small-town Texas murder emerged a landmark civil rights case. The little-known story of the Mexican American lawyers who took *Hernandez v. Texas* to the Supreme Court, challenging Jim Crow-style discrimination." The documentary is available online: http://goo.gl/8s3U.

The unassimilable races

What it means to be Asian

15

There are lots of issues that Asian Americans share, . . . one being the immigrant experience, being relatively recent immigrant arrivals. And Asians also suffer from a perpetual-foreigner syndrome, meaning that you could be a fourth- or fifth-generation Asian American but still somehow it's difficult to believe that you're an American. I get that: First they compliment me on my ability to speak English, and often I get asked, "Well, where are you from?" and for some reason people refuse to take Flushing for an answer.

John Lui, attributed

Institutionalized aggression

Formal, institutionalized policies that target Asian populations have a long history in the U.S., something that we tend to forget. A short overview:

1790   Congress decrees that "any alien, being a free white person who shall have resided within the limits and under the jurisdiction of the United States for a term of two years, may be admitted to become a citizen thereof." The "free white person" element was retained until "persons of African descent" was added in 1873. Cargile (2010) notes that while this was a major civil rights victory, it also alienated Latinos and Asians: "their status as 'outsiders' was now firmly fixed in a society only able to see in black and white" (ibid.: 60).

1882   President Garfield vetoes the Chinese Exclusion Act; Congress rallies a three-quarter majority to override the veto so that Chinese are not allowed to immigrate.

1885   Anglo miners riot against Chinese workers. Twenty-eight Chinese[1] laborers are killed in the riots.

1905   Anti-Japanese rhetoric escalates. Newspapers fuel this panic, and the Asiatic Exclusion League is formed in San Francisco.

1922   The Cable Act revokes the U.S. citizenship of any woman who marries an Asian.

1923   A Japanese immigrant challenges the Exclusion Act so that he might become a naturalized citizen (Takao Ozawa v. United States), and the Supreme Court rules that the Japanese – and all other Asians – are *unassimilable races* and thereby ineligible. A few months later the Supreme Court rules that while Bhagat Singh Thind, a native of Punjab, is Caucasian, he is not white. In accordance with the Congressional Act of 1790, this means Thind cannot apply for American citizenship, and further, all natives of India who were naturalized citizens at the time were stripped of that status.

1933   *Time Magazine* runs a story with the headline *Again: Yellow Peril*:

> Japan has driven a strategic wedge of Japanese dominion between the two American island possessions, the Philippines and the Hawaiian Islands . . . Japan's purpose is obviously to absorb both of these American possessions . . . The Philippines we are helping the Japanese to acquire through our political corruption and stupidity.

1942   A few months after the Japanese military attacks Pearl Harbor, President Roosevelt signs Executive Order 9066, which allows military authorities to take whatever action they deem necessary to contain Asian presence. There is no right to a trial or representation. The end result is the removal of Japanese Americans to internment camps.

1964   The California Initiative allowing landlords to discriminate passes with 65 percent of the vote. At that point, a property owner could refuse to lease, rent or sell housing or property on the basis of race, ethnicity, or anything else he or she cared to name.

As laws and protections have evolved, overt discriminatory acts have diminished. Of course this does not mean the end of anti-Asian sentiment or action. In earlier chapters we saw that Asians are discriminated against in the workplace, in the courts and in education, and that this is true for new immigrants who speak English as a second language, for U.S. citizens who speak Hawai'i Creole, and even for those of Asian origin who are monolingual English speakers and have no foreign accent at all.

Half the world

While immigrants from Asia were once largely Japanese and Chinese, that is no longer the case. By the time of the 2000 census, there were six large Asian groups in the U.S. (Chinese, Filipino, Indian, Japanese, Korean, and Vietnamese) that together made up 88 percent of the whole (Park 2008: 543). These six nations are both internally and externally diverse in terms of culture, politics, religion, and language. Most non-Asians are unaware of this level of complexity.

It is useful to note that taken together, the eight most populous Asian nations are home to about 3.5 billion persons, or about half of the world's population.[2]

Despite all this, the U.S. government has only one term that lumps all of these nations, ethnicities, cultures and languages from the Far East, Southeast Asia, and the Indian subcontinent together: Asian (Table 15.1).

While it may be an unreasonable burden on the U.S. Census Bureau to take note of each and every world language spoken in the U.S., the great disparity in the level of detail we employ to characterize the world's populations bears some consideration. *Asian* is not a comfortable term for many of the people we assign it to. For example, when asked about the place of India in Asia, one person of Southeast Asian heritage was hesitant:

> That's a tough one because [when] I hear the term Asian American I consider them [Asian Indians] as separate, not Asian. I know India is located [in] Asia but then I always thought of it as separate . . . because to me it seems different.

> (Park 2008)

Table 15.1 Asian household population by detailed group, 2004

Total Asian population	12,097,281
Chinese, (excluding) Taiwanese	2,829,627
Asian Indian	2,245,239
Filipino	2,148,227
Vietnamese	1,267,510
Korean	1,251,092
Japanese	832,039
Other Asian	250,666
Laotian	226,661
Pakistani	208,852
Cambodian	195,208
Hmong	163,733
Other Asian, not specified	140,571
Thai	130,548
Taiwanese	70,771
Indonesian	52,267
Bangladeshi	50,473
Sri Lankan	22,339
Malaysian	11,458

Source: U.S. Census Bureau, 2004 American Community Survey

Most non-Asians show little curiosity or even basic knowledge about the world outside the U.S. I would suggest that this is due, in large part, to the fact that geography instruction has almost disappeared from school system curricula. The National Geographic Society, concerned about this trend, hired Roper Public Affairs to conduct a study (2006) to ascertain the depths of the problem. In the resulting report, it was established that even politicians – the very people responslble for maintaining international relations – are likely to get basic facts wrong.[3] The situation is far worse for young adults. In their sample:

- 86 percent could not identify four countries in the Middle East on a map.
- 69 percent could not pick out China on a map of Asia (Figure 15.1).
- 65 percent could not locate the United Kingdom on a map.
- 50 percent could not pinpoint New York State on a map of the U.S.

One item on the poll is of particular interest here. When asked "Which language is spoken by the most people in the world as their primary language?" 74 percent answered English; only 18 percent gave the correct answer (Mandarin Chinese). The Roper Report suggests that there is a connection between the general false belief in the primacy of English and the fact that 62 percent of our young adults do not speak any foreign language (ibid.: 33).

This general lack of knowledge about the world could be attributed to the gap in the curriculum, but then we must ask ourselves how this gap came to be. In times of budgetary shortfalls, the programs that get cut are the ones we feel we can do without. While talk of diversity and a wider world, global perspective is popular, in practice, ethnocentrism is well established on the individual and institutional level (Kinder and Kam 2009). Language plays a central role in the structuring of these hierarchies:

> Underlying the intersection of language and race is a language ideology that we call the ideology of nativeness, an Us-versus-Them division of the linguistic world in which native and nonnative speakers of a language are thought to be mutually

Figure 15.1 Asia

exclusive, uncontested, identifiable groups. At the core of this ideological model is a view of the world's speech communities as naturally monolingual and monocultural, whereby one language is semiotically associated with one nation.

(Shuck 2006)

More specifically, Devos and Banaji (2005) conducted a series of six quantitative studies to answer a straightforward question: "Do people differentiate between ethnic groups within the concept of 'American'?" The data gave them a simple answer: "To be American is to be White" (ibid.: 463). The college students who participated in the study were unambiguous in their view of the relationship between race and belonging. Even when an individual subscribes to the belief that all races and ethnicities are entitled to equal human rights and liberties, there is still "an exceptionally large effect demonstrating, at least among White American students, a strong automatic association between American and White compared with American and Asian" (ibid.: 452–453).

There is a large body of scholarly work that has examined the complicated way Asians are perceived – and how they perceive themselves as residents and citizens of the U.S. Some of the findings include:

- Native English speakers are not good at identifying Asian accents on the basis of voice alone (Lindemann 2002, 2005); however, many people believe that they are, in fact, quite capable of distinguishing, for example, Japanese from Chinese, or India from Pakistan.[4] In a situation where the speakers see each other, the non-Asian will sometimes hear a foreign accent that is not there, a phenomenon called accent hallucination (Atagi 2003; Fought 2006; Rubin 1992; Rubin and Smith 1990).
- The communicative burden is usually divided unequally, the brunt of this responsibility resting on the non-native English speaker; however, it is possible to ameliorate this tendency, though few take the time and trouble to do so (Derwing *et al.* 2002).
- Native English speakers are willing to judge Asian learners of English – their intelligence, friendliness, work ethic and many other complex personality traits – on the basis of very little information – as long as there is no ambiguity about race. That is, race sometimes has more of an effect than actual English language skills when such judgments are made (Barry and Grilo 2003; Devos and Banaji 2005).
- Negative attitudes about Asians, whether they are conscious or not, can make successful communication difficult or impossible (Cargile 2010; Cheryan and Monin 2005; Lindemann 2002, 2003, 2005). Asians are still seen – and may always be seen – as the Other, and not authentic Americans (Park 2008; Pyke and Dang 2003; Rosenbloom and Way 2004; Volpp 2001; Wang 2008; Yoo *et al.* 2009).

Microagressive behaviors which may seem simply rude or uninformed are rampant and contribute to an overall atmosphere of other-ness. Examples: "All Asians look alike," "I used to have a Japanese neighbor" (Sue *et al.* 2007). It must be clear to anyone familiar with the way language subordination works that the history of institutionalized discrimination against Asians has had a broad and negative impact on self-image and self-confidence (Cargile 2010; Cheryan and Bodenhausen 2000; Cheryan and Monin 2005; Goyette and Xie 1999; Kawai 2005; Park 2008; Pyke and Dang 2003; Rim 2009; Sue *et al.* 2007; Tamura 1994; Tsai *et al.* 2002; Wu 2002).

Stereotypes

The evidence establishes that the concept *Asian* evokes an association not with a specific nation or geographical region, but with race. In the general view of things, anyone with a particular bone structure and skin color will count as Asian. Take, for example, the way Asian stereotypes are used in entertainment film as a kind of shorthand, as in the 1993 film *Falling Down*:

> The proprietor, a middle-aged ASIAN, reads a Korean newspaper . . . the Asian has a heavy accent . . .
> D-FENS: . . .You give me seventy "fie" cents back for the phone . . . What is a fie? There's a "V" in the word. Fie-vuh. Don't they have "v"s in China?
> ASIAN: Not Chinese, I am Korean.
> D-FENS: Whatever. What differences does that make? You come over here and take my money and you don't even have the grace to learn to speak my language . . .
> (1993: 7–8)

D-Fens, the white-collar worker on the edge of his sanity does not distinguish between Chinese and Korean; that is not important to him. The Korean has committed three sins in D-Fens's eyes: he has "come over here" and having immigrated, he "takes my money" by establishing himself in a social position in which he has economic capital and goods to dispense. These sins are compounded by the fact that the shop owner "doesn't have the grace to learn to speak my language."

Of course, the claims are erroneous: the shop owner does speak English. He speaks English well enough to get into a rousing argument with the customer, to assert his rights as owner of the shop, and to ask the customer to leave. But, crucially, he does not speak English to the customer's satisfaction, because he speaks English with an Asian accent. Here we are reminded of Heath's characterization of situations in which non-native speakers of English gain social or economic currency: "their language has become a focus for arguments in favor of both restrictions of their use and imposition of Standard American English" (Heath *et al.* 1981: 10).

Non-native English-speaking Asian Americans, as a large and diverse group, experience something in common, regardless of their economic status, education, or national origin: there is a special stigma attached to their presence which is externalized in reactions to the way they speak English. So conditioned are we to expect a different world view, a different accent, that we hear one where none is present. Individuals experience this regularly.

A young woman of Asian Indian heritage, but a native and monolingual speaker of English, relates a story in which a middle-aged man in a music store is unable to help her when she asks for a recently released Depeche Mode tape (Kapoor 1993). "You'll have to speak slower because I didn't understand you because of your accent," he tells her. She is understandably hurt and outraged: "I have no discernible accent. I do, however, have long dark hair and pleasantly colored brown skin. I suppose this outward appearance of mine constitutes enough evidence to conclude I had, indeed, just jumped off the boat and into the store."

The pain of this experience is real whether or not a foreign accent is present. In this case, the harm was real, but without repercussions which affected the young woman in a material way. Others are less fortunate:

In February 1992, at the Department of the Treasury building on Main Street in San Francisco, a Treasury official called down to the lobby with a question. Irritated by the quality of response that he or she received, this official made a formal complaint of "communication difficulties" based on Filipino accent. He or she did not provide the name of the security guard responsible for the poor service. Subsequent to this report, the General Services Authority directed the subcontractor who supplied the security guards to *remove all five Filipino agents who had been on duty that evening*, due to "language barriers" (Cacas 1994). The men removed from their positions were not given regular employment at another site, but were used as fill-ins on a variety of assignments, which caused them significant financial and other problems.

This kind of treatment is not unusual, but the reaction of the men in question was quite remarkable. As a group, they sued their employer under Title VII, in order to restore their honor and dignity. For Filipino Americans, the charge of insufficient or inadequate English is especially stinging, as English is one of the primary languages of education in their homeland, where in the 1975 census more than 15,000 claimed it as a first language and almost half a million listed it as a second language in 1980 (Lewis 2009). The five men in question had lived in the U.S. for most of their lives, and their public comments on the case left no doubt that the harm was as much emotional as economic: "It was a slap to my face," "It deeply hurt my feelings" (Ancheta 2006; Doyle 1994; Tiongson *et al.* 2006).

In fact, the attorneys for the security guards established that they were qualified and experienced workers, with between three and nine years on the job without any complaints about their language abilities. The Filipino security guards won their lawsuit, but a question was never raised: how was it that an anonymous official could bring about the removal of five men with solid work histories, solely on the basis of an unsubstantiated claim of an irritating and distracting accent? If the guards in question had been Italian or Norwegian speakers, would the same progression of events be imaginable?

Our relationship to the Far East and Pacific is shaped to a great degree by the facts of nineteenth-century colonialism, in which the U.S., young in comparative terms, followed the European model in targeting smaller nations to dominate – politically, economically and socially. We have a history of dealing with the Asian world as a warehouse of persons and goods available to suit our own purpose and fill our own needs, a practice rationalized by the supposition that those people are inherently weaker.

In order for such rationalizations to work, Asians must be seen as manipulative, with a tendency to use natural wiles and treachery to achieve their own ends. This kind of thinking provides a way to justify aggression. Thus a prominent Asian stereotype is of an intelligent, clever, but crafty and unreliable person. A secondary stereotype grows out of the mystification of Asia, the mysterious Orient where hard-working but simple people ply their crafts and study arcane philosophies, attaining wisdom and a spirituality specific to their race. We are uncomfortable with Asians unless they correspond to the stereotypes we have created for them.

There was a great deal of affection for Charlie Chan, the wise Chinese detective employed by the Honolulu Police Department (played first by the Swedish-born Warner Oland and then by Sidney Toler, both in "yellowface"), who dispensed calm fortune-cookie wisdom and always solved the crime. His sons, played by Keye Luke, Victor Sen Yung (both native Chinese) provided the comic foil. As Americanized second-generation types, they played the gap between expectation and reality for all it was worth. While the actors portraying Charlie Chan contrived Chinese accents, the sons (both of whom came to the U.S. as very small children) spoke English as a primary language and with a markedly urban discourse style ("Pop!"). In a similar way, the 1937 film of Pearl S. Buck's *The Good Earth* also used white actors to play the leads, to the satisfaction of reviewers who found that the main character met (stereotypical) expectations: "Physically, Muni becomes satisfactorily celestial, imbued with racial characteristics" (*Variety*, January 29, 1937).

Female Asian stereotypes focus on submissiveness, beauty, a need for strong male direction and a talent for tragedy (the opera *Madam Butterfly* is perhaps the ultimate example of this stereotype). While Asian male stereotypes have evolved (over-achieving in education and business, whether the business be a greengrocer's or computer chip research and development), female images seem to be more persistent.

The stereotypes in film linger, but there are other stereotypes that have evolved since World War II that are far more restrictive and damaging on a day-to-day basis. The most prevalent and deeply rooted Asian stereotype of all is encapsulated in a series of questions and statements often directed to Asians (Cargile 2010; Cheryan and Bodenhausen 2000; Kawai 2005; Le 2010; Lee 1994):

Where are you from?

Where are you REALLY from?

But you speak English so well!

Scholars and analysts see this as a symptom of a larger problem, often referred to as the *perpetual foreigner syndrome*: "We are figuratively and even literally returned to Asia and rejected from America" (Wu 2002: 79). Wu is affronted by such casually racist and condescending remarks which imply "that I am not one of 'us' but one of 'them' . . . I am a visitor at best, an intruder at worst" (ibid.: 80).

Our discomfort with those Asians we see as unable or unwilling to assimilate into Anglo society is balanced out and made tolerable by the contrasting stereotype, those model Asians who are unobtrusive and well behaved in their other-ness, who assimilate to the point that we can overlook (or at least, claim to overlook) issues of race and physical characteristics and language.

Today the model minority is the "most influential and prevalent stereotype for Asian Americans" (Kawai 2005: 109). The concept was first articulated in print in a 1966 *New York Times Magazine* story ("Success Story, Japanese Style") and later in the same year, a "Success Story of One Minority in U.S." about Chinese Americans (*U.S. News and World Report*). In both cases the immigrant group in question (Japanese, Chinese) were provided as examples of good immigrants, who obeyed the laws, respected the government's authority, put great value on family ties and responsibilities, pursued education and believed in hard work as the primary route to success. The two articles celebrated Japanese and Chinese Americans as the model minority groups who had close family ties, were extremely serious about education, and were law-abiding (Kawai 2003; Park 2008b). Asian American had come to mean "exhibiting cultural values that are conducive to socio-economic success" (Park 2008: 552).

More than forty years later, the condescending tone of these pronouncements published in the early1960s is hard to overlook. In the jargon of the Transactional Analysis movement of the 1960s, this would be called a "cold fuzzy," or something that sounds at first like a compliment but is decidedly less (as in "you look great – for your age"). Another negative aspect of the model minority stereotype is the implied juxtaposition of *good* (Japanese or Chinese) with *bad* (all other minority and/or immigrant groups). In the late twentieth century, both those who supported affirmative action and those who opposed it drew on the Asian-as-model-minority stereotype that set up a competition between Asians, African Americans, and Latinos/as (McGowan and Lindgren 2006).

In his interviews with Asian American students, Park found that an individual can identify with the term "model minority" while still chaffing under its restrictions:

> Asian Americans cannot perform as "normal" students, cannot be countercultural, contentious, unconventional, or lead an independent lifestyle. The ramifications are not that the image itself is threatened but that the individual is somehow less authentically Asian American if he or she diverges from it. It is an identity imposed by others and places considerable constraints not only in the area of study one selects but the very trajectory of one's work and contribution to society.
>
> (Park 2008: 552–553)

Anglos often deny or minimize the negative effect of Asian stereotypes. This becomes clear if discriminatory behavior toward Asians is compared to other stigmatized groups. For example, on a website where theater professionals discuss their work, someone posts a question:

> Topic: Caucasian to Asian makeup tips? . . . Working on a production of "Thoroughly Modern Millie" where we have Caucasian actors playing Bun Foo and Ching Ho . . .

as far as makeup, we want it to look as authentic as possible, while exaggerating it enough for an extremely large venue. Any tips or ideas? Anyone have photo examples?

The following hypothetical comparison paragraph is my composition:

> Caucasian to African American makeup tips? Working on a production of "Show Boat" where we have Caucasian actors playing African American stevedore Joe and his wife Queenie . . . as far as makeup, we want it to look as authentic as possible, while exaggerating it enough for an extremely large venue. Any tips or ideas? Anyone have photo examples?

The wording here is not overtly racist, but its offhand, casual tone is almost as disturbing as slurs heard more commonly. It doesn't occur to the writer that there might be some problem with *yellowface* (as discussed earlier in connection with film representations of Asians).[5]

Blackface was a theatrical practice in the late 1800s and into the twentieth century when Anglos performing in minstrel shows and vaudeville would appear as African American caricatures. To do this they used burnt cork or black greasepaint to change white faces to black faces. There were also actors who painted broad red lips around their mouths, outside the borders of their own lips. Later the red paint was dropped, but the space remained either flesh-colored or painted white. Some of the most persistent and virulent African American stereotypes originated with Blackface performances. It is not hard to understand that today any theater person suggesting that an Anglo play an African American – and wear makeup as part of that costume – would meet with tremendous, nationwide backlash. It is hard to imagine anyone so uninformed that they would raise the possibility of Blackface in a current day, non-satirical production in a public forum.

Yet here a number of people responded to a question about yellow face with suggestions that included using tape on the eyelids and heavy eye liner. In the first half of the discussion, very few responses addressed the racist underpinnings of the question, and those few comments ("If we ignore the history behind 'black face', why is 'Asian face' less offensive?" "Come back next year when you do Ragtime and need help turning white people black!" (ibid.)) are not responded to directly by the original writer until this exchange:

> This thread's unbelievably racist. How about just have the actors AS THEY ARE. When non-Caucasian actors are cast in traditionally white roles they don't get made up as white. Don't you grasp what it is you're actually suggesting? Creepy.

To which the original writer responds: "You obviously failed to read my post."

At a later point the thread turns to a more thoughtful discussion of race and ethnicity in casting. This is just one of hundreds if not thousands of examples that are easily found on the internet, radio, television and in print. It is a particularly good example because it makes very clear how unaware Anglos are when it comes to racism toward Asians. Many will claim that the primary image for Asian Americans is thoroughly positive.

The flip side to the model minority stereotype is an older and less ambivalent construction of Asians as the "Yellow Peril," an image which arose in the mid- to late nineteenth-century xenophobia and racism, in response to increasing numbers of Asian immigrants. This duality – model minority and threat in one – is a common feature of racial stereotypes. Whether seen as models of successful assimilation or as yellow devils,

Asians – both native to the U.S. and immigrants – are mocked and berated for their accents (real or imagined) and seen as perpetually foreign (Chou and Feagin 2008; Gee 2009; McGowan and Lindgren 2006). In extreme cases they are denied employment, or become the victims of violence (Chow 2001; Hall and Hwang 2001).

For example, two Anglo autoworkers, angry because they were about to lose their jobs due to a downturn in the industry, picked a fight with Vincent Chin, a stranger to them they had mistaken for Japanese. According to the police report, a bystander heard one of the two men of say to Chin, "It's because of you little motherfuckers that we're out of work." He was beaten with a baseball bat and died of his injuries a few days later.

As terrible as this crime was for Chin and his family, it got worse. The judge who heard the case allowed the attorneys to come to a settlement without hearing any witness testimony. The two men – who never served any jail sentence despite multiple attempts to try them – were given probation and a fine of $3,000 plus court costs (Choy *et al.* 1990, documentary, *Who Killed Vincent Chin?*). Public criticism at the time compared this sentence to similar court cases in the age of Jim Crow in the Deep South.

The outrage about such a sentence for a brutal, premeditated hate crime (a term not yet in use at the time) sparked a new wave of activism across the country and the formation of American Citizens for Justice (ACJ). This was the first time that

> [People] who traced their ancestry to different countries in Asia and the Pacific Islands crossed ethnic and socioeconomic lines to fight as a united group of Asian Pacific Americans. They were Chinese, Japanese, Korean, and Filipino; they were waiters, lawyers, and grandmothers who were moved by the incident that heightened their awareness of discrimination and racism directed toward the APA community.
>
> (Yip 1997)

The two young Anglo men who murdered Thien Minh Ly, a Vietnamese native and graduate of UCLA, were arrested when a letter written by one of them was given to the police. This small excerpt is a vivid display of matter-of-fact racism, but it is fairly calm compared to the rest of the letter:

> Oh I killed a jap a while ago I stabbed him to Death at Tustin High school I walked up to him Dominic was with me and I seen this guy Roller blading and I had a knife. We walk in the tennis court where he was I walked up to him. Dominic was right there I walked right up to him and he was scared I looked at him and said "Oh I thought I new you" and he got happy that he wasn't gona get jumped. Then I hit him . . .

Not all aggression is so overtly violent. More usually, those who speak English with an Asian accent are met with a combination of irritation, unease, distrust and condescension. One such situation was made public when Dell Computer put a new and unusual policy in place in response to customer complaints about dealing with Asian support staff on the telephone. A new level of paid customer service was introduced; for a fee, subscribers would be helped on the phone by native speakers of English from North America (Whoriskey 2008. See also Chapter 17 on linguistic profiling).

There is also a large body of public commentary with no obvious racial or ethnic triggering event, much of which is extreme and virulent, which will be considered in the next section.

Mockery

As discussed in earlier chapters, mockery can be an effective tool when the goal is subordination by means of trivialization. There are many examples of linguistic mocking on the internet targeting Latinos/as and African Americans (Calafell 2006; Chun 2004; Hill 1995, 2008; Ronkin and Karn 1999). There are fewer sources of such material for Asians, but there are many day-to-day examples. Public mockery of Asian-accented English comes from politicians (as discussed earlier in this chapter), from talk-show hosts (Jay Leno seems to be particularly fond of pseudo-Asian accented English), newspapers ("We likee Hirally! She best quality!"), news commentators (Maloy 2009), lawyers (Soo 2003), and judges speaking to petitioners (Angulo 2008). It also comes from those who simply like to participate in discussions online. An example from the *Urban Dictionary* which was made on August 14, 2006 (when it was downloaded in October, 2010, there were 180 up votes, and 82 down):

> **Ching chong bing bong:** The language of those born to the Asian countries. It is the root of all evil and when heard for an excessive amount of time, causes one to vomit uncontrollably. *Excuse me, I can't understand your ching chong bing bong, please try English when you are in America.*

Taken at face value, this kind of statement – and there is a great deal of it – indicates that the stereotypes of Asian Americans are very narrow and persistent, and discrimination is broad and unapologetic.

Certainly those who speak English with an Asian accent have the impression that they are not taken seriously, and that "native speakers deliberately chose not to understand them, and that some native speakers tended to 'shut down' or 'close up' when the L2 learners started talking" (Derwing *et al.* 2002: 247). This correlates with other research that has established the ability of native English speakers to hallucinate an accent where none exists (as discussed in Chapter 9).

To this last point must be added the odd case of not only hallucinating an accent, but mocking what has been hallucinated. A case in point is the way Senator Alfonse D'Amato mocked a prominent Asian-American High Court judge by quoting him using a stereotypical Asian accent (Henneberger 1995). The judge D'Amato was mocking is a native speaker of English, born in Los Angeles.

The inappropriate nature of this behavior is clearer if you substitute a different public figure, one from a minority population that has its own variety of English, but who speaks *SAE natively. President Obama is one such person. If during a Senate session, a Senator mocked President Obama while employing features of AAVE – and employing them badly – there would be a very large (and deserved) backlash. Not because Obama isn't a native speaker of AAVE, but because such an act lays open the speaker's true feelings about that language and the people who speak it in a way that is difficult to ignore or gloss over.

The transmission and rationalization of racism

When children play together, quite a lot of information about the world and the way it works passes from oldest to youngest in the form of chants, rhymes and games. In the seminal study of childhood games, folklorists Knapp and Knapp put this much more prosaically:

> We are so preoccupied with what we have to offer children that we overlook the education they can offer one another; yet, in the unsupervised nooks and crannies of their lives, where they perpetuate centuries-old folk traditions, children learn what no one can teach them.
>
> (Knapp and Knapp 1976: 9)

Some of the things children teach each other include turn-taking, the negotiation of rules, the difference between cheating and testing the rules (ibid.: 31), how to claim prestige or power, and how to deny prestige and power to others. Chants and rhymes are also part of the process of learning to face fears and superstitions, and the acquisition of social skills such as accommodation and resistance.

Knapp and Knapp contend that children's lore helps them cope with the day-to-day in three ways: (1) they are comforted by the assurance that everybody has the same troubles; (2) they learn how to cope with what is frightening in the present by escaping into fantasy; and (3) most important in the context of this book, folklore provides a tightly controlled frame for the expression of hostility and frustration. In connection with this last point, children learn about how to repair misunderstandings, deny culpability, and apologize. It is in this last context that children experience and begin to understand racism and xenophobia.

Collections of children's rhymes, songs and games recorded by folklorists and anthropologists between the mid-nineteenth and the mid-twentieth century contain many shocking examples of extreme, unapologetic racism, some of which promotes violence. The three groups targeted most often in the collected children's lore are African Americans, Jews, and Asians. Here is an example of one version of a very widely known rhyme that has been in circulation since the early twentieth century (as I learned it growing up in 1960s Chicago):

> Ching chong Chinaman
> Sitting on a bench
> Trying to make a dollar
> Out of fifty-five cents.
> He missed. He missed.
> He missed like THIS.

There is some speculation that *ching chong* originated as an imitation of a dialect of Chinese as heard by native English speakers. That is a perfectly reasonable – but unverifiable – hypothesis. It is also true that between the years 1850 and 1950, major newspapers in New York, Chicago and Los Angeles reported legitimate (but not necessarily unbiased) stories about Chinese nationals or residents, and that Ching Chong appeared as one of many actual given names. Undoubtedly the overtly discriminatory epithet *chink* is derived from *ching chong*. It should also be noted that while these terms were first coined in connection with Chinese immigrants and residents, they now are used more broadly in reference to anyone with an Asian appearance.

These two syllables spoken together have a history and a significance that evoke strong reactions from Asians:

[Ching Chong] comes from an ugly place deep in this country's history, when Chinese were viewed as strange interlopers, the "heathen Chinee," an economic and social scourge. Those words once accompanied violence and lynchings. "Ching-Chong Chinaman" rhymes dating to the 19th century weren't just schoolyard taunts. To be ignorant of that . . . doesn't eliminate the history.

Nor are schoolyard taunts harmless:

"I would get 'sighted' – picked out – as the 'chinky girl' and those words would come out, then fists would hit me," remembered Doris Owyang, the program manager for San Francisco State University's Center for the Integration and Improvement of Journalism. Three years ago, a group of white teenagers attacked Asian-American youths while shouting imitation Chinese, a case that ended in felony and misdemeanor convictions.

(Chung 2006)

Chung's article – and many others like it – were written in response to an exchange that took place on *The View*, a popular morning television talk show, on December 5, 2006. The panelists were discussing a guest from the previous taping who had, it seemed to them, showed up drunk for his televised interview. Rosie O'Donnell, a panel member, commented on the whole matter:

The fact is that it's news all over the world. That you know, you can imagine in China, it's like: "Ching chong . . . ching chong. Danny DeVito, ching chong, chong, chong, chong. Drunk. 'The View.' Ching chong."

(*The View*, ABC, December 5, 2006)

Objections from the Asian community followed immediately in the form of newspaper articles, letters to the editor, and television interviews and statements (Chung 2006). The complaints were unified in their shock and displeasure that O'Donnell would have used such blatant ethnic slurs, and demands for a public apology. Some Asian-Americans *performed* their disapproval; for example, ultra-conservative Filipina Michelle Malkin (infamous for her pro-government stance on the matter of the internment of Japanese-Americans in World War II) posted a video on YouTube, as did younger Asians whose anger was just as potent.[6]

Rosie O'Donnell, a comedian, actor and talk show host, is a prominent figure in the LGBT[7] civil rights movement, someone who has publicly confronted others who make homophobic statements or gestures; thus, her reaction to the demand for an apology was perplexing to many who followed the incident. Rather than end the episode by apologizing directly and clearly, she embarked on a passive-aggressive non-apology apology.

Apologizing-but-not-apologizing is a speech act that has been studied by linguists interested in pragmatics and political discourse strategies as well as by casual but insightful observers (Kampf 2009; McCall 2001; Robinson 2004). A few generalizations can be made about this kind of speech act: it is never neutral (that is, there is always an underlying power dynamic and conflict); the maintenance of "face" plays a role; the person apologizing is seeking a way to mollify – or at least to silence – the offended party while still minimizing his or her own responsibility:

Indeed, the apologizer's acknowledgment of a transgression is the most important feature for facilitating an understanding of the motive for apologizing or avoiding it. In addition to a clear acknowledgment of responsibility, an ideal apology should . . . be void of any other type of excuses and/or justifications.

(Kampf 2009: 2258)

I'm sorry, I just refuse to apologize

It is common practice to apologize while maintaining that no offense was actually given, as happened in the O'Donnell case. The strategies for pulling off a non-apology are varied:

1 *If in fact my words offended anyone, I regret that fact.* This is a gambit to save face and throw doubt on the fact of the offense itself. Just beneath the surface is denial of having caused offense at all.
2 Express regret that a statement had an adverse effect on others or was perceived as offensive: *I'm sorry that your feelings were hurt.* This puts the onus on the person who was offended. One way to think about this: *When I punched you in the face, it was not my intent to break your nose. Really.*
3 Apologize for the style alone: *I apologize for my abrupt tone.*
4 Apologize for a specific and limited component of the offense while rejecting the bulk of it; *I apologize for generalizing about Asians. It's only the Japanese who are the true model minority.*
5 Apologize using passive constructions and euphemisms to mitigate responsibility: *my words were taken out of context* (you deliberately misunderstood me); *the situation was misinterpreted* (*the situation* rather than the act itself); *people have told me I was wrong to say it* (that's what people say, but I'm not buying it); and the classic: *mistakes were made* (but not by me).
6 Apologize while using gestures and facial expressions to undermine the sincerity of the words themselves. *I'm sorry that you were [AIR QUOTES] offended.*
7 Apologize while claiming authority to do so: *I'm sorry if you were offended, but I'm a straightforward person, I call 'em like I see 'em.*
8 Often a person will simply go on the offensive: *Can't you take a joke?* or *You're the one who is racializing this discussion, not me* or *Wow, you are a drama queen, aren't you?* or *How dare you say I'm prejudiced. I am the one being discriminated against.*

In the aftermath of the December 5, 2006 performance by O'Donnell, many of these strategies and tactics were employed by herself, her colleagues and her weblog visitors. Her exchanges with people who visit her weblog were particularly interesting, because it was her policy to respond briefly to every comment visitors left.[8] In that venue her "ching-chong" joke came up repeatedly over a few weeks, with two kinds of audience comment: those who defended her performance and those who criticized her roundly and pursued the issue of an apology.[9]

A short examination of the weblog comments and her responses provides insight into what seems to have been O'Donnell's sometimes conflicted feelings about the whole incident. Please note that I have corrected typos but left abbreviations in common use across the web as they are used, and further, these are not all the comments, nor do they necessarily appear in this order. Read these with the strategies discussed above in mind.

Excerpt from www.reappropriate.com, Rosie O'Donnell blog post, October 9, 1998. Reprinted by permission of blog owner.

(1) Rosie: for someone who comes off to be so sensitive and aware of lgbt issues, why did you think it was alright to mock Chinese people and the language on The View (re: danny devito: ching chong . . .)???

RO: it was not my intent to mock / just to say how odd it is that danny drunk was news / all over the world even in china / it was not meant to mock

(2) Rosie, what made you think it was okay to make fun of the way Chinese people speak?

RO: the joke was about the danny devito drunk news / making headlines all over the world including china / just comedy folks / no intent 2 harm / peace

(3) JP writes: Hey Rosie, why aren't you getting your head out your butt and be more sensitive to Asian-Americans. Don't post this message and see how you are hiding your true facade. You suck and need to get off tv.

RO: go fuck urself, jp

(4) Leema writes: U r a great role model. I respect ur courage. I'd like 2 know what makes u imitate a foreign language as a joke. It'd be funny if u knew how 2 speak it, it sounds racist and ignorant, which u r not.

RO: i am irish / i do an irish accent / make drunk jokes / stereotypes / this is comedy / i do many accents / and probably will continue to / my mom in law impression offends some Southerners / what can u do / i come in peace

(5) Chao writes: Rosie   I am very appalled at your comments on The View regarding Asian people. They were so insensitive and hurtful. How can you possibly explain this and what can you say to help heal my wounds?

RO: sorry u were offended chao / it was not my intent

(6) Beth writes: It's so silly that Bill O'Reilly is having a segment on how you angered the Asians – you didn't do anything at all – you were saying how silly it is that Devito became world news! Don't listen to them!

RO: i don't

(7) toni writes: Ro, I can not believe that the Chinese are mad at you about a JOKE!!! Oh My God, lighten up people. Bill O'Reilly even stood up for you tonight on "The Factor"! Calm down people it was just a joke!

RO: go bill

(8) Yves writes: Rosie –I don't see the big deal about the Chinese routine. You've done English accents before on TV and the Brits didn't get bent out of shape. They took it out of context and they need to chill.

RO: the whole thing is odd 2 me

(9) Max writes: I'm a hypersensitive politically correct leftist. I checked out YouTube to see what the fuss was about. Give me a break! You were speaking Gibberish to symbolize a language you didn't know. So what?!

RO: so what is right

(10) Hiroyuki writes: Rosie, Till this latest incident I was on your side. How could you use racist stereotyping? If what you say in the past is true, what you say in the unguarded is true – then I guess you are a racist

RO: come on hirou gotta be kidding

(11) Ben writes: If the joke were about fat people and instead went: "Fat people around the world heard it. They probably said, 'Gobble gobble, munch munch, DeVito, drunk, munch view, gobble.' Would it offend you?

RO: well / it would offend me / as it makes no sense / but the joke was about / the absurdity / of danny devito drunk on the view / being INTERNATIONAL NEWS / then the offensive ching chong / and we're off 2 the races

(12) Ploy writes: Did you really think that Chinese bit was funny? Going "ching chong" is exactly how people degraded and mocked my family all our lives. It's distasteful and it hurts me that it comes from you.

RO: i am sorry it hurt u poly / all the people who made fun of u / in a negative way / for being who u r / my bad accent was not meant to insult or degrade / linguistic incompetence – guilty / mocking – never

(13) mel writes: i love you rosie and i'm not offended by your asian joke but the reason people are is because you weren't doing an accent. you weren't speaking actual chinese, just mocking their speech.

RO: i wasn't mocking / that's my best impression / accents r tough / on the whole

(14) denise writes: Rosie you would have had a cow if someone did what you did to the chinese about Gay people. For Shame.

RO: like someone doing a gay guy with a lisp / like i do / a lot / 4 shame back at ya

(15) John writes: Miss O'Donnell, I was wondering when your public apology for insulting the Asian American community will be? P.S. I will make it my personal vendetta to make this public to everyone I know.

RO: do ur best john / go in peace

(16) Ben writes: You say how you don't understand what the fuss is about, but it's hard 2 understand w/o having grown up Asian. Imagine a derogatory gay joke. If YOU got bent outta shape about it, I WOULD understand...ben

RO: i am sorry it hurt u / i didnt think of it the way it was taken / i will b more sensitive / promise

In the December 14, 2006 airing of *The View*, O'Donnell addressed the issue directly.

This apparently was very offensive to a lot of Asian people. So I asked Judy, who's Asian and works here in our hair and makeup department. I said, "Was it offensive to you?" And she said, "Well, kinda. When I was a kid people did tease me by saying ching-chong." So apparently "ching-chong," unbeknownst to me, is a very offensive way to make fun, quote–unquote, or mock, Asian accents. Some people have told me it's as bad as the n-word. I was like, really? I did not know that [. . . The joke was] never intended to hurt anyone, and I'm sorry for those people who felt hurt or were teased on the playground . . . there's a good chance that I'll do something like that again.

(O'Donnell, *The View*, ABC, December 14, 2006)

On the basis of the public record it seems that O'Donnell never issued a sincere first person, unqualified apology, one which might have gone like this: "I was wrong to use those words to imitate Chinese or Asian speakers, I understand now how offensive it was and it will not happen again. Please accept my sincere apology." Quite the opposite, she gave notice that she was likely to repeat her performance.

One of the points many critics raised had to do with O'Donnell's advocacy for LGBT rights and protections. The assumption underlying these complaints seemed to be that those who advocate for one peripheralized group should do the same for other groups who are discriminated against. In fact, this is another example of the depth and breadth of language-focused discrimination and standard language ideology. Even the most liberal people will demonstrate what they believe to be their right: to use language as a tool to establish and re-establish social boundaries and privilege.

If nothing else, this episode and others described here make clear how unaware – and unconcerned – most Americans are when Asians are the focus of discriminatory policies and practices.

In the classroom

In educational settings an unwillingness to engage in conversation with anyone who speaks with an Asian accent has been well documented. Such refusals could be due to simple laziness, disinterest, animosity, fear of being socially linked to foreigners, resentment, racism, ethnocentrism, or any combination of these.

In my own experience teaching at the University of Michigan I considered this problem at length because it was one I saw personally on a regular basis. I decided to try a small experiment when I was teaching an introductory linguistics course to 250 undergraduates in lecture format. In teaching this course I worked with graduate student teaching assistants who took over discussion sections, common practice at almost all universities. A number of my TAs were Asian non-native speakers of English who had come to the States to work on advanced degrees in linguistics. They had accents, but their English was fluent and colloquial and each one of them had been accepted into the graduate program.

The first time I taught this class, I had multiple emails and phone calls after the first discussion section. Students complained about having a TA who spoke with an accent; they couldn't understand the TA and wanted to be moved to another section. Sometimes these complaints were very harsh and accusatory in tone, as if by being assigned to an Asian teaching assistant, they were being denied some basic right. Resolving these conflicts required that I meet with each of these students individually to discuss the actual nature of their worries, and to suggest ways to ameliorate what they perceived as an irresolvable conflict. Not one of these students ever considered that they might have some work to do in order to achieve successful communication; in every case, it was seen as the TA's responsibility alone.

The next time I taught this course, I spent half an hour in the first lecture talking about accents in general and foreign accents in particular and about common-sense ways to resolve difficulties – if difficulties ever arose. These included asking for clarification in a straightforward but polite way, requesting that a word or sentence be written on the board, along with the benefits of patience, open-mindedness and empathy for those who were now in a situation that the undergraduates might someday be in themselves, if they were lucky enough to study abroad. That year I had two disgruntled undergraduates asking to be removed from a discussion section led by a native Japanese speaker, and both those individuals had missed the first lecture.

This is, of course, only anecdotal, but others have spent years researching the elements that cause communication difficulties between ESL learners and native speakers, from phonetics to ideology. In a particularly insightful study, Derwing, Rossiter and Munro set out to "determine whether native speakers' comprehension of accented speech can be enhanced through instruction. The experiment involved both cross-cultural content and explicit instruction in the characteristics of a particular accent" (Derwing *et al.* 2002). The study required pre-testing of comprehension after listening to Vietnamese accented recordings, accent lessons, cross-cultural communication lessons, and post-comprehension tests.

The students, all enrolled in a class in the social work program, were divided at random into three groups:

1   The Accent Instruction group, which received instruction in the nature and characteristics of English spoken with a Vietnamese accent *in addition to* cross-cultural training by means of readings and conversations tied to the curriculum, recorded by the Vietnamese speakers.
2   The Familiarity group did not receive instruction on the way Vietnamese influences English language learning, but they did get the cross-cultural communication instruction, which included listening to the content-related recordings made by the Vietnamese participants.
3   The Control group received neither type of training, and concentrated on the course material alone.

The experiment itself took eight weeks and consisted of the pre-test, the in-class instruction sessions, and the post-test. In the testing, students listened to a recording of Vietnamese speakers talking in English about a topic relevant to the coursework; they answered comprehension questions and transcribed sentences. Finally, they filled out a questionnaire on their attitudes and perceptions about the material and presentation.

The only difference between the Accent Instruction and Familiarity groups was the fact that the former got additional instruction in the way Vietnamese influenced pronunciation of English.[10]

On the basis of this experiment, there is some reason to believe that anti-Asian sentiment and language-focused discrimination are not immutable. Some proportion of individuals reject Asians and communication with Asians out of unfamiliarity; an effort to replace stereotype with real interpersonal experience will bear fruit. In this particular situation, the students were not given a choice of which group to join; those who found themselves in the Accent Instruction or the Familiarity groups were required to participate in the exercises which by their nature challenged stereotypical expectations.

Table 15.2 summarizes this study. Given a choice, would students participate in this kind of instruction? Should they be compelled to participate? What would be gained or lost by instituting such policies?

Table 15.2 The effect of preparation on communication between Asians and non-Asians

Question	Groups					
	Control		Familiarity		Accent Instruction	
	Pre-test	Post-test	Pre-test	Post-test	Pre-test	Post-test
Rate your ability to understand foreign accents. 1 = very poor 9 = excellent	4.71	5.52	4.27	5.70	3.10	5.25
When I hear someone start to speak with an accent, I expect that it will be difficult to understand them. 1 = strongly disagree 9 = strongly agree	5.76	5.33	5.27	4.55	6.50	4.63
Circle how confident you are that you can understand someone who speaks with an accent (0 to 100% in increments of 10)	54%	60%	47%	60%	34%	59%
I understand people with accents better now (not limited to Vietnamese accent). 1 = strongly disagree 9 = strongly agree		4.5		5.52		6.70

False speakers of language

In Chang-Rae Lee's critically acclaimed 1995 novel, *Native Speaker*, a Korean-American narrator called Henry Park tells the story of how he came to fall in love with his wife, an American who is of interest to him not just as a woman, but because as a speech pathologist she works with children who are non-native speakers of English.

"People like me are always thinking about still having an accent," he tells her in their first discussion. What he does not say, but which is clear to the character from real-life experiences is that people "like" himself must always be thinking about having an accent, because that is what is expected of them: to be different, and to externalize that difference with language. Caught between his own and public expectations, Park can please no one. When his wife leaves to travel without him, and perhaps forever, her note of explanation is a simple list of descriptors for him, which include:

> illegal alien
> emotional alien
> Yellow peril: neo-American

Later he finds another scrap of paper with a definition of himself on it that she could not quite include on the final list: *False speaker of language.*

Like African Americans, Asian Americans have more and more difficult hurdles to leap before they can transcend stereotype and be accepted as individuals. Accent, when it serves as a marker of race, takes on special power and significance. For many in the African American community there is little resistance to the language subordination process, in part because the implied promises of linguistic assimilation – while obviously overstated – are nevertheless seductive, precisely because the threats are very real.

The idea of perfect English, of belonging absolutely to the mainstream culture of choice, is one that is hard to resist for Asian Americans as well.

DISCUSSION QUESTIONS AND EXERCISES

- Consider the series of court rulings beginning in 1883 that led to the shutdown of all immigration from China for about sixty years. Look also at the related rulings that made it illegal to grant Asians naturalized citizenship. In that broader context, read the story of Bhagat Singh Thind, who came to the U.S. in 1917. What were the long-range repercussions of the Supreme Court decision that sent him back to Punjab? In linguistic terms, how factual was the Court's definition of Indo-European? The website: http://goo.gl/4wKkS.

- Look closely at Table 15.2 adapted from the Derwing *et al.* (2002) experiment. What conclusions can you draw from these figures? How do the three control groups compare to each other? Consider differences between the first and second groups, and then compare them to the third group. On this evidence alone, what measures seemed to be most effective in alleviating communication stumbling blocks? Argue for or against the proposition that all first year college students should be required to participate in an orientation session that addresses communication issues such as these.

- In 2005, a student of Asian heritage applied to Princeton. He had an excellent academic history and hit all the usual marks for admission, but he was not admitted. He enrolled at Yale, and shortly thereafter filed a lawsuit against Princeton for discrimination on the basis of national origin. In the following spring, a column appeared in *The Daily Princetonian*, the campus newspaper. A short excerpt:

    Hi Princeton! Remember me? I so good at math and science. Perfect 2400 SAT score. Ring bells? Just in case, let me refresh your memories. I the super smart Asian. Princeton the super dumb college, not accept me.

    What is the purpose of writing this in what is supposed to be the plaintiff's own language? What underlying beliefs and ideologies might be informing it?

- How aware were you, before reading this chapter, of how offensive "ching-chong" is as an ethnic slur. How did you react to this information? If you felt any irritation, can you get to the bottom of that, and figure out where it comes from? If you are Asian, what are your experiences with this term? Have you ever talked to non-Asians about the impact this term has? Why or why not?

> - If you are Asian and you are willing to volunteer to answer questions, please let your instructor know. It would be especially helpful if you were willing to talk to the other students about the various viewpoints in this chapter, and whether you agree or disagree with conclusions drawn.
> - To test your own knowledge of Asia, try the quiz you'll find here: http://www.mccollam.com/fun/geoquiz/asiaquiz.html.

Notes

1 See also a *New York Times* article from 1905 entitled "CONFERENCE INDORSES [sic] CHINESE EXCLUSION; Editor Poon Chu Says China Will Demand Entrance Some Day. A PLEA FOR THE JAPANESE Committee on Resolutions Commends Roosevelt's Position as Stated in His Message." Available at: http://goo.gl/wRxTE.

2 Consider that the government of India (a nation of almost 1.2 billion persons) officially recognizes fifteen languages, some of them with as many as fifty or more dialects. India is linguistically complex, but it is not unusual in this; it is not even extreme in the larger global view. China has 55 official minority nationalities, eight major languages and hundreds of other language families from Mongolian to Hmong. Fiji has less than a million residents but they are spread out over 7000 square miles of islands on which fifteen languages (in addition to Fijian) are spoken (Ethnologue.com; population figures taken from the CIA Factbook, the U.N. website, and from census reports of some of the nations).

3 At one point George W. Bush seemed to think that Africa is a country rather than a continent; John McCain spoke publicly about the Iraq/Pakistani border, which does not exist. There are multiple examples of politicians from both parties making similar errors.

4 A website created and maintained by a Chinese-American provides some insight into this issue, along with photos. AllLookSame? Available at: http://alllooksame.com/?page_id=2.

5 The Wikipedia entry on Blackface is especially thorough and well documented, with many excellent references for anyone interested in pursuing this subject further. Available at: http://en.wikipedia.org/wiki/Blackface.

6 Michelle Malkin: http://youtu.be/0qINiw6ub5U; Ruby Ibarra: http://youtu.be/BEZ8KbWUzP8.

7 LGBT is the common abbreviation for the Lesbian, Gay, Bisexual, Transgender communities. Available at: http://www.gaycenter.org/.

8 As is the case with most weblogs, O'Donnell reserves the right not to publish comments which violate the standards that have been established for the discussion board.

9 There were also numerous responses on other websites and weblogs, many of which were written by Asian Americans recounting their own experiences with racism. Many wrote of being taunted using "ching chong," and attempted to make clear how very offensive this term was to the Asian population. Some were angry, and some were more diplomatic. See, for example, http://mamazilla.blogspot.com/2006/12/i-wasnt-hallucinating.html.

10 This description of the research is, of course, vastly simplified. The original article is

accessible to non-specialists and makes fascinating reading for anyone interested in learning more.

Suggested further reading

Bendixen and Associates (2007) Deep Divisions, Shared Destiny: A Poll of African Americans, Hispanics and Asian Americans on Race Relations. *New American Media*. Available at: http://xrl.in/7irm.

Cheryan, S. and Monin, B. (2005) "Where Are You Really From?" Asian Americans and Identity Denial. *Journal of Personality and Social Psychology* 89(5): 717–730.

Hosoda, M. (2007) Listeners' Cognitive and Affective Reactions to English Speakers with Standard American English and Asian Accents. *Perceptual and Motor Skills* 104(1): 307–326.

Kawai, Y. (2005) Stereotyping Asian Americans: The Dialectic of the Model Minority and the Yellow Peril. *Howard Journal of Communications* 16(2): 109–130.

Reyes, A. and Lo, A. (2009) *Beyond Yellow English: Toward a Linguistic Anthropology of Asian Pacific America*. New York: Oxford University Press.

Tiongson, A.T., Gutierrez, E.V. and Gutierrez, R.V. (2006) Positively No Filipinos Allowed: Building Communities and Discourse. In *Asian American History and Culture*. Philadelphia, PA: Temple University Press.

Case study 1

16

Moral panic in Oakland

> Moral panics are about locating evildoers, establishing the poisonous influence and iniquity of their actions, and rectifying the damage they've inflicted on the rest of us. The skeptic is challenged to understand what moral panics tell us about the inner workings of the society in which we live.
>
> Goode (2008: 39)

How to build a moral panic

Moral panic is a key concept in sociology, media and communication studies, where it is used to describe a certain kind of group or communal behavior. In the simplest terms, a moral panic starts when a community of people become aware of an event or person or group which may pose a threat to societal values and interests (Cohen 2002 [1972]; Critcher 2006; Goode and Ben-Yehuda 2009). Individuals who take up the cause – agents or actors who accelerate the process – are referred to as *moral entrepreneurs* or *crusaders*. Agents must be in a strong position socially to generate public awareness and to focus that awareness on a scapegoat or "folk devil." Institutions can also act as moral entrepreneurs, so that the information media, entertainment media, schools, politicians and corporations (some or all of these) may be involved in the birth, acceleration and lifespan of a moral panic.[1]

It is crucial to remember that the object at the center of any panic is standing in for some larger social conflict which may be too controversial to raise directly.[2] One example of a recurring panic here in the U.S. has to do with dog breeds that are considered aggressive. For example, in the 1970s many communities banned Doberman pinschers, and more recently pit bull terriers have caused panics.

The event or events that trigger a panic may have been truly newsworthy and cause for increased concern, but the discussion quickly overruns the boundaries of the specific incident spirals upward.

> Moral panics then, are those processes whereby members of a society and culture become "morally sensitized" to the challenges and menace posed to "their" accepted values and ways of life, by the activities of groups defined as deviant. The process underscores the importance of the mass media in providing, maintaining and "policing" the available frameworks and definitions of deviance, which structure both public awareness of, and attitudes towards, social problems.
>
> (O'Sullivan 1994: 186)

Portrait of a folk devil

In the case of pit bull panics in the U.S., moral entrepreneurs never talked specifically about the underlying conflict, but it was immediately recognizable once articulated. Pit bulls are associated with a particular stereotype: working-class males of a lower socio-economic class who are prone to excessive and mindless violence, criminal tendencies, drug and alcohol abuse, and disregard or contempt for the common good due to a lack of human empathy (Gladwell 2006). This lack of empathy has been called "social alexithymia" and is found in many kinds of racist discourse (Hill 2008: 96). The assumption is this: Just as there is no hope of reasoning with an abused, out of control pit bull, there is no hope of appealing to the better nature of the men who own them. Using this example, we can trace the stages of a moral panic.

Ten simple steps to a moral panic

The elements of a moral panic do not follow one after the other in lock-step. There will be some variation in tone and speed of the acceleration, and on occasion a moral panic sputters and stalls in an early stage. The example here is meant to be representative of the steps in a full-fledged moral panic.

1 Something unsettling or disturbing or frightening happens. The media focus on the event in the course of their usual news cycle. There is significant reader or viewer response and interest; the cycle ramps up.	PIT BULLS ATTACK FOUR-YEAR-OLD. MAULED CHILD REQUIRES EXTENSIVE SURGERY. ATTACK DOGS HAD A HISTORY OF AGGRESSION.
2 Hostility and negativity are expressed openly. The media coverage intensifies focus and discourse on the offending person or thing.	PIT BULLS ARE CANINE EVIL.
3 A person or group standing at the epicenter of a growing moral panic is demonized and its defenders or representatives become folk devils.	OUT-OF-WORK TRUCK DRIVER JOHN SMITH CAMPAIGNS TO GET HIS ATTACK DOGS BACK; HIRES A LAWYER. SMITH'S LAWYER CLAIMS: CHILD CROSSED PROPERTY LINES TO TEASE ATTACK DOGS.
4 Individuals or institutions step forward to serve as moral entrepreneurs; evidence to the contrary ignored or buried.	JUDGE SAYS PIT BULLS ARE DEADLY WEAPONS. NUMEROUS STUDIES SHOW PIT BULLS NO MORE PRONE TO BITING THAN OTHER BREEDS.

5	The media coverage intensifies and the press looks aggressively for any stories which may be tied into the triggering event.	PIT BULL ATTACK KILLS PET. PIT BULL BITES OFFICER KRUPKE.
6	The message moves beyond its original sphere at an ever increasing speed, abetted by the media, politicians, and sometimes those with a commercial interest in the outcome.	DOG ATTACKS UP 40%. HOW SAFE IS YOUR BACKYARD? EXPERTS RECOMMEND FENCES AT LEAST 6 FEET HIGH.
7	Definers are identified. These are people who are identified primarily by their credentials and claim to authority.	MAYOR RAISES POSSIBILITY OF A BREED BAN. PSYCHIATRIST TALKS ABOUT THE EMOTIONAL TRAUMA OF DOG ATTACKS. 27 SURGERIES LATER, PIT BULL ATTACK SURVIVOR DR EVA SMITH TELLS HER STORY.
8	Criticism accelerates to mockery.	WHAT KIND OF DOG HAS FOUR LEGS AND AN ARM?
9	Consensus is reached. On a regional or national level, there is widespread acceptance and acknowledgement that the group or event in question poses a very real threat to society.	CITY COUNCIL MULLS MULTI-PRONGED APPROACH TO RESOLVING PIT BULL THREAT.
10	Reactions and suggested remedies are disproportionate, with long-term, widespread and in extreme cases, destructive results. Actual resolutions sometimes result in a change in the law, one designed to further penalize the deviants and put more stringent controls in place.	PIT BULL ADOPTIONS DOWN 80%. CITY REQUIRES INSURANCE FOR PIT BULL OWNERS. POLICE KILL TWO PIT BULLS PLAYING IN FENCED FRONT YARD.

The cycle dies down, the media steps back and the panic fades quite quickly. Because the underlying conflict has not been resolved, the issue waits for a triggering event to resurface.[3]

African American English in context

In a previous chapter we looked at AAVE from a number of directions. Beyond issues of phonology, morphology, syntax and rhetorical style, we compared definitions and theorized about what the differences in those definitions meant. We looked at racism, overt and covert, as it surfaces in all age groups, ethnicities, races and socioeconomic groups. We considered the way AAVE is subordinated, and how those who subordinate rationalize their actions by assumption of authority and reference to language mythology. The issue of linguistic insecurity was raised, and countered by the acknowledgement that AAVE persists and will continue to persevere because it fills a need.

With this background information, we turn to the events of late 1996 and early 1997 referred to as the Oakland Ebonics Controversy, a moral panic of tremendous proportions and repercussions.

The setting[4]

Oakland, California, is a large port city on the East Bay in the San Francisco area. It has an estimated 2008 population of 404,155 with a population density of 7,298.8 persons per square mile (Figure 16.1). Oakland is a very diverse city, with an Anglo population of less than 40 percent and large African American, Latino and Asian communities.

Lopez (September 2001) reports that in the East Bay area overall, those under age 18 are more racially and ethnically diverse than the population as a whole. A larger percentage of the under-18 group self-identify as more than one race. From the available figures it could be posited that some 30 percent of the school-aged children in Oakland are AAVE speakers, while another 20 percent may speak a language other than English at home (Figure 16.2).[5]

The cost of living in Oakland is well above national averages. A person moving from Chicago to Oakland would pay approximately 11 percent more for groceries, 47 percent more for housing, 6 percent more on healthcare, while the cost of utilities will go down by about 20 percent. This will have something to do with the severity of Chicago's winters and the cost of heating fuel (CNNMoney.com March 2009). At the same time, 26.6 percent of Oaklanders under the age of 18 live below the poverty line (Figure 16.3).

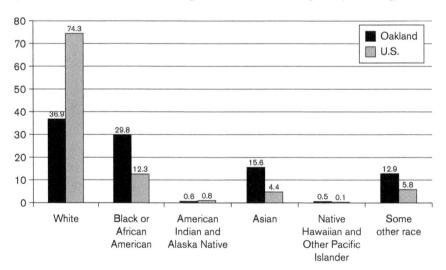

Figure 16.1 Population in Oakland and the U.S., percent by race

Source: U.S. Census Bureau, American Community Survey 2007

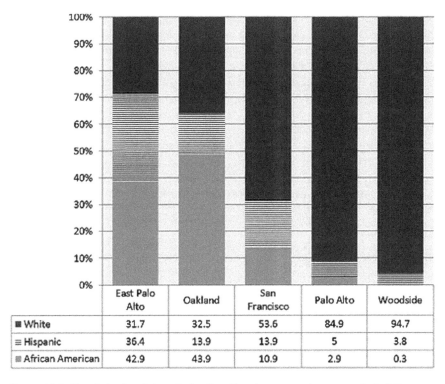

	East Palo Alto	Oakland	San Francisco	Palo Alto	Woodside
■ White	31.7	32.5	53.6	84.9	94.7
≡ Hispanic	36.4	13.9	13.9	5	3.8
■ African American	42.9	43.9	10.9	2.9	0.3

Figure 16.2 Population breakdown in five San Francisco areas, by race and ethnicity

Source: Adapted from Purnell et al. 1999 and the U.S. Census Bureau, American Community Survey 2007

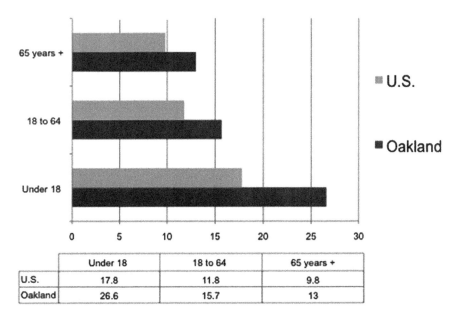

	Under 18	18 to 64	65 years +
U.S.	17.8	11.8	9.8
Oakland	26.6	15.7	13

Figure 16.3 Percent of population living below the poverty line in the U.S. and Oakland, by age

Source: U.S. Census Bureau, American Community Survey 2007

It is no surprise that there is inequality in school funding, nor is it difficult to trace the connection: richer districts provide more of everything, from audiovisual equipment to classroom assistants, while higher salaries make it possible to hire the best teachers

In Oakland, only 6.5 percent of the school population is Anglo, while Latinos and African Americans together make up about 70 percent of the total. In addition, a full 30.6 percent of Oakland's school population needs instruction in English as a second language.

If 30 percent of Oakland's students come to school without sufficient English skills, and another approximate 30 percent speak AAVE as a home language, the school district will require extra resources to provide the necessary instruction. Even with so many additional challenges, Oakland is underfunded in comparison to neighboring Pleasanton, where only 5.7 percent of the students come to school as native speakers of a language other than English.

The triggering event

A few things about the Oakland school district in 1996 which are generally agreed upon:

- The children in the district, most especially the African American children, were not doing well academically, and had not been doing well for a very long time.
- This failure to thrive was due at least in part to the fact that African American children came to school speaking a variety of English that (1) differs significantly from the academic/school English they were expected to use; and (2) was highly stigmatized.
- Teachers had not yet found a methodology that addressed these complex issues.
- The teachers and staff were looking for a way to make schooling relevant and rewarding for these children.
- The School Board recognized that it would take a great deal of funding to find appropriate ways to proceed and turn this situation around.
- There was no money for such a project; there was barely enough money to keep the classrooms staffed and provide textbooks.

In summary, if AAVE speakers were to succeed in school, two things had to happen: funding needed to become available, and they had to find a way to engage the children in the possibility of success. At the same time, the staff and school board were very much aware that there was money available for teaching English to children who came to school speaking another language entirely, as they would cite in their resolution:

> Whereas, the Federal Bilingual Education Act (20 USC 1402 et seq.) mandates that local educational agencies "build their capacities to establish, implement and sustain programs of instruction for children and youth of limited English proficiency."

At this point, a well-established theory was raised: the best way to introduce children to the idea of *SAE is to use the home language as a conduit.[6] So why not propose that AAVE be recognized as a language independent of English? If this approach worked, there would be more money to get things done, and they would have the beginnings of a program that valued AAVE as a fully functional human language. This would be a good first step toward drawing disenfranchised children back into the classroom.

The School Board wrote a proposal which said, in essence: We are failing in our primarily goal to teach AAVE-speaking children *SAE. They are resistant for a lot of complex reasons, and nothing we have tried so far has been successful. We have reason to believe that if we approach this from their perspective things will improve. If we start with what the children know, with the home language, they will understand that we're not trying to take anything away from them. They'll begin to expand their skills until the point they can code-switch between AAVE and *SAE according to situational factors.

This is what the School Board was saying, but they didn't put it this way. Note that their position is very conservative and traditional. All parties agree that schoolchildren must learn *SAE because the command of that language is crucial to success. No one raises the issue of the racism inherent to this linguistic separate-but-equal approach. The Anglo world is saying: you must assimilate linguistically, or we will systematically shut you out. Fair warning: learn our language, be like us, or we will discriminate against you.

This ideology is so deeply rooted that the lack of logic, the incongruity is left to stand unchallenged. The Oakland School Board did not question this status quo; they affirmed their commitment to it without hesitation. But there was an element of anger – certainly well placed, but counterproductive in its timing – in the way they worded their affirmation and their resolution and in the way they described AAVE. Unfortunately the approach they took hindered rather than helped their cause.

Linguist Geoff Nunberg (1997) put it quite bluntly: "The language of the board's declaration seemed calculated to play to all the worst stereotypes of education jargon and afrocentric twaddle."

A basic tenet of persuasive writing is to never give detractors an inaccuracy to focus on, because they will use it to distract away from the real issue. In this case, detractors latched onto poor wording and inaccuracies and yanked very, very hard. The original version of the resolution was made public on December 18, 1996. Despite its flaws, the first media reports were fairly even-handed, for example, this opening from *The San Francisco Chronicle* dated December 19, 1996:

> The Oakland school board approved a landmark policy last night that recognizes Ebonics, or Black English, as a primary language of its African American students . . . The district's resolution, passed unanimously, declares that all teachers in the Oakland Unified School District should be trained to respect the Ebonics language of their students as distinct from standard American English – not a dialect that is "wrong."

There is no mention here of "teaching AAVE" to the students, as would be reported later, even in the same paper. Nor is there any implication that *SAE was to be abandoned or replaced. And still, despite reasonable reports in the immediate aftermath of the resolution, the media coverage soon slipped into the realm of language mythology, and whatever good might have come from the original proposal was a lost cause.

Linguists have spent a lot of time looking at the original proposal, analyzing problem areas and addressing generalizations or factual errors step by step, documenting everything along the way. This is a reasonable and useful thing for linguists to do, but in the tradition of all such situations, the carefully researched material made available to the public was largely ignored or, in some cases, mocked.

The important point is this: in our eagerness to set the record straight on matters of linguistic science, we missed the larger, far more important underlying conflict. We addressed the symptoms rather than the disease. This is where the language subordination model might be able to shed some light on how the media firestorm came to be.

This sentence occurs early in the resolution:

> [Scholarly] studies have also demonstrated that African language systems are genetically-based and not a dialect of English.[7]

The annual meeting of the Linguistic Society of America (LSA) happened to come at the height of the Oakland controversy. During that meeting a response was drafted, the intent of which was to highlight what was factually accurate in the proposal while clarifying other points:

> What is important from a linguistic and educational point of view is not whether AAVE is called a "language" or a "dialect" but rather that its systematicity be recognized.

The phrase "African Language Systems are genetically-based" was another example of poor wording that distracted from the key issues. Shortly after the resolution was made public, the board issued a clarification: they had used "genetically-based" in the sense of "originate in." But the damage was already done, as some commentators chose to focus on other readings of "genetic."

> "Black students are genetically predisposed to speaking an inferior style of English." What would happen if a white conservative said that?
> (Rush Limbaugh, On Ebonics, *The Rush Limbaugh Show*, December 22, 1996)

The term "genetic" is used in comparative and historical linguistics in the study of inter-relatedness of language families over time and space. In that context, you might say that Latin and Italian are genetically related. This concept is not widely understood outside linguistic circles, where "genetics" is associated with highly controversial matters such as innate intelligence, DNA research and manipulation, stem cell research among others. See "Last Train to Oakland," below, for an example of a public reaction to the use of genetic linking.

Finally, the board set about authenticating their claims by drawing on what they referred to as "scholarly studies." This could be interpreted as an attempt to reach over the heads of potential detractors by establishing a link to academia and thereby claiming authenticity in a way that could be challenged on facts. If in fact the Board had consulted with linguists about the wording of the resolution, this appearance of falsely claiming authenticity could have been avoided, but they chose not to.

Thus far we have the inferred claims from the resolution:

- Our language is fully grammatical within itself; it is distinct and it links us to our African origins in a way we celebrate.
- Our children have suffered educational malpractice because others refuse to recognize or accept our allegiance to ourselves and our communities (Baugh 1999).
- We can prove it; we have academics and scholars to back us up.

Thus the stage was set for a panic of large proportions.

The panic cycle in Oakland

The following collection of media quotes and snippets originates from more than two thousand items resulting from a database search for the word *Ebonics* occurring in a headline or lead paragraph between November 1996 and 2010. Included are news reports, editorials and letters to the editor from newspapers, and news and commentary from the broadcast media.

Representative selections have been divided into rough categories that correspond with the hypothetical example provided above. As you read, pay attention to the shift in tone from neutral to hostile by keeping track of phrasing, descriptive terms, punctuation, and the evolution escalation of false or distorted reporting of facts. For example, consider the word *primary* in the extract from the December 20, 1996 issue of *The Chattanooga Times*. How might that be interpreted? Is it *meant* to be incendiary?

Some of the examples are far less aggressive than others; some are merely very subtle. Where others have researched a particular statement or issue, that work is cited.

Something unsettling or disturbing or frightening happens; the media focus on the event in the course of their usual news cycle. There is significant reader or viewer response and interest; the cycle ramps up:

1   Oakland Schools OK Black English. Ebonics to be regarded as different, not wrong. *The San Francisco Chronicle*, 12/18/1996.
2   Oakland school board declares Black English a second language. *Associated Press*, 12/18/1996.
3   "Ebonics" May Be Taught in California Schools . . . declaring that so-called "black English" is a second language. *CNN Today*, 12/18/1996.
4   Schools accept black English; Oakland board grants Ebonics primary status . . . Acknowledging that many African-American students do not speak standard English, the Oakland School Board has approved a special program – the nation's first – that recognizes black English as a primary language. *The Chattanooga Times* (Tennessee), 12/20/1996.

Hostility and negativity increase and are expressed openly. The media coverage intensifies focus on the offending person or thing:

1   Oakland school board declares black English a second language . . . Levi Smith doesn't want his three children speaking Black English with phrases like "He be at the store," even though the Oakland School Board says it's a legitimate language. *Associated Press*, 12/20/1996.
2   Here's how they be talkin. *Charleston Daily Mail* (West Virginia), 12/20/1996.
3   If you've never heard the term "Ebonics," then you probably don't live in the Oakland, California area. Oakland's school board has decided to teach Ebonics, or "Black English" as a legitimate language. Is their approach innovative, or demeaning? *CNN Newsnight*, 12/20/1996.
4   The Argument over the Issue of "Ebonics" as a Separate Language. There is a great deal of argument over the existence of Ebonics. *CNN Today*, 12/20/1996.
5   Oakland schools give black dialect status as second language. Saying it has failed to adequately educate black youngsters, the Oakland Unified School District has

declared black English a second language. It becomes the first district in the nation to give the controversial dialect official status in programs targeting bilingual students. *The Dallas Morning News*, 12/20/1996.

6   In a decision that touches on explosive educational and racial issues, the Oakland, Calif., school board declared Wednesday that many of its 28,000 black students do not speak standard English, but a distinctive language spoken by American blacks. *Morning Star* (Wilmington, NC), 12/20/1996.

7   School District Elevates Status of Black English. *The New York Times*, 12/20/1996.

8   [The Oakland school board] declared Wednesday that many of its 28,000 black students did not speak standard English, but a distinctive language spoken by American blacks. *Palm Beach Post*, 12/20/1996.

9   Thousands of Americans became instantly bilingual this week, when a California school district declared that black English is a separate language. They call it Ebonics, combining the words ebony and phonics. Tonight, the angry response grows in plain English. *ABC World News Tonight*, 12/22/1996.

10 Critics blast Oakland's Ebonics plan. *United Press International*, 12/21/1996.

11 Ebonics: A distinct language, or broken English? *Saint Petersburg Times*, 12/21/1996.

12 The "Ebonics" Tragedy. ANOTHER TRAGIC chapter in racial self-destruction is being written in Oakland, where the school board voted unanimously last week to require the teaching of "black English." Since educators of all colors apparently feel a need to puff up all sorts of ordinary things with fancy names, "black English" is now being called "Ebonics." *San Jose Mercury News*, 12/23/1996.

Individuals or institutions step forward to serve as moral entrepreneurs:

1   A decision by the school district in Oakland in California has touched a nerve across the nation . . . But state and federal educators are distancing themselves from the proposal. And many Oakland parents are outraged over the decision. *All Things Considered*, NPR, 12/20/1996.

2   Reverend Jesse Jackson urged the Oakland, California, school district today to reverse its decision recognizing Ebonics, or Black English, as a second language. Jackson called the decision, quote, "an unacceptable surrender borderlining on disgrace," end quote. *CBS Sunday Night News*, 12/26/1996.

3   . . . the reactions range from amazement to interest to the view of black poet Maya Angelou, who considers it "an awful idea," in plain English. *CBS Evening News*, 12/23/1996.

4   The hearings began on a combative note. Sen. Lauch Faircloth (R-N.C.) denounced Ebonics as "absurd" and said that the Oakland school board's decision to have teachers recognize it in classes struck him as "political correctness gone out of control." *The Washington Post*, 1/24/1997.

Definers are identified primarily by their credentials as a claim to authority:

1   Not surprisingly, the decision by school officials in Oakland, Calif., to declare black English – so-called Ebonics – to be a separate language has prompted controversy. Many black leaders denounced the move; Education Secretary Richard Riley says Ebonics is not a foreign language but non-standard English, a form of slang. "This is not an issue and I do not want it to become an issue. African American students are

very capable of using standard English in the form it is now being taught." – Sen. Ralph David Abernathy, D-Atlanta, who is sponsoring a bill that would ban Georgia's school systems from implementing language curriculum based on Ebonics. *Florida Times-Union*, 1/27/1997.

2 Arsenio Hall be no fan of Ebonics. "Malcolm X didn't need it. Martin Luther King didn't need it. Maya Angelou didn't need it. It's absurd. Absurd. I think it creates awful self-esteem in black kids to tell them they need something extra that other Americans don't need. It sends out an awful signal." *Austin American-Statesman*, 2/2/1997.

3 St. Louis Superintendent Cleveland Hammonds says city schools won't sanction Ebonics as a separate language. *St. Louis Post-Dispatch* (Missouri), 12/27/1996.

4 Treating black students who say "He bin" instead of "He has been" like foreign language students is no way to raise academic standards in American classrooms, says Education Secretary Richard Riley. *Associated Press*, 12/14/1996.

5 At a ceremony for the Congressional Black Caucus this week, [actor Bill] Cosby said: "I didn't hear any ignoromics spoken this morning. There are more than 100 people and nobody said 'liberry.' Nobody said, 'We bein' here.'" *St. Louis Post-Dispatch*, 1/9/1997.

6 The Philadelphia school board president, a board member and the deputy superintendent yesterday said there was no way their schools would recognize "slang" as a second language. *The Philadelphia Daily News*, 12/21/1996.

7 Aisha Blackshire-Belay, chair of African Studies at Indiana State University and a linguist specializing in black English, expressed serious reservations about Oakland's decision Wednesday to incorporate "Ebonics" into English teaching. *Milwaukee Journal Sentinel*, 12/22/1996.

8 Forget Ebonics – it's an insult, *Emerge* editor tells NSU group . . . "To me, it's an insult," said Curry, editor-in-chief of *Emerge* magazine. "You're saying we can't teach our kids, and I disagree with that." *The Virginian-Pilot* (Norfolk, VA), 2/5/1997.

A person or group standing at the epicenter of a growing moral panic is held up for criticism and its defenders or representatives become folk devils:

1 Oakland Schools Err with Ebonics Vote: THE OAKLAND school board is doing its students a disservice by categorizing "Ebonics" – also known as "black English" – as the primary language of African American students. *The San Francisco Chronicle*, 12/20/1996.

2 Social commentators of every hue, gender, national origin and political persuasion, up to and including Maya Angelou, the Rev. Jesse Jackson, Kweisi Mfume and Rush Limbaugh, stopped just short of advocating that the members of the Oakland school board be hind-quartered and lynched for advancing such an outrageous policy. *Pittsburgh Post-Gazette*, 1/1/1997.

3 The Academic Fad that Gave Us Ebonics. *Wall Street Journal*, 1/22/1997.

4 The recent decision by the Oakland, Calif., School Board to teach Ebonics, or black English in its public schools is at best misguided, and at worst a deliberate attempt to re-segregate our American society by keeping blacks mired in poverty and self-defeating behaviors. *The Virginian-Pilot* (Norfolk, VA), 1/27/1997.

5 THE OAKLAND, Calif., school board, backpedaling furiously, now has revised its ill-advised resolution of Dec. 18 on the teaching of "Ebonics." Good riddance to bad

rubbish. The original resolution was so poorly drafted that I am minded to venture a suggestion: While Oakland is teaching English to its children, let someone teach English to its school board. When the uproar arose, the board insisted that it had no intention of actually teaching Ebonics, or Black English, in the classroom. *The Augusta Chronicle*, 1/25/1997.

6 Public school officials in Oakland, having declared that African Americans speak a language distinct from English, defended their plan to help failing black students, while California's schools chief Thursday questioned the wisdom of the decision. *San Jose Mercury News*, 12/20/1996.

7 Schools to recognize black 'Ebonics' California district to use dialect as a bridge to proper English . . . The resolution has reignited a decades-old controversy over the legitimacy of black English. *USA Today*, 12/20/1996.

8 "Ebonics" is not a language. The School Board of Oakland, Calif., has made a disgraceful decision for which it deserves to stand in the corner until further notice. Its recognition of "black English" as a language, and directive that teachers "respect" it, is a blow to education. *The Boston Globe*, 12/21/1996.

9 Some say that endorsing a dialect as a second language would lower standards and condemn kids to a life of unemployment because standard English is the only language of the working world. *The Dallas Morning News*, 12/21/1996.

The message moves beyond its original sphere at an ever increasing speed, abetted by the media, politicians, and sometimes those with a commercial interest in the outcome:

1 Scholars debunk merits of "Ebonics." *The Herald Sun*, Durham, NC, 12/29/1996.

2 The vagary of the Oakland, Calif., political hierarchy to propose that (presumed) mature, college-educated adults stoop to the vacuous mentality of a jive-talking, callow, maligned faction of society is the ultimate level of lunacy and perversity becoming the daily norm of this drug-crazed mass of inhumanity cavalierly referred to as the human race. Are the politicians in Oakland really concerned with improving education, or are they looking to establish another bureaucratic program to help fulfill their personal agendas of nepotism? Their political prescription (Ebonics) to this "cultural cancer" is analogous to the medical community's covetous approach to the spectrum of medical maladies prevalent in this country – treating the symptom rather than the cause. *Buffalo News*, 1/27/1997.

3 The Ku Klux Klan could not have come up with a better plan to impede the academic progress of young black children than the idea of teaching Ebonics as a separate language. *Crain's Chicago Business*, 1/27/1997.

4 The "Ebonics' Fraud. If the people who have been promoting "Ebonics" with a straight face have any sense of humor, they surely are splitting their sides over the fact that they have promoted their fraud into a nationwide discussion – and even a Senate hearing yesterday. *Chattanooga Free Press* (Tennessee), January 24, 1997.

5 [letter] No Caribonics, no Ebonics. As a child in my Caribbean homeland, slang was not permitted in our home. My parents made sure that we spoke properly (like white people). So there! It is laughable to read about ebonics. If the reason for this calamity is those black folks in Oakland are special, then how do we treat the Caribbean people? Although we have a distinct accent, it has never prevented us from learning standard English. *The Atlanta Journal-Constitution*, February 6, 1997.

6 EBONICS IS BLACK-ON-BLACK CRIME. So the Oakland Board of (mis) Education has decided to drop any suggestion that Ebonics is genetically based and that students should be taught in both Ebonics and standard English. Well, too late. The damage has already been done. Not since "Amos 'n' Andy" and Mammy from "Gone With the Wind" has black America had to withstand such an assault on its collective image. This is black-on-black crime. *Daily News*, New York, 1/17/1997.

7 When the Oakland, Calif. Unified School District announced last year that it would adopt Ebonics – also called "Black-English" – as a teaching tool, a hue and cry arose throughout the land. Educators nationwide denounced the district for "legitimizing" a form of communication believed to be inferior to standard English, they raged. *Tulsa World*, 5/28/1997.

Criticism accelerates to mockery:

1 [Letter] I enjoyed the politically incorrect editorial cartoon comparing "Ebonics" with "Bubbonics" on Dec. 22. *The Herald Sun*, 12/29/1996.

2 LET us not misunderstand the Oakland School Board's intentions regarding "Ebonics," the new word for the way black people talk. A construction of "ebony" and "phonics," Ebonics is a bogus word – appropriately, I suppose, since the concept of "black English" is, too. *The Houston Chronicle*, 12/29/1996.

3 I, too, have been looking for examples [of Ebonics], but the half-dozen or so newspapers I read regularly have given us very little in the way of genuine Ebonics. The best example I found was on the Internet. English: Toys R Us. Ebonics: We Be Toys. I like the Ebonics version better. Mike Royko, syndicated newspaper column, 12/29/1996.

4 At the Virginia Polytechnic Institute, an African American student gets an email entitled "Ebonic Loan Application." The fake document was packed with stereotyped and racist images; for example, under "place of birth" were the following choices: charity hospital, free public hospital, cotton patch, back alley, zoo.

Reactions and suggested remedies are disproportionate, with long-term, widespread and in extreme cases, destructive results. Actual resolutions sometimes result in a change in the law, one designed to further penalize the deviants and put more stringent controls in place:

1 Georgia Senate rejects Ebonics for curriculum. Don't know much about science books. Don't know much about the French I took . . . Georgia lawmakers do know one thing – nobody be teaching Ebonics in state classrooms. A Senate committee has approved a bill prohibiting the controversial topic. The full Senate and the House will consider it later. *The Chattanooga Times*, February 13, 1997.

2 *Cornell Review*, a conservative student publication, published a parody – a description, in ebonics, of courses that might be taught in Cornell's Africana Studies and Resource Center. An excerpt from a prospective course, Racism in American Society: *Da white man be evil an he tryin to keep da brotherman down. We s got Sharpton an Farakhan, so who da white man now, white boy? . . . We ain t gots to axe da white man for nothin in dis class. Village Voice*, 9/30/1997.

3 A black lawmaker and former principal has drafted a bill that would prohibit Ebonics

from being taught in a South Carolina classroom or college. *The Post and Courier*, 1/4/1997.

4   School Board 24 in Western Queens last week became the first in the city to officially ban Ebonics, or so-called black English, from its classrooms. Board members voted unanimously Thursday night to "reject any recognition of Ebonics as a distinct and legitimate language" and compared it to "unacceptable grammar" and a "decimation of the English language." *Daily News*, 1/27/1997.

5   California bill would bar Ebonics from classrooms. *USA Today*, 1/27/1997. An explosive debate about how and whether to use black English in public classrooms could lead Congress to ban the use of federal funds for such instruction, Sen. Arlen Specter (R., Pa.) said yesterday. *The Philadelphia Inquirer*, 1/24/1997.

6   Last Train from Oakland. Oakland's attempt to link genes and language was both racist and idiotic. Yesterday's Senate hearing underscored the plan's weaknesses, and brought the city's superintendent under heavy attack. Outraged by the city's proposal, one Congressman even suggested restricting Federal aid to the Oakland district. *The New York Times*, 1/24/1997.

Postscript: Institutionalized mockery

On October 9, 1998, a distinctive quarter page advertisement appeared in *The New York Times*. In it, an African American figure reminiscent of Martin Luther King, Jr. stands with his back turned to a bold proclamation in white print: "I HAS A DREAM." The ad makes its case by appealing directly to African Americans:

> By now, you've probably heard about Ebonics (aka, Black English). And if you think it's become a controversy because white America doesn't want us messing with their precious language, don't. White America couldn't care less what we do to segregate ourselves. The fact is language is power. And we can't take that power away from our children with Ebonics.
>
> (The National Head Start Association)

The National Head Start Association (NHSA) is a private, not-for-profit membership organization representing some two thousand federally funded Head Start programs across the country. These educational programs address the needs of poor children to age 5.

The message underwritten by NHSA is quite clear: to succeed, the African American community must assimilate linguistically. To maintain allegiance to home and community by linguistic means is to embrace poverty, ignorance, and prejudice. The authorities called upon to give credence to this message are the men who gave their lives for equal rights. Here, Ebonics is not a fully functioning variety of English, the symbol of solidarity and allegiance, but a disaster for the African American community.

What is not generally known about this ad is that it was not conceptualized or written by the NHSA: it was the product of a collaboration between a group called Atlanta's Black Professionals and three prominent ad agencies. The ad won the 1998 Grand Prize of the annual Athena Award offered by the Newspaper Association of America; *The New York Times* ran it free, as a public service announcement.[8] According to executives at the ad agencies, the advertisement was popular when it first ran in Atlanta and was requested by schools from Miami to Richmond.[9]

It is clear that this advertisement follows directly from the national debate on the Oakland Ebonics controversy. What is unclear – and the far more important question – is this: How did we come to this place where successful African American professionals, a national education organization and the most prominent daily newspaper not only collaborate to disseminate such divisive and exclusionary rhetoric, but award each other for it? Does an organization dedicated to the education of poor children really intend to advocate that we turn our backs on speakers who cannot or will not assimilate to corporate conceptions of "good" English? And perhaps most difficult: what are linguists, parents and teachers who are dedicated to the education of all children to do in the face of such beliefs and tactics?

Speaking up

There were a number of media reports on the Oakland controversy that were particularly interesting for unusual perspectives, observations, or negative slant and factual inaccuracies. Some – but not all – of the negative or misleading articles appeared in high profile conservative publications where the Oakland resolution was treated "as just one more multiculturalist scam" (Nunberg 1997).

DISCUSSION QUESTIONS AND EXERCISES

Discussion references

Applebome, P. (1997) Dispute over Ebonics Reflects a Volatile Mix That Roils Urban Education. *The New York Times*, March 1.

Heilbrunn, J. (1997) Speech Therapy: Ebonics. It's Worse Than You Think. *The New Republic* January 20.

See also Rickford's response to Heilbrunn's inaccuracies and biases, in:

Rickford, J.R. (1999) The Ebonics Controversy in My Background: A Sociolinguist's Experiences and Reflections. *Journal of Sociolinguistics* 3: 267–275.

Rich, F. (1997) The Ebonic Plague. *The New York Times*, January 8.

See also Sclafani's analysis of the NYT coverage:

Sclafani, J. (2008) The Intertextual Origins of Public Opinion: Constructing Ebonics in *The New York Times. Discourse and Society* 19: 507–527.

Discussion exercises

- Perhaps the best popular illustration of how a moral panic originates is found in *The Music Man*, a musical comedy that first appeared on stage and later, on film. A con man comes to small town Iowa; his first step is to engage the trust of the community. Clips of this small segment can be found on YouTube (search "The Music Man" and "Ya Got Trouble" together). This is in fact a comedy, but it does a good job of demonstrating the whole process in a short time. Have a look at it and decide who Harold Hill is: moral entrepreneur or devil?

● Select two or three clips provided in the case study and do a close reading and analysis. How do they (or don't they) fit into the language subordination model?

● In his article about his own involvement in the Oakland controversy, John Rickford talks a little about how linguists experienced personal fallout from the public:

> One thing that I naively did not expect was the subtle and not-so-subtle nastiness that issues of language can elicit from the public. I encountered this in the occasionally severe distortions of information which I had shared with reporters in good faith, and in the "hate mail" which my quoted remarks in the press elicited. One example of distortive reporting was Jacob Heilbrunn's Ebonics article in the January 20, 1997 issue of *The New Republic*, to which I responded with a letter in the March 3, 1997 issue. One example of the hate mail was a postcard I received addressed to "John Rickford, Linguistics Professor (God Help Us All)" which included, alongside a newspaper report of my remarks at the 1997 LSA meeting, the comment: "It's just amazing how much crap you so-called 'scholars' can pour and get away with. Can you wonder, John Boy, why the general public does not trust either educators, judges or politicians? As a brother might say, 'Ee Bonic be a bunch a booshit man, but it get de muny offa de White man. He be a sucka.'" Geoff Pullum also got hate mail for his *Nature* piece, as did Rosina Lippi-Green for her *New York Times* letter to the editor in December 1996. It comes with the territory.
>
> (Rickford 1999)

● Below is the letter mentioned in Rickford's article, which I wrote to *The New York Times* after they published an editorial on the Oakland controversy. Following that are partial transcripts of two of the many letters I received through the mail. Questions for discussion follow.

December 26, 1996

To the Editor:

In your Dec. 24 editorial "Linguistic Confusion" you demonstrate considerable confusion of your own.

The body of research on the history of that variety of American English called Black English or African American Vernacular English is anything but "dubious." Because the school board in Oakland, Calif., prefers the term "ebonics" does not change the well-documented body of empirical, quantitative socio-linguistics that underlies what we know about the history and structure of that language. A more thorough examination of the topic would have provided you with input from linguists who could make the facts available to you.

This is yet another example of the media's biased reporting on language issues, in its self-appointed role as arbiter of a spoken "standard" language – a mythical beast you will never define with any clarity because it does not exist.

Discrimination on the basis of language variation linked to race, national origin and economics exists not because the language is worthless or less than functional, but because newspapers and other voices of authority insist that such discrimination is right and because we have been pushing that message for so long that most people no longer think to examine the false logic and spurious common-sense arguments.

You and other papers have printed strong criticism of the Oakland board's action by prominent and intellectual African Americans, but you have not sought out those who would speak rationally to the other side of this issue. There are interviews with Maya Angelou but none with the Nobel Prize winner Toni Morrison. The Rev. Jesse Jackson has drowned out James Baldwin's famous 1979 editorial "If Black English Isn't a Language, Then Tell Me, What Is?"

If you cannot look to your own archives, go to the major research universities in this country where African American and other linguists have produced a significant body of work that might have given you some facts to work with. I suggest you start with the linguists John Rickford, John Baugh and Geneva Smitherman.

ROSINA LIPPI-GREEN Ann Arbor, Mich., Dec. 24, 1996.

The writer is an associate professor of linguistics, University of Michigan.

● Responses sent through the mail to me, excerpted:

You should be ashamed of yourself. You know better. You SHOULD know better. Did you get where you are today talking Black?

I agree with you that we need to be more open minded about language. What I wish is that Pig Latin would be accepted. It fits right in there with Ebonics.

● What assumptions are the letter writers working with? Why might they have come to such conclusions? What are the primary emotions that come across?

Notes

1   Moral panics have been documented as far back as antiquity. More recent examples include the Salem Witch Trials, the McCarthy hearings, Satanic Ritual Abuse in the 1980s and the Terry Schiavo case, in which family members disagreed on whether or not to discontinue life support for a woman in a vegetative coma.

2   In *Verbal Hygiene* Cameron looks closely at moral panics in England, from dog attacks to The Great Grammar Controversy.

3   Frankfurter's *Evil Incarnate: Rumors of Demonic Conspiracy and Satanic Abuse in History* (2006) takes as a thesis that Satanic ritual abuse stories surface again and again over time because they serve an important function. In a community where individuals, groups or institutions are leaning toward dissent, a moral panic provides an excuse to persecute or root out the non-compliant.

4   All numbers in this section originate from the U.S. Census Bureau, 2006–2008 American Community Survey, unless otherwise noted. Data are based on a sample and are subject to sampling variability. Race figures do not include those who self-identify as "more than one race."

5 Not included here are those who self-identified as "more than one race." Note that the Latino population is distributed among the races also according to self-identification.
6 Linguists and educators have produced a tremendous amount of work on the theory and methodology, a great deal of which originates in Europe, where multilingualism and bidialectalism are the rule rather than the exception.
7 This is not the place to list all the problems in the original resolution; others have done that in great detail. Lakoff provides one of the clearest, most concise and accessible of such treatments, for those who are interested in analyzing the resolution more closely.
8 The NHSA accepted as a donation some portion of the money that came along with the Athena award, but they deny endorsing the advertisement for publication (Deputy Director Michael McGrady, personal communication).
9 Some of this information originates from email correspondence with linguists who were concerned enough about the advertisement to investigate. My thanks to Geneva Smitherman, Orlando Taylor, Arthur Spears, Marcy Morgan, Rebecca Wheeler and John Baugh.

Suggested further reading

Baugh, J. (2001) *Beyond Ebonics: Linguistic Pride and Racial Prejudice.* New York: Oxford University Press.
Baugh, J. (2004) Ebonics and Its Controversy. In E. Finegan and J.R. Rickford (eds.) *Language in the USA: Themes for the 21st Century.* New York: Cambridge University Press.
Cohen, S. (2002 [1972]) *Folk Devils and Moral Panics: The Creation of the Mods and Rockers.* New York: Routledge.
Critcher, C. (2006) *Critical Readings: Moral Panics and the Media.* Maidenhead: Open University Press.
Fairclough, N. (1995) *Media Discourse.* London: Edward Arnold.
Gitlin, T. (1980) *The Whole World Is Watching: Mass Media in the Making and Unmaking of the New Left.* Berkeley, CA: University of California Press.
Goode, E. and Ben-Yehuda, N. (2009) *Moral Panics: The Social Construction of Deviance.* Malden, MA: Wiley-Blackwell.
Herman, E.S. and Chomsky, N. (2002 [1988]) *Manufacturing Consent: The Political Economy of the Mass Media.* New York: Pantheon Books.
Johnson, C. (1997) John Rickford – Holding on to a Language of Our Own. *The San Francisco Chronicle*, February 16.
Johnson, S. (1999) From Linguistic Molehills to Social Mountains? Introducing Moral Panics about Language. Centre for Language in Social Life Working Papers.
Kretzschmar, W.A. (2008) Public and Academic Understandings about Language: The Intellectual History of Ebonics. *English World-Wide* 29: 70–95.
Lakoff, R. T. (2000) *The Language War.* Berkeley, CA: University of California Press.
Nunberg, G. (1997) Double Standards. *Natural Language and Linguistic Theory* 15: 667–675.
Pandey, A. (2000) Linguistic Power in Virtual Communities: The Ebonics Debate on the Internet. *World Englishes* 19: 21–38.
Popp, R.K. (2006) Mass Media and the Linguistic Marketplace: Media, Language, and Distinction. *Journal of Communication Inquiry* 30: 5–20.

Pullum, G.K. (1997) Language That Dare Not Speak Its Name. *Nature* 386: 321–322.

Rickford, J.R. (1999) The Ebonics Controversy in My Background: A Sociolinguist's Experiences and Reflections. *Journal of Sociolinguistics* 3: 267–275.

Ronkin, M. and Karn, H.E. (1999) Mock Ebonics: Linguistic Racism in Parodies of Ebonics on the Internet. *Sociolinguistics* 3: 360–380.

Seymour, H.N. and Seymour, C.M. (1979) The Symbolism of Ebonics: I'd Rather Switch Than Fight. *Journal of Black Studies* 9: 397–410.

Walsh, J. (1997) Discussing "Ebonics" in Plain English. *The Baltimore Sun*, January 7.

Wise, T.J. (2009) *Between Barack and a Hard Place: Racism and White Denial in the Age of Obama*. San Francisco: City Lights Books.

Wolfram, W. (1998) Language Ideology and Dialect: Understanding the Oakland Ebonics Controversy. *Journal of English Linguistics* 26: 108–121.

Case study 2

17

Linguistic profiling and fair housing

Douglas Massey, who has conducted extensive research on patterns of racial segregation, has noted that *America's large urban areas remain only slightly less segregated than South Africa during apartheid.* Today, 41 percent of Black Americans live in neighborhoods that are described as hyper-segregated, that is, in all Black high-density neighborhoods near other all-Black neighborhoods. Another 18 percent of African Americans also live in conditions of high segregation.

> "No Home for the Holidays," National Fair Housing Alliance,
> December 2005 (emphasis added)

In the period following World War II, one of the most pressing problems in the U.S. had to do with insufficient housing. Property owners and managers, mortgage institutions and insurance companies made a difficult situation worse by openly discriminating against potential buyers or renters on the basis of color or ethnicity. In the year 2010 it is hard to imagine that a coalition of real estate agents, banks and insurance companies would fight – openly, unapologetically – for the right to discriminate against people of color. But this is just what happened in California.

Tyranny of the Californian majority

In 1963, the California legislature passed the Rumford Fair Housing Act which prohibited racial discrimination in housing practices. The California Real Estate Commission immediately started raising money to sponsor a referendum (referred to as Proposition 14)[1] which called for a revision to the state constitution that would allow property owners to continue to discriminate any way they pleased:

> Neither the State nor any subdivision or agency thereof shall deny, limit or abridge, directly or indirectly, the right of any person, who is willing or desires to sell, lease or rent any part or all of his real property, to decline to sell, lease or rent such property to such person or persons as he, in his absolute discretion, chooses.
>
> (Noel and Cheng 2009)

That 1964 voter initiative passed with a 65 percent majority, thus nullifying the Rumford Act and "creating a California Constitutional right to discriminate against members of racial minority groups" (Oppenheimer 2020: 118). In turn, Proposition 14 was struck down when the California Supreme Court ruled it a violation of the Fourteenth Amendment,[2] and thus unconstitutional (ibid.). In May 1967, the Supreme Court of the U.S. affirmed that decision.

In Oppenheimer's history of California's anti-discrimination legislation, he notes that the courts "acted with great courage, defying the will of the voters, to protect minority rights" (ibid.: 118). This is a perfect example of the concept of the tyranny of the majority. In the U.S. the founding fathers anticipated such problems by writing the Bill of Rights, which protects individuals even in the face of overwhelming public opinion.

Subsequent legislation (most notably the Civil Rights Act of 1968, often referred to as the Fair Housing Act) extended protection to include a wider range of discriminatory behaviors and protected classes.

The Office of Fair Housing and Equal Opportunity (FHEO)[3] has a website[4] where it describes its purpose as the office that administers and enforces federal laws and establishes policies that make sure all Americans have equal access to the housing of their choice. There are state organizations which perform similar functions, dozens of non-profit civil-rights organizations and a legion of fair housing advocates and activists who are deeply involved in the pursuit of equal housing for all.

Actions based on race, color, national origin, religion, sex, familial status or handicap that are specifically prohibited by law include the following:

- refusal to rent or sell housing;
- taking steps to making housing unavailable (a landlord or owner takes the property off the market to avoid potential renters or buyers on the basis of a protected category);
- setting different terms, conditions or privileges for sale or rental of a dwelling (for example, require people of a particular race to pay a larger security deposit);
- providing different housing services or facilities (the landlord prohibits some renters from using the garden or pool);
- falsely denying that housing is available for inspection, sale, or rental;
- for profit, persuading owners to sell or rent (blockbusting) or denying anyone access to or membership in a facility or service (such as a multiple listing service) related to the sale or rental of housing;
- refusing to make a mortgage loan;
- refusing to provide information regarding loans;
- imposing different terms or conditions on a loan, such as different interest rates, points, or fees;
- discriminating in appraising property;
- refusing to purchase a loan;
- setting different terms or conditions for purchasing a loan;
- threatening, coercing, intimidating or interfering with anyone exercising a fair housing right or assisting others who exercise that right;
- advertising or making any statement that indicates a limitation or preference based on race, color, national origin, religion, sex, familial status, or handicap. This prohibition against discriminatory advertising applies to single-family and owner-occupied housing that is otherwise exempt from the Fair Housing.

And still, housing discrimination is widespread. Reasons for this fall into two categories: (1) victim vulnerabilities; and (2) property owners, managers, or contractors looking for ways to increase profits regardless of legality.

In the first case, victims of housing discrimination are often unaware of their rights, or how to pursue redress when rights have been violated. Weil (2009) conducted a long-term study of housing conditions for Latinos in Southern Louisiana shortly after Hurricane

Katrina. Latinos were especially vulnerable in the period following the disaster; when there was a lack of even rudimentary housing and tensions were high, employers – such as contractors who recruited Latinos specifically to work on reconstruction projects – were also primarily responsible for the allocation of housing. Added to these factors was insufficient government oversight (ibid.: 491).

A case in point is Natalia, a Latina teacher and a fluent speaker of English who told Weil that prior to Katrina she had no basis for complaint: "If they felt like I was inferior, they didn't let me know. But I have never felt embarrassed or humiliated or slighted in any way as a Hispanic." Any reasonable interviewer, having established a good relationship with the informant, must take such information at face value. However, Natalia also took part in a discrimination audit which provided important additional data.

Government and non-profit agencies who track housing discrimination will often perform an audit when discriminatory practices are suspected. For example, if a Korean-American applies for a mortgage and is quoted an unusually high interest rate – and reports this – an Anglo tester is sent in to apply for the same mortgage (supplying the same information on the application). This process may be repeated a number of times with different testers. If sufficient evidence can be documented, the bank or mortgage company may be charged with unlawful discrimination.

In Natalia's case, her experiences with rental agents was recorded and then compared to the experiences of an Anglo, non-Latina:

> Unbeknownst to [Natalia], she was discriminated against on several occasions; however, the discrimination was often masked by a friendly and seemingly accommodating voice . . . it is often difficult today for an individual to know whether he or she has been treated unfairly, and as a result, the vast majority of discrimination cases go unreported.
>
> (ibid.: 493)

With refinements of the laws and widening of protections, property owners, landlords, bankers and sales people have become far more subtle in the techniques used to screen out renters or buyers whom they consider undesirable. The National Fair Housing Alliance pursues unethical real estate companies and rental agents because residential segregation "results in disparities in access to quality education, employment, home-ownership and wealth accumulation for communities of color" (National Fair Housing Alliance 2009).

One of the more insidious ways that owners and managers screen out applicants or buyers who are unwelcome is to do so over the phone, on the basis of accent (Figure 17.1).

Heard but not seen

John Baugh is a sociolinguist and a professor of linguistics whose primary research areas have to do with the social stratification of English (with a focus on African American Vernacular English) and with discriminatory practices toward individuals and groups who do not command the dominant linguistic norms of their communities.

Some years ago Baugh began looking for an apartment for himself and his family in the vicinity of Stanford University, calling telephone numbers listed on real estate advertisements, in the usual way of things. Baugh is African American; he grew up in urban Los

Figure 17.1 Sounds like discrimination

Source: U.S. Department of Housing and Urban Development

Angeles and Philadelphia with parents who were both university professors, and thus grew up comfortable in a variety of language communities. In his youth and adolescence Baugh acquired three varieties of English: he is a native speaker of a formal, academic English, of AAVE, and he also has a command of Chicano English.

In contacting landlords about advertised rental properties by phone, Baugh used more formal, academic English and he was told that yes, he could come see the apartment. Only to be turned away with excuses once the landlord saw him in person.

Baugh was the same person on the phone and off, but the perception of him had shifted from a well-spoken, educated Anglo to a well-spoken, educated African American. With that shift, the apartment he wanted to see was no longer available.

Here is direct evidence that the language subordination model is built on deception. The ideology says: sound like us and you'll *be* one of us, no more trouble for you. Baugh *does* command what people think of as *SAE; but he is still discriminated against on the basis of race.

Of course, the identification of social allegiances on the basis of language traits is a normal and natural practice for all human beings; variation is built into spoken language specifically to help us situate each other in social and geographic space. The problem starts when we draw conclusions and then use them to discriminate and exclude individuals from normal life activities on the basis of race, ethnicity, national origin or any other protected category.

In a long-term study funded by the Ford Foundation, Baugh and his associates looked at these issues closely. The initial question was a simple one, on the surface at least: Is it possible to tell a person's race and/or ethnicity based on an individual's speaking voice – without any visual clues at all?[5] That is, are there specific phonological or phonetic features that are associated with a particular race or ethnicity, and if so, do specific traits trigger specific kinds of reactions?

I had you at hello

Baugh and his colleagues designed a series of four experiments to better understand some of the most basic aspects of linguistic profiling. In the first stage of this study, Baugh collected the data himself by systematically calling landlords to inquire about advertised apartments, targeting five specific areas in the San Francisco Bay area. In every case he used the same greeting: "Hello, I'm calling about the apartment you have advertised in the paper." In order to avoid suspicion on the basis of idiosyncratic features, different return telephone numbers and pseudonyms were used for each of the three calls to each landlord.[6] The hypothesis was that in communities where the population was predominantly Anglo, there would be fewer positive responses to inquiries made in AAVE or ChE.

The second study was similar to the first in that the same sentence was used, but this time twenty individuals who were native speakers of one of the targeted varieties of English recorded the sentence in question. Baugh's three utterances were also recorded for the database. More than four hundred students at Stanford took part in this experiment, in which they listened to the recorded segments and made note of their best guesses in terms of race, ethnicity, and sex.

The third and fourth experiments had to do with the measurement of very fine phonetic and acoustic detail in order to identify how sensitive listeners are to cues well below the level of consciousness. The methodology here involved isolating the single word *hello* from Baugh's three recordings. The reasons for limiting the experiment this way are important:

> We have several reasons for examining one word. This allowed us to hold external factors to a minimum. Second, it also illustrates how little speech is needed for dialect identification. "Hello" is a self-contained utterance, making perceptual studies more natural. By focusing on one short word, we are able to hold utterance duration well below one second (x = 414 msec.), making it comparable to other studies already made.

Student participants were again asked to identify race, ethnicity and sex on the basis of listening to that single variable.

(Purnell *et al.* 1999: 13)

In each of these four experiments, the authors found that they had to reject the null hypothesis. That is, they began with the expectation that there would be no correlation between language features and discriminatory experiences. However, 70 percent of the time, listeners were able to identify race, ethnicity and sex on the basis of an utterance less than a second long (ibid.: 14). After analysis of the four experiments, the authors came to four clear, statistically significant conclusions:

1   Dialect-based discrimination takes place.
2   Ethnic group affiliation is recoverable from speech.
3   Very little speech is needed to discriminate between dialects.
4   Some phonetic correlates or markers of dialects are recoverable from a very small amount of speech.

(ibid.: 11)

A human failing

In the first experiment described in Purnell *et al.* (1999), Baugh targeted five specific areas around the San Francisco Bay to see if the race/ethnicity distributions in those areas would serve as a predictor of linguistic profiling. The findings are laid out in Figure 17.2.

Note first that for each of the five areas, the population is broken down by race/ethnicity. So, for example, East Palo Alto has approximately equal numbers of Anglos, African Americans, and Chicanos/as, with a tendency toward Anglos. Palo Alto has very small populations of Chicanos/as and African Americans, and Woodside is even more exclusively Anglo. Oakland has the largest proportion of African Americans, while East Palo Alto has the largest populations of Chicanos/as.

The lines superimposed over the bars indicate the number of times Baugh was able to successfully make an appointment to see an apartment. When he spoke ChE, his inquiry calls were successful as few as 20 percent of the time. The best response to ChE inquiries came from East Palo Alto, which is also home to the largest proportion of Chicanos. However, even in East Palo Alto Baugh's ChE inquiries were successful only 60 percent of the time. Corollary to this is the fact that even in the two areas where Anglos are outnumbered by people of color (Oakland and East Palo Alto), Anglos have better success in booking these appointments.

This is a reminder that housing discrimination is not strictly an Anglo phenomenon; there are many documented cases of such practices, of violence and civil rights violations from persons of all races and ethnicities. Consider the data in Table 17.1 from a study of the relationship between race/ethnicity and racial stereotypes. Individuals were asked to judge the 'unintelligence' of different groups.

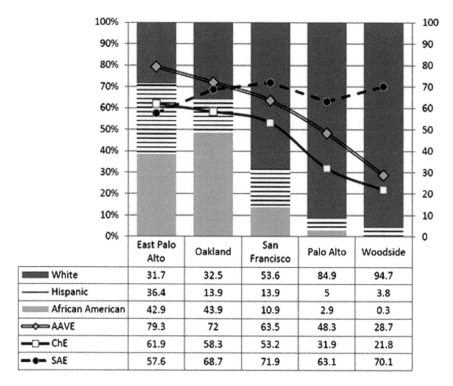

Figure 17.2 Population breakdown in five San Francisco areas by race and ethnicity, appointments to see apartments confirmed, by race and ethnicity

	East Palo Alto	Oakland	San Francisco	Palo Alto	Woodside
White	31.7	32.5	53.6	84.9	94.7
Hispanic	36.4	13.9	13.9	5	3.8
African American	42.9	43.9	10.9	2.9	0.3
AAVE	79.3	72	63.5	48.3	28.7
ChE	61.9	58.3	53.2	31.9	21.8
SAE	57.6	68.7	71.9	63.1	70.1

Table 17.1 Los Angelinos from four race/ethnicity groups judge each other on intelligence

Answering the question	Groups being stereotyped: Are people in this group unintelligent? 1 = intelligent, 3.4 = average intelligence, 7 = not intelligent			
	Blacks	Latinos	Asians	Whites
Whites	3.79	3.96	2.90	3.09
Asians	4.39	4.46	2.90	3.25
Latinos	3.93	3.57	2.74	2.87
Blacks	3.31	3.96	3.21	3.32

Source: adapted from Bonilla-Silva (2010: 191).

Housing discrimination toward Muslims

The terrorist attacks of September 11, 2001, brought with them a surge in discriminatory acts – both passive-aggressive and violent – toward Americans of Middle Eastern ancestry. The Middle East is considered one of the Asian nations by the U.S. Census Bureau. In this case discriminatory focus is primarily on religion.

The concept of a Muslim accent is less well formed than that of a Chinese or Swedish American, but it is still distinctive to many and becoming more so in the course of a decade of war in Iraq and Afghanistan.

A family of Pakistani immigrants living in San Francisco public housing was improperly denied an emergency transfer to another apartment after someone broke into their home, desecrated their Quran, defaced their passports and shredded their traditional clothing, according to a federal court lawsuit.

After the August 2005 incident – which took place during a time of intensified anti-Muslim sentiment in the country and while the San Francisco Housing Authority was under court order to better protect tenants from hate-motivated crimes – agency officials ruled that the break-in at Ashan Khan's apartment was a simple burglary and didn't qualify the family for an emergency apartment transfer, according to the family's reports (Lagos 2007).

Summary

The U.S. Department of Housing and Urban Development's National Fair Housing Alliance has been using phone auditing to examine suspected cases of housing discrimination linked to aural (rather than visual) traits with some success. Landlords advertising apartments, insurance companies offering low home insurance rates, banks eager to sell mortgages, in all aspects of the housing industry, the NFHA continues to find evidence of linguistic profiling to the detriment of people of color and people who speak English as a second language.

The growing body of literature on linguistic profiling produced by scholars, government agencies and non-profit civil rights organizations points to a simple conclusion: Anglos are more likely to have calls returned; they hear a wider range of possibilities and may be offered monetary incentives; they are quoted better rates on insurance and mortgages before the persons making these decisions have ever checked references or credit ratings. But the investigation process is long, the legal system is slow, and the fines too insignificant to have any lasting or long-term effect.

The first and best line of defense is to make sure that people are aware of their rights and how to protect those rights. Equally important is to make others aware of linguistic profiling.

DISCUSSION QUESTIONS AND EXERCISES

- Watch the advertisement produced by the Equal Housing Authority on linguistic profiling, in which an Anglo makes phone call after phone call about an advertisement for an apartment; with each call he uses a different stigmatized accent. An informal survey of my own indicates that the average person can identify all the accents (which does not, of course, mean that the accents are technically accurate; it may be that individuals recognize the portrayal of an accent). Asian and Middle Eastern accents are included, though there has been no formal investigation of how such accents are profiled in day-to-day telephone interaction. How might such an investigation look?
- Imagine that you have a friend or coworker who applied for an apartment and has been the victim of linguistic profiling, in your view of things. He or she is reluctant to register

a complaint. Investigate the process and put together the information and forms that your friend will need to pursue the issue. Consider the following issues:

● Does this process strike you as reasonable, or overly complicated?
● Why might an otherwise intelligent, well-established individual be reluctant to pursue equal treatment under the law?
● Read some of the articles about linguistic profiling provided. How would you describe the tone: Any hint of an ideological leaning in one direction or another?
● Can you recall any instances of linguistic profiling over the phone? Judgments made about the stranger on the other end? Reactions?

Notes

1 Hereafter referred to as Prop 14/1963 to distinguish from a later Proposition, also numbered 14.
2 The Equal Protection clause of the 14th Amendment requires that State governments provide equal protection under the law to all people within its jurisdiction, regardless of race or other protected category.
3 This is found within the Department of Housing and Urban Development (HUD).
4 The website is: http://portal.hud.gov/portal/page/portal/HUD/program_offices/fair_housing_equal_opp.
5 On the one hand this seems like a deceptively easy question, but in fact it is complicated by the possibility of racist applications. In the suggested readings at the end of this section there are a number of articles which explore linguistic profiling within the context of the law and court system.
6 According to Purnell *et al.* (1999):

> This procedure of anonymity parallels legally approved practices of testers used by the Department of Housing and Urban Development and similar organizations when suspecting discriminating practices by landlords (e.g., City of Chicago v. Matchmaker Real Estate Sales Center, 1992; Johnson v. Jerry Pals Real Estate, 1973; United States v. Youritan Construction Company, 1975).

Suggested further reading

Baugh, J. (2003) Linguistic Profiling. In S. Makoni, G. Smitherman, A. F. Ball and A. K. Spears (eds.) *Black Linguistics: Language, Society, and Politics in Africa and the Americas*, New York: Routledge, pp. 155–168.

Bullock, L. (2006) Testers Posing as Katrina Survivors Encounter "Linguistic Profiling." *National Newspaper Publishers Association*, August 16.

Chin, W.Y. (2010) Linguistic Profiling in Education: How Accent Bias Denies Equal Educational Opportunities to Students of Color. *Scholar* 12: 355–443.

Kim, K. (2005) Voice Profiling: Watchdog Groups Are Working to Expose Discrimination Based on How a Person Sounds over the Phone. *St. Louis Post-Dispatch*, February 6.

Purnell, T., Idsardi, W. and Baugh, J. (1999) Perceptual and Phonetic Experiments on American English Dialect Identification. *Journal of Social Psychology* 18(1): 10–30.

Smalls, D.L. (2004) Linguistic Profiling and the Law. *Stanford Law Review* 15: 579.

Squires, G.D. (2006) Linguistic Profiling: A Continuing Tradition of Discrimination in the Home Insurance Industry? *Urban Affairs Review* 41: 400–415.

On the web

Recording of John Baugh's sentences in three varieties of English are available online at http://www.stanford.edu/~jbaugh/baugh.fft.

NPR's Tovia Smith reports on scientific research that's being used to support claims of a kind of discrimination that takes place over the phone. It's called "linguistic profiling." http://www.npr.org/templates/story/story.php?storyId=11285, 13 September 5, 2001.

The Fair Housing Act at http://www.justice.gov/crt/housing/title8.php.

The National Fair Housing Advocate at http://fairhousing.com/index.cfm.

Conclusion

18

Civil (dis)obedience and the shadow of language

> Most of the greatest evils that man has inflicted upon man have come through people feeling quite certain about something which, in fact, was false.
>
> Bertrand Russell, cited in Haught (1996: 149)

> Marge, it takes two people to lie. One to lie, and one to listen.
>
> Homer Simpson

The process of language subordination targets not all variation, not all language varieties, but only those which are emblematic of differences in race, ethnicity, homeland, or other social allegiances which have been found to be less than good enough. Dedicated practitioners of language subordination do not complain about most of the variation which is active in U.S. English. There has never been an outcry about Chicagoans' inability to distinguish between "merry," "Mary" and "marry." Nor are there essays in local papers on the stupidity and unworthiness of people who say "cawfee" rather than "cah-fee" or "coo-off-ee." People do not lose jobs because they wait *on* line rather than *in* line. There may be an occasional ruffled feather about the use of *hopefully* or *healthy*, about split infinitives and dangling participles, "who" vs. "whom," but such debates – while often loud and sometimes acrimonious – eventually fade, because these are points of language variation leading to change which are largely completed, and solidly entrenched in the vernacular.

But people do lose jobs and school children are belittled because their native language makes it difficult for them to differentiate between /l/ and /r/ sounds; because their sentence intonations are Latino; because they say "y'all" rather than "all of you," "aks" rather than "ask."

The demand that the disempowered assimilate linguistically and culturally to please the empowered is – purely in linguistic terms – an impossibility. A person's accent (the bundle of distinctive intonation and phonological features) is fixed or hard-wired in the mind, and once past a certain age it can only be very laboriously changed, to a very limited degree, regardless of commitment, intelligence, and resources. Thus the constant public debate on good English, on the one right English, is as fruitless an exercise as the hypothetical congressional debate on the ideal height and weight for all adults. We cannot purge language of variation linked to social difference, but more important than that undeniable fact: it should not matter.

If as a nation we are agreed that it is not acceptable or good to discriminate on the grounds of skin color or ethnicity, gender or age, then by logical extension it is equally unacceptable to discriminate against language traits which are intimately linked to an individual's sense and expression of self.

But people are judged on the basis of language form rather than language content, every day. Without hesitation or contemplation, workers are turned away, children are corrected, people are made to feel small and unimportant in public settings. The process of language subordination is so deeply rooted, so well established, that we do not see it for what it is. We make no excuses for preferences which exclude on the basis of immutable language traits.

Having established that this process works, and having looked hard at how it works for both the powered and the disempowered, a logical question has not yet been raised: what now?

When discussing this question with my students – a racially and ethnically mixed group of bright young people of both sexes, well educated, thoughtful – this is where the deadlock will occur. Some, enraged by the practices they have studied and observed (and perhaps experienced), will demand that we stop all pretenses in the school to teach "standard" English. They contemplate passive resistance and large-scale civil disobedience, and a United States in which the equation between national unity and linguistic homogeneity has been examined and discarded as untenable and unfair. Others point out that because children are still in the language acquisition stage, they should theoretically be able to acquire more than one variety of English – and that this should become a rule. Idealism does not put food on the table, this argument goes.

It is a strong argument. Economic rationalizations are the most often raised, most loudly voiced, and the most persuasive of all common-sense arguments used to coerce the few into the ways of the many: Assimilation is the price of success.

Comparison of Figures 18.1 and 18.2 makes it clear that the U.S. has always been and will always be ethnically, racially, and linguistically heterogeneous, but it is equally true

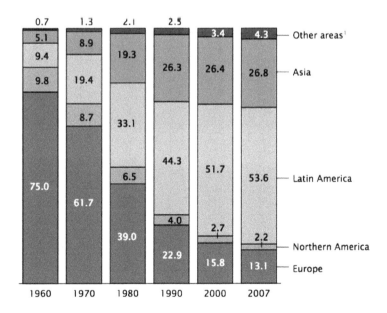

Figure 18.1 Distribution of the U.S. population by national origin, over time

Note: [1]Other areas include Africa and Oceania

Source: U.S. Census Bureau, Census of Population, 1960 to 2000, and 2007 American Community Survey

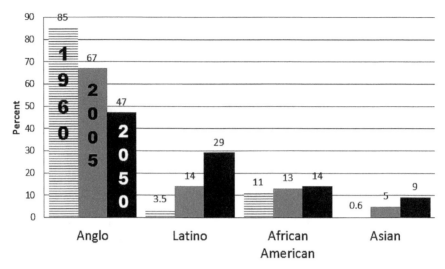

Figure 18.2 Population change over time by race/ethnicity 1960 > 2005 > 2050 (projected)

Source: U.S. Census

that the population figures are shifting. In a democracy based on majority-rule, power relationships cannot be static and will always be expressed – in part – by means of language ideology.

The question is, can this unbroken circle of intimidation truly not be broken, or do we like things the way they are? Language serves as a convenient excuse to turn away. Are we unwilling to consider a nation in which the cost of success is achievement measured by other, fairer, means?

Ideology is most effective when its workings are least visible, and standard language ideology in the U.S. functions like a silent but efficient machine. Its practitioners are terribly skillful at coercing consent and participation from those people and groups who suffer the most under the weight of language ideology. Thus the most factual stand: every language is in fact completely viable and functional, therefore we do not need and should not attempt standardization – seems to be doomed.

And if that is the case, if human nature will allow nothing else, then it is only common sense to remember that power will shift, and one day – most likely within the lifetimes of those reading this book – the power of the majority will shift too. Putting inclusive, respectful, cooperative language policies in place now is the first step toward making sure they are still in place when you, personally, need them.

In the meantime, a realistic goal must be a much smaller one: to make people aware of the process of language subordination. To draw their attention to the misinformation, to expose false reasoning and empty promises to hard questions.

If in the face of clarity and truth about standardization, the way it works, and its social connections and meanings, peripheralized language speakers and communities choose to try to assimilate to linguistic (and cultural) norms of another group, then that is a choice freely made that must be respected. But at this time, there is little or no truth in advertising the process of language standardization. Right now, people attempt to conform and to assimilate because they are inundated with promises and threats if they do not. The threats are real: the evidence is at hand in the experiences of the people whose stories are told here. The promises, however, are not so real. Because discrimination on the basis of language has not to do with the language itself, but with the social circumstances and identities attached to that language, discrimination will not go away when the next generation has assimilated. Mainstream U.S. English is a flimsy cover to hide behind in the face of serious intent to exclude on the basis of race or ethnicity.

Eleanor Roosevelt's statement on the connection between inferiority and cooperation is one that I have thought about for a long time, in the writing of this book. It captures two basic elements of the language subordination process: First, one person or group must want to make another person or group believe that their language – and hence their social allegiances and priorities – are inferior. Second, that targeted person or group must become complicit in the process.

But it also raises the important issue of language system and language content, or linguistic and social grammaticality addressed in the first chapter. I raise this topic here because I anticipate a common response to the arguments set forth in this book will be that I am – as I have been called in the past – a language anarchist. One of those lax, liberal types, for whom anything goes. Who has no respect for language or the traditions of the past, and no interest in teaching those traditions to children. No interest in aesthetics, and an unwillingness to talk of quality in spoken language, for fear that somebody will be marginalized.

In fact, I will state very clearly that in my opinion, it is not a sin against mankind to have standards and preferences about the spoken language. As a product of the institutions that I have written about in this book, I have been exposed to stereotypes for my whole life. I hope that I have learned to look beyond them to see and to hear the person behind the cultural expectations, but even then, I have preferences. I can, and I do, choose among storytellers. I can decide that Jane tells a joke better than Joan. That political candidate Park is better than candidate Goldstein in off-the-cuff debate. One song lyric may delight me while another falls flat.

As a speaker of a variety of U.S. English which is not stigmatized, on occasion I feel inferior about my own language. I can recall times when I failed to make a point because I could not articulate my thoughts clearly. I have used too many words when a few would have sufficed. Most of all, I have felt inferior on those occasions when I have been moved by spoken language which is clear, precise, vivid, and following from this, effective for me personally. But because I belong to the social (and hence, to the language) mainstream which isolates me from the process of subordination, any feelings of inferiority are of my own making. Other value systems are not forced on me; I am allowed the consolation of my mother tongue. I am free of the shadow of language, and subject only to the standards that I accept for myself.

Language subordination is not about relative standards and preferences in the way language is used. Language subordination does not say: Joan can't tell a joke, but rather that Joan is not worth listening to, because her English makes it clear that she was born on the Bayou, or in Harlem, Puerto Rico, Hong Kong or on the Pine Ridge Reservation. Whether Joan is the best or the worst teller of jokes ever born, some people will never know because they will not listen to what she has to say: how she says it is enough to know that it is unworthy of their consideration.

Language subordination is about taking away a basic human right: to speak freely in the mother tongue without intimidation, without standing in the shadow of other languages and peoples. To resist the process, passively or actively, is to ask for recognition, and acknowledgement. It is a demand for the simple right to be heard.

Shortened bibliography

The entire bibliography is available online at www.routledge.com/textbooks/lippi-green.

Agha, A. (2003) The Social Life of Cultural Value. *Language and Communication* 23(3–4): 231–273.

Alexander, L. (1992) What Makes Wrongful Discrimination Wrong? Biases, Preferences, Stereotypes, and Proxies. *University of Pennsylvania Law Review* 141(1): 149–219.

Alim, H.S. (2005) Critical Language Awareness in the United States: Revisiting Issues and Revising Pedagogies in a Resegregated Society. *Educational Researcher* 34. 24–31.

Alim, H.S. (2006) *Roc the Mic Right: The Language of Hip Hop Culture*. New York: Routledge.

Anderson, K. (2007) Constructing Otherness: Ideologies and Differentiating Speech Style. *International Journal of Applied Linguistics* 17(2): 178–197.

Armstrong, J.D. (2006) Homophobic Slang as Coercive Discourse among College Students. In H. Luria, D. Seymour and T. Smoke (eds.) *Language and Linguistics in Context*. Mahwah, NJ: Lawrence Erlbaum, pp. 219–226.

Aziz, S.F. (2009) Sticks and Stones, the Words That Hurt: Entrenched Stereotypes Eight Years after 9/11. *New York City Law Review* 13: 33 ff.

Bailey, G. and Tillery, J. (1996) The Persistence of Southern American English. *Journal of English Linguistics* 24(4): 308–321.

Baugh, J. (2000) Racial Identification by Speech. *American Speech* 75(4): 362–364.

Baugh, J. (2003) Linguistic Profiling. In S. Makoni, G. Smitherman, A.F. Ball, and A.K. Spears (eds.) *Black Linguistics: Language, Society, and Politics in Africa and the Americas*. New York: Routledge, pp. 155–168.

Baugh, J. (2007) Plantation English in America: Nonstandard Varieties and the Quest for Educational Equity. *Research in the Teaching of English* 41(4): 465.

Bonilla-Silva, E. (2009) *Racism without Racists: Color-Blind Racism and the Persistence of Racial Inequality in the United States*. Lanham, MD: Rowman and Littlefield Publishers.

Bonilla-Silva, E. and Forman, T.A. (2000) "I am not a Racist but . . .": Mapping White College Students' Racial Ideology in the USA. *Discourse Society* 11: 50.

Bono, M. (2007) Don't You Be My Neighbor: Restrictive Housing Ordinances as the New Jim Crow. *Modern American* 3: 29.

Bourdieu, P. and Thompson, J.B. (1991) *Language and Symbolic Power*. Cambridge: Polity.

Bratt, K. (2007) Violence in the Curriculum: Compulsory Linguistic Discrimination in the Arizona-Sonora Borderlands. *Journal for Critical Education Policy Studies* 5(1).

Bruch, P. and Marback, R. (eds.) (2005) *The Hope and the Legacy: The Past, Present, and Future of "Students' Right to Their Own Language."* Cresskill, NJ: Hampton Press.

Bucholtz, M. (1995) From Mulatta to Mestiza: Language and the Reshaping of Ethnic Identity. In K. Hall and M. Bucholtz (eds.) *Gender Articulated: Language and the Socially Constructed Self*. New York: Routledge, pp. 351–374.

Bucholtz, M. (2001) The Whiteness of Nerds: Superstandard English and Racial Markedness. *Journal of Linguistic Anthropology* 11(1): 84–100.

Bucholtz, M. and Hall, K. (2005) Identity and Interaction: A Sociocultural Linguistic Approach. *Discourse Studies* 7.

Cameron, D. (1995) *Verbal Hygiene*. New York: Routledge.

Campbell-Kibler, K. (2007) Accent, (ing), and the Social Logic of Listener Perceptions. *American Speech* 82(1): 32–64.

Cashman, H.R. (2009) The Dynamics of Spanish Maintenance and Shift in Arizona: Ethnolinguistic Vitality, Language Panic and Language Pride. *Spanish in Context* 6(1): 43–68.

Chomsky, N. (1959) Review of *Verbal Behavior* by B.F. Skinner. *Language* 35(1): 26–58.

Cobas, J. and Feagin, J. (2008) Language Oppression and Resistance: The Case of Middle Class Latinos in the United States. *Ethnic and Racial Studies* 31(2): 390–410.

Cobb, J.C. (2005) *Away Down South: A History of Southern Identity*. Oxford: Oxford University Press.

Coulmas, F. (ed.) (2007) *The Handbook of Sociolinguistics*. Blackwell.

Coupland, N. (2002) Sociolinguistic prevarication about "standard English." *Journal of Sociolinguistics* 4(4): 622–634.

Coupland, N. (2009) The Mediated Performance of Vernaculars. *Journal of English Linguistics* 37(3): 284–300.

Cukor-Avila, P. (2003) The Complex Grammatical History of African-American and White Vernaculars in the South. In S.J. Nagle and S.L. Sanders (eds.) *English in the Southern United States*. New York: Cambridge University Press.

Curzan, A. (2002) Teaching the Politics of Standard English. *Journal of English Linguistics* 30(4): 339–352.

Cutler, C.A. (2010) Hip-Hop, White Immigrant Youth, and African American Vernacular English: Accommodation as an Identity Choice. *Journal of English Linguistics* 38(3): 248–269.

Delpit, L. D. and Dowdy, J.K. (2008) *The Skin that We Speak: Thoughts on Language and Culture in the Classroom*. The New Press.

Derwing, T. and Munro, M.J. (2009) Putting Accent in Its Place: Rethinking Obstacles to Communication. *Language Teaching* 42(04): 476–490.

Derwing, T., Rossiter M. and Munro, M.J. (2002) Teaching Native Speakers to Listen to Foreign-Accented Speech. *Journal of Multilingual and Multicultural Development* 23(4): 245–259.

Devos, T. and Banaji, M.R. (2005) American = White? *Journal of Personality and Social Psychology* 88(3): 447–466.

Dicker, S. (2008) US Immigrants and the Dilemma of Anglo-Conformity. *Socialism and Democracy* 22(3): 52–74.

Dovidio, J., Gluszek, A., John, M. *et al.* (2010) Understanding Bias toward Latinos: Discrimination, Dimensions of Difference, and Experience of Exclusion. *Journal of Social Issues* 66(1): 59–78.

Dumas, B.K. (1999) Southern Mountain English: The Language of the Ozarks and Southern Appalachia. In R.S. Wheeler (ed.) *Workings of Language*. London: Praeger, pp. 67–80.

Duranti, A., Ochs, E. and Schieffelin, B.B. (2011) *The Handbook of Language Socialization*. John Wiley & Sons.

Eagleton, T. (2007) *Ideology: An Introduction*. 2nd edn. London: Verso.

Eckert, P. (2008) Variation and the Indexical Field. *Journal of Sociolinguistics* 12(4): 453–476.

Eckert, P. and Rickford, J.R. (eds.) (2001) *Style and Sociolinguistic Variation*. Cambridge: Cambridge University Press.

Fairclough, N. (1989) *Language and Power*. London: Longman.

Fairclough, N. (1992) The Appropriacy of "Appropriateness." In Fairclough, N. (ed.), *Critical Language Awareness*. London: Routledge.

Fairclough, N. (2009) *Critical Discourse Analysis*. London: Longman.

Feagin, C. (1990) The Dynamics of a Sound Change in Southern States English: From R-Less to R-Ful in Three Generations. In J.A. Edmondson, C. Feagin *et al.* (eds.) *Development and Diversity: Language Variation across Time and Space*. Summer Institute of Linguistics, pp. 129–146.

Finegan, E. and Rickford, J.R. (eds.) (2004) *Language in the USA: Themes for the Twenty-First Century*. Cambridge: Cambridge University Press.

Flagg, B.J. (1995) Fashioning a Title VII Remedy for Transparently White Subjective Decision Making *Yale Law Journal* 104(8): 2009–2051.

Fordham, S. (1999) Dissin "the Standard": Ebonics as Guerrilla Warfare at Capital High. *Anthropology & Education Quarterly*, 30(3): 272–293.

Fordham, S. (2010) Passin' for Black: Race, Identity, and Bone Memory in Post-racial America. *Harvard Educational Review* 80(1): 4–30.

Foucault, M. (1984) The Order of Discourse. In M.J. Shapiro (ed.) *Language and Politics*. Oxford: Oxford University Press.

Fought, C. (2006) *Language and Ethnicity*. New York: Cambridge University Press.

Gallois, C., Ogay, T. and Giles, H. (2004) Communication Accommodation Theory: A Look Back and a Look Ahead. In W. Gudykunst (ed.) *Theorizing About Intercultural Communication*. London: Sage Publications, pp. 121–148.

Gee, J.P. (2011) The Literacy Myth and the History of Literacy. In *Social Linguistics and Literacies*. New York: Routledge, pp. 22–45.

Gee, J.P. (2011) *Social Linguistics and Literacies: Ideology in Discourses*. Taylor & Francis.

Giroux, H. A. (2001) *Theory and Resistance in Education: Toward a Pedagogy for the Opposition*. Westport, CN: Bergin & Garvey.

Gluszek, A. and Dovidio, J.F. (2010) Speaking with a Nonnative Accent: Perceptions of Bias, Communication Difficulties, and Belonging in the United States. *Journal of Language and Social Psychology* 29(2): 224–234.

Goode, E. and Ben-Yehuda, N. (2009) *Moral Panics: The Social Construction of Deviance*. Malden, MA: Wiley-Blackwell.

Green, L. (2002) *African American English: A Linguistic Introduction*. Cambridge: Cambridge University Press.

Herman, E.S. and Chomsky, N. (2002 [1988]) *Manufacturing Consent: The Political Economy of the Mass Media*. Pantheon Press.

Hill, J.H. (2000) The Racializing Function of Language Panics. In R.D. Gonzalez and I. Melis (eds.) *Language Ideologies: Critical Perspectives on the Official English Movement*. Mahwah, NJ: National Council of Teachers of English.

Hill, J.H. (2008) *The Everyday Language of White Racism*. Malden, MA: Wiley-Blackwell.

Johnson, J. R, Rich, M. and Castelan Cargile, A. (2008) "Why Are You Shoving This Stuff Down Our Throats?" Preparing Intercultural Educators to Challenge Performances of White Racism. *Journal of International and Intercultural Communication* 1.113–135.

Jordan, J. (1988) Nobody Mean More to Me than You and the Future Life of Willie Jordan. *Harvard Educational Review* 58: 363–375.

Kang, O. and Rubin, D.L. (2009) Reverse Linguistic Stereotyping: Measuring the Effect of Listener Expectations on Speech Evaluation. *Journal of Language and Social Psychology* 28: 441–456.

Kawai, Y. (2005) Stereotyping Asian Americans: The Dialectic of the Model Minority and the Yellow Peril. *Howard Journal of Communications* 16(2): 109–130.

Kretzschmar, W.A., Jr. (2008) Language in the Deep South: Southern Accents Past and Present. *Southern Quarterly* 45(2): 9–27.

Kroskrity, P.V. (2005) Language Ideology. In Duranti, A. (ed.) *A Companion to Linguistic Anthropology*. Oxford: Blackwell Publishing Ltd.

Labov, W. (1972) The Logic of Nonstandard English. In A. Cashdan and E. Grugeon (eds.) *Language in Education*. London: Routledge and Kegan Paul, pp. 198–211.

Labov, W. (2006) *The Social Stratification of English in New York City*. Cambridge University Press.

Labov, W. (2010) Unendangered Dialect, Endangered People: The Case of African American Vernacular English. *Transforming Anthropology* 18(1): 15–27.

Linguistic Human Rights in the World. http://www.linguistic-rights.org/.

Luhman, R. (2008) Appalachian English Stereotypes: Language Attitudes in Kentucky. *Language in Society* 19: 331–348.

Macedo, D.P., Dendrinos B. and Gounari, P. (eds.) (2003) *The Hegemony of English*. Paradigm Publishers.

Matsuda, M. (1991) Voices of America: Accent, Antidiscrimination Law, and a Jurisprudence for the Last Reconstruction. *Yale Law Journal* 100(5): 1329.

May, S. (2008) *Language and Minority Rights: Ethnicity, Nationalism and the Politics of Language*. New York: Routledge.

Meek, B. (2006) And the Injun Goes "How": Representations of American Indian English in White Public Space. *Language in Society* 35(1): 93–128.

Mendoza-Denton, N. (2008) *Homegirls: Language and Cultural Practice among Latina Youth Gangs*. Malden, MA: Blackwell.

Milroy, J. (2001) Language Ideologies and the Consequences of Standardization. *Journal of sociolinguistics* 5.530–555.

Milroy, J. and Milroy. L. (2002 [1999]) *Authority in Language: Investigating Standard English*. London: Routledge.

Morenberg, M. (2010) *Doing Grammar*. New York: Oxford University Press.

Morgan, M. (2010) The Presentation of Indirectness and Power in Everyday Life. *Journal of Pragmatics* 42(2): 283–291.

Munro, M., Derwing, T.M. and Morton, S.L. (2006) The Mutual Intelligibility of L2 Speech. *Studies in Second Language Acquisition* 28(01): 111–131.

Ng, S.H. (2007) Language-Based Discrimination: Blatant and Subtle Forms. *Journal of Language and Social Psychology* 26(2): 106–122.

Nunberg, G. (2009 [1983/1997]. The Decline of Grammar. *The Atlantic Monthly*, 22 October.

Oboler, S. (1992) The Politics of Labeling: Latino/a Cultural Identities of Self and Others. *Latin American Perspectives* 19(4): 18–36.

Ogbu, J.U. (2004) Collective Identity and the Burden of "Acting White" in Black History, Community, and Education. *The Urban Review* 36(1): 2 ff.

Okamura, J. (2008) *Ethnicity and Inequality in Hawai'i*. Philadelphia, PA: Temple University Press.

Otheguy, R., Zentella, A.C. and Livert, D. (2007) Language and Dialect Contact in Spanish in New York: Toward the Formation of a Speech Community. *Language* 83(4): 770–802.

Perry, T. and Delpit, L.D. (eds.) (1998) *The Real Ebonics Debate. Power, Language, and the Education of African-American Children*. Boston: Beacon Press.

Pinker, S. (1994) *The Language Instinct*. New York: W. Morrow and Co.

Potowski, K. (ed.) (2010) *Language Diversity in the USA*. New York: Cambridge University Press.

Preston, D.R. (2008) Five Visions of America. *Language in Society* 15: 221–240.

Purnell, G.K., Raimy, E. and Salmons, J. (2009) Defining Dialect, Perceiving Dialect, and New Dialect Formation: Sarah Palin's Speech. *Journal of English Linguistics* 37(4): 331–355.

Reagan, T. (2006) The Explanatory Power of Critical Language Studies: Linguistics with an Attitude. *Critical Inquiry in Language Studies* 3(1): 1–22.

Reyes, A. and Lo, A. (2009) *Beyond Yellow English: Toward a Linguistic Anthropology of Asian Pacific America*. New York: Oxford University Press.

Rickford, J.R. (2005 [1999]) Using the Vernacular to Teach the Standard. In J.D. Ramirez, T. Wiley, G. De Klerk, E. Lee and W.E. Wright (eds.) *Ebonics: The Urban Education Debate*. Clevedon: Mutilingual Matters, pp. 18–40.

Rickford, J.R. (2010) Geographical Diversity, Residential Segregation, and the Vitality of African American Vernacular English and Its Speakers. *Transforming Anthropology* 18(1): 28–34.

Rickford, J.R. and Rickford, R.J. (2000) *Spoken Soul: The Story of Black English*. New York: John Wiley and Sons.

Rohrer, J. (2008) Disrupting the "Melting Pot": Racial Discourse in Hawai'i and the Naturalization of *Haole*. *Ethnic and Racial Studies* 31(6): 1110–1125.

Romaine, S. (2010) Language Contact in the USA. In K. Potowski (ed.) *Language Diversity in the USA*. New York: Cambridge University Press, pp. 25–46.

Rosenbloom, S.R. and Way, N. (2004) Experiences of Discrimination among African American, Asian American, and Latino Adolescents in an Urban High School. *Youth Society* 35(4): 420–451.

Rubin, D.L. (1992) Nonlanguage Factors Affecting Undergraduates' Judgments of Nonnative English-Speaking Teaching Assistants. *Research in Higher Education* 33(4): 511–531.

Rubin, D.L. and Smith, K.A. (1990) Effects of Accent, Ethnicity, and Lecture Topic on Undergraduates' Perceptions of Nonnative English-Speaking Teaching Assistants. *International Journal of Intercultural Relations* 14(3): 337–353.

Santa Ana, O. (2004) *Tongue-Tied: The Lives of Multilingual Children in Public Education*. Lanham, MD: Rowman and Littlefield.

Schiffrin, D. (2006) *In Other Words: Variation in Reference and Narrative*. Cambridge University Press.

Sclafani, J. (2008) The Intertextual Origins of Public Opinion: Constructing Ebonics in *The New York Times*. *Discourse and Society* 19(4): 507–527.

Skutnabb-Kangas, T., Phillipson, R. and Rannut, M. (1994) *Linguistic Human Rights: Overcoming Linguistic Discrimination*. Berlin: Mouton de Gruyter.

Shuck, G. (2006) Racializing the Nonnative English Speaker. *Journal of Language, Identity and Education* 5(4): 259–276.

Siegel, J. (2006) Language Ideologies and the Education of Speakers of Marginalized Language Varieties: Adopting a Critical Awareness Approach. *Linguistics and Education* 17(2): 157–174.

Sigelman, L. and Tuch, S. A. (1997) Meta-stereotypes: Blacks' Perceptions of Whites' Stereotypes of Blacks. *Public Opinion Quarterly* 61(1): 87–101.

Silva-Corvalán, C. (2004) Spanish in the Southwest. In E. Finegan and J.R. Rickford (eds.) *Language in the USA: Themes for the Twenty-First Century*. New York: Cambridge University Press.

Silverstein, M. (1992) The Uses and Utility of Ideology: Some Reflections. *Pragmatics: Quarterly Publication of the International Pragmatics Association* 2(3): 311–324.

Silverstein, M. (1998) Contemporary Transformations of Local Linguistic Communities. *Annual Review of Anthropology* 27: 401–426.

Silverstin, M. (2003) Indexical Order and the Dialectics of Sociolinguistic Life. *Language and Communication* 23.193–229.

Smalls, D.L. (2004) Linguistic Profiling and the Law. *Stanford Law and Policy Review* 15; 579.

Smitherman, G. (1995) *African American Women Speak Out on Anita Hill-Clarence Thomas*. Wayne State University Press.

Smitherman, G. (2000) *Talkin that Talk: Language, Culture, and Education in African America*. Routledge.

Smitherman, G. (2006) *Word from the Mother: Language and African Americans*. New York: Routledge.

Spears, A.K. (1998) African-American Language Use: Ideology and So-Called Obscenity. In S. Mufwene (ed.) *African-American English: Structure, History, and Use*. New York: Routledge.

Spears, A.K. (2007) African American Communicative Practices: Performativity, Semantic License and Augmentation. In H.S. Alim and J. Baugh (eds.) *Talkin Black Talk: Language, Education, and Social Change*. New York: Teachers College Press, pp. 100–111.

Spolsky, B. (2002) Prospects for the Survival of the Navajo Language: A Reconsideration. *Anthropology & Education Quarterly* 33: 139–162.

Strauss, C. (2004) Cultural Standing in Expression of Opinion. *Language in Society* 33:161–194.

Tamura, E. (2002) African American Vernacular English and Hawai'i Creole English: A Comparison of Two School Board Controversies. *Journal of Negro Education* 71(1): 17–30.

Tillery, J. and Bailey, G. (1998) Y'all in Oklahoma. *American Speech* 73(3): 257–278.

Tillery, J., Wikle, T. and Bailey, G. (2000) The Nationalization of a Southernism. *Journal of English Linguistics* 28(3): 280.

Umaña-Taylor, A., Vargas-Chanes, D., Garcia, C.D. and Gonzales-Backen, M. (2008) A Longitudinal Examination of Latino Adolescents' Ethnic Identity, Coping with Discrimination and Self-Esteem. *Journal of Early Adolescence* 28(1): 16–50.

Winford, D. (2003) Ideologies of Language and Socially Realistic Linguistics. In S. Makoni *et al.* (eds.) *Black Linguistics: Language, Society, and Politics in Africa and the Americas*. London: Routledge.

Wolfram, W. (1998) Language Ideology and Dialect: Understanding the Oakland Ebonics Controversy. *Journal of English Linguistics* 26(2): 108–121.

Wolfram, W. (2004) Dialect Awareness in Community Perspective. In M.C. Bender (ed.) *Linguistic Diversity in the South: Changing Codes, Practices, and Ideology*. Athens, GA: University of Georgia Press.

Wolfram, W. and Beckett, D. (2003) Language Variation in the American South: An Introduction. *American Speech* 78(2): 123–129.

Wolfram, W. and Ward, B. (2006) *American Voices: How Dialects Differ from Coast to Coast*. London: Blackwell.

Yuracko, K. (2005) Trait Discrimination as Race Discrimination: An Argument About Assimilation. *The George Washington Law Review* 74: 365–438.

Index